Family Money Book

by
The ERC Editorial Staff
(EXECUTIVE REPORTS CORPORATION)

Prentice-Hall, Inc.
Englewood Cliffs, New Jersey

Prentice-Hall International, Inc., *London*
Prentice-Hall of Australia, Pty. Ltd., *Sydney*
Prentice-Hall Canada, Inc., *Toronto*
Prentice-Hall of India Private Ltd., *New Delhi*
Prentice-Hall of Japan, Inc., *Tokyo*
Prentice-Hall of Southeast Asia Pte. Ltd., *Singapore*
Whitehall Books, Ltd., *Wellington, New Zealand*
Editora Prentice-Hall do Brasil Ltda., *Rio de Janeiro*
Prentice-Hall Hispanoamericana, S.A., *Mexico*

© 1986 by
PRENTICE-HALL, INC.
Englewood Cliffs, NJ

This publication is designed to provide accurate and authoritative information in regard to the subject matter covered. It is sold with the understanding that the publisher is not engaged in rendering legal, accounting or other professional service. If legal advice or other expert assistance is required, the service of a competent professional person should be sought.

From a Declaration of Principles jointly adopted by a Committee of the American Bar Association and a Committee of Publishers and Associations.

Library of Congress Cataloging-in-Publication Data

Family money book.

Includes index.
1. Finance, Personal.   I. Executive Reports
Corporation.
HG179.F35   1986   332.024   86-8958

ISBN 0-13-302605-1

Printed in the United States of America

WHAT THIS BOOK WILL DO FOR YOU

With your new Family Money Book in hand, your current income can feel like much, much more—instantly. That's because you're now an insider privy to shrewd, little-known money angles that squeeze more from every one of your hard-earned dollars. Whether you want to save, spend or invest, there's a "better way" to do it—and the new Family Money Book shows you how. For example, you see—

* how to boost take-home pay immediately without waiting for a raise
* how to slash thousands from this year's tax bill
* how to cut the cost of credit cards, long-distance calls, and other everyday expenses
* how to pull in a second income with low-risk, top-profit investments
* how to pay less on big-dollar items like new cars, homes, college tuition
* how to get big unexpected tax savings from a home or apartment
* how to turn the family business into a family fortune
* how to turn some of your personal expenses into tax deductions
* how to insure maximum security for your family at the lowest cost
* how to get the most from your travel and entertainment expenses

Many books deal with one or two aspects of personal finances. Your new Money Book brings them all together. It's your best all-round guide to turning what you already have into dynamic new wealth. And unlike specialty books written in technical language, the Money Book is easy to read *and* easy to use.

There's this added feature: each tip can be read on its own, whether it's a way to cut costs, save taxes, or build wealth. So you don't have to wait till you read the whole book before you cash in. You immediatley see what to do and how to do it.

And in just minutes, you recoup the low cost of the Money Book ten, twenty, even thirty times over.

One final word: Some of the ideas here may be affected by the changing tax law setup. So check closely with your personal adviser before taking action on tax saving moves that apply to you.

Just take a minute now to glance at the table of contents. You'll see that this is the kind of help you and your family can use at once and every day, an "instant answer" book that transforms your important money problems into lots of extra dollars.

The Editors

Table of Contents

Family Money Book

Chapter 1
How Your Family Can Live Comfortably For Less By Using Today's Top Cash Management Techniques

Chapter 2
Today's Best Ways to Earn A Higher Return on the Family Nest Egg

Chapter 3
Tax Shelter Investments—
Are They Right For You And Your Family?

Chapter 4
Money-Saving Ways To Buy, Sell And Own
A Family Home

Chapter 5
Key Tax Moves That Help A Family Business—
No Matter What Its Size

Chapter 6
How To Tap An Overlooked Source
Of Big Tax Deductions

Chapter 7
How To Boost Your Income And Expand Your Wealth—Without Getting A Raise

Chapter 8
How To Use IRAs To Multiply Your Family's Wealth

Chapter 9
How Social Security Helps You And Your Family—
Both Now And In The Future

Chapter 10
Family Tax Tactics That Yield Big Dollar Savings
Year After Year

Chapter 11
How To Get Bargain-Rate Insurance That Gives You Top-Dollar Protection

Chapter 12
How to Care For An Aged Parent Without Draining Your Financial Resources

Chapter 13
How To Leave Your Family In The Best Possible Financial Shape

Chapter 14
How To Save Tax Dollars And Time On Your Family Tax Returns

Chapter 1

How Your Family Can Live Comfortably For Less By Using Today's Top Cash Management Techniques

The road to financial security begins at home. By putting your own house in order, you can live comfortably for less and increase the amount of money you can invest for your family's security. That's what this Chapter is all about. For starters, we'll show you how to figure your net worth and put together a family budget that works. You'll also learn how you can slash your borrowing costs by shopping around for the lowest interest rates; how to get the best deal on your credit cards; find the best sources for financing your child's college education; take low-cost vacations; and get the fairest money deal on your consumer purchases.

HOW TO PLAN FOR YOUR FAMILY'S FINANCIAL FUTURE

Many people assume that financial planning is something that only professional money managers can do. But this is just not so. You can make the most of your family's financial resources without the help of so-called "experts." We'll show you how to take matters into your own hands with a financial self-diagnosis that tells you—
(1) What you're worth, i.e., the amount by which your assets exceed your debts;
(2) What you're spending your hard-earned cash on; and
(3) Where you can cut back—or get a better deal—on the goods and services you buy.
Most importantly, a financial self-diagnosis will give you a realistic basis for planning your family's future—whether it includes a comfortable retirement, remodeling your home, or providing a college education for your children. When you've come up with a plan you can live with, you'll be in a good position to achieve your goals.

How Much Are You Worth?

The first step in your self-diagnosis is preparing a net worth statement, such as the one shown below. With this easy-to-use worksheet you can total your assets (what you own) and liabilities (what you owe) and then find your net worth.

1

A net worth statement gives you a clear picture of the nature of your financial resources. It tells you, for example, whether your funds are tied up in personal assets such as home furnishings or if you are shortchanging your retirement accounts. You may also find out that you have too much cash sitting in a low- or no-interest checking account, or that a significant portion of your assets are underutilized. For example, you may have $50,000 or more of equity in your home (the excess of the home's value over your outstanding mortgage balance). You can borrow against your equity—at relatively low rates—and free up cash for an important family goal such as your child's college tuition.

Also, if the cash value of your life insurance policy is high, you may be able to borrow that amount at a low rate. On the other hand, if your short-term liabilities present too much of a burden, it may be time to end the shopping spree and make a change in your spending habits.

ASSETS—WHAT YOU OWN

CASH: AMOUNT

Checking accounts . . . .
Savings accounts . . . .
Cash on hand . . . .
Money market funds. . . . .
Credit unions . . . .
Time deposits . . . .
In a safe . . . .
Other . . . .

Cash value of investments:

Stocks . . . .
Mutual funds . . . .
Government savings bonds . . . .
Municipal bonds . . . .
Corporate bonds . . . .
Loans extended to others . . . .
Other . . . .

Cash that *could* be withdrawn from:

Retirement plans (pension, profit-sharing, Keogh, etc) . . . .
IRAs . . . .
Employee savings plans . . . .
Other . . . .

Cash value of business ventures. . . . .
Cash surrender value of insurance policies. . . . .

Real estate:

Market value of home and land . . . .
Market value of summer home . . . .
Market value of other real estate. . . . .
Market value of personal property:
Car, boat, trailer, other vehicles. . . . .

Household furnishings . . . .
Jewelry . . . .
Furs . . . .
Antiques, art, coins, other collections . . . .
Clothing . . . .
Other . . . .

  Total Assets: $_____

LIABILITIES—WHAT YOU OWE

Amount owed on home mortgage(s) . . . .

Installments:

Automobiles . . . .
Furniture & appliances . . . .
Credit card debts . . . .
Bank loans . . . .
Finance Company loans . . . .
Amount owed for taxes . . . .
Any other bill outstanding . . . .
Total Liabilities . . . . $_____
Total Assets . . . . $_____
Less: Total Liabilities: . . . . $_____
  TOTAL NET WORTH . . . . $_____

▶ **WHAT TO DO:** Your net worth statement is the starting point of your financial plan. You can see what you own (your assets) and what you owe (your liabilities). But as valuable as it is, it will pay off even more if you take stock of your financial situation routinely—perhaps every six to nine months—to see if you're making headway in reaching your objectives.

How To Prepare A Budget That Keeps Your Finances On Track

You can increase the funds you have to work with—even if you are now spending every penny you have. By planning and sticking to a budget that realistically reflects your spending power, you can eliminate unnecessary expenditures that are emptying your pockets. All it takes is applying a few sound management principles to your money affairs.

Your first step toward bringing your spending in line is to—

(1) figure out how many dollars you have to spend this year; and

(2) determine just where those dollars are going.

We've made it easy for you to figure out the amount of money you have to spend with the income statement that appears on the following page. Start with your gross salary; if you are a two-earner couple, include the earnings of both. Then add every item of income you expect to receive this year from *all* sources—keeping any estimates on the low side.

INCOME STATEMENT

Husband's earnings . . . . $
Wife's earnings . . . .
Earnings of other family members. . . . .
Bonuses . . . .
Interest & dividends . . . .
Rent income from property owned . . . .
Royalties. . . . .
Business profits. . . . .
Profits from sales of assets . . . .
Child support, alimony. . . . .
Gifts. . . . .
Other . . . .

Net Annual Spendable Income $_____
Net Monthly Spendable Income $_____

Part two of your financial inventory consists of measuring your expenses. Use the expense statement that follows as a guide and pull your figures from last year's checkbook, income tax returns and your paid bills and receipts. You'll be starting with fixed expenses such as rent or mortgage payments, utilities, taxes—bills that stay essentially the same from month to month. Variable expenses follow (e.g. clothing, entertainment, hobbies, etc). In some cases you'll have to make estimates, but for other items you should have exact figures. In either event, you should be able to come up with an annual and monthly figure for each expense category.

When you've filled in the chart above, you'll have a precise idea of where your money goes. There's bound to be room for improvement. You should concentrate your efforts on those mandatory and discretionary expenses that you can reduce—or at the very least, level out.

Mandatory expenses you can control: The big expenses in this category can be reduced with some simple financial planning moves. Here are a few examples:

Mortgage payments: You may have bought your home several years ago when interest rates where much higher than they are today. If that's the case, consider *refinancing* your home mortgage. This entails getting a new mortgage at today's interest rates and paying off the old, high-interest mortgage. Refinancing does involve additional one-time-only expenses, such as closing costs, points, maybe even a prepayment penalty. If you can recoup these expenses (by way of lower monthly mortgage expenses) within two or three years, refinancing makes a great deal of sense. See Chapter Four for details.

Installment and loan obligations: Bank credit cards, department store cards, gasoline credit cards, etc. are all valuable consumer aids, but some families overextend themselves with these sources of credit. Result: The monthly payments (and high interest charges) mount each month and eat up a high percentage of take-home pay. Combined with other loan obligations, the burden may in time become unmanageable.

One answer to that problem may be debt consolidation. How it works: You obtain a loan to pay off all your outstanding debts. You have one monthly loan

YOUR FAMILY'S EXPENSES

Mandatory Expenses You Generally Cannot Control:

Health insurance . . . . $

Child Care expenses . . . .

Medicine and drugs . . . .

Commuting costs . . . .

Real Estate taxes . . . .

Mandatory Expenses You Can Control:

Rent or mortgage payment . . . .

Installment and loan obligations . . . .

Income taxes and payroll taxes . . . .

Utilities (gas, oil, electric, water) . . . .

Fund for children's college education . . . .

Car costs (repairs, maintenance, gas) . . . .

Car and home insurance . . . .

Life insurance . . . .

Food . . . .

Discretionary Expenses:

Home furnishings and repairs . . . .

Family gifts (birthdays, holidays) . . . .

Clothing . . . .

Vacation costs . . . .

Charitable contributions . . . .

Personal expenses (e.g., haircuts) . . . .

Recreation, hobbies, magazines . . . .

Other (cigarettes, liquor, etc.) . . . .

CASH RESERVES AND SAVINGS . . . .

Total for year . . . . $_____

Total by month . . . . $_____

payment instead of a whole batch. Typically, the new loan is for a longer term than the old obligation, and the one monthly payment is smaller than the sum of the payments you made before debt consolidation. For additional information on how you can cut your credit card costs, see p. 12.

Federal income tax: Because of today's progressive tax-rate structure, Uncle Sam takes a larger bite out of your income as your earnings go up. That leaves less in your pocket for current consumption and for savings. Surprisingly, you have a great deal of control over the tax bill you pay each year. Your *Family Money Book* features scores of practical, easy to implement tax-saving ideas that will cut Uncle Sam's take year after year.

Utility bills: There are some simple energy-conservation measures you can take to cut costs if your heating/cooling or electric bills are high. Some examples: Caulking around windows and doors, or lowering thermostat settings in the winter and raising them in the summer. If these measures don't seem to help, then your home may not have enough insulation. Or your heating system may be old and inefficient and should be replaced.

Bolstering your home's insulation or replacing your heating system is expensive. But the money you spend now will yield steady annual dividends in the form of lower heating and cooling bills.

Fund for children's college education: Providing your children (or grandchildren) with a good college education may be one of your family's most important goals. Since college tuition is so expensive (and rising), you should start setting aside funds right now, even if college is a long way off. Fortunately, you can use tax savings to fund part of this large expense *and* cut the overall family tax bill (see Chapter Ten). And if you need financial assistance, we can tell you where to find the best sources of college aid to help you fund your child's education. See page 17.

Car costs: Few expenses can be more disastrous to the family budget than car repairs. They seem to hit you when you least expect—or can least afford—them. If your car repair bills are becoming an ongoing and expensive nuisance—the transmission one month, a valve job the next, a new alternator the month after— you may be throwing good money after bad. If your money is being eaten up in repairs, you may be better off buying a new car. See page 25 for tips on how to get the best deal on a new car.

How to level out expenses: Some of your mandatory expenses are payable annually, some quarterly, some bi-monthly, and some monthly. When several of these payments come due in the same month, your checkbook becomes a battlefield.

> ▶ **WHAT TO DO:** Allocate part of your monthly income to take care of these large expenses. Let's say you have three bills due in July: a car insurance premium of $200, a mortgage payment of $700 and an electric bill of $95. That comes to a rather hefty $995 that you have to ante up. Of course, since you know about these bills in advance you can actively plan for them by setting aside about $83 each month.

How to do it: Many banks offer automatic transfer privileges—by telephone, or by "money machine"—between checking and savings. You deposit your payroll check into your checking, transfer cash to savings, then pull cash back when it's needed (in the meantime, you earn interest). Or you can use a payroll savings plan, if your employer offers it. Upon your authorization, part of your check is deducted and deposited into a savings account.

Whatever the method, this reserve for large bills should be a separate account to avoid confusion with regular savings.

Your utility company may also have a monthly budget plan that allows you to equalize the payments for gas and electric bills. But watch out! Equalized payments are based on estimated usage and that could be higher than what you actually use. So figure things out carefully before you sign up.

Insurance costs: You may be spending more than necessary on your life, home and car insurance. Worse, you may be overpaying for inadequate coverage. See Chapter Eleven for a complete discussion on how to buy the insurance you need at the lowest possible cost.

Discretionary expenses: These expenses eat up an astonishingly high percentage of your earned income, but they're also the most amenable to cutbacks in spending. The best tactic for bringing this spending in line is to set a specific dollar amount to cover these expenses.

▶ **WHAT TO DO:** Establish an allowance in advance for your discretionary expenses and make a serious effort not to exceed it. Don't set yourself up for failure by knocking out expenditures for entertainment, say. The odds are you won't stick to your resolve. Rather, your self-imposed limits should be within reach.

Many people go overboard in spending because they have no game plan. If you know there's only so much in the pot for, say, entertainment or gifts, you're less likely to overspend. Your budget will show you that going over the limit in one area will require reduced outlays in other areas, such as setting aside less money for savings or your children's college education. Keep in mind that your initial budget is not chiseled in stone. It will take time to adjust to the new system and to find a realistic spending level for some expenses.

Planning for an emergency: Cash reserves—having a cushion to soften the blow of a financial emergency—is another essential element of your budget. An emergency fund equal to four to six months of your after-tax salary is generally recommended. On the other hand, if your employment is secure and you anticipate no major expenditures, you could get by with less. Put aside a small amount from each paycheck until your cash reserves equal the figure you've set for yourself.

Future plans: You've evaluated your basic expenditures and arrived at a plan for controlling your discretionary spending, but what about your long-range goals? If you're concerned about your future security, or your child's college education in particular, your employment years are the time to start saving.

▶ **WHAT TO DO:** Set aside between 5% and 10% of your take-home pay and put it into your savings. Think of this payment as simply another fixed obligation that comes off the top of your income. It will give you a sure shot at accomplishing your goals.

Here's An Easy Way To Boost Your Take-Home Pay

Raises aren't the only way to increase your take-home pay. If you've been getting oversized federal tax refunds the past few years, you can put more cash in your pocket each pay period by filing a revised Form W-4 (Withholding Allowance Certificate) with your employer.

If you qualify for any of the tax breaks listed below, you can probably increase your withholding allowances and your take-home pay:

• Deductible amounts to an IRA or retirement plan (see Chapter Seven and Eight).

• Special deduction for two-earner married couples (see Chapter Five).

• Deduction for job-related moving expenses (see Chapter Fourteen).

• Tax credit for child-care expenses (see Chapter Ten).

• Itemized deductions in excess of the standard allowance (for 1986, it's $3,670 for married couples filing jointly).

• Special withholding allowance (available to any single taxpayer with just one job, and a married person with a non-working spouse.)

• Losses from sales of investment property, such as stock.

Caution: In the usual instance, overwithholding doesn't make much sense since the Government doesn't pay interest on overwithheld taxes. But if your interest and dividend income is large, or if you've got other earnings not subject to withholding, it may pay to withhold more than necessary from your paycheck. This way, you can avoid a possible penalty for underpayment of estimated taxes.

HOW TO GET THE MOST FROM YOUR BORROWING POWER

The last few years have brought important changes in the way—and from whom—you can borrow money. Result: While banks are still very much in the credit picture they are certainly not the only game in town. There are many other—and possibly better—ways of borrowing money. Let's start with—

Retirement plans that allow plan loans are a good source of long-term, relatively low-cost credit. The tax law requires that plan loans (a) bear a reasonable rate of interest, (b) be adequately secured, and (c) be available to all employees on a non-discriminatory basis.

Loans repaid over a period of more than five years are considered taxable distributions from the plan, rather than a tax-free loan transaction. Loans that are required to be repaid within five years are not taxable distributions as long as the loan doesn't exceed the lesser of (1) $50,000, or (2) one-half of the employee's vested benefit. (If one-half the employee's vested benefit is less than $10,000, the employee may still borrow up to $10,000 tax-free.)

▶ **SPECIAL BREAK FOR HOME LOANS:** A housing loan is not subject to the five-year rule. In other words, the repayment period can be longer than five years without the loan being tagged a distribution. But note that a housing loan is fully subject to the dollar limits.

What is a housing loan? It's a loan made to enable an employee to buy, build, or substantially rehabilitate a home to be used as a principal residence by either the employee or a member of his or her family.

Retirement plan investment loans: These are different from regular retirement plan loans in that they're not based on the borrower's own retirement plan account. They are part of the general investment activities of the plan. In addition to conventional investments, a plan may allow its trustees to invest in obligations of employees—usually secured by home mortgages.

Although these loans are not subject to the same requirements as to amount and duration as regular retirement plan loans, security requirements are apt to be stringent. Reason: The plan is obligated to limit itself to prudent investments.

How You Can Borrow Against The Equity In Your Home

You can turn the equity in your home—the current fair market value less the amount still due on your mortgage—into a revolving line of credit that you can tap at your convenience, simply by writing a check.

And, unlike a traditional second mortgage, which also uses your home as collateral, you pay interest only on the funds you actually use. You're not required to take a lump-sum mortgage and pay interest on the entire amount.

Here are three important reasons for the popularity of home equity loans:

Liberal loan amounts: Your maximum credit line is generally pegged at either 70%, 75% or 80% of the value of your home less the balance remaining on the first mortgage. So, if your home is worth $120,000 and you have $30,000 left outstanding on the first mortgage, you would be able to borrow between $63,000 and $72,000, depending on the plan.

Low cost: As a general rule, the home equity loan will cost you less than other forms of borrowing. But your interest charge is not fixed. That's because the home equity loan carries a variable, floating interest rate. Interest is normally charged at the prime rate plus between 1.5% and 4% and is computed daily. Result: The cost of your loan follows the prime rate—down or up. And while there is no floor for how low the interest rate can fall, there is no ceiling on how high it can rise, either. Most lenders make a monthly adjustment if the prime rate changes, but some adjust the rate every two weeks.

Flexibility: Once your application is approved (approval is based on the amount of unencumbered equity in the home, credit history, and ability to successfully carry additional debt), you receive a supply of checks or a bank credit card (or in some instances, both) you can use to tap into your account. You can use all or part of the credit line available, but you are charged for only the amount you actually borrow. And you can pay off the principal at any time without a prepayment penalty.

▶ **APPLY ONLY ONCE:** Since equity access is a revolving credit line, funds repaid are automatically available to the user. And once you've been cleared for credit, you don't need to reapply or reveal the purpose of the loan. (If you get your home equity loan from a brokerage house, however, loan proceeds cannot be used to buy securities.)

If this sounds too good to be true, be advised that the many appealing benefits of home equity access also contain the kernels of potential financial difficulty.

If you've had trouble handling run-of-the-mill credit in the past, an unstructured, essentially open-ended home equity loan is probably not for you. Reason: Missing a lot of payments *could* lead to default and the loss of the home—and possibly worse. Reason: Your home's current value is the basis for the loan amount. If the value of the home decreases, you could be required to turn over additional assets to meet the obligation.

Another disadvantage: Like any other loan that carries a variable interest rate, you won't know at the beginning how much it will end up costing you.

Consumer action: If you decide to get a home equity loan, make sure you:

1. Have a specific and *significant* purpose for the borrowed funds (e.g., funding a child's college education, making costly home improvements, or refinancing high-interest debt, or second mortgage);

2. Do some comparison shopping. Check out what additional fees are involved in the different equity access plans: Some hit the borrower with origination fees (points) and annual account-maintenance charges that can drive up loan costs, especially if the amount you plan to borrow is small.

How To Borrow From Your Insurance Policy

Your insurance policy may be the most accessible source of credit. If it's a whole life policy (not a term insurance policy) it builds up a cash surrender value that you can borrow against—at extremely low interest rates that are specified in the insurance contract. The rates range from 5% on older policies to 8% or 10% on newer policies. You pay interest on the loan at the same time that you pay your premiums. There is no schedule for repayment of loan principal. You can pay off the loan in installments, or just make interest-only payments.

Generally, you can borrow up to 95% of the policy's cash surrender value. Since the cash value of the policy increases each year, so does the amount you can borrow.

Borrowing against your policy's cash value *is* easy, but before you plunge ahead, keep these factors in mind:

● Policy borrowing can be a good idea if you need cash for a worthwhile investment. But it's a bad idea if you will be consuming the cash (to buy a new car, go on a vacation, etc.) Remember that you are, in effect, paying interest to the insurance company for the use of your *own* money.

● The policy loan's very flexibility may work against you in the long run. Since there's no schedule for repayment of principal, your natural inclination will be to make interest-only payments as long as possible. Result: The total cost of the interest will be high.

● Any portion of a policy loan balance at your death will be deducted from the amount paid to your beneficiary. Suppose there's a $30,000 loan balance outstanding on your $100,000 life insurance policy. If you die, your beneficiaries receive only $70,000.

Five Basic Rules That Will Help You Slash Your Borrowing Costs

Besides shopping around for the best possible loan terms, there is a lot you can do to ensure that you pay the lowest possible charges on all your loans. Here are the six basic rules to keep in mind:

1. The cost of borrowing is obviously a function of the interest rates and loan amount. An equally important factor is *how and when you repay the loan.* The longer the loan balance is outstanding, the more the loan will cost you. A short-term loan at a high interest rate may cost *less* than a longer-term loan at a lower interest rate. For example, if you borrow $4,000 at 16% and pay it off over three years, total interest charges are $1,062.61. If you borrow the same amount at 18%, but pay it off over two years, total interest comes to only $792.71.

Shoot for the shortest manageable repayment time. And make sure any loan agreement allows you to repay the loan, preferably without penalty.

2. A loan's interest rate doesn't tell you how much you really pay. For example, the lender may tack on "closing fees" that drive up the total cost. Or the loan may be discounted (the interest is deducted in advance) and bear a true rate of interest that's *double* the stated interest rate.

The Federal Truth in Lending Law requires that the lender tell you what the loan's Annual Percentage Rate is. The APR represents the true cost of the borrowed money. It relates the finance charge to the amount of money you borrow, the amount of time you borrow it for, and also factors in any extra fees such as "points."

3. Don't sign any credit agreement before you understand the following elements and can identify them in the document: cash price of the item you buy; downpayment (or trade-in, if any); amount to be financed; the finance charge in dollars; the Annual Percentage Rate; the number, amount, and due date of the payments.

4. Beware of credit life and credit accident insurance. This type of policy pays off your loan balance if you die or become disabled while the loan is outstanding. It sounds like a good idea, but it's not. The insurance is almost always overpriced.

5. If interest rates fall—or if a better deal comes along—*refinance your debt.* Suppose you've got a $3,000 total balance on your store charge and credit cards and that your interest charge averages out to 19.8%. Bank X comes out with a new 16.8% card. If you refinance—borrow from Bank X and pay off the $3,000 balance on your old cards—you'll save $90 a year. That doesn't sound like much, but it's better to have the cash in your pocket than a lender's.

HOW TO COME OUT A WINNER IN THE CREDIT CARD GAME

Credit cards are convenient. You can carry a minimum of cash and rely on your cards to bail you out of money emergencies. And you usually need a major credit card to pay by check in a store. Finally, credit cards also give you—

▶ **VALUABLE PROTECTION:** If you buy defective merchandise with a credit card, you don't have to pay the charge when it comes due as long as (1) you make a good faith effort to return the merchandise or try to convince the merchant to make good on the product, (2) the item costs more than $50, and (3) you bought the goods in your home state, or within 100 miles of your home address.

But you can pay dearly for all this convenience. When you buy something with a credit card and don't pay the bill promptly, you are actually taking out a loan that can carry a sky-high 18%-22% interest rate. If you make minimum monthly payments you could wind up paying more in interest than the total cost of your purchases. And the family that comes close to its credit limit may be given an even larger credit limit to encourage spending. So it's easy for a family to get deeper and deeper in debt without realizing it.

Here's how you and your family can use credit cards conveniently, economically and intelligently, beginning with—

How To Choose The Best Credit Card Deal

If you think all credit cards are the same, think again. Interest rates, finance charges and fees vary greatly from one bank credit card to another. In fact, rates can vary by as much as 10%

How can you find the best deal? By taking advantage of the competition and shopping around. You don't have to get a credit card from a local bank. You may find the best deal from a bank in another state where the interest rates are low. All you do is write to the bank for an application, fill it out, and send it in. Ask your bank for the American Services Association's *Summary of Consumer Credit Laws and Rates*. That publication will give you a list of all the low-interest states.

Unfortunately, banks can *also* shop around for a better lending environment. Watch out for a letter in the mail informing you that your bank has moved its credit-card operations to another state. In all probability, the switch means a higher interest rate, unless, of course, you switch your business to another lender.

Also, you may want to check out a mid-sized bank rather than one of the larger, more aggressive banks that are out pushing their cards through the mail. Often, the rates at the smaller banks are more competitive. Credit unions usually offer lower rates, too.

Premium credit cards. Gold or platinum premium cards offer a higher credit line and additional features. But the annual fee is usually higher than for a regular card. So if you don't intend to take advantage of the extra perks—the gold or platinum card is just another costly status symbol you can do without.

What to look for in a travel and entertainment card. While travel and entertainment cards don't charge interest on most purchases, there is an annual fee for use of the card. However, you must pay your bill *in full* within 30 days.

> ▶ **CONSUMER ALERT:** Being forced to pay off the balance at the end of each month could work to your benefit. You'll be less likely to run up large bills if you know they have to be paid off promptly. And you will avoid interest charges.

Should you get a debit card? When you use a debit card to make a purchase, the money is deducted from your bank account (some debit cards are linked to a money market account at a brokerage house). So why would you want one? Answer: You gain some—

> ▶ **CONTROL OVER EXPENSES:** Because you use a debit card just as you use a checking account, there is no chance that you will forget to pay. Result: Psychologically, you won't be as tempted to get in over your head as you might if you were using a credit card.

Debit cards, however, have two drawbacks: (1) You can't withhold payment should a retailer sell you damaged goods and (2) should your debit card be stolen, your liability can go as high as $500.

How To Keep Your Credit Card Spending In Hand

With banks mailing out pre-approved credit cards to prospective customers across the country, the lure of easy money and ready spending may be hard to resist. The best way to keep credit cards from wrecking your finances is to set an installment payment limit—and stick to it.

One rule of thumb: First substract from your monthly take-home pay all your fixed expenses, i.e., mortgage payments and the like. (For this purpose include food, car or commuting expenses as fixed expenses.) Installment payments (including finance charges) shouldn't exceed 10% to 15% of what's left over. This is a conservative approach to installment spending.

> **Example:** Let's say your family has a take-home income of $3,000 a month. Your fixed monthly expenses comes to $2,000. *Result:* You'd be in the clear if your monthly installment payments were in the $100-$150 range.

Of course, if you charge a little here and charge a little there, your spending is liable to exceed the 10-15% limit you've set for yourself. To remove that possiblity you must—

▶ **KEEP RECORDS:** Treat your credit cards as you do your checkbook. Maintain a running balance of what you charge on each card. (Your best bet is to maintain separate index cards for each credit card noting the date, the purchase amount and the balance on the card.) *Result:* You focus in on exactly how much you owe and when you owe it. (Missing a payment date usually leads to late charges and higher interest payments.)

How To Protect Your Credit Cards

Credit card fraud is on the rise and it's costing consumers a bundle in higher fees and retail prices. It can also take money out of your pocket in a more direct form. If your credit card is lost or stolen, *you* pay for the first $50 of losses. You are not liable for the unauthorized use of your bank or telephone card *account numbers*, but you must notify the company as soon as you know of the illegal usage. Your liability on a lost or stolen automated teller machine card or debit card is $50 if you report the loss or theft within two days. If you don't meet the two-day reporting deadline, your liability jumps to $500. If you don't make a report within 60 days of getting a statement, there may be no limit to your liability.

▶ **WHAT TO DO:** You can protect your cards—and yourself—by making sure family members stick to these rules:

1. Don't carry more cards than you intend to use while shopping. Carry them separately from your driver's license or other types of identification. Reason: A thief with these items in his or her possession has all the identification necessary to cause a big dent in your pocketbook.

2. Keep or destroy any carbon copies of bills charged to your credit cards at stores, restaurants, and gas stations. Reason: Thieves rummage through trash of business establishments and use customers' names and numbers to charge merchandise.

3. Hang up on telephone callers who ask for your credit card number (some pose as survey takers or contest promoters). Chances are they're up to no good.

4. Make copies of each credit card you own and write down the issuer's phone number on the same sheet. The faster you report lost or stolen credit cards the better.

5. If you have an automated teller card, money card or access card, NEVER carry the access number around with you. Memorize it.

6. Save all your credit card slips. Reason: It's a good move to reconcile individual charges with what's reported on the credit card statement. That way, you'll know immediately if an unauthorized use of your card has been made.

PRODUCT WARRANTIES—WHAT THEY MEAN AND HOW THEY CAN HELP YOU

Product warranties are a major source of confusion for consumers. *Reason:* Many people are unaware what the warranty covers, how long its coverage lasts, and what rights they have if the manufacturer fails to make a repair under the warranty.

Background: Manufacturers who offer written warranties are required to clearly label them as either ''full'' or ''limited.'' The difference between the two designations lies in what the maker must do if the product does not perform satisfactorily. (Later on, we'll cover what protection you have if the manufacturer chooses not to affix a written warranty to its product.)

• Full warranty: Under a full warranty the manufacturer must repair or replace a defective product without charge and within a reasonable period of time during the warranty period. And it must give consumers a new product or a refund if the original product hasn't been repaired after several attempts.

▶ **TOO LARGE TO SEND BACK?** If a product is too large or too heavy to ship back to the store, it must be repaired or replaced right in your home. You pay nothing for either parts or labor.

You are protected by the ''full'' warranty even if you are *not* the product's original purchaser.

▶ **BUYER ACTION:** By law, copies of the complete warranty must be available in the store where a warrantied product is offered for sale. If a warranty isn't on the product itself or displayed nearby, ask the manager for a copy.

In general, you can measure the value of a ''full'' warranty by two things:

1. Duration: A two-year warranty is certainly more valuable than one for, say, 90 days. By the way, a ''life-time'' guarantee may not be as valuable as you think. Reason: The product may be guaranteed for its life—not yours.

2. Parts covered can cover so little of the product as to be practically worthless. For instance a ''full'' two-year warranty on the casing of a food processor is not very valuable. But one on the motor, container, and blades would be.

• Limited warranty: A manufacturer who uses a ''limited'' warranty can restrict his liabilities in ways not permitted under a ''full'' warranty. A ''limited'' warranty can require that you return the product to the store for repair. It may cover only the cost of parts, not labor. You may have to pay handling charges. Or you may be entitled to only a pro-rata refund under the warranty. A product could be warrantied for home use only. An air conditioner installed in your office might have no coverage. The warranty may not cover you if you are not the original puchaser. And, even if you are, you may be required to return a registration card to the manufacturer to get coverage.

▶ **WHAT TO DO:** Weigh the duration, extent of coverage, and restrictions of a ''limited'' warranty when you decide to buy a product. Keep in mind that the duration and coverage of a "limited" warranty can make it a better deal than even a "full" warranty.

Now let's talk about what happens if a manufacturer exercises the right *not* to expressly warranty its product. Are you out of luck if the product turns out to be a lemon? Fortunately, the answer is no. *Reason:* You are still protected by an—

▶ **IMPLIED WARRANTY:** Implied warranties are created under state law and exist automatically without being written down. The most common implied warranty— the warranty of merchantability—is a promise that a product is not defective and is fit for ordinary use at the time it is sold.

Another type of implied warranty requires that the product be suited for the particular purpose for which it was bought. To prevail under this warranty you must be able to show that the seller had reason to know: (1) that the product will be used for a specific purpose and (2) that you as the buyer are relying on his skill or judgment in selecting or furnishing suitable goods.

The duration of implied warranties varies from state to state. Some states enforce limited warranties for up to four years.

▶ **BE CAREFUL:** A *written* warranty may contain a phrase such as "Implied warranties on this product are limited to three months." If the written warranty itself extends for only three months, this could mean you have no legal recourse should you discover the product is defective after three months.

How To Protect Your Claim When A Product Goes Sour

By law, the following information must be given to you if a written warranty is provided for a product costing more than $15: Who is entitled to the protection and when it begins (unless it is the date of purchase); identification of the parts covered by the warranty; what will be done to correct defects or failures (including which items of service will be paid by the warrantor and which expenses must be borne by you). Finally, you must also be told of the steps to take in order to get satisfaction (including the company's name and address and a toll-free phone number you can use to get warranty information). The rest is up to you. For instance, don't throw away the sales receipt. You'll need it to prove the date you purchased the product. You might even save the ad that led you to buy the product. If may include guarantees that add ammunition to your complaint. And, obviously, keep the warranty itself in a file for future reference.

Extra protection: If you requested service, write down the dates—and keep a folder of your service receipts. *Reason:* If the warranty period runs out before the product is fixed, you will have proof that the defect was discovered while the warranty was still in effect.

What To Do When Things Go Wrong

It's a rare person indeed who hasn't fought with a store, credit card company, or bank over a billing error. Computer (or human) mistakes can lead to seemingly endless runarounds that succeed only in elevating your blood pressure—next month the error is still on the bill.

Does that mean you're powerless? Not at all. In fact the law gives you a potent weapon to help you fight back. It's called the Fair Credit Billing Act (FCBA).

The main purpose of the Fair Credit Billing Act is to force companies to resolve quickly consumer complaints about their bills. "Billing errors" may arise in a variety of ways. For example, the clerk may fail to credit a returned purchase, or the computer may bill you for the same item twice, or the store may mail the periodic statement to the wrong address.

▶ **CONSUMER ACTION:** Write—don't call—the company at the address given on your bill for billing error notices. Do so no later than 60 days after the initial bill containing the error is received.

The letter must include your name, address and your account number. You must also indicate that (1) an error exists on the bill, (2) its amount and (3) why you think the error has been made. (If you send along an documentation, a sales receipt, for example, make sure you retain a copy of it yourself.) You may want to send the letter "return receipt requested" to ensure that the company received it—and when. In any case keep a copy of the letter for your own records.

What happens next: The store, bank, or credit card company has thirty days to respond to your letter (unless, of course, the error is corrected before then). The dispute must be resolved one way or another within two billing cycles (but no later than 90 days) from the time the notice was received. *Important:* The notification letter you send activates the resolution process and shifts the burden of solving the problem to the creditor. A creditor can't retaliate against you for exercising your rights on a billing error. Once the creditor has your letter, it *cannot*—

- Try to collect the disputed amount or charges (by instituting court action or attachment proceedings, for example).

- Make or threaten adverse credit reports, or report the contested amount as delinquent to a credit bureau. The amount may, however, be reported as disputed.

- Close your account or accelerate the debt.

- Levy finance charges or late penalties on the amount in dispute.

▶ **IF YOU WERE RIGHT:** The store, bank, or credit card company must correct its mistake, credit your account, if necessary, and send you a correction notice.

HOW TO GET HELP IN PAYING FOR YOUR CHILD'S COLLEGE EDUCATION

Do you have a son or daughter about to apply for college? Then maybe it's time for you to do a little studying of your own. The subject: How to defray the ever-increasing cost of a college education—which currently runs about $50,000 for four years of room, board and tuition at a private university. You'll need to know as much as possible about the loans, grants and scholarships that are available for your child. The help is there. It's just a matter of knowing how and where to look.

How to get started: Once your child has been accepted by a college, you should obtain a financial aid form from the school. The form is used to record your family's income, assets, living expenses, family size, and your child's earnings, savings, and other sources of income.

Fill out the form and send it to a needs analysis service (the financial aid office will tell you which one). The service will examine your family's financial picture in relation to your child's college expenses and determine how much of the cost you will be expected to bear. That amount, known as your Family Contribution, will be subtracted from total college costs to arrive at your Family Need. That's the maximum amount of financial aid you can ask for.

Financial aid can come from a wide range of sources—federal, college or private, to name a few. Let's start with—

The Federal Government

Traditionally, Uncle Sam has been the most generous source of loans and grants for college-bound students. Because of budget cutbacks, this may no longer be true in the coming months and years. While all the following programs were available at presstime, you should check with the financial aid officer of your child's college to get the latest word.

National Direct Student Loan (NDSL): This is a low-interest (currently 5%) loan for undergraduate or graduate studies. The maximum amount an undergraduate can borrow is $6,000. Graduate students are eligible for an additional $6,000.

A student begins repayment of the loan six months after graduating, leaving school, or dropping below half-time status. Generally, the loan must be repaid in ten years.

However, a recipient may defer repayment for up to three years if he or she is a member of the Armed Forces or the Commissioned Corps of the U.S. Public Health Service, or a volunteer in the Peace Corps, VISTA, or comparable service. Deferments are also available for up to three years for students who are disabled or who are caring for a spouse in such a condition.

NDSL has one key limitation: As a general rule, it is available only to families with incomes of under $25,000.

Guaranteed Student Loan (GSL)

A GSL is a low-interest loan made by a bank, credit union, or savings and loan association. The loan is subsidized by the Federal Government. The amount you can borrow depends on family income.

• Under $30,000: Undergraduates can get loans of up to $2,500 for each year of study. Cumulative loans can't exceed $12,500. For *graduate students*: $5,000 per year with a cumulative ceiling of $25,000, minus what was borrowed as an undergraduate.

● Over $30,000. You must undergo a ''needs analysis'' to see how much money your child is eligible to borrow.

How the needs analysis is carried out: The school your child applies to will calculate need based on the following three factors: 1) the cost of education; 2) other aid your child might be receiving; and 3) expected family contribution. The school will take the sum of the last two factors and subtract it from the cost of education. The remainder represents student need.

The third factor—family contribution—is based on Government tables that take into account family income, family size, and the like. But before we go into greater detail on this, let's take a look at how a needs analysis would be carried out in this—

Example: Mary and John Smith have three dependent children, the oldest of whom will be attending State University in the fall. The cost of a year at State U is $7,000, but part of that cost will be defrayed by a $1,500 scholarship. The Smith's adjusted gross income, based on their Federal tax return, is $36,000. We assume their expected family contribution is $3,010.

Needs Analysis

Cost of education		$7,000
Expected family contribution	$3,010	
Financial aid	$1,500	
	$4,510	
Available resources		− $4,510
Student need		$2,490

▶ **IMPORTANT:** Students who qualify for a GSL must pay an "origination fee" of 5%, which is subtracted from the loan amount. Lenders are also authorized to require an insurance fee of 1%.

Parent Loans to Undergraduate Students (PLUS): Like GSLs, PLUS loans are made by a private lender. However, unlike GSLs, these loans are available to any family regardless of income.

Parents can borrow up to $3,000 a year, up to a total of $15,000 for each child who is a dependent undergraduate student enrolled at least half-time. Graduate students may borrow up to $3,000 a year up to a total of $15,000. This amount is in addition to the GSL limits.

Independent undergraduate students can take out their own loans for up to $2,500 a year. However, the PLUS loan, combined with the undergraduate's GSL, cannot exceed the yearly and total GSL undergraduate limits ($2,500 and $12,500).

▶ **KEY DISTINCTION:** A dependent student is one who is at least partially dependent on his or her parents for support. An independent student is someone who (1) is not claimed as a dependent on the parents' tax return, (2) does not live with his or her parents for more than six weeks during each year, and (3) does not receive more than $750 in annual assistance from his or her parents.

Repayment of a PLUS loan must begin 60 days after the loan is made. Payments are then made each month for the remainder of the loan. Graduate and professional students as well as independent undergraduates can defer repayment of the principal while they attend school full time. Interest payments, however, are due after 60 days.

Pell Grants: The Pell Grants Program provides undergraduates with cash awards which do not have to be repaid. Furthermore, a student can supplement a Pell Grant with other forms of federal and non-federal aid. For more information, write to the Public Documents Distribution Center, Department DED-87, Pueblo, Colorado 81009. Ask for the "Formula Book" for Pell Grants.

Supplemental Educational Opportunity Grant (SEOG): This is an undergraduates-only award which does not have to be repaid. Students are eligible for up to $2,000 a year, depending on need, the availability of SEOG funds at the school, and the amount of other financial aid the student is receiving.

Unlike Pell Grants, a set amount of money for SEOGs is given to each participating school. When that money is gone, there are no more SEOGs for that year. That's why it's critical that your child apply for an SEOG as soon as possible.

College Work Study (CWS): The College Work-Study Program provides jobs for both undergraduate and graduate students in need of financial aid. A student's total CWS award depends upon need, the amount of money the school has to dispense, and the amount of other aid received from other sources.

In order to qualify, a student must: (1) exhibit financial need and demonstrate that he or she can hold down a job and do well academically; (2) be a citizen or a permanent resident of the United States; and (3) be accepted for enrollment or be enrolled at least half-time at a qualifying college.

The school decides on the student's work schedule, based on class schedule, health and academic progress.

▶ **IMPORTANT:** Regardless of which Federal aid program your child applies for, keep in mind that money is usually distributed on a first-come, first-served basis. It's crucial that your child submit his or her application as early as possible. January 1 of the year in which your child plans to enter college is the earliest application date. And remember that federal aid does not automatically continue from year to year. Your child must reapply for aid each year he or she is in college.

Military Scholarships

If your child is interested in a career in the military, he or she may be able to get one of the Armed Forces to pay for college. Four-year ROTC scholarships, in amounts ranging from $25,000 to $45,000, are available to qualified applicants who are willing, upon graduation, to fulfill a six-year military obligation. The scholarships cover tuition, books and fees, and also include a monthly allowance of $100.

To qualify for a scholarship, an applicant must: (1) be a U.S. citizen and at least 17 years of age; (2) be a high school graduate or have equivalent credit; (3) meet certain physical standards; and (4) complete college and commission requirements by a certain age, depending on the program.

For more information on ROTC scholarships, contact your local recruiter or write to one of these addresses:

Army ROTC Information Center
P.O. Box 7000
Larchmont, NY 10538

Navy/Marine Opportunity Information Center
4015 Wilson Boulevard
Arlington, VA 22203

Air Force ROTC Advisory Service
Maxwell Air Force Base
Montgomery, AL 26112

Scholarships

There are a number of ways a student can turn academic achievement into dollars for college. Here's a look at some of the available college scholarship funds:

National Merit Scholarships: Thousands of college-bound students qualify each year on the basis of their scores on the Scholastic Aptitude Test. A student can get one of three awards:

1. One-time-only awards of $1,000, based solely on merit.

2. Renewable four-year scholarships, sponsored by participating colleges. These awards range from $250 to $2,000 per year, and are based on the student's need.

3. Renewable four-year scholarships, sponsored by corporations for the children of their employees. If your child is a national merit finalist and your employer sponsors an award, the National Merit Scholarship Corporation will send the company your child's name. Awards are based on need, and range from $250 to $2,000 per year.

Private scholarships: These are scholarships available in virtually every field of study, from aerospace to real estate, from private foundations and associations. To find out what scholarship money is available, here's—

▶ **WHAT TO DO:** Go to your library and ask to see Gale's *Encyclopedia of Associations*. This guide will give you the information you need on the amounts and requirements of scholarships and awards given to students with particular career interests.

Parent's Loan Programs

These plans have been set into motion by a number of organizations nationwide. They are specifically designed to aid middle-income families. Repayment schedules are established which are keyed into the family's income and the amount that the family wants to borrow on a per year basis. The annual figure can be adjusted up or down. Payments to the colleges are made through the bank and repayment schedules are quite generous (often up to six years). Many plans include an insurance policy. *Reason*: In case the parent becomes disabled or dies, the student is protected. He or she won't be forced to drop out of college.

Here is a list of plans and their sponsors: The Knight Agency Plan. The Knight Agency, Boston, Massachusetts.

Girard Bank's Educ-Check Plan. Girard Bank, 2nd & Chestnut St., Philadelphia, PA 19106.

Parents' Loan of Princeton University, Princeton Parents' Loan Plan, Office of the Controller, P.O. Box 35, Princeton, NJ 08534.

The Collegeaire Program, Student's Financial Services, One Perimeter Way N.W., Atlanta, GA 30339.

State Loans

Every state offers some kind of financial aid for college students; some are more generous than others. Depending on where you live, your son or daughter may be eligible for the following types of assistance: loans, merit awards, grants for specializing in a particular field of study, work-study money, or veterans benefits.

Some of these programs are based on need; all require the child to establish and prove residency. To find out about the educational assistance programs your son or daughter may be qualified for, contact your state's Department of Education or similar office. They should be able to give you the rundown on available state aid.

Other Cost-Cutting Strategies

Grants, loans and scholarships are all key parts of a college student's financial aid package. But there are other, less publicized, methods of keeping your son or daughter's college bill within reason.

Advanced placement: Advanced placement allows students to take college-level courses in high school and receive college credit for them. By accumulating enough of these credits, the student can skip one or two college semesters and thereby cut overall costs. The Advanced Placement Program is administered through the College Board. For more information, contact your high school guidance center, or write: CLEP, Box 2815, Princeton, NJ 08541.

In addition, you may be able to enroll your child in the College-Level Examination Program. If he or she scores high enough on a CLEP exam, say in mathematics, many colleges will grant credit in the subject. Your child gets the credit for an introductory college level course without your having to pay for it.

College cooperative programs: Students who qualify for this program alternate periods of study with periods of work in their chosen field. Although it may take longer to graduate, tuition costs are distributed over, say, five years rather than four. And co-op deals help to spread the burden because the student shares financial responsibility with both his or her parents and the college.

For more information on cooperative education programs, write to the National Commission for Cooperative Education, 360 Huntington Avenue, Boston, MA 02115.

HOW TO GET THE BEST LONG-DISTANCE TELEPHONE SERVICE AT THE LOWEST POSSIBLE PRICE

For as long as most of us can remember, if you wanted to make a long-distance telephone call, you picked up your AT&T phone and made use of AT&T's network to complete your call. But times have changed, and a stiff competition is now underway for your long-distance dollars.

▶ **WHOLE NEW BALL GAME:** Because of an agreement coming out of an anti-trust suit, AT&T's long distance competitors must be given equal access to local Bell operating company networks by late 1986. As a result, the competitors will be able to offer the easy dialing access that formerly only AT&T could offer. In other words, they can deliver the same type of service as AT&T. Net effect: If you choose, you can have your long distance calls carried by a company other than AT&T simply by dialing "1" plus the area code and the number.

▶ **IT'S YOUR DECISION:** It's up to you to pick which long-distance company you want as your primary carrier. If you don't make a choice, you will be assigned, at random, to any of the carriers serving your area.

How the decision process works: Three months before equal access goes into effect in your area, your local phone company sends you a ballot notifying you of your choices and asking you to make a selection. This ballot is returnable in 30 days.

Important: You're not locked in to your primary long-distance company, regardless of whether it's your choice or a random assignment. And it doesn't have to cost you anything to change. If you select another long-distance company within six months of equal access coming to your area (nine months from your first notice), there is no fee. If you switch after that time, your local phone company will charge you $5.

What's more, you may be able to use one or more long-distance companies other than your primary long-distance carrier. Another carrier may have a particularly good rate to a certain area or at a certain time of day.

What are your choices? They will be listed on your ballot and may vary in different parts of the country. There has been a shake-out in the industry due to the intense competition, and the top three, currently, are AT&T, MCI and GTE-Sprint. Before you decide on a company, check whether the numbers you commonly call are "on" or "off" the network of the carrier you select—especially if it's one of the smaller long-distance carriers.

Reason: While most of the major carriers will connect you with any phone in the U.S., some may charge you premium rates to reach more remote locations that are "off" their network. That means the last link of a call will have to be completed over another carrier's lines. This could cost you more. AT&T will continue to carry long-distance telephone calls from every exchange in the country. It will also provide worldwide service; other companies provide service to only some foreign countries, if at all.

Which company offers the lowest price? The best way to answer this question is for you to look at a typical long-distance bill. Make a list of the destinations of your calls, their length and the time made. Then consider the rates the various long-distance carriers charge. You can compare companies directly by asking them just what they would charge for those calls.

▶ **ANOTHER WAY TO COMPARE:** For a fee, you can have a computerized comparison of your long-distance bills done by the Center of the Study of Services, a non-profit consumer group in Washington, D.C.

How it is done: You send the Center a typical long-distance bill. Their computer produces a report showing how much you would have paid using various long-distance plans available in your area. For more information on this consultation service and its costs, call the Center at (800) 441-8933 or (202) 347-7283.

What features should you consider? There's more to choosing a long-distance carrier than rates per minute. The following list outlines other features to consider.

● As we said, a crucial consideration is whether the plan serves the locations you commonly call. Are those locations "on-net"? (i.e., will the calls be billed at the company's lowest rates?)

● Is there a startup fee or a minimum monthly charge?

● What are the per-minute rates? Many companies, such as AT&T, charge a higher rate for the first minute of a call, less for additional minutes.

● How is the length of a call rounded off? Most plans round up to the next highest minute. Others round up to the nearest tenth of a minute. This latter method saves you money.

● Are there any time-of-day restrictions on calls? In exchange for a lower startup fee, lower monthly fee or lower per-minute rates, some plans restrict you to certain calling periods.

● What are the discount periods? Most companies give discounts for calls made at certain times of the day or night. These discounts should coincide with the times when you tend to make most of your calls.

● Are there discounts for volume or prompt payment?

● What is the basis for setting rates: mileage or area code? One or the other may cost more, depending on where you are in your area and the locations you are calling in another area. Other plans don't consider distance at all; some have special rates to neighboring states. Again, to be sure of getting the best rates, you have to know your particular calling pattern.

● How good is a company's transmission quality? Even with equal access, some differences in quality will occur. Various factors are involved, including: how well a carrier maintains its facilities, i.e., circuits; whether transmission is through cable (AT&T), satellite (SBS), or microwave (MCI); etc. The truth is in the talking. But you can get an impression of a particular carrier's quality by asking friends or colleagues who use it if they are satisfied.

● If you spend $30 or less on your long-distance bills, you should avoid companies with monthly fees, minimum usage charges and startup fees.

For more information: If you want to know more about slashing your phone costs, you can read ''The Complete Guide to Lower Phone Costs,'' written by Robert Krughoff, the president of the Center for the Study of Services. You can obtain the book by writing to: Lower Phone Costs, 806 15th St., N.W., Suite 925, Washington, D.C. 20005.

HOW TO DRIVE HOME THE BEST DEAL ON A NEW CAR

Although interest rates on car loans are lower than they have been in recent years, car prices are still sky-high. How do you get the most for your money? The best way is to arm yourself with the facts on how to buy at the lowest price, how to trade in your old car, and how to inspect the car before you accept delivery.

How to buy at the lowest possible price: Here are ways you can save money buying a car: (1) Be prepared to haggle: the car salesman does not expect you to buy at the first price he quotes. Typically, you'll make a lower offer and then negotiate from there. Take the time to find out what the car (and options you want) cost the dealer. You can get this information, and the range of dealer mark-ups, from independent sources such as Consumer Reports.

(2) Consider using an auto broker: This is a buying service which orders a car for you at a price as low as $50 or $75 over invoice price. In return, you pay a fee, ranging from $20—$400, or a share of the markup. For example, a national service called Car/Puter (800-221-4001) will, for a $20 fee, refer you to a dealer

near you which sells cars to Car/Puter clients, at prices typically $50 to $150 over invoice for domestic cars and $500 over invoice for imports.

(3) Buy late in the year: You've bound to get a lower price since dealers want to clear out "old" inventory before the new models arrive.

(4) Look into used rentals: The three major car rental companies, Avis, Hertz and National, sell cars that have been used as rentals. Prices are low, each car comes with a complete maintenance record, and major components are warranted for a period of time.

(5) Corporate twins: If you're thinking of buying an American car from one the the big three automakers: Ford, Chrysler or GM, check whether the model you want has a "corporate twin," which is mechanically the same car as one marketed by a less expensive division of the same corporation. The cars differ in name, trim *and price*.

(6) Buying a car in Europe: You can save between 5—10% off the price of a European car if you pick it up in Europe and have it shipped back to the United States. Caution: Be sure the American subsidiary will honor your warranty as a car purchased in Europe.

How A Special Kind Of Car Loan Can Help You Buy A Luxury Car

You may be able to buy the car you want at a cost you can afford with a new kind of car loan.

▶ **INNOVATIVE FINANCING:** You take out what's called a balloon auto loan. This means you pay substantially lower monthly payments during the first year of the loan than you would with a conventional loan. And a higher percentage of each payment is deductible interest.

Result: When you figure in the greater tax savings, the edge over conventional loans is even bigger.

The best part is that you are not required to make the balloon payment if you don't want to.

Why don't you have to pay the balloon at the end? To answer that, let's first take a look at how the typical balloon auto loan works.

You make a downpayment on the car you want and apply to a local bank for a balloon loan for the balance. The bank makes an estimate of what the value of the car will be at the end of the loan period—say, three years from now. It then agrees to buy back the car from you at that price. That buy-back price equals the balloon payment on the loan. The difference between the car's actual price and buy-back price is called the residual.

Each month you pay interest and principal on the residual (less downpayment), and only interest on the buy-back amount.

Result: Your monthly payments are smaller than they would be with a conventional loan.

The low monthly payments you make with a balloon auto loan are comparable to lease payments. But unlike a personal car rental, a good part of your payments is deductible interest. (Of course, if you rent a car for business purposes, the lease payments may be deductible as a business expense.) This deductible feature makes balloon loans especially attractive to car users in high tax brackets.

What happens after three years? You get—

▶ **THREE CHOICES:** You can: (1) Pay the buy-back price in cash and keep the car, (2) refinance the buy-back price as a used car loan, or (3) give the car back to the bank and forget about the balloon payment.

In other words, you—and not the bank—are in the driver's seat. If you feel the car is worth more than the buy-back price, you can keep the car or sell it to someone else at a profit. If you feel it's worth less, you can simply turn the keys over to the bank and walk away from the deal.

Example: Mr. Benson is buying a new car for $12,000. He has $1,800 for a downpayment and will borrow the remaining $10,200. If he gets a conventional three-year loan at 13%, his monthly payments would come to about $344.

During the first year of ownership, Benson will lay out $4,124—and 28% of that will be deductible interest. So, assuming he's in the 44% tax bracket, Benson will be out of pocket $3,617 the first year, including the tax savings.

▶ **ALTERNATIVE MOVE:** Instead of getting a conventional loan, Benson gets a three-year, 13% balloon loan for $10,200. The car is estimated to be worth $5,400 at the end of the three years, so the residual on the car is $6,600. Benson pays principal and interest on $4,800 ($6,600 less the $1,800 downpayment), and interest only on the remaining 45,400.

New result: Benson's monthly payments drop to less than $221. His payments for the first year total $2,643—and a full 47% of that is deductible. This slashes the out-of-pocket cost of his first-year payments to $2,095. So by going the balloon loan route, Benson can have the same car for 42% less in actual cost.

Looking at it another way: Suppose Benson didn't want to spend more than $221 a month on a new car. If he took out a conventional loan, he would have to settle for a car costing less than $8,400. But, by getting a balloon loan, he can "buy up" to a $12,000 car.

Ground rules: The bank imposes certain rules when it makes a balloon car loan. A minimum downpayment is required (usually 10%). And you must keep the car well-maintained. You are responsible for making your own repairs, getting insurance, etc.

Also, you cannot exceed a certain mileage limit over the term of the loan. Typical limit: 18,000 miles a year for the length of the loan. So if you drive 50,000 miles over a three-year loan period, you are under the limit no matter how many miles you drive in any one year.

If the car is damaged or you exceed the mileage limit, you may have to make an additional payment to the bank before it will take the car back. Or you may have to pay more than the car is worth if you want to keep it.

Note: Although the interest charges on the loan should be deductible, the Government hasn't ruled on this either way.

Not all banks offer balloon auto loans, and those that do have slightly different requirements and interest rates. So you will have to shop around for the best available deal.

How To Trade In Your Old Car

If you intend to trade in your old car, don't bring up the subject until you've nailed down the price of the new car. Then ask the salesperson what you'll be given on a trade-in. If you tell the salesperson at the outset that you're trading in, he or she will quote you a high figure for your old car. But the salesperson will also jack up the price of the new car.

On the other hand, if you get the trade-in price after you know what the new car will cost, he'll have to give you a more realistic figure. And, you may be able to beat his trade-in price by selling your old car privately.

If your trade-in car is only a couple of years old and well-maintained you may be in for a pleasant surprise. You may be able to sell it privately for nearly as much as you paid for it a few years ago. To determine this value, go to the financial institution where you do most of your business. The loan manager can look up the pricing figures in the "Blue Book." These figures are compiled on the wholesale value of cars or what the bank or other financial institution would lend you to buy the car.

Expect hundreds, not thousands, of dollars more on the trade-in of a car in extremely good condition.

▶ **ALTERNATE ROUTE:** You may want to donate your old car to a nonprofit organization rather than trade it in. Reason: You can take the car's current market value as a charitable deduction on your tax return.

The New Car Closing Deal Checklist

Picking up a new car is exciting—it's also the time to make sure that it lives up to your expectations. Here are some of the things to look for *before* you take delivery:

☐ Is the car *exactly* the model you ordered and does it have the options you ordered? Check your order form to confirm this.

☐ Is the body damaged in any way? Sometimes the sheet metal gets nicked and dented in transit. Check to see if repairs were made before it got to the showroom to be sold as new. Daylight inspections are a must if want to detect paint problems.

☐ Are any parts loose or missing? These might include bumpers, hubcaps, oil dipsticks, gas caps, etc.

☐ Are there any signs of engine, transmission and brake leaks?

☐ Do all the outside doors, glove compartment door, hood lid and all windows close securely?

☐ Does the car body leak? Ask to have the car washed just before you take delivery and feel and look around for water leaks near the windows and doors, in the trunk and under the dashboard.

☐ Do all the controls and accessories (heater, radio, brake and turn signals, windshield wipers, lights and so on) work?

☐ Take the car for a short test drive. Don't limit yourself to a spin around the block. Take the car out to the turnpike to see how it performs at various speeds. Does it perform to your satisfaction?

☐ Ask the dealer to sign a delivery service form that states that all pre-delivery services have been completed. Get a copy for yourself.

☐ Ask the dealer to sign and date all warranties.

☐ After you've gone through the checklist to your satisfaction, then, and only then, do you turn over your check to the dealer (or, sign the loan agreement, if you get financing through the dealer). At that point you can feel confident that you've done everything possible to prevent a lemon from sitting in your driveway.

HOW TO GET THE BIGGEST BANG FROM YOUR VACATION DOLLARS

Going on vacation doesn't have to be an expensive proposition—if you follow a few simple rules:

● Travel off season: If you know the right time to go, you can get your vacation at a discount. And there's always an off-season somewhere. For instance, high-season in the Caribbean starts in Mid-December and ends in Mid-April. *Reason:* That's when residents of colder climes want to migrate south. But the weather will generally be just as good (and often better) during the "off-season." And the prices for air fare, hotel rooms, restaurants, etc. will be lower. You'll get better service and you'll have the place to yourself.

● Go where the crowds don't: Most tourists meekly follow fellow vacationers to the most overcrowded and underserviced locations around. And they are guaranteed to be miserable. So stay away from tourist traps and get off the beaten path.

● Always ask for lodging discounts: It's worth the cost of a long-distance phone call to learn about a "Supersaver Discount Weekend" or "Off-Season Specials." Use a motel or hotel chain's toll-free reservation number to make inquiries, too. And pay attention to ads in the travel sections of newspapers for dollar-saving arrangements.

● Play the exchange rate game: Try to visit a country where the cost of living is low and the rate of exchange for the U.S. dollar is high. Since this information changes, ask someone at your bank to give you a rundown of the most up-to-date exchange rates for the countries you might like to visit.

● Shop where the locals do: It's fine to window shop the exclusive stores around the world. But stick to department stores and out-of-the-way places where the locals do their shopping. Money-saving tip: Many countries have a Value-Added Tax (10% to 18% added automatically to the purchase price). If you spend more than $55 in one store, you can usually get refund forms to present to customs when you depart. Note: Don't pack your gifts; they may be inspected.

● Check out tourist discounts: Bus, subway and train tickets for unlimited travel can be bought cheaply in many countries. Some foreign restaurants feature specially priced tourist menus or fixed-price menus. So, before you leave for your trip abroad, ask the tourist offices of the countries you'll be visiting what special discounts are available.

● Call home collect: To avoid those huge service charges that hotels routinely add to your bill, call collect when you call home. And don't assume that calls from U.S. hotels are any better. They're not. You can wind up spending more than four times as much for a local phone call from your hotel room than from the public phones in the lobby or out in the street.

● Look into plans that help you if you are injured or ill when traveling abroad: Membership in such a program entitles you to (1) qualified free medical service or evacuation if such service is not available nearby, (2) free legal assistance if required in connection with an accident and (3) assistance in such nonmedical travel emergencies as lost luggage, tickets or travel documents.

How To Get The Most From A Timesharing
Arrangement

Whether it's a condo on the beach in Hawaii or a ski resort in Vail, timesharing may be a money-wise way to go on vacation and avoid the ever-increasing cost of a room at a hotel or resort.

How it works: Timesharing is an arrangement whereby you pay, in advance, to reserve a week or more of vacation at a location for the next 20 to 50 years. For that reason, the idea is particularly attractive to people who are interested in returning to the same spot year after year.

In general, there are two types of timesharing arrangements:

1. Fee simple plan: This gives you ownership of your week and a piece of the property. For example, if you select the first week of April at The Sunshine Resort under a fee simple plan, you have exclusive use of a room for that week, and a 1/52nd interest in the resort.

Ownership of a timesharing unit gives you the right to rent, sell, loan or will your share. You pay property taxes and are able to deduct interest and taxes proportionate to your share of the property.

2. Right-to-use plan: Here, you do not own your unit: You simply have the right to use it for a specified period each year for a number of years. At the end of that time, the timesharing privilege expires.

Potential pitfall. The big problem with non-ownership plans is that they can leave you without any protection should the resort go bankrupt.

▶ **WHAT TO DO:** Ask that a non-disturbance clause be added to the timesharing agreement. This forces the resort's lender to recognize your occupancy right in case of foreclosure. Make sure the clause is in writing, is recorded with the local deed office, and is also included in the mortgage or construction loan.

Added precautions: Regardless of what type of timesharing arrangement you choose, you can protect yourself further by taking these steps:

● Make sure that the developer has set up an escrow account to ensure that the facilities will be completed and free of claims.

● Get a written commitment from the seller that any facilities that have not been completed will be built as promised.

● Have your lawyer read over the timesharing agreement. Find out what your rights are if the builder or management company has financial problems or defaults.

● Obtain a complete breakdown of the annual assessments before you buy. These should include management of the property, taxes, utilities, upkeep, etc.

● Contact local real estate offices, the Better Business Bureau and consumer protection agencies and find out what they know about the project and the developer.

● Examine the facilities. Make sure the buildings are of quality construction, that they are kept clean and in good condition, and that recreation facilities are properly maintained and adequate for the size of the resort.

● Find out if you can trade your timesharing week for another time at the same resort, or for a week at another resort run by the same developer. But keep in mind that timesharing exchange networks usually let you swap your week only for one of the same or lesser desirability.

● Check to see if the developer is a member of the National Timesharing Council of the American Land Development Association (ALDA). ALDA is the national trade association for recreation, resort and residential real estate developers, and is located at 604 Solar Building, 1000-16th Street N.W., Suite 604, Washington, D.C. 20036.

Here's A Vacation Idea With A "Homey" Touch

Capturing the charm and flavor of a foreign country—or even another part of the U.S.—can be difficult when your hotel is in a well-known tourist area. In order to find out how the other side really lives, you might want to—

▶ **EXCHANGE YOUR HOME:** There are a number of firms that arrange home swaps. For instance, they match Americans who want temporary homes in Europe with homeowners there who are looking for a similar arrangement in America. Many agencies will also set up swaps for Americans travelling in this country.

Added benefits: Living in a home while on vacation lets you bring the entire family at no extra cost, unlike a hotel or motel. What's more, you'll enjoy the comfort, convenience and privacy of a private home away from home. Many deals also include cars, household help, country club privileges and child care services.

▶ **WHAT TO DO:** For more information, write: Vacation Exchange Club, Inc., 12006-111th Avenue, Unit 12, Youngtown, Arizona 85363. Or call 602-972-2186.

Chapter 2

Today's Best Ways
to Earn A Higher Return
on the Family Nest Egg

The rich get richer for a reason: They have the means and the know-how. You may not have the same financial resources, but you can certainly use the same know-how. Astute individuals like yourself can take advantage of many of the same money-makers used by the rich without putting up large amounts of capital or taking unnecessary risks.

This Chapter covers a number of investment options that are within your means. You'll see how to make the most of the traditional money-makers such as money market accounts, mutual funds, municipal bonds and Government securities. You'll also get the straight story on the rewards—and risks—of the more sophisticated techniques, such as buying on margin and short sales.

LOW-RISK WAYS TO INVEST YOUR CASH RESERVES

All of us have cash we can't afford to lose, money we rely on for unforeseen expenses and emergencies. You want to invest these dollars and see them grow. But above all you must have safety. That's what this section is all about. It discusses those money-makers that put a premium on safety. There are no absolute 100% guarantees—there never are. But there are ways you can build your wealth with a minimum of risk—and a maximum of peace of mind.

Why Money-Market Funds Are A Good Place
To Park Your Cash

If you keep lots of cash in a regular savings account, you are losing money. There is an alternative you should consider looking into: Money market funds.

What are money market funds? They're akin to mutual funds—you deposit your money in the fund and let the fund's management do the investing for you (they spread the risk around through a number of money market securities). Money market funds offer three advantages:

#1—Low initial investment: The initial amount required to invest in a money market fund is generally $500 or $1,000. And some funds now allow you to make subsequent deposits of as little as $50.

33

#2—Liquidity: You can usually write an unlimited amount of checks on your money market balance with no charge involved. Some funds allow you to write checks for any amount; others have a small minimum requirement ($50 or $100).

Result: Money market funds give you flexibility other investments—for example, six-month CDs—don't have. You have access to your money and can earn interest at rates comparable to those paid by bank CDs. It's like having a high interest-paying checking account.

#3—Safety: Although money market funds are not federally insured you can buy yourself protection by using a money-market fund that invests 100% in Federal obligations (i.e., Treasury bills, notes and bonds), or a fund that is insured by a private company. Finally, you can put your nest-egg cash in a bank money market fund. These funds combine higher rates with—

> ▶ **GOVERNMENT INSURANCE:** Depositors in bank money market funds are covered by Federal insurance (up to $100,000 per account). That appeals to investors who like the security of savings accounts and the convenience of dealing with their local banks.
>
> The drawback: You may have to accept a slightly lower interest rate than you could get with a non-bank money market account. And you may have to keep your account above a certain level to earn the high interest rate that the bank offers. If your account drops below a minimum amount (e.g., $2,500), you earn interest at only the passbook rate (and you may also have to pay a service charge). The banks generally permit you to write up to three checks a month on your account balance.

How A Certificate of Deposit Allows Investors To Play The Money-Market Game

Unlike a money market account where the yield fluctuates constantly, bank certificates of deposit (generally called CDs) allow an investor to lock in a yield for a fixed period of time. When it appears that interest rates have peaked or are falling, you can lock in current yields by buying a two, three, or even five year CD. On the other hand, if you think interest rates are heading up you can purchase a short-term CD say for 90 days or six months—and then reinvest the proceeds in a higher yielding CD.

Let's take a closer look at these popular wealth-builders.

● *Maturity dates:* Before CDs were deregulated, they came with standard maturities—for example, six months (actually, 182-days) or one year. Now many banks offer what are sometimes referred to as "designer" CDs—you can design the CD to last for as long as you want. If your child's tuition bill is due in 150 days, for example, you can set up a CD to last 149 days and use the earnings to help pay the tuition.

● *Minimum deposit requirements:* Previously, the amount required to purchase, say, a six-month CD, was $10,000. Now small investors—those who don't have $10,000 of cash on hand—can take advantage of CDs too. However, most banks still require some sort of minimum deposit. General rule of thumb: Short-term CDs (those maturing in a year or less) may require deposits of $1,000 or $2,500; long-term CDs (maturing in more than a year) only $500.

● *Compounding:* Some CDs are compounded at a simple interest rate; others are compounded daily. All other things being equal, you are better off with a CD that is compounded daily. Reason: Your interest earns interest every day and your overall return is higher.

How You Can Earn Interest On A CD In 1986 And Defer Taxes Until 1988

As a general rule, you have to pay tax each year on the interest earned by your CD, even though you haven't withdrawn the interest. But there is a big exception: Interest on a short-term CD (maturity period of 12 months or less) can be tax-deferred if (1) you can't withdraw the interest until the CD matures, or (2) you can't withdraw interest without incurring a substantial penalty. Result: You owe no tax on the interest until maturity.

Bottom line: If you buy a short-term CD in 1986 that doesn't mature until 1987, you pay no tax on the interest until you file your return in April, 1988.

Of course, if the CD permits penalty-free withdrawals of interest in 1986, the interest is taxable income for 1986 even if no actual withdrawal takes place.

This technique will work anytime during the year, but the earlier during the year that you purchase a CD that doesn't mature until the following year, the more tax you will defer for a year.

Investing in this kind of CD has an obvious drawback. You can't get at your money before maturity without paying a penalty. But you can minimize the drawback. Some banks offer a CD that permits you to free up your money as soon as you have accomplished your tax goal. It's a—

▶ **DO-IT-YOURSELF CD:** You—and not the bank—set the maturity date for the CD. As long as you set the maturity date after December 31, 1986, the interest isn't taxable until 1987 (assuming no penalty-free withdrawals are allowed before then).

Payoff: You tie up your funds for the minimum amount of time needed to get tax deferral.

How To Get High Yields And Tax Benefits From A Super-Safe Investment

What are you looking for in an investment? Safety is number one with some investors, others want tax savings and still others prefer a high yield. If all three are important to you, you may want to consider U.S. Treasury Bills (T-Bills).

▶ **SAFETY:** T-Bills are backed by the full faith and credit of the Federal Government. You can't get any safer than that.

▶ **HIGH YIELD:** The rate of return on a T-Bill is competitive with many other money-market investments.

▶ **TAX-SAVINGS:** The income from T-Bills is exempt from state and local taxes. And, depending on the maturity date of the bills, you may be in line for Federal income tax deferral.

How to invest: You can purchase T-Bills that mature in three, six or twelve months for a minimum investment of $10,000. You submit a bid to the Federal Reserve Bank along with your check for $10,000. The purchase price is set at an auction held every Monday (or preceding Friday if Monday is a bank holiday). The Treasury then sends you a "discount check" for the difference between the purchase price and $10,000 face value. When the bill matures you get $10,000 back.

Since Treasury Bills are sold at a discount price and are redeemed at face value upon maturity, the return is the difference between the purchase price and the face value (assuming you hold the T-Bills until maturity). Here is how you can compute the approximate yield:

$$\text{Investment yield} = \frac{(100 \text{ minus price}) \ 365}{\text{price (number of days to maturity)}}$$

What are the tax angles? As we've already mentioned, T-Bills are exempt from state and local tax. That may not sound like much, but it can be significant. For example, a resident of New York City with a taxable income of $40,000 purchases a T-Bill with a yield of 10%. The equivalent yield (before Federal tax) for an investment subject to state and local tax—say, certificates of deposit—is only 8.4%.

▶ **TAX BREAK:** The interest income from T-Bills is not taxed until the year it matures, even though most of the interest may have accrued in a prior year. So some astute timing on your part can defer the tax on interest income for a year.

For example, a 12-month T-Bill bought in June of 1986 will mature in 1987 and you won't owe any tax on it until you file your 1987 return in 1988. But a six-month T-Bill bought before July, 1986 will mature in 1986 and you will have to report the interest on your 1986 return.

How to buy T-Bills by mail: You can buy Treasury bills directly from the U.S. Government by mailing a noncompetitive tender form (obtained from any Federal Reserve Bank) to a Reserve Bank or branch, along with your certified check for $10,000.

Or you can send a letter with your check stating: (1) that your bid is noncompetitive; (2) the face amount of the bills you want; (3) the maturity (3, 6, or 12 months); (4) your Social Security number and business telephone number. Print or type "TENDER FOR TREASURY BILLS" along the bottom of your envelope.

▶ **EXTRA REQUIREMENT:** Your tender must be accompanied by a completed W-9 Form (Payer's Request for Taxpayer Identification Number). The Form is available from any IRS office or from your local Federal Reserve Bank or branch. If you don't include a completed Form W-9, your tender will be rejected and your money returned to you.

Treasury Notes and Bonds: They are similar to Treasury Bills in that they are IOUs backed by the full faith and credit of the U.S. Government. And the interest rate on the Notes and Bonds is also determined by an auction.

▶ **LOW-COST, HIGH-YIELD OPTION:** Notes generally have a maturity of two to ten years. Bond maturities are longer than that. However, Notes and Bonds are available in denominations lower than T-Bills—as low as $1,000—and, as a general rule pay higher interest than T-Bills.

For more information on currently available Treasury Bills, or Notes and Bonds, check your phone book for the number of the Federal Reserve Bank in your area. They'll have a recorded message and another number to call if you still have questions.

Government Savings Bonds Offer the Best of Both Worlds to Smaller Investors

U.S. Government Savings Bonds—known as EE Bonds—have always been attractive because they offer:

● Safety. They are backed by the full faith and credit of the U.S. Government.

● Low cost. A $50 Bond can be purchased for as little as $25.

● Tax shelter. There is no tax on the interest until the bonds are cashed in or mature.

There's yet another key feature that makes EE Bonds a standout in today's unpredictable money-market climate. This is one investment that offers a—

▶ **FLOOR ON YOUR INTEREST, BUT NO CEILING:** Here's how the yield works on a Series EE Bond held at least five years. For each six-month period a Bond is held, it pays the *greater* of (1) 85% of the average interest rate of five-year U.S. Treasury securities issued during the immediately preceding six months or (2) 7½% compounded semiannually.

Bottom line: If interest rates go up, the EE Bond rate goes up, too. But if interest rates drop, EE Bonds can't drop below 7½%. In other words, while the yield on, say, money market funds may drop below 7½%, EE's will continue to yield 7½%.

Important: The variable rate feature applies only to Bonds purchased after October 31, 1982.

▶ **GOOD NEWS:** If pre-11/1/82 Bonds are held for five years past that date, it's a can't-lose proposition. You pocket the greater of the yield promised when the Bond was issued or the variable investment yield. In other words, an EE Bond bought in October, 1982, will pay no less than 9% (eight-year maturity) and may pay more if 85% of the average rates for Treasury obligations is higher than 9%.

Of course, like Series EE Bonds purchased after November 1, 1982 older E and EE Bonds must be held for five years after November 1, 1982, for you to get the choice between the guaranteed and the variable investment yield.

All Savings Bonds sold at a discount, new or old, Series E or EE, have one key attraction from the tax standpoint.

▶ **TAX DEFERRAL:** You don't owe any tax until you cash the Bonds in (unless you elect to pay tax annually on the Bond's increase in value). In fact, you can defer taxes past the maturity date of your Bonds by rolling the proceeds over into Government HH Bonds.

HH Bonds are straight interest-bearing obligations that pay interest (7½% on new issues) every six months. After November 1, 1982, HH Bonds were only issued in exchange for Series E or EE Bonds. Tax break: You can trade in your EE Bonds for HH's without paying any current tax on the accrued interest from the EE Bonds.

How To Lock In High Yields On Treasury Bonds

Stripped Treasury bonds are an interesting opportunity for investors looking for a safe way to lock in a high yield. When you buy stripped Treasury bonds, what you get is U.S. Treasury bonds with the interest coupons removed. You buy the bond at a low price and wait until it matures. Your return comes solely from the difference between the purchase price and the value at maturity.

The absence of interest payments is a key feature. If you buy a 9%, 10-year stripped Treasury bond, you have locked in that yield until maturity. In contrast, if you buy a 10-year coupon Treasury with a quoted yield of 9%, you must reinvest the semiannual interest payments at that rate to realize a 9% return over ten years.

But don't U.S. Treasury bonds pay interest semiannually? The answer, of course, is "yes." That's where the "stripping" comes in. Every Treasury bond is composed of two elements: (1) the bond itself, which is redeemed at face value at maturity, and (2) the right to semi-annual interest payments. What happens is that the interest payments are stripped from the bond.

Example: A stripped Treasury bond that matures at $61,600 in the year 2005 sold for $10,000 in early 1986. That works out to 9.3% yield to maturity.

What happens if interest rates go higher in the future? Then you would be better off with a coupon bond where you can reinvest the interest payments at the higher rate. On the other hand, interest rates may go lower. In that case, you are sitting pretty. In the case of the stripped bond in the example above, you know you will bet 9.3% over the entire 19-year period.

There are two kinds of stripped Treasurys.

Broker stripped bonds: Here, a broker buys U.S. Treasury bonds and strips them. The bonds are held by custodian banks in an irrevocable trust, and the banks issue certificates for the interest payments and for the principal. The certificates are sold separately by the broker. Brokers give various names to these receipts and market them by their acronyms: TIGRs (Treasury Investment Growth Receipts), CATs (Certificates of Accrual on Treasury Securities), etc.

Government stripped bonds: These bonds—called STRIPS (Separate Trading of Registered Interest and Principal Securities)—are stripped by the U.S. Government itself. The bonds are delivered directly to brokers and banks, who sell them to the public. Because STRIPS are direct obligations of the U.S. Government to the individual bondholder, they are even safer than a CAT or TIGR. Because a STRIPS is less risky, the yield on a STRIPS is slightly lower.

Stripped bonds certainly sound attractive. But they may not be a good idea for all investors. Reason: You must pay tax as if you received interest payments each year, even though there is no actual income until the bond matures. That's why stripped bonds are bought mainly by tax-exempt buyers, such as pension funds, Keogh plans and IRAs.

Another use: Stripped Treasury bonds are also effective for building a child's or grandchild's college fund. For example, you could purchase a stripped Treasury bond for, say, $1,000 and make a gift of it to your new grandchild. When the bond matures in 19 years, the child has an instant $16,160 fund for college. In the meantime, the child can use his or her personal exemption deduction ($1,080 for 1986) to shelter the taxable yearly accrual in the bond's value.

▶ **FOR MORE INFORMATION:** Contact your broker. He can tell you more about stripped U.S. Treasury bonds and recommend a receipt that's tailored to your needs.

HOW TO GET HIGH INTEREST ON YOUR SAVINGS DOLLAR—PLUS TOP SAFETY

Is there a way to get a return on your savings that reflects the relatively high interest rates homebuyers are paying? Fortunately, the answer is "yes." Not only can you get the higher mortgage-market rates, but the Government guarantees your investment.

▶ **MORTGAGE-BACKED SECURITY:** You invest in a pool of home mortgages. It's actually a mortgage-backed security. And by far the most popular is a certificate guaranteed by the Government National Mortgage Association, a Government agency better known as Ginnie Mae.

Three-way payoff: (1) Ginnie Mae certificates are safe because they're backed by the full faith and credit of the U.S. Government. (2) They offer a high yield—the highest interest rate of any Government security. (3) And Ginnie Maes are liquid. There is an active and well established secondary market for Ginnie Maes; $175.6 billion were traded or re-registered during a recent year.

Ginnie Mae certificates are issued by private firms (typically a mortgage company or a bank) and are backed by a pool of Government-insured mortgages. (Veterans Administration, Federal Housing Administration, and Farmers Home Administration home loans). They usually mature in 30 years.

An investor in a Ginnie Mae receives a return that reflects the interest rates that individual homeowners in the mortgage pool are paying. Each month, the investor receives a check that's a passthrough of interest and principal on the pooled mortgages. Ginnie Mae guarantees that you get this monthly payment, whether or not payments are made on the mortgages by the homeowners.

Ginnie Mae also guarantees the full repayment of principal if the certificate is held to maturity. But if a certificate is sold before maturity and rates go up, it may be sold at a loss. Reason: A Ginnie Mae is generally a fixed-rate instrument, so it may lose value if rates go up. If rates drop, however, the certificate will sell at a premium.

▶ **ADJUSTABLE MORTGAGES:** The fluctuations in value can be avoided with a Ginnie Mae certificate backed by an adjustable rate mortgage pool. Reason: Since the interest rate on the certificate is adjustable, the certificate should trade at prices close to its original issue price.

Another point: The buyer of a Ginnie Mae certificate can't be sure of the size of his monthly payments. Reason: His payments include not only scheduled payments of principal and interest, but also unscheduled prepayments of principal that reflect foreclosures and prepayments made by the homeowners in the mortgage pool.

What to watch out for: While Ginnie Maes offer attractive features to investors, there are several potential drawbacks.

The unwary investor may spend his monthly Ginnie Mae check thinking it is all interest income and expecting to get his entire principal back later. But he won't. Since the payments received are actually the payments on house mortgages, the monthly check consists of both principal and interest—just like the monthly morgage payment made by a homeowner. When the certificate payments end, there is no principal left. In the meanwhile, the investor must re-invest his principal to maintain his nest egg.

Investment facts: Ginnie Mae certificates can be purchased from a securities firm. Minimum denomination: $25,000 (with $5,000 increments for additional investments above $25,000). If that's too rich for your blood you can invest in a unit investment trust or buy mutual fund shares. One important point to keep in mind: Neither funds nor trusts are guaranteed by the government; only Ginnie Mae certificates are.

Unit investment trust: You buy a unit of a trust that invests in a pool of Ginnie Mae certificates. Minimum initial purchase is $1,000, with $100 increments above that.

Drawbacks: An investor can't be absolutely sure how long a Ginnie Mae investment trust will stay in business. Reason: Although the home mortgages in the underlying pool have 30-year terms, many of them are prepaid (for example, when a home is sold). These prepayments are funneled through to unit holders as a return of capital. A lot of prepayments (and/or a number of redemptions by unit holders) can cause a unit trust to terminate and immediately pay back each unit holder's remaining principal. Result: Your "long-term investment" may not last as long as you thought it would.

Mutual funds: You can pay as little as $1,000 (with $100 increments) to buy shares of a mutual fund that invests in Ginnie Mae certificates.

▶ **IMPORTANT DIFFERENCES:** A unit investment trust is locked into the same Ginnie Mae certificates during the life of the trust. A mutual fund, on the other hand, is actively managed and its Ginnie Mae holdings can change. Another plus: If some of the underlying mortgages are prepaid, the fund can immediately reinvest the proceeds in other Ginnie Maes.

Other features: Some funds automatically reinvest principal and even interest income into the fund. And others have special features, like automatic transfers to other funds, and special minimum purchase arrangements.

Of course, you pay for all this convenience. As a general rule, a fund's yield will be less than the yield paid by a unit trust or Ginnie Mae certificate.

Another way to buy high-paying home mortgages: "Freddie Mac" Certificates are first cousins to Ginnie Mae Certificates. The Freddie Macs are issued by the Federal Home Loan Mortgage Corporation and are also backed by a pool of home mortgages, and make monthly payments made up of both principal and interest to investors. Both types of Certificates are readily marketable.

▶ **BIG DIFFERENCE:** Unlike Ginnie Maes, Freddie Macs are not insured by the Federal Government. However, they are insured by the Federal Home Loan Mortgage Corporation, a publicly held company, and have a triple-A rating. However, because they are a relatively higher risk investment, Freddie Macs carry higher yields than Ginnie Maes.

Investment facts: Freddie Mac Certificates are issued in $25,000 denominations. If that's too high, investors may be able to buy an existing Certificate (one that's been partially paid off) on the open market for something less than $25,000.

INVESTMENT TECHNIQUES FOR THE SMALL INVESTOR

There are a number of ways a small investor can accumulate wealth in the stock and bond markets without taking big risks, and without committing large chunks of cash. Here are some time-tested strategies that place a high premium on safety, or have special angles, such as convenience, low initial cash requirements, or special tax breaks.

How You Can Invest In The Stock Market For As Little As $25 A Month

If you would like to invest in the stock market on your own but feel that you can't come up with the necessary capital to get started, you might want to consider a—

▶ **SYSTEMATIC PURCHASE PLAN:** There are two immediate benefits: (1) You can invest in stocks of your choice by making monthly payments of as little as $25. (These payments may actually be less than the price of a single share.) (2) You pay a smaller brokerage fee than if you buy shares in the normal fashion.

How the typical plan works: After contacting a brokerage firm and obtaining an application form, you start your account by sending a minimum investment of $25. The broker uses the money to purchase shares or fractions of shares in a stock or stocks of your choice. From then on, you may invest as frequently as you wish (with the same $25 minimum). It's as simple as that.

Example: Ms. Johnson decides to invest $100 per month in a blue-chip stock. Her broker suggests XYZ, selling at around $150 per share. Ms. Johnson sends her first $100 and goes along with the broker's recommendation of XYZ. The broker then purchases $100 worth (minus brokerage fees) of XYZ stock for a custodial account under Johnson's name.

Result: Ms. Johnson would be credited with about ⅔ of a share of XYZ on her first purchase. (Ordinarily, the broker wouldn't handle an account as small as Johnson's.)

Here are some frequently asked questions—and the answers—about systematic purchase plans.

Q. Are there any limits on the kinds of stocks I can purchase under this plan?

A. No. You can choose from among the stocks listed on the New York and American Stock Exchanges, plus the major issues that trade over the counter (OTC).

Q. What happens to dividends paid on the stocks I own?

A. You can have the broker reinvest your dividends in the stock you have selected, or you can have the proceeds mailed to you.

Suggestion: You would probably be better off reinvesting dividends in the early going, when they amount to only pennies. Later you can have the dividends mailed to you.

Q. Why can't I just buy $25 or $50 worth of stocks each month on my own—why do I need to enroll in this plan?

A. First of all, many brokers will not handle transactions as small as this. Secondly, most brokerage houses have a $25 commission charge, so to invest $50 you'd have to pay $75.

In contrast, a systematic purchase plan overcomes these problems and offers three pluses:

1. You can get "a piece of the action" on Wall Street for a relatively small price.

2. You can purchase fractions of shares and, thus, buy into companies whose stock sells for $75, $100, $150 and more per share.

3. You pay a smaller commission than if you invested on your own through the same broker. (The commission on monthly investments of less than $300 runs around 6%.)

Q. What if I decide to stop investing?

A. There's no requirement that you keep investing in a systematic purchase plan. Here's—

▶ **HOW TO CASH IN:** You can contact the broker and tell him to discontinue your automatic investments. You direct him to send you your stock certificates or the proceeds of the sale of your shares.

How To Increase The Odds Of Making Money In Stocks

Dollar cost averaging can boost your odds for success if the stock or mutual fund you invest in (and the stock market in general) heads upward over the long term. Here's—

▶ **HOW IT WORKS:** You invest the same amount of money in the same stock (or fund) at regular intervals—say, quarterly or monthly—no matter what the market is doing. You purchase as many shares as you can for that amount.

For example, if you have $100 to invest, and the price of a stock you want to purchase is $20 a share, you can buy five shares. If the price drops down to $10, you buy ten shares. And if the price goes up to $25, you purchase only four shares.

What's so earth-shattering about that? Absolutely nothing—it's simple, dull arithmetic. Your purchase of shares at a lower cost (when the stock or the market in general is down) will even out your high-cost per-share purchases. Over the long run, your cost per share should average out below the average price per share at the time of each purchase.

Example: Ms. McGee wants to purchase stock in General Corporation, a blue chip company. She has $1,000 for an initial investment and plans on adding $150 every month thereafter. Assuming a normal fluctuation in the price of the stock, here's how McGee's investment looks over the next ten years.

Year	Annual Amount Of Investments	Average Price Per Share	Number Of Shares Purchased	Average Cost Per Share
1	$2,800	$13.30	215.054	$13.02
2	1,800	14.78	122.449	14.70
3	1,800	13.58	132.062	13.63
4	1,800	15.93	114.723	15.69
5	1,800	13.46	133.038	13.53
6	1,800	14.24	127.660	14.10
7	1,800	15.55	116.279	15.48
8	1,800	16.22	111.801	16.10
9	1,800	15.94	112.782	15.96
10	1,800	17.85	101.408	17.75
Totals	$19,000	$15.09	1,287.256	$14.76

Result: The average price per share is $15.09, compared to an average cost per share of only $14.76. And the figures above reflect a fairly steady market. The difference between the average price per share and the average cost per share will be bigger if there is more fluctuation in the market.

If the market price of General at the beginning of the eleventh year is $17.93, McGee would realize $23,080.50 (1,287.256 shares × $17.93 a share) if she sold all her General stock. Subtracting her total cost of $19,000 leaves her a $4,080.50 profit before commissions. Of course, she also received dividends on her stock while she held it.

In spite of its advantages, dollar-cost averaging is not without its perils. If the stock you pick keeps declining, or if the market declines over the long term, you are throwing good money after bad.

▶ **IMPORTANT:** Stick with your hand. Dollar cost averaging won't work if you get cold feet in the middle. If you discontinue the plan when the value of your shares is less than your cost, you may wind up with a loss.

How A Dividend Reinvestment Plan Can Multiply Your Family Nest Egg

Buying shares of stock in various companies is one way to build the family nest egg. But for the smaller investor, commissions paid on small lot purchases eat up a lot of profit.

One way to alleviate this problem is to use a discount brokerage house. This type of broker will do your buying and selling at lower rates—frequently much lower—than the regular brokerage houses. However, the discounter won't offer services provided by other firms, like investment counseling and up-to-the-minute reports.

Another approach is to use a—

▶ **DIVIDEND REINVESTMENT PLAN:** The plan allows an investor to buy additional shares of stock without paying commissions. Close to 1,000 companies offer such plans. There is generally a nominal service charge on the transaction. And the company whose stock is being purchased by the plan sometimes pays the service charges, itself.

How it works: A shareholder participating in a dividend reinvestment plan gets additional shares of stock instead of cash dividends each quarter. Some even allow shareholders to buy stock at a discount (say 5% or 10%).

▶ **MULTIPLIER EFFECT:** An investor's initial investment can build up quickly. Dividends paid on the original shares are used to buy additional shares in the company. And the new shares also give off dividends that are in turn reinvested in still more stock, and so on. This is known as the power of compounding.

There is also a beneficial side effect to investing in a dividend reinvestment plan. The dividend reinvestment plan is a form of forced saving. When people take quarterly dividends in cash, they often fritter that money away. With the dividend reinvestment plan, your money is socked away automatically.

Tax angles in dividend reinvestment plans: When a shareholder has the option of taking dividends in the form of cash, they are taxed to him as ordinary income—even if they are automatically reinvested in additional shares of stock. Taxable amount: The full cash dividend rate. Where stock is purchased at a discount, the taxable dividend is increased by the discount.The service charges or fees connected with a reinvestment plan are deductible investment expenses.Your basis in the shares is equal to the fair market value as of the dividend payment date. Your holding period begins the day after that date.

▶ **WHAT TO DO:** Keep careful records of when and how many shares you purchase through dividend reinvestment, the fair market value of the stock on the dividend payment date, and the amount of your service charges.

Reason: When the shares are eventually sold, you will need the records to determine the amount of taxable gain and whether or not the shares qualify for long-term capital gain treatment.

How To Get In On The Market On A
Shoestring

Investors who want to get in on the stock market action without investing a lot of cash should look into an investment club. This is simply a group of investors who pool their resources and expertise in order to make stock and bond investments.

▶ **SAFETY IN NUMBERS:** With an investment club, you are not going one-on-one with the stock market. You have the comfort of knowing the other investors in your club—there are usually around 15 of them—are in the same boat as you. And the amount you contribute to the club—generally on a monthly basis—is minimal (it can be as little as $10 per month; it is rarely above $50).

Of course, in an investment club you tie your fortunes to the rest of the club, for better or for worse. Result: It is not surprising that most investment clubs pursue a conservative investment strategy.

Ten key points: Whether you intend to join an investment club that is already in existence or you are looking to start one up, there are ten key points to keep in mind. They can help you make your investment club a success.

1. Keep your club small. Anything over 20 members starts to become unwieldy.

2. Contributions should be made on a regular basis (e.g., monthly).

3. Contribute at least a minimum amount each month. That way you'll spread your risk out over the long run.

4. Reinvest the dividends. You can't make money without investing money.

5. Aim for diversification. In this respect, your club will act much the way a mutual fund does.

6. Adopt an overall policy. You and the other members of the club will have to arrive at a consensus.

7. Set reasonable goals. Don't expect to get rich quick. Remember: This is the safe approach.

8. Provide for contingencies. For example, you should be prepared in case several members drop out.

9. Do your homework. You and the other members must keep on top of trends, P/E ratios, and so forth.

10. Get advice. Don't try to do it all on your own—you can consult brokers, attorneys and accountants for all the investment, legal and tax ramifications.

▶ **FOR MORE INFORMATION:** Contact the National Association of Investment Clubs, 1515 East Eleven Mile Rd., Royal Oak, Michigan 48068. They can send you and your club valuable publications explaining how to set up an investment club, including a model portfolio.

WHY SOME ASTUTE INVESTORS CHOOSE PREFERRED STOCK OVER COMMON STOCK

Preferred stocks—they are identified with ''pfd'' in the daily stock market quotations—are popular with some investors. Reason: Preferred stocks often pay higher dividends than do their common stock counterparts.

▶ **WHAT'S A PREFERRED STOCK?** A preferred stock is so named because it's preferred as to dividends. That doesn't mean it always pays a higher dividend. It does mean the issuing corporation must make dividend payments on its preferred before it pays dividends on its common. The dividends are usually locked in—either as a stated dollar amount or as a stated percentage of the stock's par value.

In general, the return on your investment is fixed, though with some so-called "participating" preferred issues, you may receive extra dividends if earnings are high. With a "cumulative" preferred, a corporation that doesn't pay dividends one year and resumes the next must pay the accumulated arrearage before it begins paying common stock dividends.

▶ **HIGHER YIELD:** The yield on preferred stock is usually higher than the yield on the issuing corporation's common stock. In general, the preferred may pay anywhere from 1% to 5% more than its common stock counterpart.

Other side of the coin: Your preferred stock dividends don't usually fluctuate with corporate earnings. While common stock dividends may increase, preferred dividends won't (unless they are participating preferreds).

If you purchase a preferred issue when interest and dividend rates are high, you may be able to lock in the yield for a longer period of time than you could with, say, a corporate bond. Reason: As long as the stock is outstanding—and as long as the company keeps paying dividends—a fixed amount will be paid each year. So if the stock isn't called (redeemed by the corporation), your yield, theoretically, is perpetual.

Whether or not a preferred issue will be redeemed depends on its terms. Typically, a corporation is able to redeem the preferred only at or above its par value. This makes it unlikely that certain issues will be redeemed. For example, in an 11% yield climate, a preferred stock issued 15 years ago and paying 5% on its par value of $100, is unlikely to be called.

The situation is different with "sinking fund" preferred stock. Here, the issuing corporation must redeem a specified percentage of the issue each year. For example, a 10-year sinking fund preferred may call for 10% of the entire issue to be redeemed each year at par. At the end of 10 years, the entire issue is redeemed. Some 20% of the total preferred stock market consists of such issues.

There are two basic types of sinking funds: (1) "lottery sinkers" (shares to be redeemed are determined by chance), (2) "pro-rata sinkers" (each shareholder must surrender a certain proportion of shares each year). Often, the issuing corporation has the option of buying shares on the open market to fulfill its redemption requirements. This opens up an interesting profit opportunity where the stock is trading below issue price.

Example: ABC Utility's sinking fund preferred was issued at $100 and pays 5%. ABC must redeem 10% of the issue in December of each year. Because the dividend is low, the stock may trade at, say, $50 in January. But as the redemption date draws closer, the share price will bid up. Reason: The corporation will try to purchase preferred stock shares on the open market to avoid redeeming shares at $100 a piece.

Result: A shareholder who bought at $50 a share can stand to profit in a big way in a short period of time. Holders of preferred stock should tell their brokers to keep an eye out for such quick-profit opportunities.

Another investment feature: Convertible preferred stock can be converted at the holder's option into the corporation's common stock at a stated price. Suppose you bought 100 shares of ABC preferred when ABC common was selling for $10 a share. The preferred is convertible into 125 shares of ABC common at $20 a share. If ABC common goes to, say, $25, there's an opportunity for an instant, built-in profit. The built-in profit is already reflected in a higher price for the preferred, which you can sell. Alternatively, you can convert your preferred into common and sell.

▶ **TAX-FREE SWAP:** Your conversion of preferred to common is not taxable. Your cost basis for the common shares is the same as it was for the preferred. And the amount of time you held the old preferred shares is added to the time you hold the new for purposes of meeting the more-than-six-month-holding period requirement to get low-taxed capital gain treatment on any profit from the sale of the common shares (60% tax-free).

See your stockbroker: Talk things over with your stockbroker before making a move into preferred stock. Despite its "preferred" label, a preferred stock isn't inherently better than common stock. A preferred is safer in that the dividends are paid first, the dividends are cumulative, and the preferred owner has a preferential call on the assets of the corporation. Dividends are also higher on preferred stock. But, obviously, a big dividend isn't much good if a corporation must suspend dividend payments on all classes of stock because of poor business conditions.

NEW INVESTMENT IDEA ALLOWS YOU TO BOOST DIVIDEND INCOME FROM YOUR BLUE CHIP STOCK

One mark of a blue chip stock is steady dividend payments, quarter after quarter, year after year. Now a new investment allows owners of some blue chip stocks to boost their dividend income by giving up their chances at big capital gain later.

▶ **NEW TYPE OF TRUST:** It's called the Americus Trust. How the trust works: In exchange for his stock, the investor gets a unit in the trust that splits the blue chip stock into two parts: one part gets all the dividends and a small amount of future appreciation in value; the other part gets the right to any value appreciation over a certain price level. The Trust holds only the stock of one company.

Payoff: You can own more of the part that best suits your investment objectives—more dividend income or more capital gain appreciation. How? By selling the component you're not interested in and reinvesting the proceeds in the other component.

More details: The Trust allows an investor in a specified blue chip stock to swap shares of stock for an equal number of units in the Trust. (At least 100 shares must be swapped.) Each Trust unit consists of two components: a Prime and a Score.

A Prime component entitles the holder to all cash dividends (and most stock dividends) on the stock. In addition, he is entitled to a limited portion of the appreciation in value of the Trust units (which, of course, depends greatly on the stock's performance) up to a set amount called the ''Termination Claim.'' A Prime holder is entitled to vote his proportionate shares of stock held by the Trust.

A Score component holder, on the other hand, gets no dividends. But he does get any appreciation over the Termination Claim. A Score is like a long-term call option.

Trust units and the separate components are traded on the American Stock Exchange.

▶ **DIVIDEND STRATEGY:** You can sell your Score (appreciation) components and use the proceeds to accumulate more Prime (dividend) components. Result: You can increase dividend income while still keeping the opportunity to get some appreciation.

Alternative move: If you don't currently own shares of the blue chip stock, you can still obtain a dividend position in the stock by buying Prime components on the AMEX. You also have the chance of pocketing appreciation in a stock you don't own.

To see how a dual purpose trust can offer attractive investment features to an investor who owns blue chip stock, let's take a look at an example.

Facts: Blue Chip stock trades at $51 and pays a dividend of $3.40 per share per year. An Americus Trust is set up for Blue Chip, and the Termination Claim is set at $60. Let's say Prime trades at $45 and Score at $6 when the Trust is set up.

The yield on a Prime component is higher than the yield on a Blue Chip share: 7.44% ($3.40 divided by $45) vs 6.67% ($3.40 divided by $51). And by selling Score components and reinvesting the proceeds in more prime components, the investor can concentrate his investment on the dividend side.

You can even get your shares back: The Trust allows the investor to redeem complete Trust units (consisting of both Primes and Scores) for shares of stock. So if an investor wants to take advantage of, say, a trade offer, he is free to do so. However, it takes some time to receive the shares from the Trust (up to one week), so the investor may be delayed from taking advantage of such investment opportunities.

Of course, an investor doesn't have to trade his Trust units for stock. If, for example, the investor wants to liquidate his investment in a hurry, he can sell his separate components on the AMEX, and thereby avoid the up-to-one-week waiting period.

The Trust is designed to last five years, at which time the investor receives shares of stock for his units or components based on the net asset value of the Trust. (Fractional shares are paid off in cash.) Trust termination is the only time that separate components can be exchanged for shares of stock. You receive stock in exchange for Prime and Score components.

The Americus Trust has received a private ruling from the Revenue Service regarding the tax consequences for Trust investors. Here is a rundown of the important tax rules:

• The Trust is not taxed on dividends and other payouts to the investors. They are taxed to the investor only.

▶ **INVESTOR TAX TRAP:** Under the Trust agreement, some dividends paid on stock are not currently paid to Prime holders; they are retained by the Trust and paid out at termination. Prime holders may, nevertheless, owe current tax on these dividends.

• No tax is owed when stock shares are exchanged for trust units. Your tax basis (cost for tax purposes) in the stock is carried over to the trust units. And the time you held the stock is added to the time you hold the units when figuring the holding period for long-term capital gain tax treatment.

• The sale of a component may result in taxable gain or loss. Your tax basis in the unit must be apportioned between the components according to their fair market values at the time of sale.

• You pay no tax when you receive shares from the redemption or termination of a unit. But you may have a gain or loss on the cash received for fractional shares.

An Americus Trust may appeal to investors who want more dividend income. (Remember: You don't have to be a stockholder. You can get in on the action by purchasing units or components on the AMEX.) But investors who are interested in the dual purpose trust concept currently face one big drawback. As of now, there have been only two Americus trusts: one was offered several years ago for pre-divestiture AT&T stock; and one was recently introduced for Exxon.

The Americus Trust is the brainchild of Mr. Joseph Debe of Americus Shareowner Service Corporation. And Mr. Debe is in the process of introducing 28 other trusts, covering such stocks as IBM, General Motors, American Express, Coca-Cola, Du Pont, General Electric, and Xerox.

Investors can obtain more information on the dual purpose trust idea by contacting Americus Shareowner Service Corporation, 15 W. 39th St., New York, NY 10018.

▶ **WORD OF CAUTION:** Investing in an Americus Trust is not without risk. Since a Trust is involved with only one stock, the Trust is subject to the same risks as those involving the blue chip stock. There is no guarantee the value of the Trust will go up, or that dividends will continue to be paid.

How To Accumulate Wealth Without Putting All Your Eggs In One Basket

Variety is the spice of life. And when it comes to investing your money, it may be the safest way to go. How to do it: You might consider—

▶ **OPEN-END MUTUAL FUNDS:** Open-end funds allow you to spread your investment in a variety of stocks and bonds. How it works: You purchase shares in a mutual fund—a federally regulated investment company—which in turn buys stocks and bonds. Your investments are chosen by a group of professional advisers. The minimum initial investment is typically $500 or $1,000 (there are some that allow a minimum of $200) and subsequent investments can be as little as $50.

Result: The amount you are risking is small, but the payoff can be big. Are there any other advantages to mutual funds? There sure are. To name just a few—

• Diversification: Instead of sinking or swimming with a few stocks and bonds, you cut down your risk by spreading out your investment.

• Top-notch management: With a mutual fund, you have access to the same top professionals that larger investors do.

• Convenience: Owning shares in a mutual fund is like doing one-stop shopping. You get the benefit of diversification without having to put up with paperwork hassles.

• Easy investment and divestment: It's generally easy to invest or reinvest in a mutual fund. For example, most funds allow you to purchase shares over the phone. And redemption orders can be easily placed, so your cash isn't needlessly tied up if you need it.

• Fund switching: Most funds permit you to transfer from one fund to another within the same family of funds—also by phone. For instance, if the stock market is bullish you may want to switch into a growth stock fund; if it is bearish you could choose a diversified fund.

• Smorgasbord of funds: There are many types of investment funds. Some have specific investment purposes: for example, municipal bond funds, money market funds, growth stock funds, etc. Others are speculative: "junk" funds (high-risk bonds), hedge funds (put and calls), etc. The most common type is the balanced fund, which is just what it sounds like—the investments are balanced between many different stocks and bonds.

Q. How do you decide what type of mutual fund to invest in?

A. It depends on your priorities. For example, you might want to concentrate on long-term growth. Then you can pick your fund accordingly.

Of course, you should also check out a fund's investment record, management structure and fee structure before putting your money in any mutual fund. You also have to consider whether you prefer a "load" fund or a "no-load" fund.

▶ **THE DIFFERENCE:** Load funds are sold to you by a salesperson. You have to pay a sales charge—that's the "load" for this service. No-load funds, on the other hand, have no sales charge. The only cost is the management fee (you also have to pay management fees with load funds). That gives the no-load investor an immediate advantage—which is compounded over a number of years.

Example #1: Ms. Green invests $5,000 in a load fund that has an 8% sales charge. The fund yields 8% a year. After subtracting her sales charge, Green has $4,600 working for her. At the end of the first year, Ms. Green's shares are worth $4,968. If the yield remains the same and she makes no deposits or withdrawals, at the end of ten years Greeen will have $9,931 in her account.

Example #2: Mr. Grey invests $5,000 in a no-load fund that also yields 8%. Grey doesn't have to pay a sales charge so he has his entire $5,000 investment working for him. At the end of one year, he will have $5,400 in his account ($432 more than Ms. Green). Again assuming that the yield remains constant at 8% and no deposits or withdrawals, at the end of ten years Grey will have $10,795 in his account ($864 more than Ms. Green).

Note: These examples assume equal yields. A load fund that outperforms a no-load over the course of a few years may be a better deal. It does illustrate, however, how the no-load investor gets a head start on the load investor.

How To Make the Most of the Tax Breaks Available on Mutual Fund Investments

Most distributions from mutual funds to their shareholders are ordinary dividends. These dividends are eligible for the $100 ($200 for married couples) dividend exclusion, but are otherwise subject to tax as ordinary income. But there are other types of distributions from mutual funds that are eligible for—

▶ **BIG TAX BREAKS:** Some distributions from mutual funds are eligible for long-term capital gain treatment even if the shareholder has held the mutual fund shares for less than six months. Other types of distributions are completely tax-free to the shareholders.

● *Capital gain distributions:* These distributions are paid out by mutual funds from the net capital gains they have realized on the fund's portfolio. It is the fund's holding period that controls. So if a transaction results in a long-term capital gain for the fund, it is treated as a long-term capital gain when it is distributed to fund shareholders. That's true even if the shareholder has not held his shares for more than six months.

On the other hand, if a fund distributes a short-term capital gain, it is ordinary income even to shareholders who have owned the mutual fund shares for more than six months.

● *Undistributed capital gains:* Some mutual funds retain part or all of their long-term capital gains rather than distributing them to shareholders. Each shareholder in the fund is responsible for paying tax on a pro rata portion of these capital gains even though they were not distributed in cash. However, the mutual fund itself must also pay taxes on undistributed capital gains and shareholders get a credit for their pro rata share of the tax paid by the fund. Result: Since most mutual funds pay a 28% capital gains rate and the maximum rate for individuals on long-term capital gains is only 20%, most shareholders get a special break.

The tax credit for taxes paid by the fund in excess of the shareholder's own liability for capital gains can be used to shelter other income from tax.

▶ **ON YOUR TAX RETURN:** Report undistributed capital gains just as if they had been received. They are entered on Schedule B and as long-term captial gain on Schedule D. However, a taxpayer who does not otherwise have to file Schedule D may simply enter 40% of the distribution on page 1 of Form 1040.

You get the credit for the tax paid by the fund, by filling out Form 2439 (it is supplied by the fund) and attaching it to your return.

The shareholder can also increase his or her basis in the mutual fund shares (and thus reduce future taxable profits on sale of the shares) by the difference between the amount of undistributed capital gain reported and the pro rata portion on the fund's tax on the gain.

● *Tax-exempt distributions:* Some mutual funds invest a portion of their money in tax-exempt securities such as municipal bonds. The tax-free earnings on these securities are also generally tax-free to shareholders of the fund when distributed to them.

Mutual funds do not report tax-free dividends on Form 1099-DIV along with taxable dividends, Instead the mutual funds send separate statements showing the amount of tax-free dividends paid.

Return of capital distributions: Sometimes a mutual fund will make a distribution that does not come from its earnings and profits. In this case it is actually returning a portion of the shareholder's investment in the fund to him. These distributions are generally tax-free to shareholders. But if total return-of-capital distributions exceed the shareholder's basis in the shares, then the excess is taxable to him as a capital gain (long or short term depending on how long the shares have been held).

Example: Brown purchased shares of XYZ mutual fund in 1984 for $10 a share. In 1985 he received a return of capital distribution of $2 a share. This distribution reduces his basis to $8 a share. In 1986 he receives a further return of capital distribution of $9 a share. Result: His tax basis in the shares is reduced to zero and he has a long-term capital gain of $1 per share.

Sales, exchanges and redemptions: When a shareholder sells his mutual fund shares, exchanges them for shares in another mutual fund or has them redeemed (repurchased) by the fund, a taxable transaction has occurred. The amount of the gain or loss on the transaction is the difference between the shareholder's adjusted basis in the shares and the amount realized. These are capital transactions and are therefore eligible for long-term capital gain treatment if the shares have been held for more than six months. If the amount received is less than adjusted basis, the shareholder has a deductible capital loss.

The adjusted basis is generally the purchase price (including any commissions). You also add the difference between the amount of undistributed capital gain apportioned to you, and the pro rata share of the tax paid by the fund on the gains. Finally, you subtract any return of capital distributions.

How Corporate Bonds Lock In High Investment Yields

If you're looking for high yields—and you're willing to accept some risk as part of the bargain—you ought to look into—

▶ **CORPORATE BONDS:** When you buy corporate bonds, you are banking on the corporation's promise to pay (1) a fixed amount of money over the remaining life of the bond, and (2) the par value of the bond at maturity. The three key figures you must know are the bond's coupon rate, its current yield, and its yield to maturity.

Coupon rate: This shows the amount of the money that the bond is paying out. It is expressed as a percentage of the bond's par value of $1,000 and is found in the financial papers right after the bond's name, and before its maturity date. For example, XYZ 8⅛ 07 pays $81.25 a year until the bond is redeemed by the issuer for $1,000 cash in the year 2007.

Current yield: If you buy a bond at par value, the coupon rate will equal your current yield. More often than not, however, you will buy a bond after it is issued. If the bond's coupon rate is lower than today's rate for new bonds, you will pay less than par for the bond. If the bond's coupon rate is higher than the new-bond rate, you will pay a premium (more than par).

Current yield tells you how much of a return you'd get by purchasing an existing bond. Suppose our XYZ bond is quoted at 85. The bond will cost $850 and the annual $81.25 payout will throw off a 9.56% current yield on your invested dollars. You can find current yield by dividing the coupon rate by the purchase price.

Yield to maturity: This figure takes into account not only the bond's current cash yield but also the payment you will receive when the bond is redeemed by the issuing corporation. A bond broker will tell you what the yield to maturity is on a particular bond. If you want to arrive at an *approximate* yield-to-maturity figure for a bond bought at discount, use this formula:

$$\frac{\text{Annual interest plus (discount divided by years to maturity)}}{\text{(Current price plus par value) divided by two}}$$

Example: Mr. Smith buys a 7% bond selling for $820 with 15 years remaining until maturity. The par value (principal on which interest is paid) is $1,000. Smith figures his yield to maturity as follows:

$$\frac{70 + {}^{180}\!/_{15}}{(820 + 1000)/2} = \frac{70 + 12}{910} = 9.01\%$$

Result: Even though the current yield is only 8.54%, Smith's yield to maturity is about 9.01%

Note: When bonds sell at a substantial discount (here, $180) it increases the yield to maturity. The bigger the discount and the shorter the period to maturity, the higher the yield to maturity.

▶ **HOW TO BUY:** Usually, you buy corporate bonds through a broker and pay a commission of about 1%. If the broker already owns the bonds, you have to pay the so-called "spread"—the difference between the bid and ask prices for the bond. Minimum bond investment is usually $1,000 (although sometimes you can find bonds for $500).

▶ **HOW TO COLLECT:** It depends on whether the bond is a bearer or a registered bond. If it is a bearer bond (it belongs to whoever owns it), you clip a coupon off the bond and cash it in at your bank. If the bond is registered in your name, you get an interest check through the mail. All new corporate bonds must be issued in registered form (this rule went into effect in 1983). However, there are still plenty of pre-1983 bearer bonds available.

Caution: Corporate bonds pay higher rates than, say, Treasury issues or money market funds, but your risk is greater too.

The first and most obvious risk is that the issuing corporation may be unable to meet its bond obligations. True, bonds are rated for investment quality by Moody's and Standard and Poor's. If you buy a bond rated A and up, and the issuer's a major Fortune 500 corporation, the likelihood of your losing your investment is small. But there's no guarantee that a bond rated A and up when you buy it will retain its top rating until maturity. If the corporation's fortunes ebb, so will the rating and the bond's market value.

The more likely risk is *market risk*. If interest rates go up after you have purchased a bond, its market value will drop. So if you need cash in a hurry and must sell the bond, you will have a (tax-deductible) loss. On the other hand, of course, interest rates may drop after you buy. In that case, you will be able to sell the bond at a profit.

The Tax Aspects of Your Corporate Bond Investments

The interest paid on corporate bonds is fully taxable, just like bank passbook interest. But corporate bonds can also yield a capital gain or loss, if they are sold (or redeemed) for more or less than their purchase price. Let's take a look.

Bonds bought at par: If your purchase price equals the par or face value of the bond, you will have neither gain nor loss if you hold the bond until it is redeemed. Reason: The amount you will receive from the bond's issuer equals what you paid for the bond. However, if you sell the bond before it is redeemed you will have capital gain if the bond is worth more than par (this can happen if interest rates decline after you purchase the bond). If you sell at a loss (for example, if rates go up after your purchase) you will have a capital loss. Your gain or loss will be short- or long-term depending on your holding period for the bond.

Discount bonds: A bond bought for less than its issue price is said to be selling at a "market discount." This does not mean the bond is not a sound investment—it may be rated triple A. It's caused by interest rates having gone up after the bond was issued. The discount is a built-in profit if held to maturity. You pocket the difference between the discount price paid and the higher amount received when the issuer redeems the bond at its full face value.

▶ **BIG DOLLAR DIFFERENCE:** This built-in profit can be either fully taxable or 60% tax-free, *depending on when the bond was originally issued*. The key date is July 18, 1984. The profit on the redemption of a market discount bond that was issued after that date is fully taxed ordinary income—just like salary or interest income. But the profit on the redemption of a bond selling at a discount that was issued on or before July 18, 1984 is low-taxed capital gain—only 40% of the profit is subject to income tax.

There is a similar result if a market discount bond is sold at a profit before redemption. If the bond was originally issued on or before July 18, 1984, the profit is low-taxed capital gain. If it was issued after July 18, 1984, the profit is fully taxed ordinary income to the extent of the market discount attributable to the time you owned the bond. Your broker should be able to help you figure the capital gain and ordinary income elements.

▶ **WHAT TO DO:** Before you buy a bond selling at a market discount, check on its issue date with your broker. The tax break on the older bonds can make a big difference in your after-tax yield. And that's what really counts. This break will, of course, be available to those in the know for many years to come.

Some corporate bonds are *issued* at a discount price. Key difference: Part of the so-called original issue discount is subject to tax each year during the time you own the bond. These bonds are generally not suitable for an individual investor's portfolio. Reason: Although interest is not received until the bond matures, the investor must pay tax each year—at ordinary rates—even though he receives no interest until the bond matures or is sold. But these bonds are suitable IRA investments, since IRAs are not subject to current tax.

Premium bonds: Sometimes investors pay more than face value for corporate bonds—in other words, they buy at a premium. This can happen if the bond was issued when interest rates were higher than they are when you buy the bond.

If you purchase a bond at a premium you can elect to amortize the premium (deduct it ratably over the remaining life of the bond). Result: Each year that the premium bond is held, a proportionate share of the premium is taken as an itemized deduction (investment expense). The amount deducted must also be subtracted from the bondholder's basis in the bond.

> *Example:* In January, 1985 Smith purchased an XYZ Corp. bond with a face value of $1,000 maturing in 1995. Smith paid $1,300 for the bond. Each year Smith deducts and reduces his basis by $30 ($300 premium divided by 10 years).

If Smith sells the bond in December, 1986 for $1,400, he will realize a long-term capital gain of $160. Reason: His basis in the bond will be $1,240 ($1,300 original cost less 2 years amortization at $30 a year). Sales price of $1,400 less basis of $1,240 equals $160 gain.

Note: Once you elect to amortize the premium on a single bond, you are required to begin amortizing the premiums on any other bonds you hold at that time or purchase in the future. A taxpayer has to get permission from the IRS before he can stop amortizing bonds purchased at a premium.

Q: What happens if I don't elect to amortize the premium?

A: If you don't elect to amortize the premium you pay over par value on a bond, you get no current deduction. On the other hand, you don't have to reduce your basis in the bond either. So if you hold the bond until it is redeemed at maturity for par value, you will have a capital loss equal to the premium.

HOW YOU CAN BUY A CORPORATE BOND THAT LETS YOU CASH IN ON THE ACTION IN COMPANY STOCK

You get something extra if you buy a convertible corporate bond. These securities have all the standard bond features: a fixed interest rate and a fixed date when paid off. A convertible bond is a debt of the corporation that issued it (interest must be paid on the bond, whether there are earnings or not).

> ▶ **SOMETHING EXTRA:** The bonds are convertible into common stock—thus the name convertible bonds. Convertible bonds can be exchanged for a predetermined amount of common stock of the issuing corporation. This can't be done with regular bonds.

> *Example:* Mr. Grant pays $1,000 for a convertible bond of XYZ Corp., with a conversion privilege of 50 shares of common stock. This means Grant can convert his bond into 50 shares of XYZ stock at no extra cost. The stock is selling at $15 when Grant buys the bond. If the stock goes over the $20 mark, Grant comes out ahead. He can convert the bond into common stock or sell the bond at profit.

Grant is a potential winner when his stock goes up, but he doesn't have a comparable risk when the stock goes down. That's because convertible bonds have this—

▶ **BUILT-IN SAFEGUARD:** When the price of the common stock underlying a convertible drops, the convertible's price may fall—but not as much as the price of the common stock. Reason: Convertible bonds have an intrinsic value as bonds. When the common stock is selling below the conversion price, the bond won't sell for any less than its value as a bond.

On the other hand, when the stock rises above the conversion price, the bond price goes up. Let's go back to Mr. Grant.

Example: Grant bought the bond for $1,000 when the stock was $15, but the stock has fluctuated since then. First it dropped to $12 (a 20% decrease). The bond did not drop at the same proportionate rate; it fell by considerably less than 20%. Then the stock rose to $25—and the bond shot up to $1,250.

So the convertible can be a two-way winner for the smart investor. There's a brake on losses and the bond picks up if the stock turns around.

▶ **TAX BREAKS:** (1) The conversion from the bond to the common stock is tax-free, and (2) the bond's long-term gain holding period is tacked on the time you hold the stock. Let's say you hold onto the bond for more than six months before you convert it. You can sell the stock immediately after conversion, and have your profit treated as lightly taxed long-term capital gain.

Investment considerations: There may be some drawbacks to convertibles. For some convertibles, the value of the common stock you get on exchange is so low in relation to the conversion price that it may be years before the conversion privilege is worth anything. For others, the price of the common is so high that you may have to pay a premium of 50% or 100% to buy the convertible. In that case, your yield will be low—and if the common stock sinks, you can lose as much as if you owned the common.

ADVANCED STOCK MARKET TECHNIQUES

Most investors buy stock for cash in the hope their investment will appreciate over time. But there are other ways to make money in the stock market. Those who are willing to take the risk and up the ante can leverage their stock purchases, generate current income by selling the *right* to purchase stock and even make money when a stock goes down. Here's a rundown of some of the more important advanced stock market strategies.

How to Use Leverage to Buy Stocks or Bonds

Using borrowed funds to finance investments is a time-tested strategy. In the stock-and-bond field, it's called—

▶ **BUYING ON MARGIN:** You write a check for only part of the cost of the stock. Your broker extends you credit for the rest. Of course, you have to pay the broker an interest fee on the borrowed funds.

Result: Any profit you make is increased by the amount of stock you bought on margin.

Example: Mr. Able buys 100 shares of ABC stock at $40 a share. So Able puts up $4,000. If ABC goes up to $50 a share, Able has a profit of $1,000. That's not bad.

But let's say that instead of buying 100 shares, Able buys 200 shares of ABC on 50% margin. He puts up the same $4,000 and his broker puts up the other $4,000. When ABC goes up to $50 a share, Able has a $2,000 profit (less interest and commissions)—twice as much as before.

Of course, buying stock on margin has a comparable downside risk. In our example, if ABC stock plummeted to $30 a share, Able would lose $2,000 instead of $1,000.

Your initial investment must be no less than 50%. On the New York Stock Exchange, you must make a minimum deposit of $2,000. And your equity cannot fall below the level of 25% (your brokerage house may set a higher limit). If your equity falls below this level, you will get a "margin call" from your broker. You will be required to bring your equity back about 25%. In other words, you have to sink in more cash. If you fail to meet the margin call, your broker has the right to sell the stocks in your account to replace the credit he has given you.

Stock you buy on margin is registered in what is called "street name"—in other words, in the name of the brokerage firm. But you will be sent all the dividends you earn.

You only have to put up 30% for corporate bonds (50% is required for convertible bonds) and 8% for Treasury bonds. If you are interested in purchasing bonds on margin, you may want to buy bonds that will yield enough to cover your interest costs. This is called a "positive carry."

Result: You can factor out interest charges in deciding how long you want to hold onto the bond.

Q. How much interest do you have to pay when you buy on margin?

A. It depends. In the past, the rates have ranged from 6½ to 13%. You will find a difference of ½ to 1½% between brokers. You'll have to shop around. If you combine all your margin accounts with one broker, you are likely to get a better rate than if you scattered them around.

Reminder: There is a big downside risk to buying on margin. Neophyte investors should tread carefully here. (Caution: If you buy a discount bond with borrowed funds, you may lose part of your interest deduction. See your professional adviser.)

▶ **CUT THE RISK:** You can always place a stop order with your broker. What to do: You instruct your broker to sell when the stock reaches a specified price. That way, you put a ceiling on your loss.

How To Take Advantage of Short Sales

Suppose you anticipate—based on strong factual research—that the price of a stock is about to fall. So you sell the stock short—you sell it even though you don't own it. So that you can deliver the stock to the buyer, you borrow shares from your broker (who gets them from one of his customers). Eventually, you have to replace the borrowed stock. By then, hopefully, you can buy the shares on the market at a lower price and replace the borrowed shares.

▶ **PAYOFF:** Your profit is the difference between the proceeds from the short sale and what you pay for the replacement shares. So you make money when the stock goes down.

Example: Mr. White strongly feels that XYZ stock is about to drop. He sells short 100 shares at $50 a share. (*Note:* White is required to put up a good faith margin of 50%, to be held by the broker.)

Say White is right about the stock and it drops to $30 a share. White then "covers" (buys replacement stock) his short position by purchasing 100 shares for $3,000. Result: White has a profit of $2,000 (before commissions and interest charges) by selling short.

What happens if the price of XYZ goes up? Then White comes out on the losing end. If the price rises to say, $70 a share, and White covers, he is out $2,000. And, of course, he still has to tack on commissions.

▶ **NOT FOR THE FAINT-HEARTED:** As you can see, selling short is a highly speculative undertaking. Theoretically, the possibility for loss is much larger than that for gain. *Reason:* Your gain is limited because the stock can't drop any lower than zero. On the other hand, your loss is unlimited because there is no ceiling on how high the stock can go.

Important: In order to place a short sell order, two conditions must be present. (1) Obviously, the broker must be able to borrow the stock, and (2) you have to meet the up-tick rule (the latter is required by the New York Stock Exchange and the American Stock Exchange). Simply put, the up-tick rule says the last price of the stock you are selling short must be up from the previous price.

Example: You want to sell short on ABC stock. The stock is now at 25¼, down from the previous price of 25½. *Result:* You can't sell short. However, if the price goes up to, say, 25⅜ (from 25¼,) you then can sell short.

Reminder: We can't emphasize enough that selling short is a high-risk venture. If you decide to sell short, you may want to minimize the risk by—

▶ **PLAYING IT SAFE:** Arrange to buy the same stock at a higher price at the same time that you sell short. That way, if the stock does go up, you take some of the sting out of your loss by offsetting it with a gain.

How You Can Get Extra Dividends From Your Stock Portfolio

It's possible to increase the annual return on the value of your stock portfolio by as much as 15% without an increase in dividends or buying new stock. How? By using a tried-and-tested investment strategy that's been growing in popularity—the selling (or writing) of call options on your stock.

▶ **WHAT IS A CALL OPTION?** It is the right to buy 100 shares of a stock at a set price (called the striking price) for the life of the option. The length of the option can range anywhere from 30 days to one year, but the most common length is nine months and ten days.

You are paid a premium for selling the right to buy your stock. The buyer of the call option expects a rise in the price of the underlying stock. You, the seller, on the other hand, don't expect the price of the underlying stock to go much above the striking price—if at all.

Example: You own 100 shares of ABC stock, which you bought at $45 a share. You place an order through your broker to sell an ABC option. A buyer of an ABC call has the right to buy 100 shares of ABC from you at $60 before the end of next December. The stock is also worth $60 a share today. You get, say, $500 for the option. Even after paying commissions, that may be equivalent to an annual return of about 15% on the value of the stock.

A month or two goes by, and the value of the stock goes down (or stays the same). What happens: The option is not exercised since the market price is lower than the striking price. So the option eventually expires. You pocket the $500 premium (less commission) and hold on to your stock. You can then sell another option on the ABC stock if you so desire—and continue the high yield.

▶ **TAX PICTURE:** Premiums from lapsed call options are short-term capital gains. That means they are fully taxable as ordinary income. But unlike interest and dividends, call option premiums can be completely offset by losses from stock sales.

''Wait a minute!'' you're probably saying. You bought ABC stock in the first place because you thought it would go up. If you sell a call and the stock's value goes up, don't you miss the profit from the short-term rise?

Answer: You will—but with good reason: There's money to be made taking that sure, quick cash up front. Remember: If you sell a call on ABC and pocket an immediate $500, that $500 is yours no matter what happens to the price of the stock.

Let's say ABC goes up to $68 a share. An investor who bought an ABC option at 60 can sell the option at a profit. Or he can ''call'' the option. In other words, he has the right to buy the actual shares at $60 a share. In this situation, you have two choices.

1. You can let the stock go at 60. You lose out on the $800 gain—from 60 to 68 (but not the $1,500 gain you had before selling the call). But remember, you have the $500 premium.

▶ **TAX CONSEQUENCES:** The call option premium is treated as part of the proceeds from the sale of the stock. So if the stock is entitled to long-term capital gain treatment (you've owned it more than six months), only 40% of the proceeds (including the option premium) are subject to tax.

2. You can close out the option. This allows you to hold on to your ABC stock if you think it's going up further. You go out and buy another ABC call option with a striking price of $60. That cancels the call you sold, so you still have your ABC stock. However, since the ABC stock has gone up in value—from $60 to $68—so has the value of the ABC call option with a 60 striking price. As a result, you'll have to pay more for the replacement call than you received for the call you sold. So if the replacement call cost you $1,400, you have a $900 loss ($1,400 cost less the $500 premium income).

▶ **CAPITAL LOSS:** The loss you have on the sale and repurchase of the call is currently deductible as a short-term capital loss. A $900 loss can shelter from tax up to $900 of your salary, interest, dividends or other ordinary income (up to $3,000).

Important benefit: You still get dividends when you sell call options on your stock. Any dividends declared on your stock while an option is outstanding go in your pocket. So, in effect, you get double dividends—the ones the corporation declares, plus your option premium income.

The Tax Law includes an important rule for call option writers: If you write an ''in the money'' call (striking price is less than stock's trading price), the holding period for your stock is *suspended* until the call option lapses, is exercised or is closed out (by purchase of offsetting option).

▶ **WORST THAT CAN HAPPEN?:** As we said before, the stock can go up and be called away. In that case, you lose out on the stock's appreciation. On the other hand, the stock could nosedive and you must hold it to cover the call. In that situation, you can close out the call and free up your stock. Result: The replacement call costs less than the call you sold, so you come out ahead on the calls, which thus reduces the loss on your stock.

Bottom line: Selling call options can pay off in extra income—if you know the right strategies. But as with almost any investment, there are risks. What this all means is that you absolutely must get the help and advice of a broker who specializes in buying and selling options.

HOW MUNICIPAL BONDS HELP YOU BUILD FAMILY WEALTH WITH TAX-FREE INCOME

Municipal bonds have long been popular among investors. Reason: They are the premiere source of—

▶ **TAX-FREE INVESTMENT INCOME:** Most state, county, and municipal bonds pay interest that is free of federal income tax. In addition, if the bond is issued by the state you live in, there isn't any state tax in most instances, either. What's more, in many cases, municipal bonds are a relatively safe investment.

Just glance at the comparison chart on page 65 to see the power of tax-exempt bonds. It shows the rate of taxable interest which "traditional" bonds must yield before taxes to equal various tax-exempt bond yields.

For example, suppose Mr. Brown, a married taxpayer filing jointly, has taxable income of $51,000. For Brown, a municipal with a tax-free yield of 10% is the equivalent of an investment (such as a corporate bond) throwing off a 16.13% taxable yield.

Of course, tax-free interest isn't the whole story on municipals. There are a couple of other tax angles to keep in mind.

● *Capital gain:* If you buy a bond at a discount and hold it to maturity (or if you sell the bond at a profit), the gain is taxed as capital gain. If the bond was held long enough (six months and a day), you have low-taxed long-term capital gain (only 40% of long-term capital gain is subject to tax).

● *Capital loss:* There may be a capital loss when you sell a bond (interest rates may be higher than your bond's rate). As with other assets, the loss is either long-term or short-term. The capital loss from the sale of a tax-exempt can offset gain from the sale of taxable investment. Or it can offset as much as $3,000 of ordinary income.

● *Bond premiums:* Sometimes you may pay a premium for a municipal bond—in other words, you pay more than the bond's face amount. The premium is amortized ratably over the remaining life of the bond. The premium is non-deductible and reduces your tax basis in the bond.

Example: In January, 1984, Mr Quinn paid $1,200 for a $1,000 face value municipal bond that will mature in 1994. Each year Quinn must reduce his basis in the bond by $20 ($200 premium spread over ten years).

If Quinn sells the bond for $1,300 in December, 1986, his basis in the bond is $1,140 ($1,200 cost less 3 years amortization at $20 a year). Quinn has a $160 long-term capital gain ($1,300 sales price less $1,140 basis).

● *Zero coupon bonds:* Some municipals are issued at a discount and pay no interest. The difference between the face value (payable at the bond's maturity) and the discount price is equivalent to the interest an ordinary municipal pays. Key advantage: You don't have to reinvest interest payments. You can just sit back and watch your investment grow.

● *Investment expenses:* Commissions and brokerage fees you incur buying and selling a tax-exempt are added to your basis (the cost of your investment). That decreases your taxable profit and increases your capital loss when you sell. However, the tax law prevents you from deducting expenses you incur in obtaining tax-free interest. As a result, you lose deductions that stock and corporate bond investors have locked up, such as safe deposit and custodian fees. In addition there's—

▶ **NO INTEREST DEDUCTION:** You can't deduct interest on debt that's incurred or continued to carry tax-exempt securities, such as municipal bonds. In fact, the borrowed money doesn't even have to be used to buy tax-exempts for the rule to apply. As long as there's a "sufficiently direct relationship" between the indebtedness and the tax-exempts, the deduction is barred.

How To Lock In Tax-Free Profit With A Low Cost Municipal Bond

In recent years, a different kind of municipal bond has appeared on the scene. Now you can purchase—

▶ **ZERO COUPON MUNICIPAL BONDS:** Municipals are now being offered that have no coupons to clip. The bonds are issued at a discount and pay no interest. You might buy a $5,000 bond for only $2,500. You are paid the full $5,000 when the bond matures in eight years. That's a 9.05% rate of return locked in right from the start.

The difference between the face value and the discount price—called original issue discount, or OID—is equivalent to the interest income that an ordinary municipal pays. The difference is also equivalent to the interest income for tax purposes. No tax is owed on the amount paid to you at maturity. Key advantage: Since the holder of a zero coupon municipal sees his money only when the bond reaches maturity, his investment yields—

▶ **TROUBLE-FREE GROWTH:** An investor in a zero coupon municipal bond doesn't need to reinvest interest payments. The bonds act as a low-cost tax-free investment you can squirrel away for your family nest egg—and forget about.

Special tax angle: If you sell your bond before maturity, you will probably realize an economic profit (the difference between the original cost and the value of the bond the year you sell). But you may have a taxable capital gain or a deductible capital loss. Reason: To the extent interest rates have gone up since you bought the bond, the value of the bond lags behind its fixed yield—and you have a capital loss on the sale. If, on the other hand, interest rates are lower, the bond's value will be greater than the fixed yield—and you have a capital gain.

If you bought a zero coupon municipal bond before March 1, 1984, you subtract from your amount realized the build-up in original issue discount that occurred during your bond ownership. It is figured on a linear basis. Thus, if you bought a $5,000 municipal issued at $2,000 to mature in ten years, the OID is $3,000. The annual adjustment is $300 ($3,000 total discount divided by 10).

TAXABLE YIELDS EQUIVALENT TO MUNICIPAL BOND YIELDS

Tax-Exempt Yields

Single Return*	$16.19-19.64		$19.64-25.36		$25.36-31.08		$31.08-36.8		$44.8-59.7		$59.7-88.3		Over $88.3
Joint Return*		$26.55-32.27		$32.27-37.98		$37.98-49.42		$49.4-64.8	$64.8-92.4	$92.4-118.1		$118.1-175.3	Over $175.3
% Tax Bracket	23	25	26	28	30	33	34	38	42	45	48	49	50
7	9.09	9.33	9.46	9.72	10.00	10.45	10.61	11.29	12.07	12.73	13.46	13.72	14.00
7½	9.74	10.00	10.13	10.42	10.71	11.19	11.36	12.10	12.93	13.64	14.42	14.71	15.00
8	10.39	10.67	10.81	11.11	11.43	11.94	12.12	12.90	13.79	14.54	15.38	15.69	16.00
8½	11.04	11.33	11.49	11.80	12.14	12.69	12.88	13.71	14.65	15.45	16.35	16.67	17.00
9	11.69	12.00	12.16	12.50	12.86	13.43	13.64	14.52	15.52	16.36	17.31	17.65	18.00
9½	12.34	12.67	12.84	13.19	13.57	14.18	14.39	15.32	16.38	17.27	18.27	18.63	19.00
10	12.99	13.33	13.51	13.89	14.28	14.92	15.15	16.13	17.24	18.18	19.23	19.61	20.00
10½	13.64	14.00	14.19	14.58	15.00	15.67	15.91	16.93	18.10	19.09	20.19	20.59	21.00
11	14.28	14.67	14.86	15.28	15.71	16.42	16.67	17.74	18.96	20.00	21.15	21.57	22.00
12	15.58	16.00	16.22	16.67	17.14	17.91	18.18	19.35	20.69	21.82	23.08	23.53	24.00
13	16.88	17.33	17.57	18.06	18.57	19.40	19.70	20.97	22.41	23.64	25.00	25.49	26.00
14	18.18	18.67	18.42	19.44	20.00	20.90	21.21	22.58	24.14	25.45	26.92	27.45	28.00

*Based on 1986 tax rate schedules

► **KEY CUTOFF DATE:** For zero coupon municipals issued after September 3, 1982 and purchased after March 1, 1984 the yearly adjustment is figured on a compounding interest basis. Result: Smaller accruals in the early years of ownership, and larger accruals in the later years. The basis of a zero coupon municipal bond is increased by the accrued interest. Result: Larger capital gain or smaller capital loss if you sell the bond before maturity.

"Zeroes" have maturities that range from seven to 33 years. In other words, you can choose the date you want your capital returned.

Typical uses: A bond maturing in 16 years could help finance a two-year-old child's future college education. Or you can buy bonds that mature in a year a child is likely to be married, or mature in the year you intend to retire.

Word of caution: Because zeroes do not pay any current interest, they are more volatile than interest paying bonds. If interest rates go up after you buy a zero-coupon municipal, its market value will take a big drop.

How Some Municipal Bonds Offer Tax-Free Income—Plus Extra Financial Protection

A long-term municipal bond locks in tax-free interest income over the long haul. The problem is that if interest rates rise before the bond matures, the value of the bond declines. Investors won't pay face value for a bond that pays lower interest than the prevailing rate. If you want to sell such a bond to get into a higher-yielding investment, you have to sell at a loss. That means having less to reinvest.

How can you protect yourself? What can you do to avoid a loss if you want to reinvest your funds at a better rate of return?

► **ONE SOLUTION:** You might want to consider tender-option bonds or put bonds. They have maturities that range up to 30 years and pay tax-free interest, just like other bonds issued by state or local governments. But put bonds have one feature that sets them apart: You have the option of "putting" the bond to the issuer at least once a year, beginning at a specified date after the bond is issued. That means you can make the issuer redeem the bond at full face value, even if the bond is selling at a discount at that time.

Result: Put bonds take the risk of reduced face value out of interest rate fluctuations. You know you can get the par value of the bond from the issuer at least once a year.

► **IDEA IN ACTION:** If interest rates rise, you can get your full investment back from the issuer and buy another bond that pays higher interest. And if interest rates fall, you may be able to collect the higher interest rate for the life of the bond.

In effect, a put bond is comparable to a series of short-term municipal bonds that mature on the dates the bond can be redeemed. The interest rate on a newly issued put bond is usually higher than short-term bonds. That's another reason put bonds are popular with investors.

Are there any disadvantages to put bonds? The interest paid on these bonds is a bit lower than on long-term bonds of equal quality. And the issuer of put bonds often has the right to call the bonds—to redeem them before maturity. The issuer may even be required to do so on a regular schedule. This may prevent put bonds from rising above par value, the way other bonds do when interest rates fall. So although these bonds won't decline in value if interest rates rise, they generally won't increase in value if interest rates fall.

▶ **WHAT TO DO:** You may want some put bonds in your portfolio as a hedge against rising interest rates. If you're interested, check with your investment adviser. He or she will be able to point out which bonds offer the put feature, and whether they fit into your overall investment strategy.

How One Kind of Municipal Bond Can Produce a Tax-Sheltered Nest Egg

You may be after more than just tax-free interest. For instance, you may have a specific financial objective in mind—say, building a college fund for your child. There's a particular type of bond that meets this need.

▶ **DEEP DISCOUNT MUNICIPALS:** These bonds carry low interest rates and, sell at big discounts. The interest is, of course, tax free. But when the bonds mature at face value, the investor gets something extra—a handsome, built-in profit, taxed at low capital gain rates.

"Wait a minute," you may be saying. "These bonds pay relatively little interest. How can I be better off with less—rather than more—tax-free interest?"

First off, let's make it clear that discount bonds aren't for everybody. But they may fill the bill for someone who wants to build a special family nest egg with a minimum of trouble. You put your money away and it's done—period. Month after month, year after year, your tax-sheltered profit grows.

Secondly, when we say a discount bond has a "low" interest rate, we're talking about the interest rate of the face value—not the actual current yield. This may be a lot higher. *Reason:* With a discount bond, your cash investment is much lower than the face value of the bond. So your real current return is much higher than the stated interest rate. Let's see how the tax benefits of discount bonds can pay off with this—

Typical example: You have a child (or grandchild) who'll be ready for college in 16 years. You want to build a custom-designed fund for his education by buying some discount municipals now and putting them away till maturity.

▶ **WINNING MOVE:** You buy three XYZ municipal bonds. For simplicity, let's say each bond has a stated interest rate of 4%, a face value of $10,000 and sells on the market for $7,000. The bonds mature in 16 years.

How you profit: You get $1,200 a year in interest ($400 interest on each bond). That means you get a current yield of about 5.7% on your total $21,000 investment. And, as with all municipals, you get the benefit of tax-free income: If you're in the 42% tax bracket, a 5.7% tax-free yield is equivalent to a taxable yield of about 9.8%.

How your child profits: You have a $30,000 fund (the maturity value of the three bonds) ready for him when he goes to college. In other words, you've made a $9,000 profit on your investment—without your having to do a thing. This profit is taxable when you cash in the bonds—but at the low capital gain rates.

HOW TO BUY TAX-FREE MUNICIPALS THAT PAY BETTER THAN TAX-FREE BONDS

Municipal bonds are popular for good reason: Municipal bond interest is exempt from Federal income tax and usually state and local income tax (if the bond was issued by your state or a town or city in your state). But because they are tax-free, municipal bonds don't pay as well as taxable bonds (e.g., corporate bonds and U.S. Government securities).

▶ **GOOD NEWS:** There is a new kind of investment that pays tax-free interest at a higher rate. They pay anywhere from one-half to three or more percentage points higher than municipal bonds of comparable maturities.

They are called municipal leases, and here's how they work: A municipality (town, city, county, state, etc.) needs equipment (e.g., police car, fire truck, computer) but doesn't want to lay out the cash or float a bond issue. Instead, the government agrees to buy the equipment under a short-term installment sales contract. The installment contract is called a municipal lease, but the goverment actually purchases the equipment and ends up with clear title to the equipment at the end of the lease period.

The lease is the security that is sold to investors. The investment is secured by a first lien on the equipment. Each month, the investor receives payments made up of both a return of capital and interest. And that interest is—

▶ **TAX-FREE INCOME:** Here's why: Any interest paid on a municipal obligation—whether it's a bond or an installment contract—is tax-free, says the Government.

Why is the rate higher than that paid by municipal bonds? You receive a higher rate in exchange for taking a bit more risk. A municipal lease arrangement, unlike a municipal bond, is not backed by the municipality's taxing authority. It is based on annual appropriations. Each year, the state or local government must vote to spend the money necessary to make the lease payments. If it doesn't, it defaults on the deal. The equipment would then have to be repossessed and sold (or released) for the investor to avoid a loss.

A municipal lease arrangement sounds risky. But keep in mind that if the equipment is vital, the government will do its best to make the payments. To be safe, you should request from the state or local government an ''essential use'' statement, which states why the equipment was chosen and explains its use. In addition, most municipal lease arrangements contain a non-substitution clause.

▶ **INVESTOR PROTECTION:** This clause prevents a defaulting government from purchasing another piece of the same type of equipment for a stated period of time. Assuming the equipment is indeed essential, the clause should serve as a strong incentive for the government to make its payments.

But pick your lease carefully. Municipal lease arrangements are usually not rated. Nor are they privately insured.

How to invest: There are two ways to invest in a municipal lease arrangement.

● Certificate: You can buy a certificate of participation in a municipal lease arrangement from a stock brokerage firm. The minimum cost is $5,000. There is no organized secondary market in municipal lease arrangements, so you have to hold the investment until maturity (usually three to seven years). And since you are getting a return of your investment as part of each payment, you have to reinvest your principal if you want to add to your nest egg.

● Mutual fund: You can buy shares in a mutual fund for a minimum investment of $2,500, with increments of $500 permitted. Not only is this a smaller minimum than if you buy a certificate, but it is also more liquid. You have unlimited withdrawal privileges from the fund. In addition, you get professional management, diversification and automatic reinvestment of your capital. Of course, you pay for these features—an upfront sales charge and monthly management fees.

How Swapping Municipal Bonds Can Produce Current Tax Savings And Higher Yields

As year-end approaches, the municipal bond market is often swamped with a wave of bond-swapping. Why swap bonds? There are many good reasons, but the most important is—

▶ **TAX SAVINGS:** Astute bond swapping can give you a tax loss that will shelter your other highly-taxed dollars. Net effect: More money in your pocket, less in Uncle Sam's.

Here's the story: Suppose you bought a municipal bond years ago when interest rates were lower than they are today. Because your bond's coupon rate is lower than today's current bond yields, the bond's current value is less than its par value. As a result, you are sitting on a paper loss.

You can sell your bond, pick up a tax loss, and use the sale proceeds to buy another bond with a comparable yield, current price, and maturity date. Of course, you may pay a tax if you hold the bond until it matures or if you sell it at a profit. But the gain may be years down the road, so the tax will be postponed and you'll only pay at the favorable long-term capital gain rates. In the meantime, the loss you take this year offsets some of your current income.

> *Simplified example:* Mr. White bought an Apple City bond years ago for $10,000. The bond will mature in the year 2000 and has a 4½% coupon rate. The bond's current value is only $5,700. White sells the Apple City bond and buys a Peach City bond with the same face value, maturing in 2003 and paying 4⅝%. The value of this bond is also down to around $5,700. Mr. White also has a $4,300 short-term capital gain from a stock sale earlier in the year.

Dollars-and-cents benefit: White has a $4,300 tax loss this year ($10,000 cost less $5,700 current value) that he can use to shelter his $4,300 short-term capital gain from his stock transactions. Assuming for simplicity's sake that White is in the 50% tax bracket, the $4,300 tax loss saves him $2,150 in taxes.

Suppose Mr. White holds the Peach City bond until it matures. Result: White will have a long term capital gain of $4,300. At current rates, the maximum tax on that gain will be $860. Result: White's swap yields him big dollar savings now at the price of a low-taxed capital gain when the bond matures.

All in all, White comes out of the trade looking pretty good. But his current tax-free income is almost unchanged. He was earning $450 in annual interest on the Apple City bond (coupon rate: 4½%) and now he's pocketing $462.50 (coupon rate of 4⅝%). That's a $12.50 net gain—peanuts.

What can White do to kick up his investment yield? Answer: He can—

> ▶ **PUT HIS TAX SAVINGS TO WORK:** White takes his $2,150 in tax dollars saved, plus his $5,700 proceeds from the Apple City sale, and buys a Western State bond for $7,850. The Western State has a 6¾% coupon rate and matures in the year 2000.

Results: (1) White increases his current tax-free yield to $675 a year, (2) shelters his short-term stock market gain from tax, and (3) nails down a $2,150 long-term capital gain if he holds the new bond until maturity.

Important: The bond-swapping technique works only if you can take a current loss deduction on your bond sale. But if the bonds you buy are "substantially identical" to the bonds you sell, and the two transactions take place within 30 days of each other, you can't deduct your loss currently under the "wash-sale" rules. What's "substantially identical?" There's no clearcut answer. One brokerage firm suggests that bonds of the same issuer have at least a ½% difference in the yield to maturity and 5 years difference in maturity dates to avoid the wash-sale rules. However, bonds issued by different states or municipalities are not "substantially identical."

▶ **MAKE YOUR MOVE EARLY:** Every December there's a swapping boom in the bond market as investors rush to nail down losses before year-end. Result: trading fees—the cost of buying and selling bonds—go up. So it pays to do your swapping before the annual crunch.

One Kind Of Municipal Escapes All Income Taxes No Matter Where You Live

The interest from a municipal bond is free of Federal income tax, but not necessarily free of state and local taxes. You pay state and local taxes if the bond is issued by a state other than your own (and a few states even tax their own bonds).

▶ **TAX-SAVING EXCEPTION:** Bonds issued by some U.S. holdings are tax-free across the board—no matter where you live. They are specifically exempted by law from Federal tax *and* state and local tax. Owning one of these bonds is just like owning a bond issued by your state or municipality (assuming it doesn't tax its own issues).

Prime example: Commonwealth of Puerto Rico bonds. Other bonds that receive full tax-free treatment include bonds issued by the U.S. Virgin Islands and .Guam.

With states and localities taking an ever-increasing share of your income, this total tax-free break can be a big plus. If municipal bonds are your cup of tea, some of these fully tax-free bonds may be well worth looking into.

Chapter 3

Tax Shelter Investments—Are They Right For You and Your Family?

Tax shelters have been getting a bad press lately because of the IRS crackdown on so-called "abusive" shelters. But there are plenty of legitimate profit-making tax shelters around that allow you to build up your family's wealth with the tax law's help. This Chapter highlights the most popular tax shelters around today and shows how to put them in action.

WHY REAL ESTATE IS CALLED THE NUMBER ONE TAX SHELTER

In the opinion of many experts, real estate can't be beat as a money-making tax shelter. Reason: It offers a combination of benefits that few other investments can match:

● *Appreciation and inflation protection:* Over the long term, well located, well managed and well maintained property has appreciated at a rate that outpaces the increase in inflation.

● *High leverage opportunity:* Leverage basically means using other people's money—instead of your own cash—to make money. Real estate gives you better leverage opportunities than most other investments. You can buy many properties with a low cash downpayment—25%, 10% or even less—and borrow the rest of the purchase price.

● *Equity buildup:* In the usual self-amortizing mortgage, part of each payment is for interest and the remainder reduces the principal (the unpaid balance of the loan). As the investor reduces the loan's balance, he builds up equity in the property without any additional out-of-pocket cash. *Reason:* The mortgage will be paid off by the rent roll. The greater the equity buildup, the more of the property the investor actually owns. And you need not sell the building to tap a growing equity. For example, you can refinance the mortgage and obtain additional cash to buy additional properties.

● *Tax shelter benefits:* Few investments offer as many tax saving opportunities as real estate. Here's a detailed look at—

How to Build a Tax-Sheltered Fortune in Real Estate

One of the major tax attractions in real estate is the deduction for depreciation. This deduction enables you to write off the cost of a building even while the property itself is increasing in value—as is so often the case today. And you're entitled to these deductions on the full cost of the building (including borrowed amounts) even though you may have put up a minimal amount of cash. In other words, you create a big tax shelter for yourself, mostly with someone else's cash.

There are two big reasons why depreciation makes real estate a top tax-saver.

1. Since depreciation is a deduction from otherwise taxable income but does not require an ongoing cash outlay, as most expense deductions do, the result is tax-free cash. Even when you're amortizing a mortgage (the cash outlay for amortization is not deductible), the depreciation deduction may be large enough to blanket the amortization and part of the remaining income, resulting in tax-free cash. The amortization payment, since it reduces the mortgage, goes to build up equity in the property.

2. With depreciation and the ability to deduct amounts in excess of your equity, economically profitable real estate operations can produce substantial tax losses. Thus, you may be able to shelter from income tax the economic profit of your real estate operation and even shelter some of your other income—like salary and dividends—from tax.

How to write off the cost of your building: Generally, the date you placed your property in service governs your writeoff period:

• Property placed in service before 1981 must be depreciated over its useful life (20 to 35 years).

• Property placed in service after 1980 and *before* March 16, 1984, can be written off over 15 years.

• Property placed in service after March 15, 1984 and *before* May 9, 1985 must, as a general rule, be written off over 18 years.

• Property placed in service after May 8, 1985 must be written off over 19 years.

At-risk-rule exemption: As a general rule, the tax law's "at-risk" rule limits an investor's tax-loss writeoffs to the cash he has invested plus borrowed amounts on which he is personally liable. But under current law, real estate is *not* subject to the at-risk rules. So a deal financed with a non-recourse loan (the lender can look only to the property in case of default or foreclosure) can offer you writeoffs in excess of your cash investment.

Important: If you invest through a limited partnership, the loan must be non-recourse to all partners (including the general partner) and the partnership, or your writeoffs are limited to your cash contribution.

Low-taxed capital gain profits: Your writeoff for depreciation will eventually start to run out. So you may decide to sell your property. If you make a profit (your proceeds exceed your adjusted basis in the property) on the sale—

which is likely—you will discover the "hidden" tax shelter of real estate: conversion of high-taxed ordinary income into low-taxed capital gain.

> **Example:** Mr. Brown built a new apartment house in 1983 with a basis of $500,000. Using straight line, Brown has an annual depreciation deduction of $33,333 ($500,000 divided by 15). After ten years, his adjusted basis in the property is $166,667 (original basis less $333,333 total depreciation taken). Brown sells the building for $900,000. He has a $733,333 gain (proceeds less adusted basis), all of which is long-term capital gain.

> ▶ **INCOME CONVERSION:** Mr. Brown has converted $333,333 of ordinary income into $333,333 of tax-sheltered capital gain. *Reason:* Brown's $333,333 of depreciation decductions shelter an equal amount of ordinary income. The $333,333 of depreciation deductions also reduces Brown's basis by $333,333. So when he sells the building, his gain is larger by that amount. However the $333,333 is brought back into income as capital gain. In other words, it is taxed at 40% of the rate that applies to the income that was already sheltered by the depreciation deductions.

How the "recapture" rules work: The recapture rules for property placed in service after 1980 are as follows: If you use the straight-line method, all of your gain will be capital gain when you sell (regardless of whether the building is a residential or a nonresidential property). And if you use an accelerated method for residential property, some of the gain may be taxed ("recaptured") as ordinary income. The amount recaptured is the excess of the total deductions taken over the deductions that would have been allowable if the straight-line method had been used.

But if you take accelerated depreciation on *nonresidential* property, the recapture rules are tough: Your gain will be recaptured to the full extent of the recovery deductions taken (*including* straight line).

Another problem: If you sell a building and receive payment in installments (e.g., you take back a first or second mortgage), you could wind up with phantom income. Reason: Sale profit "recaptured" and treated as ordinary income is taxed in full in the year of sale—whether or not you receive payments in that year. Under prior law, the recapture portion of your profit was taxed as ordinary income ratably—as you received installment payments from your buyer.

> ▶ **WHAT TO DO:** Consider using straight line depreciation when you buy real estate. That way you have no ordinary income—and therefore no phantom income—when you sell the property.

How to Cash In on the Boom in Condo and Co-op Conversions

All you have to do is pick up the real estate section of most newspapers to see that condos and co-ops are the hottest thing in real estate right now. Whether you're interested in a unit for yourself or not, you can turn the condo and co-op boom to your advantage.

▶ **BE A LANDLORD:** You buy condominium or co-op units in bulk—five, ten, or even more and rent them to tenants. It's like buying a small apartment complex, except you own a group of apartments located in a large apartment development.

Like any landlord, you pocket income sheltered by depreciation deductions. Then when the time comes, it should be easier to sell your apartments than it would be to sell an apartment building. Reason: There are many more buyers for condo or co-op units than there are buyers for a whole apartment building.

▶ **HOW TO GET A BARGAIN PRICE:** Consider buying apartments in a large high-rise or garden-apartment complex that has been purchased by a converter specialist. Make your move as soon as possible after the converter has bought the property.

Reason: The converter has made large cash commitments: cash for the seller of the property, more cash for improvements to make the units saleable, and still more cash to carry the property while the building is being completely converted and all apartments sold. In short, the converter needs working capital—and in a hurry.

Here's where you come in: You offer to buy a number of the converter's units—*for cash*. In return, you bargain for a substantial discount off market prices—say 20 to 25% off. The typical investor in this field finances part of the purchase with a short-term personal loan. Your rental income should cover the financing and any other expenses. You can expect only a modest return. But even if you simply break even on a cash basis, you get a return in the form of tax savings.

Example: In January, you buy five units with a fair market value of $300,000. You buy them for $240,000 (a 20% discount). You lay out $120,000 cash and finance the rest. You break even (income equals expenses). Since $40,000 of the purchase price is attributable to the land, you can write off $200,000 under the Accelerated Cost Recovery System (ACRS). First-year ACRS writeoff: $17,600. That writeoff shelters $17,600 of highly-taxed income. Dollars saved in the 50% bracket: $8,800.

Rapid profits are the key: Investors who buy condo and co-op units in bulk get in and out of their investment in two or three years. If you buy units at a substantial discount off true market value, you don't need extraordinary appreciation in value to take down a big profit.

Using the example above, suppose the units appreciate to $350,000 in two years. You would have a pre-tax profit of $110,000—a 91.6% return on your $120,000 cash investment, 45.8% a year.

▶ **NOT FOR THE FAINTHEARTED:** Your profit depends on whether the conversion project as a whole is a commercial success. And the Government may say you are a "dealer" whose profits are taxed as ordinary income, not capital gain. So consult your tax and investment advisers before you make a move.

Why Historic Structures Offer A Unique Tax Shelter Opportunity

There's a great deal of history in the real estate of the United States, from the mansions of colonial times to the rowhouses of the early 1900's. The history can be fascinating—and rehabilitating such property can also be a prime source of—

▶ **TAX SHELTER:** An investor is entitled to a tax credit equal to 25% of qualifying rehabilitation expenses. Typically, these expenses account for a major portion of the total project cost.

Example: In January, a group of five investors buys a historic property for $300,000 ($150,000 for land, balance for the building). They spend $500,000 rehabilitating the property for use as commercial office space. The investors make a downpayment of $300,000 ($60,000 from each) and finance the $500,000 balance with a loan. The rehabilitation is completed and the offices are rented by year-end.

The investors are entitled to an investment tax credit of $125,000 (25% of the $500,000 rehabilitation cost). That works out to $25,000 for each investor. Since a dollar of credit reduces tax liability by a dollar, each investor gets back $25,000 of his $60,000 cash investment when he pays his tax bill. Taking the credit into account, each investor has, in effect, made only a $35,000 downpayment.

Basic requirements: Four key conditions must be met to claim the rehabilitation credit for historic structures:

1. The building must be listed in the National Register of Historic Places, or located in a historic district and certified by the Secretary of the Interior as significant to the district.

2. At least 75% of the existing external walls must be retained, OR (a) at least 50% of external walls are retained as external walls; (b) at least 75% of external walls are retained as external or internal walls; and (c) at least 75% of the building's internal framework is retained.

3. The rehabilitation must be "substantial." That means expenditures within a 24- or 36-month period ending with or within the tax year must exceed the greater of the building's adjusted basis or $5,000. And the rehabilitation must be approved by the Department of the Interior.

4. You must use straight-line depreciation on the rehabilitation cost. And a historic structure's basis is reduced by one-half the 25% tax credit claimed.

The rehabilitated building can be used for commercial, industrial, or residential-rental purposes. Rehabilitation of a residence used for personal purposes does not qualify.

The credit is strictly for restoring buildings. Adding a new wing to a structure does not qualify, and neither does the addition of building-related facilities, such as a new parking lot.

Result: The investors can depreciate $587,500 ($650,000 building and rehabilitation cost less one-half the $125,000 credit). Assuming straight-line depreciation is used for both the building shell and the cost of rehabilitation, the average annual depreciation deduction is about $30,860 for 19 years.

You can also rehabilitate a building that is not a historic structure, and still qualify for a rehabilitation tax credit. But it is a smaller credit. The credit is equal to 15% of the cost of the rehabilitation expenses if the building is at least 30 years old when the rehabilitation commences. The credit is 20% if the building is at least 40 years old. To qualify for the 15% or 20% tax credit, you must meet the same conditions listed above for historic structures (except for the first test, which qualifies a building as historic). And you don't have to obtain certification of the rehabilitation, either.

▶ **MAJOR DIFFERENCE:** If you rehabilitate a non-historic building, you must reduce your tax basis—for all purposes, including depreciation—by the *full* amount of the credit claimed. The tax basis of a historic building is reduced by ony half the credit claimed. And your non-historic building must be rehabilitated only for commercial or industrial purposes. Unlike historic buildings, you get no credit if you rehabilitate a building for residential rental use.

TWO LESSER-KNOWN TAX SHELTER OPPORTUNITIES IN REAL ESTATE

If you're thinking about investing in real estate, apartment or office buildings usually come to mind. But there are other lesser-known, offbeat real estate investments that are proving to be highly successful. Here are two of the more popular ones—miniwarehouses and private mailbox centers.

#1 Miniwarehouses

Storage space is at a premium these days. Investors can supply such space—in units of 10′ by 10′ or 10′ by 20′—in a secure, compact but economically constructed one-story building that's like a series of single-car garages set side by side—the *miniwarehouse*.

▶ **BIG PROFITS:** Investors can average a 20% return in well located, sensibly constructed miniwarehouses. And a good deal of the profit should be sheltered by depreciation deductions. Units that cost as little as $7 to $10 a sq. foot to build have been rented for as much as 50¢ a sq. foot per month. When kept to a tightly managed "no-frills" operation, these structures can bring in a healthy cash flow and provide all the standard tax advantages of commercial real estate.

Keeping costs low: Miniwarehouses can be built comparatively cheaply. Cinderblock construction is perfectly acceptable; it can be painted in bright colors and requires virtually no maintenance.

Units need neither windows nor insulation. Doors should be the standard overhead models used on garage, but they need not be the most elaborate model available; a door will get very little use since the average customer rarely visits the unit more often than once a month. Experts in the field recommend using the least expensive model that is (a) secure and (b) watertight.

▶ **SMART STRATEGY:** Movable partitions can be used to divide interior space. While these cost more than walls, they allow an investor to shift the design according to the market—creating 10' by 20' units if demand for those is high; dividing large units into 10' by 10' ones if those become popular. Miniwarehouse experts suggest devoting 15% of the space to units 5' by 6'.

Picking the right site: An investor should expect to draw about 75% of all customers from within a five-mile radius and pick a site accordingly. A market survey will be needed to answer such questions as: How many houses do or do not have basements? How many boats and recreational vehicles are owned? How many people live in apartments? In mobile homes? The answers reveal the need for storage space and the kinds of storage space in your community. This market research can also be used by investors to raise financing from lenders.

Commercial tenants may account for up to 30% of the space, so an investor shouldn't concentrate only on spots near residential areas. In fact, commercial tenants are, on the whole, preferable to individual tenants. They tend to be long-term customers. Access to a main highway is essential, but the miniwarehouse need not be seen from the road; a tall sign over the structure or a large sign near the freeway exit can pull in the patrons.

#2 Private Mailbox Centers

You can make money by buying sites or buildings that can be used for *private post offices*—small buildings where the public rents individual mailboxes.

These "centers" are catching on fast because they fill a growing need. U.S. post offices are running out of space just when more people are wanting to rent mailboxes. A center is strictly a "no-frills" operation, since all the public wants is a place to pick up its mail. And this means you can make a top profit at a minimum cost. A sorting room, a lobby and four walls of boxes—those are the "facilities" required.

This growing demand gives an investor at least three ways to earn big profits:

● You can lease a commercial property you own (or buy) to someone who will use it as a private mailbox center;

• You can convert all or part of a property you own (or rent) to a mailbox center and operate the business yourself.

• You can buy or rent a property for conversion to a mailbox center.

Another advantage of a mailbox center is that you might be able to acquire property at—

▶ **A BARGAIN PRICE:** You don't need very much space to operate a mailbox center. So you might be able to buy an oddly shaped vacant lot or an undersized storefront at a bargain price.

Profit potential: Some operators are reported to net 30% to 40% of the gross before taxes. One investor with only 312 boxes reportedly grosses $42,000 a year. He opened just a few years ago with a $5,000 investment.

Another operator said his business doubled in a year; customers are people who travel or people who are opening new businesses and like to have their mail addressed to "Suite No." such and such at the address of the mailbox center.

Few management problems: Because of its simplicity, this is one business that can prosper under absentee ownership. A dependable manager or assistant manager would be a former postal worker who is conscientious and knows the system. And it's not hard to find part-time or moonlighting postal clerks to sort mail and serve customers. This makes the business perfect for many real estate investors.

Here's a Low-Cost Way to Buy Into Real Estate With a Minimum of Trouble

How would you like to own a piece of world-famous Rockefeller Center? You can—and for less than $20. How to do it: You buy into a Real Estate Investment Trust—better known as REIT. In essence a REIT is an investment company that invests in real estate. When an investor buys shares of REIT stock, he also invests in professionally managed real estate—the underlying properties of the REIT.

In other words, a REIT operates much in the same way that a mutual fund does. For a minimal investment, you can own an interest in a big real estate property like Rockefeller Center.

Big advantage: Unlike other ways to invest in real estate (for example, an interest in a limited partnership), a REIT investment is completely liquid. Reason: You're buying stock that is publicly traded on the stock market.

Tax angles: Dividends paid out to shareholders in REITs are genrally taxed as ordinary income. However, shareholders may be in line for this—

▶ **TAX BREAK:** Dividends paid from long-term capital gains of the REIT are eligible for preferential long-term capital gain treatment on your tax return.

However, shares held six months or less that are sold at a loss are characterized as long-term capital loss to the extent of any prior long-term gain. Also, the other portion of dividends received by the REIT does not qualify for the $200 dividend exclusion ($100 if filing singly) on your tax return.

There are three basic types of REITs. Let's look at the pluses and minuses of each.

● **Mortgage REITs:** These REITS basically make only mortgage loans. As a result, the shares in these REITs offer little or no growth potential. But they do offer a high annual return—the current average is over 11%. Mortgage REIT shares perform much like bonds. Their prices go up and down in response to swings in interest rates.

Mortgage REITs can be the most risky of the three types of REITs. Reason: Their return comes almost exclusively from lending money, so if the borrowers default, the investors lose their money—even though the property may have appreciated. For example, the borrowers may have mismanaged a perfectly good property. One type of mortgage REIT, however, can allow investors to benefit from property appreciation, and thereby cut the risk factor somewhat.

▶ **LOWER-RISK REITS:** There is one type of mortgage REIT that allows you to benefit from property appreciation, the Participating Mortgage REIT. In addition to lending money, these REITs also participate in the property's growth. They collect a portion of the property's profits or own a stake in the property.

● **Equity REITs:** Investors who want an ownership position in real estate may prefer an equity REIT. The REIT owns the property itself, so investors can share in an increase in the property's value. An equity REIT does especially well when property values grow. But in times of low inflation, the investor may be stuck with low yields.

● **Hybrid REITs:** These invest in both properties and mortgages. A hybrid offers investors a sampling of both worlds—a good annual return and a shot at future appreciation. The price of hybrid REIT stock should be more stable than mortgage REITs.

A new development in REITs is called the "finite" REIT (FREIT). It attempts to have its shares better reflect the value of its underlying property by being self-liquidating. A FREIT promises to liquidate its assets and distribute proceeds to shareholders within a specified period of time (usually 7 to 15 years). This promise of a large chunk of money in the near future is supposed to keep the FREIT's stock prices up. The problem with a FREIT, however, is that when the liquidation deadline comes, the real estate market may be in a slump.

After talking things over with your investment adviser, you may decide REITs make sense for you. But which REIT?

▶ **KEY TO SUCCESS;** The key to a good REIT is the management team running the REIT. Be sure to check out their track record in other real estate projects. And their philosophy should be to improve REIT properties. Experts recommend that you avoid new REITs that do not specify the properties they will own (or lend money to). In fact, you may be better off going with an older REIT over a new REIT. They are established, have ongoing management, a track record, and many are selling at a discount.

OTHER TOP TAX SHELTERS

While real estate may be a champion tax shelter, there are other viable alternatives. A number of tax shelters have gained prominence over the years: oil and gas, equipment leasing, timber, cattle breeding and farming. While these tax shelters are certainly not without risk, many have proved successful in the past.

▶ **IMPORTANT:** Unlike real estate, the amount of tax loss from these investments that is currently deductible is limited to your "at-risk" amount. Under the tax law, your at-risk amount consists of: (1) cash you put up; plus (2) the adjusted basis of property you contribute to the deal; plus (3) borrowed funds that you are personally liable to repay (so-called recourse notes). So if the deal is highly leveraged with nonrecourse funds, your tax writeoff is limited.

Most of the top tax shelter deals are set up as limited partnerships. The arrangements can be complex, so we'll just give you the basics here. We recommend that you consult with the appropriate expert before you get into any tax shelter deal. Reminder: By their very nature, tax shelters are more risky than other investments.

HOW TO FILL UP ON TAX-SHELTERED INCOME FROM AN OIL AND GAS INVESTMENT

In most parts of the country, it costs you less to "fill 'er up" at the local service station than it did at this time last year. Reason: The price of oil has fallen. So you may figure that now is not a good time to get in on an oil and gas tax shelter. But that's not necessarily true. You may be able to buy valuable, producing oil and gas property at a bargain price. And you also get tax shelter from (1) depletion, (2) depreciation deductions, and (3) long-term capital gain on the sale of the investment.

(1) Depletion: You get a deduction for the depletion of your oil reserves. Your deduction is computed either under the cost depletion method or the percentage depletion method. You must use cost depletion if you drill a "proven area." For drilling in other than proven areas, either cost or percentage depletion may be used. But you must use whichever method benefits you the most each year.

With cost depletion, your deduction for any given year depends on how much of the potential oil reserves are recovered in that year. Your deduction is computed in two steps: (1) You divide your adjusted basis in the reserves by the estimated number of barrels remaining to be produced, and (2) then multiply that figure by the year's production. When you've recovered all your basis in the well, cost depletion stops.

Percentage depletion allows you to recover your cost of the well by deducting a percentage of your gross income from the well each and every year. This percentage is 15%.

The percentage depletion deduction cannot exceed the lesser of (1) 50% of the taxable income (gross income less allowable deductions other than depletion) of the oil of gas property, or (2) 65% of the investor's taxable income. You can continue to deduct percentage depletion as long as the well continues to produce income and even after you have fully recovered your cost basis. (Note: To the extent your percentage depletion deduction exceeds your cost basis, it's treated as a "tax preference" subject to the minimum tax. See Chapter 14 for details.)

(2) Depreciation: A large part of the tangible costs of the wells go toward salvageable assets, e.g., derricks, tanks and the like. Such assets qualify for the—

▶ **FAST WRITEOFF:** Equipment can be written off under the Accelerated Cost Recover System over a very short period of time (usually, 5 years).

(3) Low-taxed profits on a sale: Even if the well turns out to be a big winner, a taxpayer may want to get out of his investment. Why? Tax-sheltered capital gain on the sale proceeds may produce more after taxes than depletion- and depreciation-protected income will yield over the production years.

Reason: Even when you combine depletion and depreciation deductions, maybe two-thirds of your oil income will be unsheltered and taxed at full ordinary income rates. In addition, you can also have a "minimum tax" problem with depletion. Part of the percentage depletion allowance is considered a tax preference subject to the special alternative minimum tax.

Here's what happens if you sell: Ordinary income deductions for intangible drilling costs (IDCs), depletion, and depreciation reduce a partnership's basis in the property (and the investor's basis in his or her partnership interest). This, of course, increases the potential for gain on the sale of the property (or the sale of the investor's partnership interest). But, assuming the long-term holding period requirement is met, this gain is generally taxed as long-term capital gain.

There are two exceptions to this favorable capital gain treatment. The first is that the gain is taxed as ordinary income to the extent of prior depreciation under the usual recapture-of-depreciation rules. The second is a recapture of the gain attributable to the election to deduct intangible drilling costs. The amount subject to recapture is the total amount of the IDC deduction reduced by the amount which would have been deductible had the intangible costs been capitalized and recovered through cost depletion. However, the amount recaptured can't exceed the gain realized or, if no gain was realized, the excess of the tranferred property's fair market value over its adjusted basis.

Why Equipment Leasing Is A Favorite Tax Shelter

Progressive companies are on the lookout for the latest equipment to hit the marketplace. However, a company may not always be able to buy new equipment. And that's where you—the tax shelter investor—come in.

▶ **TAX SHELTER WITH A TWIST:** You buy the equipment and *lease* it to a company. Assuming that the deal is set up properly—a big assumption—here's what you can get: An immediate tax writeoff that exceeds your cash investment and— sometime down the road—profit.

Typical deal: Mr. Smith buys new electronic equipment from XYZ Inc. for $50,000. Smith makes a $5,000 downpayment and gives XYZ five personal notes for $9,000 each, due over the next five years. ABC, Inc. signs a five-year lease with Smith and agrees to pay him $1,500 a year plus a fixed fee each time the equipment is used.

If things turn out as planned, Smith's lease income allows him to pay off the notes and pocket a profit. In any case, he gets—

▶ **MULTIPLE WRITEOFFS:** Under the Accelerated Cost Recovery System, Smith is entitled to a first-year depreciation deduction of 15% of cost (with deductions of 22%, 21% and 21% in the following four years), regardless of when during the first year the system is put into service. So his first-year deduction comes to $7,500 (15% of $50,000).

In addition, Smith is entitled to an investment credit—a dollar for dollar reduction in his tax bill. If Smith claimed a 10% credit, he would have to reduce his basis in the equipment—for all purposes, including depreciation. Instead, he claims a reduced 8% credit to avoid reducing his basis. This gives him a credit of $4,000. If he is in the 50% tax bracket, his $4,000 credit is equivalent to an $8,000 deduction.

▶ **TAX SHELTER PAYOFF:** Assuming the lease generates no income before year-end (it will probably generate some income), Smith has a tax loss writeoff of $15,500 for the first year ($7,500 depreciation, plus $8,000 deduction equivalent from the credit). So he can shelter the $5,000 of income he uses for the downpayment plus $10,500 of his other income.

Q. What are some of the risks in equipment leasing deals?

A. One obvious risk is that you are personally liable to the seller on the notes, whether or not the lease turns out to be successful. You must be "at risk" on the notes to get the writeoffs. If the lease income isn't sufficient to pay off the notes, you have to dig down into your own pocket to make up the difference. Of course, the chances of this happening depend largely on whom you are dealing with. So you and your investment adviser will want to look into the background of the seller and his equipment and the prospects for obtaining a profitable lease.

There are tax complications in addition to the at risk rules: For example, there are special rules that come into play if you ''net lease'' the property (the user pays all the operating and maintenance expenses). In addition, if the user has a right to buy the property at the end of the lease, the Government could characterize the arrangement as a conditional sale instead of a lease. Because the user would be considered the owner, you would lose the investment credit and your depreciation deductions.

▶ **WHAT TO DO:** Sit down with your investment adviser before you sign up for any equipment leasing venture. He's familiar with your financial situation and can advise you whether equipment leasing is right for you. And he can help you find the deal that will give the tax benefits you want.

How to Rope In Tax-Sheltered Income From a Cattle Deal

We all know that the price of beef goes up—and down—and up again, and so on. Investments in the cattle breeding business are subject to the same sort of risks. But there's money to be made if you get in with the right bunch of professionals.

▶ **KEY POINT:** We're assuming you're not a cowpuncher yourself. So you'll need a top-flight cattle deal promoter, one who is experienced and has had success in the past. Even more important: The rancher who'll be in control of the cattle. You'll want to be doubly sure of his expertise. (Be careful if a rancher offers to limit your risk of loss; he'll undoubtedly want up to 50% of any profit from the herd in return.)

Cattle are often sold to investment groups at inflated prices. Be sure to check that what you're being charged reflects the going rates. And be sure to check the costs of feeding the animals. The deal won't show a profit if the feeding costs are astronomical.

How it works: Mr. Green buys a herd of cattle for $30,000 this year from a company that specializes in cattle breeding (the company also manages the operation for Green for a flat fee). He makes a $3,000 downpayment and gives a personal note for $27,000, secured by the cattle. The note is a recourse note, so Green is personally liable. Green has to spend another $10,000 this year for operating expenses and carrying charges—cattle feed that will be consumed this year, breeding and management fees, interest on the note and so forth. Total cash outlay this year: $13,000.

Green's first year writeoff is $23,563. Where does the first-year writeoff come from? A large part ($10,000) comes from deductions for his operating expenses and carrying charges. But Green also gets the following tax breaks:

1. "Expensing" deduction: Green can elect to "expense"—deduct immediately—up to $5,000 of his cost for the cattle.

2. Investment credit: Green can claim an investment credit on the $25,000 non-expensed portion of his cost ($30,000 less $5,000). Green claims a $2,500 credit (10% of $25,000). If Green is in the 50% bracket, that credit is the equivalent of $5,000 in deductions.

3. Depreciation deductions: Green's depreciation basis in the cattle is $23,750. That his $30,000 cost minus the $5,000 "expensed" portion and minus $1,250 (half the investment credit claimed). His first-year depreciation deduction is $3,563.

Bottom line: Green winds up with $13,563 in first year deductions ($5,000 expensing, plus $5,000 in deduction equivalent from the credit, plus $3,563 in depreciation deductions) in addition to his deductions for operating expenses and carrying charges.

Under the tax law, the credit can only be figured on amounts that an investor has "at risk" (the cash he puts up plus borrowings on which he is personally liable). In other words, if Green had financed his purchase on a nonrecourse basis (Green would not be personally liable on the note), his credit would be limited to 10% of his downpayment, or $300. Because Green is personally liable on the note, he can compute his credit on the downpayment *plus* his note.

How to Grow Tax-Sheltered Profits in Timber

Besides being one of our great natural resources, timber can be a great source of tax-sheltered income. However, assuming you're not a lumberjack, you're going to need advice if you invest in timber. Like most tax shelters, the best place to start is by finding a competent professional.

▶ **IDEA IN ACTION:** Once you find a parcel of timberland, hire an independent appraiser. His report will tell you whether the property is a good investment. He'll also help you allocate the cost of the property between the timber and the land.

Caution: Even if the land is loaded with valuable timber, you must also check to see how accessible the land is. No matter how much timber is on the land, it's not worth investing in if there is no way to ship the timber out to the markets.

If after investigating the deal you decide to invest in timberland and plant trees on the land, the tax breaks begin right away.

▶ **DOUBLE TAX WINNER:** (1) You are entitled to an investment credit equal to 10% of the first $10,000 of each year's planting costs. (2) You can also elect to write off the first $10,000 of planting costs ratably over a seven-year period.

Important: If timberland is sold within 10 years of planting timber, the profit from the sale will be ordinary income to the extent the planting costs were deducted under the seven-year writeoff setup.

More tax breaks: Every penny of operating costs is fully deductible—whether your timber operation is harvesting already grown trees or planting new trees (or both). Currently deductible operating costs include management services, labor costs, fire protection and the like.

Sale of timber: Unlike some other investments (such as cattle), you can pretty much decide when to take your profit from timber. In addition, you can get tax-sheltered long-term capital gain treatment on the profit when the timber is sold.

▶ **THREE OPPORTUNITIES FOR CAPITAL GAINS TREATMENT:** You can nail down favorable capital gains treatment on your timber whether you: (1) sell the timber outright, (2) cut the timber yourself, or (3) grant cutting rights and retain an economic interest, such as a royalty.

1. *Outright sale of standing timber:* The investor gets a capital gain or loss, since timber is a capital asset. Assuming he's held it more than six months, the gain is long term.

2. *Cutting of timber by owner:* The owner-investor who cuts the timber himself can elect to treat the timber as a Sec. 1231 asset. In general, gains are capital gains under Sec. 1231 and losses are ordinary losses. Gain is derived when you cut (in effect, it's as if you were selling to yourself). Gain is the difference between the value of the standing timber as of the beginning of the year in which the timber is cut and its cost.

Important: To get capital gain treatment under Sec. 1231, you must have owned the timber more than six months before you cut it.

3. *Disposal under a cutting contract:* An owner-investor who disposes of his timber under a cutting contract treats his gain or loss as a Sec. 1231 gain or loss if:
   (a) He retains an economic interest in the timber.
   (b) He has held the timber for more than six months before disposal. *But note this:* the date of disposal is the date the timber is cut (not the date it's sold).

▶ **THINK IT OVER:** Timber is used in many ways, but a major use is for construction. So if there's a construction slowdown you may have a hard time selling your trees. And of course, any one of a number of natural disasters can reduce your tax shelter to just so much ash. Finally, the tax law is very complex in this area, so you must consult with your tax adviser.

How One Tax Shelter Lets You Postpone Taxable Income As Long As You Want

Investing in a farming shelter allows you to take advantage of the many special rules available to farmers. In fact, one type of tax shelter deal allows you to—

▶ **PAY TAX WHEN YOU WANT:** You get a big tax loss writeoff in the year you invest in the farm operation—a writeoff that shelters other income from tax. But here's the key: Your farming income is taxed to you only when you want it to be.

Other types of tax shelters give you the writeoffs, but they don't usually give you control over the taxable income. And it may be taxed to you in a year when you already have a lot of taxable income. That's not the case with the farming deal we're talking about.

Tax shelter in action: Mr. Black invests $10,000 in XYZ Farm Partnership this year. XYZ leases farm land from owners of farm land. Then it enters into sharecropping agreements with selected farmers. The agreement is also a kind of lease: The farmer farms the land in return for a share of the crops that goes to XYZ. As part of the deal, XYZ pays the farmer's crop expenses—planting, fertilizer, insect control and so forth—incurred during the year.

▶ **TAX WRITEOFF:** The payments for crop expenses and land rentals are fully deductible by XYZ. This produces a tax loss that XYZ can pass through to Black and XYZ's other partner-investors. Black's share of the loss comes to, say, $9,000. So he has $9,000 that he can use to offset his other business and investment income.

Next year the farmers harvest the crops and give XYZ its share of the crops. Ordinarily, this is the time the investors would have to pay tax on their share of partnership profits. But not here. Black can postpone his tax bill indefinitely by taking advantage of two special tax breaks.

Tax break #1: As a general rule, rental income is taxable to a partnership (and thus to its investors) in the year the partnership receives it. But here is an exception to the rule for crop shares.

▶ **NO CURRENT TAX:** A farm landlord (in this case XYZ) owes no tax on crop shares until the shares are sold or otherwise reduced to cash. So the receipt of the crop shares in the second year has no tax impact on XYZ and Black.

After receiving the crop shares, XYZ distributes them to Black and the other investors in the third year. (XYZ doesn't distribute the actual crops; warehouse receipts are merely credited to Black's partnership account.)

Tax break #2: Let's say Black received $12,000 in cash instead of crops in the third year. He would then owe tax on $11,000, the difference between the $12,000 cash and his $1,000 tax basis for his partnership interest (the $10,000 he invested less the original $9,000 tax loss). But since Black is paid in crops instead of cash, there is—

▶ **AGAIN, NO CURRENT TAX:** Property distributed by a partnership is taxed to an investor only when the investor sells it. So the mere fact that XYZ distributes the crop shares to Black in the third year should not result in taxable income for him that year.

Net result: Black can hold on to the crop shares and sell them when it suits his tax picture. Then—and only then—will he have to pay tax on the income from his farm investment.

Important: If you are interested in a farm deal like this, there are two things you should do: (1) The results we have described here are those expected by the people setting up the deal. As always in a tax shelter deal, the Revenue Service, of course, may not necessarily be in agreement. So you will want to discuss the tax consequences with your tax adviser before investing. And (2) keep in mind farming is a boom-or-bust business. You will want to make sure that people managing the deal are experienced and have a good track record. Another reminder: You are investing to make money in farming as well as save taxes.

NEW TAX SHELTER VENTURES

Here are four new tax-shelter ventures that have been attracting investor attention—research and development equipment, thoroughbred horses, and computer leasing. All of them involve high risk. But the payoff is big if the deal is successful: an immediate tax loss to shelter your income and tax-sheltered income down the road.

How to Get In on the Ground Floor of a "State of-the-Art" Tax Shelter

The allure of getting in on the ground floor of the next IBM, Polaroid or Xerox is strong. Buying stock in companies that have a shot at big technological break-throughs is the usual approach. But there's another one for the more adventurous.

▶ **NEW APPROACH:** An investor can become a limited partner in a research and development venture. As a limited partner, you get a direct stake in several new technological developments. If things work out as expected, the investor gets a big first-year writeoff—say, 85% to 90% of his investment—and profits down the road.

Simplified example: ABC Limited Partnership contracts with independent consultants to locate new technological and scientific products that (1) are in the embryonic stage and (2) stand a chance at being successfully developed and profitably marketed. Once a number of these products—say, five—have been found, the investors are brought in. The purchase price of a limited partnership interest is payable in cash. Most of the investor's money is used to pay for research and development of the new products. The actual research and development is performed by outside contractors and supervised by ABC.

Source of the writeoff: The tax law's Sec. 174(a) allows a business to deduct costs for research and experimentation in the year they are paid or incurred. This is an exception to the general tax rule that requires business start-up expenses to be capitalized whether the business conducts the research itself, or pays someone else to do it.

▶ **FIRST-YEAR WRITEOFFS:** The contractor doing the research and development may require complete cash payment when the agreement is signed, even though the work won't be finished for several years. So a partnership can pay the entire research and development cost late in the year and deduct the entire amount.

Result: Since the partnership has no income, it has a loss which is passed through to the limited partners. Let's say each limited partner puts up $10,000 and $9,000 of that contribution goes into research and development. If a limited partner's top dollars are taxed at the 50% rate, the writeoff saves $4,500 in taxes and lowers his investment in the venture to $5,500 ($10,000 less $4,500).

Looking down the road: If all goes well, the partnership will have a number of new, technologically innovative and marketable products. Even if only one or two of its five products succeed, the partnership can still make money. It can market the new products itself (creating fully ordinary income for the partners), or sell the rights to someone else.

The risks: Technological advances are made every day. So when the R&D partnership's products get to the working model stage, they may already be obsolete. If not obsolete, they may face stiff competition from already established products. The point is that new products, even if successfully developed, may have only a modest success in the marketplace or even be unmarketable. Unlike, say, an oil and gas or real estate deal, where it's possible to analyze projections and estimates, the R&D venture is very much a shot in the dark. The investor would need a technical analysis of the proposed new products, as well as careful reviews by his or her legal and tax advisers before putting up a penny.

How to Win Off-Track Profits With an Investment in Thoroughbred Horses

Going to the track isn't the only way to bet on a horse. A horse fancier can get into the high-risk, high-stakes world of thoroughbreds through a tax-shelter partnership. These are limited partnerships that have been set up just to invest in horses.

▶ **TAX PARLAY:** By purchasing an interest, the individual investor has a shot at making money in the sport, while limiting his risk to the cash he puts up (or agrees to put up). Plus, there are tax benefits (which, of course, should not be the determining factor).

Breeding partnerships are the most prevalent type of horse deal. Here's how they work. The partnerships buys a number of good blood-line mares that are bred to stallions. The partnership pays a stud fee. The partnership keeps the offspring, so new value is created as new foals are delivered. The foals eventually are sold off; the mares themselves may be sold at some later point. Providing the revenue from the sales exceeds partnership expenses, there are cash distributions to the partners.

There are also racing partnerships, which are exactly what they sound like. Through his limited partnership interest, the investor owns a share of a horse's winnings—if any. Some partnerships are set up as combination breeding/racing deals.

Tax breaks: There are two main sources of deductions in thoroughbred partnerships:

(1) *Depreciation:* Horses bought for breeding or racing are depreciable. The writeoff period is three years for (a) horses older than 12 years and bought for breeding, or (b) more than two years old and bought for racing. Other purchased horses are written off over five years. Foals born to a partnership's broodmares cannot be depreciated since their cost basis is zero.

Important: The cost of a horse is not eligible for the investment credit.

(2) *Operating expenses:* Horses—winners or losers—are expensive to keep. But many operating costs—hay, training, vet fees, etc.—are currently deductible by the partnership.

Thoroughbred partnerships do not yield multiple writeoffs (losses in excess of invested cash). The typical deal is set up to yield a first-year writeoff that comes close to equalling an investor's cash contribution. Result: The writeoff reduces the amount that each limited partner-investor is risking in the deal.

Looking down the road: The thoroughbred partnership may sell off some or all of its horses—hopefully, at a profit. How this profit is taxed depends on the type of horse that's sold:

Foals: Unless they were held for racing or breeding, a partnership's foals are considered inventory (held for sale in the course of business). Result: Sales proceeds are taxed as ordinary income.

Breeding mares and racehorses: If held more than 24 months, profit from the sale of these horses is treated as low-taxed long-term capital gain. (Note: The full amount of depreciation taken is recaptured and taxed as ordinary income.)

Don't let the glamour fool you: The world of thoroughbreds is a tough, high-risk business that operates by its own special set of rules. And the limited partner-investor's role will be strictly passive. Result: The general partner will make most of the day-to-day decisions.

Tax Court Okays Tax-Sheltered Investment in Computer Leasing

This is the computer age. So it should come as no surprise that the tax experts have zeroed in on computers as a potential source of tax-sheltered profits.

▶ **GOOD NEWS:** In a recent case, investors in a limited partnership that bought and then leased out computers were allowed to claim big tax writeoffs—though the partnership was not set up to show an economic profit during the lease period.

Facts of the case: Taxpayer invested in a limited partnership formed to buy computers for lease and then sale. The partnership was designed to provide high bracket taxpayers with tax benefits, modest cash distributions during the lease terms and an opportunity for profits on the sale of the computers at the end of the leases.

The general partner found financially sound lessees, who placed their orders directly with the computer manufacturer. The order was then transferred to the partnership, which took title to the computers. The purchase was highly leveraged with the equipment and leases pledged as security.

The partnership leased the equipment under a net lease (the lessee is responsible for insurance, maintenance, repairs, etc.). The leases were for an eight-year period and called for reasonable rentals. It was expected that the rental fees would cover partnership expenses and permit a modest profit. But there was little or no profit during the lease periods.

Upon expiration of the leases, the partnership planned either to re-lease or sell the computers. They would have a remaining useful life of three years and an expected residual value of about 20% of their original cost. (A 14% residual value was necessary for the partnership to show an economic profit.) Unfortunately, the partnership's computers became obsolete and their residual values were lower than expected.

Taxpayer and the other investors claimed tax losses from the partnership. But the Government disallowed the losses. Reason: The setup lacked economic substance and the partnership did not really own the computers. Result: The partnership was merely a financing arrangement through which the investors bought tax writeoffs.

▶ **TAXPAYER VICTORY:** The Tax Court allowed the investors to claim their tax losses. Reason: The partnership was the bona fide owner of the computers and the transactions did have economic substance. The fact that the investors were also offered attractive tax benefits does not affect the partnership's economic substance [Est. of Thomas, 84 TC No. 32].

Chapter 4

Money-Saving Ways To Buy, Sell And Own A Family Home

For most families, a home is not only the most expensive but the most important puchase they make. A home—whether it is a house, a cooperative apartment or a condominium unit—represents more than shelter. Along with protection against the elements, it provides security for the future, an investment that can grow in value and importance. A home can provide another form of shelter, as well—tax shelter: Homeowners can keep more of their income in their pocket or at work for them instead of the I.R.S.

In this chapter, we concentrate on how you can get the most for the money that you have spent, or will spend, on your home, and how you can pay the minimum tax on the profits that homeownership can create.

HOW MUCH HOME CAN YOU AFFORD?

Before you go home-shopping, you must have some idea of how much you can afford to pay for a home. You'll find the answer by adding two sums: (1) the biggest mortgage you can obtain, and (2) the downpayment you can afford to make.

To determine how big a mortgage you can afford to carry, you must determine how much you can spare for monthly payments. There are a number of different "formulas" that supposedly tell you how big these payments can be. Some common formulas: mortgage payments can't be more than 25% (or 28%) of gross monthly income, or 33% (or 36%) or net after-tax income.

Actually, in matters like this, there's no accurate formula: the real question to answer (and it's one a lender will ask) is: How much money do you have left after meeting all other expenses each month to spend on shelter? If you haven't run up huge credit-card bills, aren't making car payments and have few expensive habits, you could well afford to put 30% or 35% of your monthly salary into mortgage payments, or buy a home that costs three times what you earn.

> ▶ **FIRST MOVE:** To get an idea of how much you can set aside for mortgage payments, total up right now all other expenditures you make in an average month leaving out rent (or your present mortgage payments if you already own your home). Subtract that total from your monthly take-home pay. Then subtract an estimate for property taxes and insurance. The result: a fairly accurate idea of what you can afford to spend on monthly mortgage payments.

To learn the amount of money you can borrow with that figure, see the chart on page 95. The chart, furnished to us by Financial Publishing Company of Boston, shows how big a mortgage you can carry at various interest rates if you devote 25% of your income to principal and interest. The chart assumes you get a 30-year mortgage. For example, suppose your total annual income is $40,000. If the current mortgage rate is 11%, you can afford to carry a mortgage of $85,799. If the mortgage is for a shorter term than 30 years, or your lender wants you to devote a higher percentage of income to payments, the top mortgage amount would be less.

To your mortgage amount, add the total cash you can afford to put into a downpayment. The result is the maximum price you can afford to pay for a home.

▶ **CHECK THE ADS:** After these calculations, you are now in a better position to make good use of the real estate classifieds in your local paper. You've flipped through them before, surely, but without any clear picture in mind about what your budget permitted you to buy. Well, now you know what to look for.

HOW TO PICK THE BEST MORTGAGE FOR YOU

Many homes bought today are still purchased with long-term, fixed-rate mortgages; but other kinds of home loans are now available—loans with adjustable interest rates, terms and monthly payments. In many cases, homebuyers have been able to nail down below-market interest rates for years because of the steady fall in interest rates since 1982. But rates can rise and there is always the risk that buyers who had a bargain rate one year could find themselves crushed under steeply increased interest payments the next.

To help you get the kind of mortgage that keeps a roof over your head—instead of bringing it down about your ears—here are the key questions you need to answer about the popular ways of financing a home.

IS THE ARM THE RIGHT MORTGAGE FOR YOU?

Once a financing novelty, adjustable rate mortgages—or ARMs, as they're commonly called—account for close to a third of all U.S. home mortgages each year. At best, the ARM can help you buy a home you couldn't otherwise afford, *and* save you big money in the early years of the mortgage. At its worst, the ARM could be a millstone that weighs you down with ever-higher mortgage payments and little prospect of relief.

What Can A Borrower Expect From An ARM?

An ARM is a long-term (typically 25- or 30-year) mortgage that does not have a fixed interest rate. Instead, the interest rate is adjusted—up or down—according

MONTHLY MORTGAGE AFFORDABILITY TABLE

Table shows how much you could spend on a mortgage assuming 25% of income is devoted to mortgage payments

Int Rate	TOTAL ANNUAL INCOME $15,000	$20,000	$25,000	$30,000	$35,000	$40,000	$45,000	$50,000	$55,000
10%	35,610	47,480	59,350	71,220	83,090	94,959	106,829	118,700	130,569
10¼	34,874	46,499	58,122	69,747	81,372	92,996	104,620	116,245	127,869
10½	34,163	45,551	56,938	68,326	79,714	91,101	102,489	113,877	125,264
10¾	33,477	44,637	55,795	66,954	78,113	89,272	100,431	111,590	122,749
11	32,815	43,753	54,691	65,629	76,568	87,505	98,444	109,382	120,320
11¼	32,175	42,900	53,625	64,350	75,075	85,799	96,524	107,250	117,974
11½	31,557	42,076	52,594	63,113	73,632	84,150	94,670	105,189	115,707
11¾	30,959	41,279	51,598	61,918	72,238	82,557	92,877	103,196	113,515
12	30,381	40,508	50,635	60,762	70,889	81,015	91,143	101,270	111,396
12¼	29,822	39,763	49,703	59,644	69,585	79,525	89,465	99,406	109,346
12½	29,281	39,042	48,801	58,562	68,322	78,082	87,842	97,603	107,363
12¾	28,757	38,343	47,928	57,514	67,100	76,685	86,271	95,857	105,442
13	28,250	37,667	47,083	56,500	65,917	75,333	84,750	94,167	103,583
13¼	27,759	37,012	46,265	55,518	64,771	74,023	83,277	92,530	101,782
13½	27,283	36,378	45,471	54,566	63,661	72,754	81,849	90,943	100,037
13¾	26,822	35,763	44,703	53,643	62,584	71,524	80,465	89,406	98,346
14	26,375	35,166	43,957	52,749	61,540	70,331	79,123	87,915	96,705
14¼	25,941	34,588	43,234	51,881	60,528	69,174	77,822	86,469	95,115
14½	25,520	34,027	42,533	51,039	59,546	68,052	76,559	85,066	93,572
14¾	25,111	33,482	41,852	50,222	58,593	66,963	75,333	83,704	92,074

Int Rate	TOTAL ANNUAL INCOME $60,000	$65,000	$70,000	$75,000	$80,000	$85,000	$90,000	$95,000	$100,000
10%	142,439	154,309	166,178	178,049	189,919	201,788	213,658	225,529	237,398
10¼	139,494	151,118	162,742	174,367	185,992	197,615	209,240	220,865	232,489
10½	136,651	148,039	159,426	170,814	182,202	193,589	204,977	216,365	227,752
10¾	133,908	145,067	156,225	167,385	178,544	189,702	200,861	212,021	223,179
11	131,258	142,197	153,134	164,073	175,011	185,949	196,887	207,826	218,763
11¼	128,699	139,424	150,149	160,874	171,599	182,323	193,048	203,774	214,498
11½	126,226	136,745	147,263	157,782	168,301	178,820	189,339	199,858	210,376
11¾	123,835	134,155	144,474	154,794	165,114	175,433	185,753	196,073	206,391
12	121,523	131,651	141,777	151,904	162,031	172,158	182,285	192,412	202,538
12¼	119,287	129,228	139,168	149,109	159,050	168,990	178,930	188,871	198,811
12½	117,123	126,884	136,643	146,404	156,164	165,924	175,684	185,445	195,205
12¾	115,028	124,614	134,199	143,785	153,371	162,956	172,542	182,128	191,713
13	113,000	122,417	131,833	141,250	150,667	160,083	169,500	178,917	188,333
13¼	111,035	120,288	129,541	138,794	148,047	157,299	166,553	175,806	185,058
13½	109,132	118,226	127,320	136,414	145,509	154,602	163,697	172,792	181,885
13¾	107,286	116,227	125,167	134,108	143,048	151,988	160,929	169,870	178,810
14	105,497	114,289	123,080	131,871	140,663	149,454	158,245	167,037	175,828
14¼	103,762	112,409	121,055	129,702	138,349	146,996	155,643	164,290	172,936
14½	102,078	110,585	119,091	127,598	136,105	144,610	153,117	161,624	170,130
14¾	100,444	108,815	117,185	125,555	133,926	142,296	150,666	159,037	167,407

to fluctuations in the financial index used by the lender. An ARM may be adjusted at one-, three-, or five-year intervals.

There are four key reasons why these loans have caught on with homebuyers:

1. All ARMS offer an initial below-market rate. For example, if lenders are charging 11% on fixed-rate mortgages, the initial rate on a three-year ARM may be 9.75%.

2. This initial below-market rate is locked in until the adjustment period comes around. Even if interest rates go up, the lender must wait, say, three years to adjust the interest on a three-year ARM.

3. An ARM may enable a family to purchase an otherwise unaffordable home. That's because a lender looks at a buyer's ability to make the first year's mortgage payments. Since an ARM's first year payments are low, a family can qualify for a bigger mortgage.

> ▶ **CAUTION:** At the initial adjustment, the interest rate (and the monthly payments) will go up. What's more, if the lender's financial index keeps going up, your interest rate will increase at each subsequent adjustment period.

4. The ARM interest rate can be adjusted downward as well as upward. Homebuyers may save money if rates drop when their ARMS are adjusted: they may lock in a lower rate for another period. (Don't count on this, though.)

> ▶ **WHEN AN ARM MAKES SENSE:** A homebuyer who expects to move again within a few years is an ideal prospect for a three- or five-year ARM. The initial interest rate is bound to be lower than that of any fixed-rate mortgage currently offered. And since the buyer plans to move anyway—to a bigger place or to another city for job-related reasons—there is less concern about any jump in interest after the adjustment.

How Will The Rate Be Adjusted?

Not all lenders use the same method, but the most common adjustment is to take (1) the financial index agreed upon—interest on one-year Treasury bills, say—and add (2) an amount called "the spread" (or "margin"). Forget your initial interest rate: the "spread" is not added to it.

Make certain you ask about this device; the "spread" is one of the most important—and least publicized—features of the ARM.

Say you took out a one-year ARM at 8.5%. Your spread is 3% and the lender uses the one-year T-bill rate at his index. One year from now T-bills are offered at 11%. Your new adjusted rate: 14%—11% plus 3%. That's quite a jump!

> ▶ **REMINDER:** As we've said, the big advantage of taking out a one-year ARM at a bargain rate is that it's easier to qualify for such financing. Just make certain that you are prepared for an increase when the adjustment period rolls around. Over the long haul, a three- or five-year ARM at 10.5% might save you more interest than the one-

year ARM above. ARMs with longer adjustment periods give you a smaller initial interest-rate bargain. But they also lock in a rate for a longer period.

You may have to pay points when you get an ARM (one point is one percent of the mortgage). For example, a one-year ARM may have a stated interest rate of 8.9% but require a payment of three points at the closing. The points push up the *effective* interest rate you pay. The lender is required to tell you the *annual percentage rate*, a figure that takes into account the initial points payment. For example, the 8.9% ARM with three points has an annual percentage rate of 13.2%—not much of a bargain.

What Protection Should An ARM Borrower Demand?

Never take out an ARM that offers no protection against runaway borrowing costs. Such safeguards, or "caps," include:

● *Payment cap:* The lender sets a ceiling on the monthly payment increase after adjustment: 7½% has become standard. Suppose you take out a one-year ARM. If your first-year monthly mortgage payment is $500, a 7½% cap would limit your adjusted monthly payment during the second year to $537.50.

● *Adjustment cap:* This cap limits the interest increase from adjustment to adjustment; 2% is the most common. If your three-year ARM has a 2% cap and your introductory interest rate is 9.5%, then your new adjusted rate for the next three years will be no more than 11.5%, even if your spread plus your index totals more. (Caution: Some lenders do *not* apply this cap to the *initial ARM increase*—read the fine print!)

● *Interest cap:* The lender pledges that you will never be charged more than a specified rate. This ceiling is set fairly high, of course, but in most cases is below the peak that rates hit a couple of years ago—roughly 15%.

Useful as these safeguards are, there's one that is more important than any of the above. Be sure to ask about a safeguard against:

● *Negative amortization:* This condition develops when a borrower owes more money at the end of the year than he owed at the beginning of the year. An ARM with no other borrower protection but a 7½% payment cap is vulnerable to negative amortization: the ARM may need 9% more in payments to be amortized at the adjusted rate.

▶ **IMPORTANT:** Never take out any ARM that lacks a safeguard against negative amortization. Many lenders now pledge that a borrower's payments will be set at a rate that can pay off the loan within a fixed period. If adjustment and interest caps limit your adjusted rate to, say 15% three years from now, then the lender pledges that your three-year ARM will be amortized at that rate—even if the index-plus-spread totals more than 15%. This pledge from a lender is your most effective protection.

• *Prepayment:* You should also try to take out an ARM that permits you to prepay it and refinance at any time you choose—preferably without penalty. If you do expect to sell your house before adjustment, find a lender that permits assumptions.

Above all, shop around: Take notes so you can make comparisons among lenders. For instance, suppose Lenders A and B are each pledging no negative amortization and use the same index on three-year ARMs:

	Lender A	Lender B
Introductory rate	8.5%	9.0%
Spread	2%	2%
Adjustment cap	3%	2%
Interest cap	16%	15.5%

▶ **WHAT'S YOUR BEST CHOICE:** *Lender A* may be better if you plan to move within three years. But if you plan to remain in your home, *Lender B's* adjustment and interest caps can better hold down interest costs in the long run.

A New Kind Of ARM—The Convertible

If interest rates start back up again, lenders should begin pushing an ingenious variation on the ARM that came on the market a couple of years ago. It's the *convertible ARM*, a mortgage that has a low introductory rate tied to an index (just like an ARM) but gives the borrower the option to switch to a fixed-rate mortgage within a set time.

▶ **THE BEST OF BOTH WORLDS:** Many buyers still prefer the security of the fixed-rate mortgage but don't want to be stuck with high rates. With the convertible ARM, they can: (1) buy the home they want now at below-market interest on the gamble that they can (2) convert that ARM into a fixed-rate mortgage with a lower rate locked in place years later.

A typical loan: Federal National Mortgage Ass'n (Fannie Mae) through its participating lenders is offering borrowers an ARM of up to $133,250 that can be converted to a long-term fixed-rate mortgage after the first five years.

• The initial interest rate is below-market, by as much as 2%.

• The monthly payment is the same for all five years, though the interest rate is refigured annually, with a 2% cap each year. If the interest rate goes up, the unpaid interest is added to the loan's principal amount.

• Downpayments may be as low as 5% for resident owners and 10% for investors.

• Buy-downs are also permitted.

Both the increase in payments and the increase in interest rates are capped if the borrower decides to continue the loan for another five years. The new rate will be an average of past rates to cushion the shock of any steep increases. The interest rate cannot increase by more than 4.5% over the life of the loan. There is also a 20% cap on the payment increase when the loan continues as a five-year ARM.

▶ **CHECK WITH LENDERS:** Many variations on the convertible ARM are possible. Availability, of course, is determinted by market conditions. And be sure to ask about conversion costs when you are comparison shopping.

Rollover Mortgages

This type of mortgage carries a fixed interest rate. Monthly payments are based on a long repayment period (20, 25, or 30 years). However, at the end of, say, ten years, the outstanding mortgage balance must either be paid off or refinanced (''rolled over'').

This hybrid mortgage locks in the current mortgage interest rate for a fixed number of years. When the ''rollover'' period comes around, the homebuyer can pay off the remaining mortgage balance. In the alternative, the homebuyer can refinance the outstanding loan balance with a new mortgage.

HOW YOU CAN TAP A TOP SOURCE OF MORTGAGE MONEY BY TELEPHONE

The telephone has always been a big timesaver when you are hunting for mortgage money to buy your home. Now, thanks to computer hookups, your phone can put you in direct contact with one of the bigger sources of home financing, once you have a specific property in mind.

The Prudential Insurance Company has set up a nationwide lending service that lets homebuyers arrange almost all of the details of financing *by phone*. Borrowers may choose among 15- and 30-year fixed-rate mortgages and three types of ARMs. You can shop for loans from your home or office in three easy steps:

1. You phone Prudential's toll-free number, 1-800-CALL PRU, and receive instructions from a taped message. You are told what other numbers to dial for various services. For example, by dialing ''1,'' you can get the latest interest rate on all five home loans:

2. If you wish to apply for a mortgage while you are on the line, dial ''4'' to get an operator who will take your order for the *Application Packet*, which costs $10.

3. After receiving the *Packet* and filling out the forms, you call the toll-free number again to apply for your mortgage. The operator goes over all the information with you and takes your application fee, which is $350. All fees may be charged by phone on any major credit card.

▶ **FAST ACTION:** Prudential phones you within days to report whether your application is approved. If it isn't, your $350 fee will be refunded. If your loan falls through, the unused portion of the fee will be refunded. If the mortgage goes through, the full $350 will be applied toward your closing costs. Some loans are made within 15 to 20 days.

Plenty Of Eligible Properties

Prudential will make loans on one- to four-family homes—including homes bought as *investments*. Also eligible are second or vacation homes, units in planned urban developments and condos (but not co-ops).

The top mortgage amount depends on your income, the property's use and the size of the downpayment. On a single-family residence where the buyer wishes to put no more than 5% down, the top mortgage is $133,250. If you put 10% down, the top mortgage can be up to $250,000. All loans with downpayments of less than 20% require private mortgage insurance.

Prudential delegates most of the groundwork on these loans to a title company. While you may select any title company you wish, you will pay lower closing costs by selecting one within the network of cooperating companies Prudential has set up across the country. The title company takes care of the appraisal and most of the other duties of a lender. You mail your monthly checks to Prudential.

▶ **COST SAVINGS:** Prudential tells us that its rates vary day by day to keep pace with the market. It tries to shave a fraction of a point off its fixed-rate 15- and 30-year mortgages to beat the competition. You can, if you wish, lock in the current rate when you pay the application fee for up to 45 days. However, by waiting till the closing to set your interest rate, you get a discount on closing costs.

SPECIAL FINANCING FOR UNUSUAL SITUATIONS

Some unusual financing methods were developed by the real estate industry a few years ago when many homebuying prospects could not afford conventional financing. Hundreds of thousands of buyers fell back on the arrangements we describe below. Keep them in mind—whether you are buying or selling a home. They could be brought back into play to suit your special situation.

"Buy-Down" Plan

This method is so called because someone—often a relative of the buyer but sometimes the homeseller or the homebuilder—advances cash needed to pay part of the mortgage interest in the initial year of the loan. In short, the interest rate is reduced, or "bought down," so the buyer can qualify for a mortgage. Please understand that lenders consider a borrower qualified if he or she has the income to meet the *first year's* mortgage payment. It doesn't matter that the first-year rate paid by the borrower is below the true rate of the mortgage.

Example: Buyer needs $60,000 to buy a new home. His current income qualifies him for a mortgage at 10%, but lender is asking 12½%. Solution: Builder sets up a three-year buy-down plan; he supplies enough cash to absorb 2½% mortgage interest the first year, 1½% the second year, and 1% the third and last year.

Buyer can afford 10% mortgage the first year; so lender, who will get paid the full 12½% interest, anyway, agrees to the deal. By the fourth year, buyer will be responsible for the full 12½% and by then he should be able to afford it.

The buy-down is a good way for a parent to help a child buy a home. But if the buy-down is financed by the seller or homebuilder, you can expect they buy-down amount to be reflected in a higher purchase price.

Seller-Held Second Mortgage

Up to 70% of all existing-homes sales made during the early-1980's mortgage interest crunch involved seller-held mortgages.

Here's an example of how it works: You want to buy a home for $70,000. You can make a downpayment of $20,000 and get a first mortgage for $40,000. That leaves you $10,000 short. You ask the seller to "take back a mortgage" for the $10,000 balance. If effect, the seller is accepting your IOU, secured by the home, for part of his selling price.

Rent With An "Option To Buy"

This arrangement permits you to move into your home and live there as a "tenant" while you raise financing. Try for an agreement that permits all, or at least some, of the rent to be applied toward the purchase price. And try to lock in a purchase price, too, when you begin your tenancy.

Graduated Payment Mortgages

The GPM is a great favorite among young homebuyers who expect their income to increase steadily in coming years but who can spend very little on housing at the present.

Homebuyers whose jobs require them to move every few years should also find a GPM an economical way to buy a home. The GPM is a long-term, fixed-rate mortgage, but its actual interest cost is not reflected in its initial payments. For the first year, the monthly payments are unusually low, perhaps $150 below those of a fixed-rate loan for the same amount. The next year, the monthly payment increases and continues to increase each year for the next five to ten years, until it stabilizes for the life of the mortgage. This stabilized amount is higher than the payment on a fixed-rate loan, to make up for the initial difference, but buyers with rising incomes should be able to afford it.

▶ **MONEY-SAVING MOVE:** Take out a GPM during a time of high interest rates and take advantage of its extra low payments as long as you can—then pay it off with a new fixed-rate loan—ideally at a time of lower interest rates.

Shared Equity Plan

Under this method, the homebuyer *shares* the costs of homebuying. The monthly costs and the downpayment are split between the buyer and a partner— either an investor, friend or relative. A 50/50 split is most common, but any split is permitted. In return for such assistance, the buyer shares any profit from the home sale with the partner.

Under some plans, the partner is considered the landlord and the buyer is the tenant whose share of the monthly payments is considered rent. The partner gets investor tax breaks from this set-up and the opportunity to sell the home at a big profit within a set time (under many arrangements).

▶ **GROWING POPULARITY:** The complexities of equity sharing initially prevented its catching on. Now, however, many banks have come to realize that having a co-signer on a home loan (i.e., the non-occupant partner) is a big plus. Several national firms now operate as consultants or intermediaries on these deals. They can provide the necessary documents and expertise. Some also have cross-country contacts with sources of cash.

For example, Family Backed Mortgage Association, Inc. (FBMA), an Oakland outfit, specializes in analyzing and developing arrangements between relatives. Its equity sharing program is called *Daddy Mac*. FBMA has provided this typical example to show the advantages that equity sharing has over, say, an outright gift of cash from a relative. The cash will reduce the size of the mortgage needed, it's true, but the homebuyer still must meet the full monthly payments. And there will be no investment return or tax benefit for the relative. But that's not the case in this—

Example: Father and Son, who wants to buy a home, have a 50/50 equity-sharing setup. They agree to divide the downpayment, all monthly costs and any future profit equally. Son also pays Father 50% of the going market rent—an essential step if any relative is to qualify for investor tax breaks. Even with the rent added, Son cuts his monthly costs by 25%. Father—the owner-investor—can be out little or no expense after taxes, and should make a profit later, when the home is sold.

FBMA charges $100 to analyze a home purchase by relatives to see if equity sharing is feasible. If it is and if they want to set an arrangement under Daddy Mac, the relatives then pay FBMA an additional $650 to have the deal set up FBMA's using forms. (The owner-relative may deduct his or her share of the fee.)

▶ **FOR MORE DETAILS:** Along with supplying counselling and proper forms, FBMA may arrange 90% FHA-insured loans through mortgage consultants across the country. For more information, call toll-free *800-323-3262* (California readers should call *800-232-3737).*

HOW TAX BREAKS MAKE HOMEOWNERSHIP POSSIBLE

The tax breaks of home ownership can actually make it possible for you to buy a home. Reason: The lion's share of your costs—property taxes and mortgage interest—are tax deductible. The tax dollars saved on each year's return go a long way toward reducing homeowner costs.

> *Example:* Let's take the Smith family. They have one child and an adjusted gross of $36,000. They pay $500 a month rent. They file a joint return and have $2,000 in itemized deductions (sales tax, charity, interest, medical expenses, etc.) So at tax return time they use the higher standard deduction ($3,670). Total tax bill (discounting any allowable credits) is $5,307 at 1986 tax rates.

Now let's see what the picture would be if the Smiths decide to buy an $70,000 home. To keep things simple, let's say Smith had the savings (and the generous relatives) to make a $10,000 downpayment. He got a $60,000, 30-year mortgage at 12% at interest. Monthly payments are $617.40.

> ▶ **BIG TAX SAVINGS:** In the first year, $7,189 of Smith's payments to the bank are deductible currently as interest. His property tax bill of $700 is also deductible. When Smith adds his other "itemized" deductions of $2,000, he winds up with a total of $9,889 in deductions for the first year.

The deductions slash Smith's tax bill to $3,738. That's $1,564 less than it would have been without his buying a home. That works out to a dollar savings of $130.75 a month. Subtract that from Smith's monthly $617.40 mortgage payments and you're down to $486.65—less than Smith's present rent bill. Meanwhile, Smith's payments on princpal—unlike monthly rent payments—are building up his equity in a home.

Savings pile up: Smith doesn't have to wait until tax return time to realize his tax savings. By filing an amended IRS Form W-4 with his employer, he can realize savings with each and every paycheck. He increases his withholding allowances from four to 10 (due to the boost in his itemized deductions) and thus increases his take-home pay.

SHOULD YOU SHOP FOR A HOME, YOURSELF, OR USE A REAL ESTATE BROKER?

The vast majority of families look for a home with the aid of a real estate broker. A real estate broker, or Realtor (if the broker is a member of the National Association of Realtors), can save you time and money. He or she should ideally be an expert on your community's property values and the current home-mortgage situation, as well as an experienced salesperson attuned to the needs of others.

First-time homebuyers (who account for over 30% of today's buyers) often feel they need a broker to ease them into the novel and often confusing experience of homebuying. Certainly a broker who lists desirable properties and has good lender contacts can can be most helpful. And, of course, the broker's commission is paid by the seller—not by the buyer.

However, don't assume that a broker's househunting services are "free." As we pointed out, the commission is almost always paid by the seller, who has included it in the asking price. Or, to put it another way, *you* pay for the broker's services, in the end, even though he or she is not hired by you.

Q. Can I hire a broker to work for me, the homebuyer?

A. You may be able to. More and more firms are offering "buyer brokerage" as an extra service. They charge either a flat fee or by the hour, and accept no commission from the seller. That arrangement automatically increases your chances of saving money.

A. Here's why: A home sale often involves two brokers—one who lists the home for sale, another who brings in the buyer. Generally, the 6% commission is split between them.

Let's say you want to buy a home costing $70,000. The commission comes to $4,200. The home is listed by Broker A, but you are shown the listing by Broker B. Ordinarily, each broker would get $2,100 from the seller.

But if "Broker B" is a buyer-broker, he or she will not share in the split. In fact, your buyer broker will insist that the owner in this case *cut his $70,000 price by $2,100.* If you paid, say, $1,000 for his or her services, then using a buyer-broker saved you $1,100.

▶ **BIGGER SAVINGS:** You could save even more if—as can happen—you buy a home listed by your buyer-broker's firm. In that case, the full 6% commission would be deducted from the price. A buyer-broker does not charge sellers a commission if the client buys one of the broker's listings.

If No Broker Is Involved

Thousands of homes are bought every year without the aid of a real estate broker. Many homesellers handle the sale, themselves, to save the commission (usually 6% or so). To ward off brokers, these owners stress the fact in their ads and on their "For Sale" signs that their home is *For Sale By Owner.* You should have no difficulty spotting these FSBOs, as they are known in the trade.

▶ **BUYER ADVANTAGE:** You automatically have plenty of leeway for haggling when you buy a FSBO. You know that the seller won't have to give a broker 6% of his sales price, so don't hesitate to knock at least 6% off your offer. And let us emphasize that haggling over the price is expected and essential. This is doubly true when dealing with owners who act as their own broker.

MONEY-SAVING CHECKLIST FOR BUYERS OF OLDER HOMES

Whether you are househunting with a broker, or on your own, you can avoid making a costly mistake by following the checklist below. It alerts you to matters you must consider, and questions you should ask, as well as preparations you should make before starting:

☐ Keep a notebook for jotting down likes and dislikes, pluses and minuses of each home. And review the classifieds regularly to get a good idea of the price range for the neighborhood and the property you're about to see.

☐ Inspect the neighborhood as well as the home. The neighborhood may not be for you if two of the three following questions can be answered "Yes"; Are there many For Sale signs up? Are there many commercial establishments about or being built? Are many of the houses and lawns poorly tended?

☐ What is the condition of the yard? Look past the fact that the lawn has been mowed and raked to note the texture and evenness of the grass. And the shrubbery. Does everything look well watered and cared for? Are there dead limbs in the trees? Can you see yourself paying for landscaping or pruning soon?

☐ Does the basement contain these signs of past—and future—trouble: cracked floor tiles? items stored on wooden blocks? water stains? If so, you can bet it floods occasionally.

☐ Are the water pipes copper? Copper pipes are the best. Do the pipes show signs of repair and patching?

☐ What's the condition of the fusebox—new? outdated? After seeing a few homes, you can build up a good standard of comparison for this particular trouble spot. Does it look as if the owner has been playing electrician on his own, or has a professional serviceman left his business card glued to the box?

☐ Is the furnace new or old? Is the house centrally air-conditioned? Or does it have window units, instead? If so, is the owner planning to leave these behind?

☐ Has the owner displayed all fuel, utility and repair bills for the past year? Will he or she show them to you if they are not out for inspection?

☐ Are there enough electrical outlets? Or is the owner using many extension cords or multiple plugs?

☐ Did you note the number of appliances and pieces of electronic equipment the owner uses? If you own considerably more, you may require extra outlets—or even rewiring the house—to suit your needs. Is the home worth such added expense?

☐ What about the condition of the fixtures or appliances in the kitchen and bathroom? Of the tile and cabinets? These rooms can be quite expensive to modernize. If considerable renovation or replacement is required, you've got a major bargaining point for a price cut.

☐ Do all doors open smoothly? Extensive, consistent sticking indicates the house is out of plumb, or unevenly aligned on its foundation. A bad sign.

☐ What about storage space? If the house suits you in most respects but lacks adequate storage space, you had better keep looking or brace yourself for some renovation.

☐ Check the heating system. What kind of repairs are needed, how old is it, and how long will the system last?

☐ Choose a home that is connected to a public sewer system in preference to one served by a septic tank or a cesspool. Check with the plumber who last serviced the house to determine condition of the plumbing and ask him to test the water pressure.

☐ Check the type and capacity of the hot water tank to determine if there will be sufficient hot water for family needs (30-50 gallon tank is needed for most families). Look for any signs of rust or leaks.

☐ Were the walls of the house insulated with expanding foam that contains toxic urea formaldehyde? If so, the home is to be avoided.

☐ Is the attic well furnished and ventilated? At least six inches of fiberglass batting is needed for the attic, with the vapor barrier on the bottom. An inadequately insulated attic can be a major source of heat loss in the winter. Extra insulation should be installed about the attic door or on top of the trapdoor, but all vents and electrical outlets should be fully exposed. Cross ventilation in the attic is essential to allow any accumulated vapor to escape.

☐ Is the garage attached to the house? An attached garage is another drain on a home's heating and air-conditioning units unless the common wall and the door are additionally insulated.

☐ Bring a flashlight with you and wear old clothes when you return for a second look. Be prepared to inspect the place on your hands and knees. Make careful note of any flaw—cracks in the foundation, possible termite damage, mold, water stains, flaking paint, loose downspouts on the raingutter. All these can be used to persuade the owner to reduce the price. Try to return to the property during bad weather, particularly during heavy rain, to see if the roof leaks, how the yard drains and whether the basement floods.

▶ **NECESSARY EXPENSE:** Don't cut corners by trying to be an "all-around expert" when househunting. It is possible to dispense with the services of a real estate broker, but if you lack such training, don't try to be your own lawyer or termite inspector or conduct your own title search (if no one has performed that service). Be prepared to pay professionals to perform these services. It's dangerous "penny wisdom" to try to save money by not hiring these experts.

WHAT TO LOOK FOR WHEN BUYING
A NEWLY BUILT HOME

When you buy a *new* home, you deal with a builder or contractor. In some cases, you may select a recently constructed home in a new development. Or the builder may offer you a choice of several models and erect whichever one you choose in a subdivision under development. You may even hire an architect to create your very own custom-built dream home.

In virtually every instance, the new home will cost you *more* than what you would pay for a comparable existing home. However, you should have far fewer maintenance headaches.

Below is a checklist covering the key items you must consider when buying or building a new home. You will stand a better chance of getting money's worth if you:

☐ Talk to other customers of the builder, contractor or architect. Visit other owners in that new subdivision to learn how they like their new homes. Ask about services and unexpected costs.

☐ Find out what warranties are offered on the home. What about the kitchen equipment? The furnace? Hot-water heater? How long do these warranties last?

☐ Know precisely what you get for your money. Don't go by the appearance of a model home. Ask the builder's salesperson exactly which features are provided with your new house and which are "extras" displayed in the model. Get it in writing. Any extra features that are to be included in the finished house should also be specified. Don't assume an item is included and later learn it wasn't.

☐ Will the new community have paved streets, water and sewer lines, and sidewalks? Make sure you know whether you or the builder will assume the costs. Find out about charges for water and trash collection.

☐ Does your contract with the builder set forth the total sales price?

☐ Does the contract definitely stipulate the completion date of your new house? Will the builder compensate you for delays?

☐ Check out the zoning uses permitted for the area in which you plan to buy a home. The neighborhood may be zoned for certain commercial uses. Such zoning may eventually lower property values. Ask at the city, county, or township clerk's office about zoning.

☐ If you are building, be sure you check your lot site in advance. Is it the size and setting you signed up for? Find out before the bulldozer and crew arrive.

☐ Visit the construction site regularly while your house is being built.

☐ Before you actually take title to your new house, make a thorough inspection. Check all equipment, windows and doors.

☐ When you take possession, insist upon receiving: (1) warranties from all manufacturers for equipment in the house; (2) certificate of occupancy and

(3) certificates from the Health Department clearing the plumbing and sewer installations, plus all applicable certificates of code compliance.

Money-Saver: If you are having your new home built for you, specify in your agreement with the contractor that the building materials are to be paid by you, personally. Then arrange with your contractor to get a list of what he needs and get in touch with the suppliers. This move enables you to deduct all sales taxes, which can run into big money, and big tax savings.

Reminder: You can deduct sales tax on big-ticket items (such as building materials) in addition to the automatic deduction for sales taxes based on your income for the year.

> ▶ **TAX-SAVING MOVE:** You *must* pay for the materials, yourself. If you merely reimburse the contractor, you may lose the deduction. Tell your tax expert that two recent cases covering this area are *Bennett*, TC Memo 1983-183, and *Petty*, 77 TC No. 34.

COOPERATIVES AND CONDOMINIUMS—HOME OWNERSHIP, FOR THE '80s

The *cooperative* and the *condominium* are two concepts that permit the purchase of "space" in a multifamily property or development of ownership. In some cases, tenants of existing buildings have become owners of their apartments after the building "went co-op" or "condo." In others, apartment houses (or townhouse developments or vacation-home communities) are built and sold as cooperatives or condominiums. In all cases, owners pay monthly maintenance fees for the upkeep of common areas (elevators, grounds, etc.)

> ▶ **A SPECIAL WORLD:** Condo and co-op owners are "citizens" in a separate community and are expected to abide by strict rules concerning everything from financial responsibilities to pets. Some owners cannot renovate their unit without the approval of the co-op's board of directors or the condo's owners' association. Your board or association may insist on the right of first refusal when you later try to sell. In many co-ops or condos, every purchaser must meet with the association's approval. Get expert legal advice about such rules before you purchase a co-op or condo.

Owning Shares In A Co-op

A cooperative apartment house is one where the tenants buy *shares in the corporation* that holds the mortgage on the building: their monthly payments are applied to the mortgage payments and maintenance. Should any tenant default on his obligation and move, his share of the payments is spread out among the other tenants (if another tenant isn't found right away).

Co-op money-savers: There are two reasons for the urban dweller's continuing interest in cooperative housing: (1) Instead of paying rent, the tenant-owner pays a carrying charge based on the actual cost of operating the property. The landlord's profit is eliminated; so are demands for increased rentals when the usual short-term leases are renewed. (2) Through ownership of stock in the cooperative corporation, tenant-owners also get tax shelter not available to he ordinary tenant. You can deduct that portion of your monthly payments applied to the cooperative's real estate taxes and mortgage interest. This helps reduce your housing cost. At the same time, part of your payments build up equity in the property.

▶ **KEEP THIS IN MIND:** While you face little risk as a tenant-owner of a cooperative apartment during booming prosperity, a recession or a similar time can cause some of your fellow tenant-owners to default. Getting another shareholder could be difficult. In such times, each person remaining in the project would have to assume a proportionate share of the vacant apartment's maintenance and mortgage payments.

Owning Space In A Condo

The condominium is a form of outright ownership of real property, quite different from a cooperative. Each condominium apartment is actually *owned* by the individual occupant. The title to each unit may be separately transferred and insured. Together with other apartment owners, the condominium tenant is co-owner of the common elements such as land, foundations, main walls, halls, lobby, stairs, corridors, elevators, roof, lawn, parking lot, trees, and such. The condominium apartment has advantages similar to that of a co-op's. For example, maintenance responsibilities such as heating, outside cleaning, and lawn tending are shared and delegated to skilled employees. And the condominium owner gains an income tax deduction for mortgage interest and property taxes.

▶ **BIG DIFFERENCE:** In a condominium, each person actually owns his unit, so he can get a mortgage on it to suit his needs. Getting a loan on a co-op is generally more expensive. In a condominium, if an owner defaults, the others are not responsible for his mortgage payments. In a cooperative, the others must take over his obligations. The condo concept has become increasingly popular over the years because of these differences.

Surprise costs: If you are buying a unit in a new condo—whether it's an apartment or townhouse or whatever design—don't leave yourself open to unexpected expenses. Here are some potential trouble spots:

● Your condo dues may be unusually low because the developer underestimated the maintenance.

● It's also possible that the developer cut the dues to sell the units faster—beware of "bargains" when you are pricing condos.

● Does the condo association maintain a healthy reserve fund to cover such expenses? Well-run associations will do so.

● Ask about the "enabling declaration," a master deed or a plan of condominium ownership. If you are not a lawyer, have an attorney study this deed and tell you exactly what's involved. You want to know how the declaration can be amended. Does it require 100% approval by all condo owners? If so, you are protected against having to accept changes you may find intolerable.

▶ **KNOW YOUR NEIGHBORS:** Ask yourself what kind of "neighborhood" you are buying into when you become a condo owner. If you are a young single person, you won't object to parties about the pool and neighbors who keep late hours. But if you are older, these good times can become bad times. Learn who will live above and below you before you buy.

WATCH FOR THESE SPECIAL TAX BREAKS
AT THE CLOSING

When your home purchase is officially "closed"—that is, when you, the buyer, actually take title to the seller's property—you will find yourself responsible for several expenses, or "closing costs." Naturally, you must demand an accounting well in advance so you can have a cashier's check already drawn up for the amount. The bank is required by law to give you an estimate of all charges.

▶ **GOOD NEWS:** Some of these costs are deductible in full in the year you buy. Here are the most common ones to watch out for and keep track of:

● *Property taxes*: You probably will have to pay a part of the property taxes for the year of the sale. That's a currently deductible expense.

● *Prepayment penalty*: If you owned a home and sold it to buy your new one, and your old mortgage had a prepayment-penalty clause, you're going to be out some cash for that, too. Keep the bank's statement showing how much you paid. This is another currently deductible expense.

● *"Points"*: Any "points" you pay your lender are deductible as an interest charge. Your lender may not use the term, "points." Instead, you may be charged a "mortgage origination fee" or something like that—but no matter. If it's a fee paid for the use of the money, it's currently deductible. Always pay for "points" separately—do not include them as part of the mortgage. Specify points on your check.

Q. What about my other closing costs?

A. Not all closing costs are currently deductible, but many of these costs will give you tax relief when you sell your house. The total cost of your home now helps determine your taxable profit years later when you sell. And the higher that cost—or, in tax terms, the higher your basis—the smaller your taxable gain when you eventually get around to selling. Most of the increase to your basis comes from improvements made after your purchase. But it can be increased at the time you actually buy the home by a number of closing costs. Here are some that can reduce your gain when you sell the home: legal expenses; title insurance; survey expenses; title search; appraisal. To make certain that you get full benefit from all your buying costs, you must always remember to—

▶ **HANG ON TO YOUR CLOSING STATEMENT:** You'll lose all these money savers if you can't prove you paid them. In fact, it's a good idea to start a Home Expenditure folder for costs that beef up your basis (see page 124).

HOW TO SLASH YOUR INTEREST COSTS ON HOME MORTGAGES

Whether you are about to buy your first home or still have years to go on your mortgage payments, you can make a massive reduction in your total interest costs by *prepaying your mortgage*. Of course, the biggest saving comes for the home-buyer who prepays from the very first, or as soon as the lender permits. However, a homeowner who has just decided to prepay can still make a difference in his interest costs.

▶ **HOW TO DO IT:** Prepayment involves your paying a portion of the mortgage *principal* in advance. Since the lender now has recovered part of its money ahead of schedule, it does not charge you interest on that portion of the principal. The longer the mortgage has to run, the bigger the amount of interest saved.

How Prepayment Works

You can make huge savings with small prepayments. Let's say you decide to prepay your principal right from the start of your mortgage. You can probably cover the next month's principal by adding anywhere from $10 to $30 to your initial payment.

Here's an amortization chart that breaks down the monthly payment of $476.17 which you would pay on a 30-year fixed-rate mortgage for $50,000 at 11%. (No escrow payments are included under Payment #1).

Payment	Interest	Principal	Total
#1	$458.33	$17.84	$476.17
2	458.17	18.00	476.17
3	458.00	18.17	476.17
4	457.84	18.33	476.17

As you can see, the bulk of these initial payments is devoted to *interest*, so you won't have to spend much to make a double payment of *principal*. Let's say your prepay from the start. Your first check, then, will be for $494.17—Payment #1

($476.17) plus the principal of Payment #2 ($18). With that one move, you save $458.17—believe it or not, that's what 11% interest on $18 comes to compounded over 30 years.

> ▶ **IMPORTANT:** Prepayment of Payment #2 does not mean you pay nothing the next month. That's when you will make Payment #3. And if you wish to continue prepaying, you include the principal for Payment #4 ($18.33) and pay $494.50. And now you save an additional $457.84 in interest—$916.01 *in just two months*.

Massive Interest Savings

If you continue to prepay in this fashion, you would pay off this 30-year mortgage in 15 years and save yourself a total of *$60,585 in interest!*

> ▶ **PREPAY AT ANY TIME:** You can probably begin paying off your present mortgage now—but always check with your lender before you begin. Explain what you intend to do at least a month in advance. Always include a note with each prepayment explaining how the amount of your check is to be broken down, and note each prepayment in your own records, too. Keep in mind that prepayments can also consist of a set amount each month. Even a prepayment of only $25 could pay off the above loan a third faster.

See for yourself: Financial Publishing Company, a Boston outfit, prepares a *Prepayment Comparison Chart* that contrasts a long-term mortgage with four kinds of prepayments. You can see at a glance how much more you can save with by prepaying.

Let's say you have a sample chart made for a $50,000 mortgage at 12.5% for 30 years, with a fixed monthly payment of $533.63. Your *Chart* shows that:

• Paying the next month's principal in advance each month would pay off the loan within 15 years and save around $71,000 in interest. The first payment (regular payment plus principal) would be $546.56, and the last would be $1,058.51.

• $500 extra each year pays off the loan in 20 years and saves $59,000.

• $200 extra each quarter pays if off in 16 years and saves $74,500.

• $100 extra each month pays it off in 13 years and saves $86,500.

> ▶ **WHERE TO WRITE:** Financial Publishing can make up a prepayment chart for you, no matter how much time you have to pay off your loan. For services and fees, write it at: 82 Brookline Avenue, Boston, MA 02215. Or telephone: (617) 262-4040.

RAPID-PAYOFF MORTGAGE PLANS

Many people want to own their home free and clear in as short a period of time as possible. After their mortgage is paid off, they can begin accumulating more money for other important family goals, like a child's college education or a financially secure retirement. As we've seen, the mortgage prepayment technique is one good way to accomplish this result. In addition, there are at least three types of mortgage plans designed with a built-in rapid pay off. Each will yield a significant savings. Reason: Since the mortgage is being paid off in a relatively short period of time, total interest costs are much less then they would be with a long-term mortgage.

1. Short-term fixed rate mortgages: For example, a homebuyer can obtain a home mortgage that is paid off in 15 years rather than the usual 25 or 30 years. However, monthly payments are higher than payments on a longe-term mortgage.

2. Growing-equity mortgages (GEMs): This type of mortgage carries a fixed interest rate for its term. But each year, monthly payments increase by an agreed-upon amount. For example, payments may go up $50 or $100 each year. The increase goes entirely towards paying off the mortgage principal.

▶ **RESULT:** Since the borrower is accelerating his repayment of the loan, the GEM is paid off in about half the time a normal fixed-rate mortgage is retired. For example, a 30-year mortgage can be repaid within 13 to 17 years, depending on the terms.

The GEM is similar to a 15-year fixed rate mortgage, except that payments during the first years are usually lower.

3. Frequent payment plans: This is the newest twist in rapid payoff mortgages. Instead of making one mortgage payment a month, you make one payment every two weeks. Each payment is one-half the usual monthly payment. Since 52 weeks of a year divided by two equals 26, that's the number of payments you make. Because each two-week payment is equal to one-half of a regular monthly payment, you wind up making the equivalent of 13 monthly payments each year.

▶ **BIG CASH SAVINGS:** The mortgage is paid off much quicker. A regular 30-year mortgage could be paid off in about 20 years using the two-week payment plan.

DOES REFINANCING YOUR MORTGAGE PAY OFF FOR YOU?

Refinancing has become a fairly common maneuver for many homeowners. In fact, a full one-third of all home loans made by S&Ls in a recent year were refinancing transactions.

Why did so many homeowners make this move? The main reason: to save money. Some refinanced to lower their current mortgage costs; others needed cash and found that refinancing costs less then other forms of borrowing. Still other homeowners refinanced to pave the way to a profitable sale. But before you refinance—

▶ **CONSIDER THE COSTS:** The rule of thumb is the new mortgage should be at least 2% below the old, and all costs must be absorbed in two years. Don't assume you will instantly save money simply because your new mortgage loan carries a lower interest rate than your old. There are lots of extra charges involved in refinancing that can offset your lower costs. You may be hit with a penalty for paying off the old mortgage early. (Fortunately, the prepayment penalty is deductible in full in the year it's paid.)

Expect These Charges

Brace yourself for a new round of closing costs when you sign that new mortgage loan agreement. You may have to pay "points" at the closing. And, unlike points paid in connection with a home purchase, points paid on a refinancing transaction are not deductible currently.

Instead, you deduct the points charged ratably over the life of the new mortgage. You will also have to absorb a whole list of "standard" closing costs, for such items as attorney's fees, survey, recording, bank application fee, etc. On a $50,000 mortgage, for example, you may have to pony up around $2,750 for closing costs (that figure includes points).

▶ **HOW TO CUT COSTS:** If possible, try to refinance through the same lender that gave you the old mortgage. Since you and your property are known entities, the lender may waive some of the usual closing costs. Some banking experts counsel homeowners *not* to refinance unless they can recover the extra refinancing costs over two or three years (in the form of lower monthly payments). If the recovery period is longer, it may pay for you to wait for an even lower rate.

CHECKLIST OF BASIC 'HOME IMPROVEMENTS' THAT SAVE YOU MONEY

Homeowners are always puttering about their "castle," making minor repairs here and touching up there. At times, they have to call in a professional for a major repair job. It's a penny wisdom not to hire a skilled carpenter or plumber who comes highly recommended during an emergency. But there are many unskilled tasks any amateur can do in only a few minutes to save cash.

One sure-fire way to conserve cash is to do anything that cuts back your electricity, gas or fuel oil bills. Here are several simple steps you can take:

☐ *Caulking:* You can make a significant difference in your energy bills by spending a couple of weekends caulking the cracks in your house. The U.S. Department of Energy reports that *up to 70% of heat loss* could be prevented with caulking wherever wood meets brick or two different materials are joined. Other trouble spots: where pipes and utility outlets are attached; trimming; window and door frames.

Don't go by appearance only. Make probing spot checks with a pencil or screwdriver to see how firm existing caulking actually is. Unusually large gaps should be filled with oakum before you add caulking.

Check out the kind of caulking that you're buying. Read the label on the compound you're getting. Will it take paint? If it won't, expect trouble later when you're having your place painted.

Oil-based caulking compounds are cheaper but have shorter lives than the new ones made of latex, vinyl or silicone.

Caulking should never be done when the temperature is under 50 degrees.

☐ *Weatherstripping:* Weatherstripping comes in sheets or strips of foam, vinyl or felt that can be stapled or nailed or merely stuck in place around windows and doors. Before application, surfaces should be dry, clean and at a moderate temperature. If you have double-hung windows, apply weatherstripping around the entire frame and where one sash meets the other. For casement windows and doors, apply it around the frame and across the threshold.

☐ *Storm doors and windows:* Maybe you should replace the storm doors and windows in your home. Check out the latest models with double-pane glass. Consider replacing entire windows or doors with new insulated models. The Energy Dept. says that 20% of heat loss in the standard house can be prevented by installing double-pane glass. Jalousie windows or doors are notoriously inefficient.

☐ *Insulation:* Insulation involves more than lining the attic floor or adding material between the outer and inner walls. It's also a good idea to use duct insulation (it comes in thick blankets) to sheathe exposed hot-air and cooling ducts (and pipes). Similar insulation can be wrapped above the hot-water heater, too—but be certain not to block any vents.

As for the walls of your house, there's no need for you to insulate every area uniformly; you can get the same value for less money by using less insulation at the proper spots. For instance, if you live where there are prevailing northwest winds in winter, the south and east walls require less insulation than the north and west ones. Insulating all four walls uniformly would be wasteful.

▶ **CHECK THE "R" RATING:** The "R" rating in insulation refers to a material's ability to resist heat flow; the higher the rating, the better the resistance. By law, it must be plainly stated on the packaging. For moderate climates, insulation rated R-19 will be sufficient; extremely cold regions can require R-38. Your contractor and your local utility should tell you what your region's recommended rating is. You'll know then whether your home is over- or under-insulated.

☐ *Light switches with dimmers:* Along with lowering the lights to give a room a more restful mood, a dimmer switch can save you as much as $10 a year for each 100-watt bulb affected. Selecting the old-style dimmer, however, will save you nothing; you will lower the lights but not the amount of electricity you use, or the electric bills you pay.

Ask for the latest in solid-state dimmer switches. These actually cut back the amount of juice consumed; the old ones did not but instead dissipated the unused electricity as heat.

If you installed a dimmer a few years ago, check it out. If it feels warm, then it's probably not saving you any money when it's in use. Worse—it could be overworked because too much wattage is under its control. Double check a dimmer's wattage rating and never exceed it.

Fluorescent lights require special switches for dimming; specify the kind of bulb involved when you're buying dimmers.

▶ **DO IT YOURSELF:** Replacing a standard light switch with a dimmer is a relatively simply job. You can do it, yourself, if you take the proper precautions and have the knack for such chores.

☐ *Meters and timers:* For as little as $25 to $35, you can buy devices that indicate exactly how much energy your home consumes. You can also buy special timers that turn your furnace or air-conditioner on or off when you're away, saving you fuel without causing discomfort.

☐ *Fireplace damper:* If you have that most charming—and inefficient—of amenities, the fireplace, you may be losing a lot of heat. It might pay you to have its damper inspected to prevent the loss of heat up the chimney. Up to 6% of all heat loss can be prevented with a damper, says the Energy Dept.

☐ *Oil furnace:* Experts tell us that the latest in oil burners can considerably improve the efficiency of any furnace that's over six years old. The new line is described as "high-speed,flame-retention burners," which means that they create more heat for each gallon of oil consumed.

These burners also deliver more heat to the house and allow less to escape up the flue. The best can run at 80% to 86% efficiency, or as much as 20% for each $100 spent on heating oil.

The burners cost from $200 to $350 but save you up to $20 for each $100 spent on heating oil.

▶ **DON'T DUPLICATE SAVINGS:** Installing one of these burners costs about the same as installing an automatic vent damper to your existing furnace. This damper prevents heat from escaping up the flue when the furnace is off. However, the new high-speed, flame-retention burners already cut back such heat loss because of their design. If you're thinking of improving your oil furnace, then the economical step to take is to install one of these new burners—you'll still cut back on heat waste and get more efficient fuel consumption, too.

☐ *Natural gas furnace:* In older gas furnaces, the pilot light is a steady drain on your pocketbook (anywhere from $30 to $60 a year). Installing an automatic spark igniter for $125 to $200 would eliminate that expense (which could become much more costly if and when natural gas prices are decontrolled).

▶ **IT ALL ADDS UP:** All of these suggested improvements can create savings for years to come. Some can pay for themselves many times over. And now let's consider another form of home improvement—

HOW REMODELING CAN INCREASE THE VALUE OF YOUR HOME

Remodeling can often be an economical way to meet your needs. It's cheaper to modernize your kitchen and add another bedroom to your two-bedroom house than it is to buy a new three-bedroom house with the latest in kitchen fixtures. Remodeling may also be the best way to increase your home's value, if inflation continues to subside. The right kind of home improvement or new addition can pay for itself two or three times over.

Below is a checklist of the more common forms of improvements and remodeling. You or your family will sell the home eventually. If you remodel it extensively to suit your taste, do not expect others to be willing to pay for your precious improvements. You may have a hard time getting your money back. Keep that possibility in mind when you are thinking of:

☐ *Re-doing the basement:* This area is losing its popularity for some reason. You risk over-improving your property if you spend a lot of money on your basement; your buyer may not be interested in that space at all.

☐ *Repainting:* A $2,000 paint job can probably increase a home's value by anywhere from $3,500 to $4,000, regardless of the inflation rate—but not if the color scheme is one very few homebuyers favor.

☐ *Landscaping:* You will probably get your money back and then some from resodding your lawn; just beware of indulging yourself in expensive and exotic shrubs and plants. Not every buyer will pay extra for the greenery.

☐ *Modernizing the kitchen or bath:* If you confine your remodeling to new cabinets and fixtures for the kitchen or bathroom you can't go wrong. But if, say, you spend a lot of luxury appliances or a sunken tub in the master bath, you probably won't get your money back.

☐ *Adding extra rooms:* If you need that fourth bedroom, build it on to your place—but if your community is one where three bedrooms is the norm, you may be building a sales barrier at the same time. On the other hand, if your home has only two, then adding the third should pay off.

☐ *Energy savers:* Modest improvements like those previously discussed are definitely an asset; however, professional appraisers say that high-cost installations, like solar-energy panels for heat or hot water, cost too much for their price to be recovered quickly, if at all.

☐ *Luxury improvements:* Swimming pools, saunas, tennis courts, fully equipped game rooms and the like can "personalize" your home right out of the market, if yours is a fairly modest neighborhood.

▶ **KEEP A RECORD OF ALL IMPROVEMENTS:** Enter every home improvement you make in a Home Expenditure Record Book and hold on to all your bills. This recordkeeping gives you an idea of just how much your home is costing you. Review it to see if it's time to sell. It can show future buyers what you've spent on it to justify your asking price. And, as we'll show, it's essential for tax purposes.

THE DOLLAR-SMART WAY TO SELL YOUR HOME

Many homesellers successfully act as their own real estate broker and save themselves the cost of a commission. You can succeed, too, if mortgage money is easily obtained, your home is in sterling condition, and your price is reasonable. If you are willing to spend the time and take the trouble to be at home whenever anyone shows up to inspect your place—then by all means handle your home sale, yourself. You can wind up keeping the commission a broker will charge.

But before you decide, think back over your days as a homebuyer. Ask yourself these key questions:

☐ Did I use a broker?

☐ How helpful was he or she?

☐ Could I perform such services for buyers?

☐ What unusual problems came up at the last minute?

☐ Can similar ones occur now?

☐ Would I know how to handle them?

Even if you don't actually hire a broker you can still avail yourself of one valuable service—without having to pay for it.

▶ **ASK FOR A FREE APPRAISAL:** Many brokers will help you price your home correctly, without charge. Check the classified ads to see which ones are offering owners a "free appraisal" or "free home evaluation service," or some such term. Brokers make this offer for a reason: They want to look over properties just coming on the market and to ingratiate themselves with owners, like yourself. By all means, take them up on these "appraisals," but make certain that no obligation is involved.

Be prepared to haggle: Don't expect to get every dollar you're asking for your place. Selling a home involves considerable haggling. Be prepared to bargain about:

☐ *The selling price:* A buyer will expect you to come down a bit from your asking price (5% to 12%). Price your home accordingly.

☐ *"Points" paid to the lender:* You may be expected to pay the lender "points" to help your seller get a mortgage ("points" are 1% of the mortgage amount—on a $50,000 loan, a "point" is $500). Agreeing to pay a couple of "points" to reduce your buyer's closing costs can actually cost you less then dropping your price; this move could also save your sale.

☐ *The broker's commission:* If you do list with a broker—and most sellers do—haggle over paying 6%, or the "standard fee." There is no law that says a real estate broker must receive 6% of the selling price; but there *are* laws about price fixing for professional services. The Federal Trade Commission has taken some real estate brokers to court over such practices; let your broker know that you realize this. Or you can set conditions upon your paying the broker's commission—agree, say, to a full 6% commission if the sale is made within 60 days.

Know the differences in "listings": Before you sign any listing agreement with a broker, have your attorney check it out. You must know the precise conditions under which you must pay a commission.

A listing is a contract between a seller and a real estate broker authorizing the broker to act as the owner's agent in the sale of his property. Under the contract, when the broker produces a buyer ready, willing, and able to buy, under the terms specified by the seller in thc listing, or other terms to which the seller may later agree, he will pay the broker a stated commission.There are three principal types of listings that you should be familiar with:

● *Exclusive right-to-sell listing:* A listing given to *one* broker, giving him or her the sole and exclusive right to sell the named property during the listing term and to collect a commission when it is sold, regardless of who sells the property. Even if you were to find the buyer, yourself, during the listing term, you would still owe the broker a full commission. This is the listing that brokers prefer; they say that they work harder to sell such listings because they stand a better chance at earning a full commission.

● *Exclusive agency listing:* A listing given to *one* broker exclusively, as above, but with the seller retaining the right to sell the property himself without having to pay commission.

● *Open listing:* This is a listing that may be given to as many brokers as the sellers wishes, with the seller agreeing to pay a commission only to the broker who sells the property. Under an open listing, the seller may sell the property himself, without having to pay a commission.

● *Multiple listing:* This isn't really a listing but rather a term used to describe an exclusive right to sell listing that the broker has agreed to pool with the listings of other brokers (who are co-members of an area multiple listing service) to gain maximum exposure for the property. When one broker lists a property for sale and another broker sells it, the two brokers share the commission. The seller does not have to pay each a full commission apiece.

▶ **GOOD NEWS FOR SELLERS:** The Federal Home Loan Bank Board, which regulates federally chartered S & Ls, issued new regulations covering the touchy situation where the seller's loan has a due-on-sale clause: (1) The homeseller finds a buyer who wants to assume his loan. (2) The S&L refuses and invokes the due-on-sale clause when seller pays off the loan. (3) The S & L then hits him with a *prepayment penalty*. The new regs forbid Federally chattered S & Ls to have it both ways—

they cannot invoke the due-on-sale clause *and* then impose a prepayment penalty. And the new regs override any state banking law that permits this practice.

HOW YOUR HOMEOWNERS' UNIQUE TAX SHELTER PROTECTS YOUR HOMESELLING PROFITS

Valuable as on-going home-ownership tax savers like interest deductions are, they are minor compared to the tax-saving advantages you get when you *sell your home*.

That's when you learn the real beauty of owning a home as an investment. When you sell your home, you—

1. Can avoid paying current tax on your profit, if you meet certain conditions, regardless of how many homes you buy and sell, and finally—

2. You get a once-in-a-lifetime opportunity to escape all tax on up to $125,000 in gain!

The "Tax-Free Rollover"

This special tax break is for people who sell one home and buy another. There is no current tax on your home-sale profit if you: (1) Spend at least as much for replacement home as you got for the old; and (2) Buy the replacement home within two years before or after the sale and use it as your principal residence within that time.

"Home," incidentally, includes co-ops and condos and mobile homes. If you buy a home that costs less than what you sell the old one for, you pay tax only on the *difference* between the sales price of the old home and the purchase price of the new (assuming the difference is less than your profit).

▶ **MULTIPLE TAX SAVINGS:** You are not limited to the number of times you can roll over. You can keep postponing the tax as long as you comply with those two requirements. It's one of the major tax-cutting devices around, and it's yours when you become a homeowner.

More breaks: The expenses you incur selling your home such as a broker's commission and "fixing-up costs," can reduce the amount you'll have to spend on your replacement home: This amount, your "adjusted sales price," is your sales price *less* two big items: (1) *direct selling costs* (commissions, legal fees, etc.); and (2) *fixing-up expenses* (painting, papering, replacing gutters, etc.) provided the work is done within 90 days before the sale and paid for within 30 days after.

▶ **ADDED BREAK:** Your direct selling costs (other than fixing-up expenses) do more than just help you delay your tax on your profit—they *cut back the amount on which you could eventually be taxed.*

How these costs add up: Let's say Romberg paid $35,000 for his home years ago. His broker tells him he can easily get $70,000 for it if he fixes it up a little. He spends $1,400 doing just that. His broker sells his place within two weeks for $70,000, as promised, and he pays the broker a $4,200 commission.

Now let's look at the result. First, his adjusted sales price—the price he'll have to pay for his new home to get the roll-over break—is only $64,400. That's $70,000 reduced by $4,200 and by $1,400.

And his gain is cut back, too. Instead of $35,000, it's $30,000—the $70,000 selling price reduced by his $35,000 cost and that $4,200 commission.

▶ **REMODELING TAX BREAK:** Your basis can include the *cost of capital improvements*—such as those remodeling expenses we have discussed: adding a bedroom or bathroom or replacing your old oil furnace with a new gas one. And when you make such additions to your home, you get something else at the same time. Since these improvements directly increase your tax basis in a home, they also *directly decrease* the tax you may ultimately pay when you sell a home and don't replace with another.

Once-In-A-Lifetime $125,000 Exclusion

This massive tax break lets you *exclude up to $125,000 in gain—completely tax free!* Since it's an exclusion you can elect only once, you should wait till you've built up a substantial amount of taxable profit—then wipe it out. There are three major conditions you must meet:

1. You must be 55 or over *at the time* you sell—not in the year you sell your house or condo or co-op. There is some leeway in this rule, though. Say you are under 55 but your spouse is 55. If your home is jointly owned and you file a joint return, the sale qualifies.

2. Your home must be *a principal residence*—not a vacation cottage or summer place—and be used as your home for three of the five years before the sale.

3. This is a *once-in-a-lifetime exclusion.* If you use it to shelter only $80,000 of tax-free gain, you can't carry over the unused $45,000 to a later sale.

Winning Combination

Because the rollover can be used as often as you qualify for it, you may want to combine both breaks if you have a massive untaxed gain and want to buy a smaller replacement home.

Example: Let's say you've rolled over several times and deferred tax on your gain each time. Now you get an offer of $180,000 for your present home. If you take it, you'll have an untaxed gain of $150,000. That means if you elect the exclusion, you'll still pay tax on $25,000. However, if you buy another home, the chances are *you won't have any taxable gain.* That's because you can combine the rollover *and* the exclusion.

▶ **TAX-SLASHING PARLAY:** You elect the $125,000 exclusion and *reduce the amount you have to roll over dollar for dollar.* Instead of having to buy a $180,000 replacement home, you can buy one for $55,000 and the rollover break allows you to escape any current tax on the $25,000—even after getting your once-in-a-lifetime break.

Five Special Exclusion Winners

The rules covering the $125,000 exclusion appear to be pretty straightforward, but this once-in-a-lifetime break may be more widely applicable than you think. Here are five situations where the exclusion was available:

1. The home wasn't used as a principal residence at the time of the sale: The home must be used as principal residence for three of the five years immediately preceding the sale. It does not have to be the principal residence at the time of the sale. So a homeseller can use the exclusion even if he hasn't lived in the house for the two years before the sale.

> *Example:* Mr. and Mrs. Smith retired and moved to Florida a year ago. They rented out their old home because they couldn't get the price they wanted. Now their broker located a prospect willing to pay the Smiths' price.

> ▶ **TAX-SAVING RESULT:** The Smiths can sell their home and qualify for the home-sale exclusion: Reason: As long as the home is sold within two years after the Smiths moved out (and the house was their principal residence for the three years before they moved), they can shelter from tax up to $125,000 of profit from the sale. The Revenue Service has already approved the idea under the former exclusion for homesellers 65 or over [Ltr. Rul. 7825067].

2. Seller hasn't lived in his present house three of the past five years: Let's say that Mr. Wade was eligible for the exclusion when he sold his home at a $50,000 profit in '85. However, later that year he purchased a more expensive house, so there was no tax owed on the profit from the sale. Now Wade has to relocate because of his job. He sells the new home and moves into an apartment. Wade wants to use the once-in-a-lifetime exclusion.

However, Wade doesn't meet the three out of five year residency requirement in his present home. He can't add on the years he lived in his old home to the time he has lived in the new one.

> ▶ **WINNING MOVE:** Wade should amend his 1985 tax return, and elect the exclusion on the previous sale. The tax law gives taxpayers three years from the date for filing their tax return for the year of sale to elect the exclusion. Result: Wade's only taxable profit from the sale of the new home is the difference between the cost of the new home and its sale price.

3. Seller has already claimed the $125,000 exclusion: The tax law says that the $125,000 exclusion is a once-in-a-lifetime break. For purposes of this exclusion a married couple is considered as one person. For example, if the husband used the exclusion on another sale, his wife can't claim it. But suppose Mr. Allen and Mrs. Martin are both widowed (or divorced) and over 55. While Mr. Allen has previously used the $125,000 exclusion, Mrs. Martin has not. They plan to marry and sell Mrs. Martin's home after their marriage.

▶ **TAX-WISE MOVE:** Mrs. Martin should sell her home before she marries Mr. Allen. That way, she can use her $125,000 exclusion—even though her future husband has also used his.

4. Seller is not 55 years old at the time of the sale: Mr. Black will not be 55 years old until July 15. He plans to sell his home on July 1. Does he lose out on the exclusion?

▶ **TAX-SLASHER:** Black sets the closing date for the sale on July 16 or later. As long as he is 55 years old before the date of the sale—the closing date—he gets the exclusion.

5. Only one spouse meets the requirements: Mr. and Mrs. Brown own their home jointly. When they sell their home, Mr. Brown is 56, but Mrs. Brown is only 53. Since Mrs. Brown is not yet 55, do they lose the exclusion?

▶ **TAX-SAVING EXCEPTION:** As long as one spouse satifies all the requirements for the home sale exclusion, the other spouse will also be treated as meeting the requirements. To get this break, however, the Browns must file a joint income tax return. So if the home was Mr. Brown's principal residence for three of the five years before the sale, the Browns get the exclusion.

HOW REMODELING CAN FURTHER SLASH YOUR TAX BILLS

When you remodel or modernize your home, you do more than improve its looks. You also enhance and increase the tax breaks of home ownership. As we've seen, you pay *no tax at all* if you reinvest your sales proceeds in another home that costs at least as much as the selling price of the previous home within two years of the sale. And you can eventually escape all tax on up to *$125,000* in *taxable gain* if you are 55 or older when you sell.

This gain is not just your profit from the last home sale but the cumulative, deferred profit from home to home. And your starting point for figuring it is the tax basis of your first home—its cost plus the money you spend on remodeling and improvements.

▶ **KEY MOVE:** We advised you to keep a *Home Expenditure Record Book* and save bills, receipts, cancelled checks, etc., because it was up to you to prove to the Government what you actually spent on your home over the years. If you cannot prove your basis and show how it was adjusted from year to year, you cannot prove your taxable gain or get your maximum homeowner breaks. Now you can see—

How tax savings add up: Mr. Anderson and his wife bought their first home 30 years ago for $20,000. They added a patio and finished off the basement for $3,000. They sold the home in 1960 for $30,000. Result: A gain of $7,000—the difference between the selling price and $23,000 (the $20,000 cost plust the $3,000 capital improvement). The Andersons bought a new home for $30,000—the same amount they received for the old one—so the tax on the gain was postponed. However, the tax basis for the new home is not $30,000 but the $23,000 adjusted basis of the old one.

During the course of his career, Anderson sells and replaces twice more. Let's take a look at his *Home Expenditure Record Book* below to see how the basis has changed since 1960.

Naturally, we show simplified entires, without such specifics as the names of the contractors and purchasers, actual dates, breakdown of amounts, etc., but it gives you an idea of how remodeling can improve your tax breaks, as well as your home's appearance.

Biggest tax break of all: This year, the Andersons decide to retire. Assuming they are over age 55, and meet all the other requirements on the special one-time exclusion, they can get tax-free treatment on up to $125,000 of gain from the sale of their residence. Let's say they sell their residence for $165,000 and rent an apartment.

• *If they keep records:* The computation is not very difficult. Mr. Anderson merely subtracts the adjusted basis ($58,000) from the selling price ($165,000) and arrives at a gain of $107,000. The entire gain is tax free to the Andersons, due to the once-in-a-lifetime exclusion.

• *If they didn't keep records:* Without complete records, Anderson would have a hard time reconstructing the cost of the improvements. In addition, the Government could question the amounts the Andersons received when they sold their homes, and the amounts spent on the purchases. As a result, the Government could assign an approximate basis to the house lower then its true adjusted basis.

Year	Transaction	Adjusted Basis
1960	New home purchased ($30,000)	$23,000
1961	Landscaping ($2,000)	$25,000
1962	Swimming pool ($4,000)	$29,000
1965	Home sold ($45,000)	$29,000 ($16,000 taxable gain)
1965	New home purchased ($50,000) and tax deferred	$34,000 (Cost less deferred gain)
1967	Added bedroom ($10,000)	$44,000
1970	Home sold ($70,000)	$44,000 ($26,000 taxable gain)
1970	New home purchased ($75,000) and tax deferred	$49,000 (Cost less deferred gain)
1972	Added tennis court ($9,000)	$58,000

And that could result in a taxable gain for the Andersons, even counting the $125,000 exclusion.

▶ **WHAT TO DO:** In your *Home Expenditure Record Book*, enter the original cost of your first home. Then as capital expenditures are made, enter these too. Attach to the book proof of purchase prices, purchasing and selling costs (these can affect basis, too), and capital improvements for all homes bought and sold. Also attach your tax returns for the years that you sold and replaced homes.

HOW TO GET MEDICAL-EXPENSE DEDUCTION FOR HOME IMPROVEMENTS

The medical-expense deduction is hard to get these days; your expenses are deductible only to the extent they exceed 5% of your adjusted gross income. As a homeowner, though, you may find some *home improvements* counting toward this deduction—if a doctor says they are medically necessary for you or your dependents.

▶ **TAX-LAW PRESCRIPTION:** To be deductible, a home improvement must: (1) Be prescribed by your physician; (2) Be directly related to medical care; and (3) Exceed any increase in value to your property.

Case in point: The Geralds' 9-year-old daughter suffered from an illness that made it dangerous for her to be exposed to dry, dusty air. Their physician prescribed an air-conditioning unit so that the temperature and humidity of the home could be controlled. And, since it would be psychologically harmful for the child to be confined to just one room, he advised that a central air conditioning unit be installed. The installation cost $2,000 and increased the value of the home $1,000. The $1,000 *difference* is deductible.

Other home improvements that have been held to be deductible: chair-seat elevator for heart patient; swimming pool installed for emphysema sufferer; home health spa for arthritis patient; computerized visual alert system in home of deaf person; installation of device to add floride to home water supply (advised by dentist); attached garage constructed at the home of a handicapped person.

Further break: Your annual expenditures for running and maintaining these medical improvements also count toward the medical expense deduction. So does the *entire* cost of upkeep and maintenance even though none or only part of the original cost of the improvement gave you a medical deduction.

▶ **WHAT TO DO:** Get a written recommendation for the improvement from your doctor and an estimate of its value from an appraiser. The Government insists on written proof.

HOW TO MAKE THE MOST OF THE BIG MOVING EXPENSE DEDUCTION

Whether you're self-employed or an employee, you can get a large deduction for both the direct and the indirect costs of moving to a new job location. Let's see how this big break stacks up today, and how you can get maximum tax mileage out of it:

There are two types of moving expenses: "direct" and "indirect."

Direct moving expenses: The definition of direct moving expenses covers the cost of moving your furniture and the like from your old to your new residence. However, it is much more comprehensive. It specifically also covers the reasonable cost of:

(1) Moving household goods and personal effects from the old to the new home (including your car and the family pets). Furthermore, it also covers the cost of packing, crating and in-transit storage of goods and effects. However, it doesn't cover certain other expenses such as the cost of refitting rugs and drapery.

(2) Traveling to the new job site—including meals and lodging en route—for you and all members of your family is fully deductible. A "member of the family" qualifies if he or she lives in your home both before and after the move. If you go by car, you can either itemize your actual expenses or deduct a flat nine cents per mile—plus tolls and parking.

Indirect moving expenses: These deductions fall into three categories.

(1) Pre-move househunting expenses include the cost of transportation and meals and lodging for you and members of your household paid during a search for your new residence. In order to qualify for the deduction you must have already obtained employment at the new job site and must travel from your former residence to the general area of your new employment and return.

(2) Temporary living expenses at the new job location include the cost of meals and lodging for you and the family which are incurred within any 30 consecutive days after you obtain your new job.

(3) Expenses of leasing, purchasing or selling a residence include costs of settling an unexpired lease, acquiring a new lease, real estate agent's commission, escrow fees, attorney's fees, appraisal fees, title costs, loan placement charges, and the like.

▶ **OVERALL DOLLAR LIMIT:** While direct moving expenses are completely deductible, there's a $3,000 overall dollar limit on the deduction of indirect moving expenses. Of this $3,000, not more than $1,500 can be deducted for househunting and temporary living expenses.

How To Qualify For The Deduction

To get the moving expense deduction, you must satisfy two simple tests:

(1) The new job must be at least 35 miles farther from your old home than the old job was, and (2) you must be employed at your new job location (or in the general vicinity) for 39 weeks during the 12 months following your move.

▶ **THREE BREAKS:** (1) You meet the 39-week test even if you switch jobs after you reach the new job location—as long as you continue to work in the general vicinity. (2) If you file a joint return, you get the deduction if either you or your wife meets the 39-week test. (3) The 39-week test is waived if a taxpayer can't comply because of death or disability or because he is laid off.

Tax strategy: Suppose you pay the expense in one year, but don't meet the 39-week test by April 15 of the next—when your return is due. How do you handle things? *Answer:* You can either: (1) Take the deduction on your return; or (2) file an amended return (and claim a refund) as soon as you meet the 39-week test.

"Recapture" of the deduction: Suppose you take the deduction on your return for the year in which you move—even though you still haven't met the 39-week test. Then, in the following year, you find out you won't meet this test. What do you do then? *Answer:* You must report the amount you deducted as added income on the following year's return.

▶ **IMPORTANT:** If your employer reimburses you for your moving expenses, you must include the reimbursement in your income and then take your moving expense deduction on your return.

▶ **TAX BREAK FOR SELF-EMPLOYED:** As we've said, self-employed taxpayers get the same moving expense breaks that employees enjoy. However, they must work at the new job location for 78 weeks out of the 24 months following their move in order to qualify.

How To Parlay A Tax-Free Sale Of Your Home And The Moving Expense Deduction Into Extra Tax-Free Income

The sale and replacement of your home, as we've explained, is tax-free to the extent that the purchase price of the new covers the selling price of the old. In addition, the tax rules grant some deductions for expenses incurred in selling and purchasing a home in connection with relocating your job, such as attorney's fees and real estate commissions. If you handle things the right way, you can create this:

▶ **TAX-FREE INCOME PARLAY:** (1) Deduct the sale and purchase expenses of your old and new homes as moving expenses and (2) claim the tax-free break on the sale of your old home.

Tax-saving result: The deductions offset ordinary income. True, the selling expense cannot then be used to reduce the gain on the old house nor can the purchase expenses be used to boost the basis of the new. However, if your purchase price is high enough, the extra "gain" on the old house will still be completely tax-free! And, even if the purchase price of the new home isn't enough to cover the extra gain, you still get this—

▶ **TAX BREAK:** Assuming you've held your old home long enough, any gain you have will be tax-sheltered capital gain. On the other hand, the deductions are still offsets against ordinary income. In effect, you've converted ordinary income into capital gain.

Example: Brown works in Chicago. He commutes from the suburbs, where he lives with his family in a home which cost him $54,000 several years ago. This year, Brown takes a new job in the Los Angeles area, so he sells his Chicago home for $80,000 and, within a year, purchases a new residence in Los Angeles for $90,000. Brown's selling expenses come to $5,400—real estate commission of $4,800 and legal fees of $600. His purchasing expenses are $600—legal fees of $400 and appraisal and title fees of $200. For simplicity, let's assume Brown has no moving expenses other than the $6,000 of expenses directly connected with the sale of his old home and the purchase of the new one.

Let's compare the results Brown gets doing things in the "usual way" with the results he can get doing things the "tax-free way."

Usual way: If Brown capitalizes his selling and purchasing expenses, his gain on the sale of his old residence will be $20,600 ($80,000 selling price less his $54,000 cost and $5,400 selling expenses). However, Brown's entire gain is completely tax free because the purchase price of his new home ($90,000) exceeded the selling price of the old ($80,000). Brown's basis for his new home is $70,000 ($90,000 cost plus $600 purchasing expenses less his $20,600 tax-deferred gain). Brown gets no deduction for the expenses incurred on the purchase and sale.

Tax-free way: Brown deducts $2,700 of his selling expenses, and $300 of his buying expenses, as moving expenses (there's a $3,000 overall dollar limit on "indirect" moving expenses).

Now his gain on the sale of the home goes up to $23,300 ($80,000 sales price, less $54,000 cost, less $2,700 of his selling expenses not deducted as moving expenses). However his gain is still completely tax-free because the cost of his new home exceeds the sales price of the old home. Brown's "extra" gain on the sale of his old home won't be taxed until he sells the new house, and maybe not even then, if he rolls over into another residence (or is over 55, and elects to use the home-sale exclusion).

Meanwhile, Brown—thanks to the moving expense deduction—gets a $3,000 offset against his highly taxed income.

Here's how Brown figures his tax basis in the new home.

New home cost	$90,000
Plus buying expenses not deducted as moving expenses (½ of total)	300
Less tax-deferred gain	(23,300)
Tax basis	$67,000

THREE WAYS TO GET TAX-FREE INCOME FROM
A VACATION HOME

You may own a vacation home—a lakeside cabin or a seashore cottage or a ski lodge—in addition to your regular residence. If so, you are in line for some extra tax breaks, along with extra income.

▶ **HOW TO GET BOTH:** Rent out your vacation home when you and your family aren't using it. Renting your place entitles you to one of three tax breaks:

1. If you really restrict your personal use of the vacation home, you may not only be able to shelter your rental income from tax, but even some of your other income.

2. If you use the property extensively for personal use *and* also rent the property out on a regular basis you also get a big break: Assuming you have enough in allowable deductions, you can shelter all your rental income from tax.

3. If you rent out the vacation home for not more than two weeks you get to keep all your rental income. That's right, it's completely tax-free.

Tax-saver #1: The Tax Law grants the maximum vacation home deduction to the owner who makes clear that his property is an investment—a profit-making enterprise—rather than a home he uses as his residence.

Question: How do I go about proving this?

Answer: What matters most is the amount of time you personally use the vacation home. You are considered to use the property not as a residence—but, rather, as a profit-making enterprise—if you and your family use the home for not more than: (A) 14 days, or (B) 10% of the number of days in the year the property is rented out, whichever is greater.

Example 1: Say you rent out your property for 48 days. You can use the home personally for up to 14 days—the greater of (A) or (B).

Example 2: Now let's say you rent out for 210 days (30 weeks). You can use the home personally for not more than 21 days. Limit (B) is greater in this case.

Question: What do I as an owner get for restricting my personal use in this manner?

Answer: You are entitled to deduct all the maintenance, upkeep, and depreciation related to your rental use of the home.

Example 3: You own a vacation home in an area where the season lasts three months. You and your family use the property for two weeks; and rent it out at $200 a week for the remaining ten weeks for a total of $2,000. Yearly expenses: $300 interest; $600 taxes; $600 for maintenance; and $300 for utilities. There's also $1,600 in depreciation every year.

Question: What can I deduct?

Answer: You can deduct all your rent-related deductions: ten-twelfths (rental use over total use) of your total payment for interest and taxes ($750), plus ten-twelfths of the total maintenance, upkeep, and depreciation ($2,083), for total rent-related deductions of $2,833.

▶ **TAX SAVING RESULT:** The total deductions completely shelter your $2,000 rental income from tax. In addition you are left with an $833 tax loss that you can use to shelter other income. Finally, you are also entitled to a $150 deduction for the portion of the interest and taxes related to your personal use of the vacation home ($900 less $750).

Tax-saver #2: Owners who are considered to hold their vacation homes "as a residence" are still able to shelter all their rental income from tax.

The Tax Law considers an owner to be holding his vacation home "as a residence," that is for personal rather than business use, if he uses it for more than the greater of (A) 14 days; or (B) 10% of the number of days the property's rented out.

Example 4: Let's say that your family used the vacation home for one month; and rented it out for the other two, for a total rental of $1,600. The Tax Law would now consider you to be holding the property "as a residence." Result: Your deductions would be slimmed down.

What you would get: You would now figure up 2/3rds (rental use of 2 months over the total usable three months) the interest, taxes, upkeep, utilities, and depreciation, for a new total of $2,266. But the Tax Law says that where property is held "as a residence," rental-related deductions can't exceed rental income, less taxes and interest attributable to rental use. Your rental income in Example (2) is $1,600. Subtracting $600 (2/3 of your $900 deductions for interest and taxes) from that figure leaves $1,000.

Result: You take $400 in maintenance deductions (2/3 of $600), plus $200 for utilities (2/3 of $300)—plus only $400 in depreciation. Though the rest of the depreciation is non-deductible, you still wind up with—

▶ **TAX-FREE INCOME:** Your $600 in rental related interest and taxes, plus $1,000 in other rental-related deductions still complete offset your $1,600 in rental income. You don't pay a penny of income tax on it! Plus, of course, you get a $300 deduction for the interest and taxes related to personal use of the property (1/3 of $900).

Tax-saver #3: The Law provides a special break for owners who rent out their vacation homes for two weeks or less. Such taxpayers do not have to report their rental income on their return. In exchange for this tax-free income, the taxpayer can't claim any rental-related deductions. He can, however, deduct all his interest and property taxes.

Chapter 5

Key Tax Moves That Help A Family Business—No Matter What Its Size

Whether the family business is a full-time occupation or a sideline activity, you can dramatically increase your profits by lowering the company's Federal income tax bill. The chart below is graphic evidence of how tax savings can boost your company's financial well-being. It assumes your business is incorporated.

IF YOUR PRE-TAX PROFIT MARGIN ON SALES IS	AND YOUR COMPANY'S TOP TAX RATE* IS				
	15%	18%	30%	40%	46%
	THEN $1,000 IN TAX SAVINGS NETS YOU AS MUCH AS SALES OF				
25%	$ 4,706	$ 4,878	$ 5,714	$ 6,667	$ 7,407
20%	5,882	6,098	7,143	8,333	9,259
15%	7,843	8,130	9,524	11,111	12,346
10%	11,765	12,195	14,286	16,667	18,519
9%	13,072	13,550	15,873	18,518	20,576
8%	14,706	15,244	17,857	20,833	23,148
7%	16,807	17,422	20,408	23,809	26,455
6%	19,608	20,325	23,809	27,778	30,864
5%	23,529	24,390	28,571	33,333	37,037

*The 15% rate applies to taxable income up to $25,000; 18% rate to income between $25,000 and $50,000; 30% rate, to income between $50,000 and $75,000; 40% rate to income between $75,000 and $100,000; and the 46% rate applies to taxable income above $100,000.

This chapter zeros in on proven income tax saving strategies. You'll find out how to slash taxes with investment credits, how to boost depreciation writeoffs, and how to keep more of your company's investment earnings. As you'll see, there's one type of corporate setup that can eliminate the tax on corporate profits. And there are also some strategies for cutting Social Security and unemployment taxes. These are only a few of the tax cutting possibilities you will find in the following pages.

THE TAX-WISE WAY TO SET UP A NEW CORPORATION FOR YOUR NEW BUSINESS

Many closely-held businesses are organized as regular corporations. And for good reason: The shareholders are shielded from personal liability and enjoy the many tax benefits that come from incorporation: retirement plans for shareholder-officers and other employees, and a host of tax-free fringe benefits (such as medical reimbursement plans and group-term insurance coverage).

There are two important steps you should take when you incorporate—the first gives you maximum tax protection if your new business plans don't work out well. The second helps you put more profits in the family's pocket (and less in the tax collector's) when your new venture turns out to be a great success.

#1—How to Get Special Tax Insurance for Your New Corporate Venture

The tax law contains a special provision—Section 1244—designed to encourage people like yourself to invest in small companies. Under Section 1244, you can get a form of no-cost tax insurance to protect you should your investment turn sour.

When you set up your new corporation, you put cash into the business in return for stock. By treating the stock as Section 1244 stock, you are really getting the best of both worlds from a tax standpoint. If your investment does well, your profit on the eventual sale of the stock is low-taxed capital gain. On the other hand, if things don't pan out, your loss is a fully deductible ordinary loss, not a capital loss of limited tax benefit. (A capital loss can only offset up to $3,000 of ordinary income each year.)

▶ **HOW TO QUALIFY:** Section 1244 stock is stock issued for money or property by a "small business corporation" (in simple terms, one that has less than $1 million in contributed capital when the stock is issued). There are no special forms to fill out. Just have the new corporation's minutes designate that all of your stock (and your family's stock) is Section 1244 stock.

The company should keep the following records: the date the stock was issued, how much you paid for it, and the total amount the company has received for its stock.

#2—How To Siphon Off Corporate Profits As Low-Taxed Capital Gain

If you're about to incorporate, you have the opportunity to achieve one of the best kinds of tax savings. You can convert high-taxed ordinary income into low-taxed capital gain by following a simple blueprint set forth right in the tax law. The technique will enable you to unload a substantial portion of stock at capital gain rates, while keeping full, undiluted control over your family business.

Example: You set up a business venture in corporate form. You own 55% of the corporation; your wife 20%; and your two children 12½% each. The business is successful and begins generating a substantial income.

Part of this income is distributed as dividends. (There's some intra-family tax-savings here, since the dividends that go to your kids are taxed in their low brackets). The balance of the income has been accumulating; and the corporation has substantial cash on hand.

Problem: How to get this cash out of the corporation without paying a huge tax.

▶ **WHAT TO DO:** Have the corporation buy back *all* of your spouse's stock, using some or all of its cash on hand. Finally, see to it that your spouse does not acquire any more stock in the corporation for the next ten years.

Tax-saving result: The gain your wife realized on the redemption of her stock is *capital gain* —not ordinary income—and you still control the corporation.

Important: Your spouse gets capital gain treatment only if she has held the corporate stock for at least ten years. So if you just set up your corporation, you have to wait ten years for this tax-saver to work.

Q. Why does my spouse have to hold on to the stock for ten years before the stock is redeemed? Why can't he or she redeem after five years, if the stock's value has increased?

A. The redemption must be complete. And it isn't if the stock is redeemed from your spouse within ten years of him or her acquiring it. If your spouse hasn't held the stock for at least ten years, the attribution rules say that stock owned by you and your children is considered owned by your spouse. *Result:* Your spouse will not have completely terminated his or her interest, and the entire amount will be taxable as a dividend.

Just as important: A redemption is complete only if your spouse does not reacquire any of the corporate stock for ten years following the redemption.

Q. Why couldn't I just redeem the stock I own myself?

A. You could, of course, if you meet the ten-year rule. However, it means you must be willing to give up all your interest in the corporation (except as a creditor). This includes such things as being an officer, a director or an employee.

Q. Wouldn't I get capital gain if I simply sold some of my stock to someone else?

A. Sure, you would. But you also dilute your control of the corporation. As a matter of fact, you might have to *give up control* of the corporation.

▶ **WATCH THIS:** There is one more requirement. Your spouse must file an agreement to notify the Revenue Service if he or she acquires any of the corporation's stock within ten years from the date of the redemption. What's more, your spouse must file it on a timely return in the year of the redemption or the entire capital gain break is lost. Be sure you talk things over with your tax adviser before you make your move.

WHY A SPECIAL KIND OF CORPORATION MAY BE AN IDEAL CHOICE FOR CLOSELY-HELD BUSINESSES

More and more business people are turning to the benefits of the S corporation. Why? Because for the closely-held business, it offers a package of—

▶ **TAX-SAVING FEATURES:** Ordinarily there is no tax at the corporate level. The corporation's profits, losses, deductions and credits are passed directly through to the shareholders as if they were partners.

How to qualify: A corporation must meet certain requirements before it can make a valid election:

• It must be a domestic corporation which is not a member of an affiliated group eligible to file a consolidated return with any other corporation. (Owning a corporation that has not begun business during the tax year, and which has no taxable income, does not disqualify a corporation.)

• The corporation can't have more than 35 shareholders. But note that a husband and wife are considered one shareholder—regardless of how they own the stock.

• All shareholders must be either individuals, decedents' estates, or certain types of trusts (like grantor trusts and voting trusts). Nonresident aliens cannot be shareholders.

• The corporation can't have more than one class of common stock. However, differences in stock voting rights do not create separate classes of stock.

• As a general rule, an S corporation must be on a calendar year (a tax year that ends December 31), unless it can establish a business purpose for a non-calendar tax year.

None of the benefits of electing S corporation treatment are available if the election is not made currently or on time. A corporation may file its S corporation election (Form 2553) along with a statement of consent of each shareholder with the Revenue Service at any time during the entire taxable year preceding the election year, or on or before March 15 of the election year.

The election is retroactive to the beginning of the year if all the eligibility requirements for the pre-election period are met and if all persons who held stock during that period consent. The election continues in effect until revoked or terminated.

If the election is made, say, on March 16th, the filing is late, and the election is effective for the next calendar year.

Final word: Despite its advantages, the S election isn't the right solution for all businesses. For example, if your new business turns out to be a roaring success, you (and the other shareholders) will be taxed like clockwork on business income. There's no way to accumulate money in an S Corp. and avoid current shareholder taxation. Expert tax advice is a must *before* you set up your business.

HOW THE FAMILY PARTNERSHIP CAN MEAN MORE AFTER-TAX DOLLARS FOR YOUR FAMILY

Let's say you own an unincorporated business. You want to save taxes by splitting the profits with your child each year.

▶ **HOW TO DO IT:** Form a family partnership and make your children your partners. If things are handled correctly, a family partnership can be a double taxsaver: (1) Some of each year's profits are taxed to your children, so the family's overall income tax bill goes down. (2) The partnership interest you give to your children now won't be part of your taxable estate. So your family's estate tax is less than if the property passed under your will.

You may have to pay a gift tax when you set up a family partnership. However, you can make a $10,000 gift to each of your children every year ($20,000 if your wife joins in the gift) that's exempt from tax. On top of the exemption, you can use part of the generous unified estate and gift tax credit to offset any tax.

But even if there is a tax on the transfer, you may be better off making a gift rather than leaving it in your estate. *Reason:* Part of the property's later appreciation in value—the part attributable to the children's partnership interest—won't be taxable in your estate.

How to set up a family partnership: You'll need written documents and a deed if you're transferring real estate assets to the partnership. Your children will then be given an interest in the partnership. You'll want a written partnership agreement, stating each party's interest in the transferred assets. You can create a partnership by oral agreement, but that may mean trouble with the IRS.

Minor children can be partners, but you must set it up carefully. Unless your children are old enough to handle their own business affairs, you'll have to set up trusts to handle their interest until they reach their majority. You can even be the trustee—but you must keep accounts, books, and records for the children.

▶ **WHAT TO DO:** With minor children as partners, you might be wise to consider a limited partnership. Make your children limited partners with you as the general partner. As general partner, the management of the property remains completely in your control. As limited partners, your children get their share of the profits each year.

How should profits be split? First, you, as the managing partner, must get reasonable compensation for your services. What's reasonable? What you would pay an outsider to do the same work. Second, what's left over must be allocated according to each partner's interest in the partnership. You and your child will be taxed on your respective shares of the partnership's profits.

Important: Your business must be one in which "capital is a material income-producing factor." If you own rental real estate or a business with inventories, you're okay. But it won't work if you own a personal service business.

HOW YOU GET A TAX EDGE WITH A FRANCHISE SETUP

Franchising is one of America's major success stories in marketing. A franchise is a license you obtain to sell a brand name product or service owned by the franchiser. The actual selling adheres to the franchiser's marketing methods, and the raw stock, appearance of your outlet, etc. are in accordance with guidelines established by the franchise. For this license you pay a fee and a percentage of the gross.

Whether or not a franchise is right for you depends on many factors—such as the quality of the franchise product, the company's track record and financial strength, and the up-front capital required. But if you do decide to buy a franchise, you can look forward to—

▶ **SPECIAL TAX ADVANTAGES:** Buyers of franchises (i.e., franchisees) are governed by tax rules that by and large give them more favorable tax treatment than buyers of other types of business property. Net effect: Part of your purchase price may be currently deductible, and the rest may be written off over a short period of time.

Exactly how you handle a purchase payment depends on the answers to two questions: (1) Is it a payment of a flat amount or is it a contingent payment (for example, you pay the franchisor a percentage of gross sales)? (2) If it is a flat amount, is it one of a series of periodic payments or is it a lump-sum payment?

Contingent payment: Any contingent payment you make to a franchisor is currently deductible as a business expense—the same as wages or any other operating expense. You do not have to capitalize the payment and write it off over a period of time.

> *Example 1:* Mr. Green, a franchisee of Tastee Family Restaurants, is required under the franchise agreement, to pay 3% of his gross annual sales to the franchisor. His annual gross sales come to $1,000,000 and he makes a $30,000 payment to the franchisor. Result: Green can deduct the entire $30,000 immediately.

Fixed payment: If you are paying off a fixed amount in a lump sum, you can write off the payment ratably over ten years or the length of the franchise agreement, whichever is less.

> *Example 2:* Mr. Quinn buys a franchise for an up-front fee of $24,000 plus future contingent payments. The franchise agreement lasts for 18 years. Result: Quinn can deduct the initial fee at the rate of $2,400 a year over the first ten years of the agreement.

If a fixed obligation is paid off in installments, things get a little more complicated:

● If the installments are equal in amount and paid over the life of an agreement of more than ten years, each payment is deductible in the year it's paid.

● Whether equal or unequal in amount, payments over a period of less than ten years are deducted ratably over the franchise period or ten years, whichever is less.

> **Example 3:** Same facts as Example 2, except that the $24,000 is paid in installments over five years—$6,000 in each of the first three years and $3,000 in the next two years. Result: Quinn still deducts $2,400 a year over ten years. If, however, the franchise agreement lasted only six years, Quinn could deduct $4,000 a year.

● If the payments are unequal and are paid over the life of an agreement of more than ten years, they are deductible when made as long as (1) no payment exceeds 20% of the total and (2) no more than 75% of the total obligation is paid over ten years or the first-half of the contract period, whichever is less.

> **Example 4:** Same as in Example 2, except that Quinn pays the $24,000 in installments over 14 years—$1,000 a year for the first four years and $2,000 a year for the next ten. Result: No single year's payment exceeds $4,800 (20% of $24,000). And payments for the first nine years (one-half of the franchise period) do not exceed $18,000 (75% of the total). So Quinn can write off each payment as it is made.

Important: In a few cases, fixed payments for the purchase of a franchise may not qualify for this special writeoff treatment (contingent payments always qualify). This happens when the franchisor gives up all significant rights and powers as part of the franchise agreement (the franchisor can't set quality standards, can't require the franchisee to buy supplies from him, can't veto the transfer of a franchise, etc.).

Result: You get no writeoff at all for the fixed payments if the franchise has an unlimited life (e.g., the agreement can be renewed indefinitely at the franchisee's option). The payments are merely used to offset your profit when (and if) you sell your franchise interest. On the other hand, if the life of the franchise can be reasonably estimated, you can write off the payments over that estimated life.

> ▶ **WHAT TO DO:** If there is a possibility of writeoffs—in other words, your franchise doesn't have an unlimited life—get together proof to back up your case. The franchisor or a trade association may be able to help you here. If they can provide statistics indicating a low rate of renewal, that will help you prove a limited life for your franchise.

HOW YOU AND YOUR FAMILY CAN COME OUT TOP TAX WINNERS BY PUTTING YOUR CHILD ON THE PAYROLL

Your children are probably doing odd jobs for your business already. If that's the case, make them legitimate employees. Put the children on your payroll and pay them wages for the work they do. That way, your family will benefit from income splitting. You are taking money that your company would otherwise pay to you as salary or dividends and shifting it into your children's low bracket. At the same time, you are building up a—

> ▶ **TAX-FREE COLLEGE FUND:** Children with low earnings do not owe any federal income tax (for 1986, the tax-free income level is $3,560). This money can be put into the bank until the child is ready for college.

There's even a way you can have your children increase their take-home pay immediately. They can bank their full wages now and earn more interest right away, instead of waiting until tax refund time.

▶ **WHAT TO DO:** Have your children's wages exempted from federal income tax withholding. All they have to do is write the word "exempt" on Line 3 of the Form W-4 that they are required to file with your company (their employer). To qualify, they must (1) have had no income tax liability for the prior year, and (2) expect to incur no tax liability for this year. (Note: Social Security tax must still be deducted from wages paid by your corporation.)

Of course, everything must be business-like when your children work for you. The wages must be reasonable and paid for actual services. If you don't handle things in a business-like manner, your children may owe tax on their earnings or your company could loose its deduction.

Q: Does this idea apply only to college-age children?

A: No. Younger children can qualify, too, as long as they are capable of rendering meaningful services to your company and receive reasonable compensation. In fact, in one recent case, the Tax Court ruled, and the Internal Revenue Service later agreed, that a business was entitled to deductions for wages paid to a seven-year-old child.

Facts: Mr. Eller owned and operated several trailer parks through partnerships and sole proprietorships. He had a son John, age 7, and two older children. Eller put the children to work at the trailer parks after school, on weekends and during the summer vacations. The children were assigned various tasks: maintenance of swimming pool and park grounds, sweeping and cleaning trailer pads and new mobile homes put up for sale, mopping and cleaning the recreation hall, doing minor repair work and so forth. The children were paid for their services. Over a period of three years, John received a total of $5,150. Eller's partnerships and sole proprietorships claimed a deduction for this amount.

Winning result: Eller is entitled to a deduction, said the Tax Court. Though John's services weren't worth $5,150, they did have value. The Tax Court granted Eller's businesses a partial deduction of $4,002 [Eller, 77 TC 934 acq., IRB 1984-52].

How about you? Eller's partnerships and sole proprietorships operated trailer parks. Suppose, however, you're the owner of a business and frequently spend Saturdays at the office. You bring the children along. You have them run errands, do the filing, clean up and otherwise act as office help. *Result:* As long as your company pays them a *reasonable* salary for work acutally done, it should be able to deduct it.

▶ **WHAT TO DO:** Comply with any requirements of your state's Child Labor Law. Furthermore, pay any withholding and other employment taxes the law requires and keep accurate records of the work your children do for you.

Reminder: No matter how much your child is paid in wages, you can still claim a dependency deduction for your child. *Reason:* Your child is still your dependent as long as you provide more than half of the child's support and he or she either (1) won't reach 19 this year, or (2) is 19 or older but is a full-time student during any five calendar months of the year.

Caution: You can lose your child as a dependant if he or she spends earnings on support and thereby provides for half of his or her total support. If that's a possibility, make sure your child banks some of the earnings, so you can meet the more-than-half-support test.

HOW YOU CAN GET MORE TAX-SHELTERED MONEY OUT OF YOUR BUSINESS BY PUTTING YOUR SPOUSE ON THE PAYROLL

Many family corporations—and their owners—may be missing out needlessly on tax deductions. The owner's spouse helps out in the business, but doesn't get a salary. They figure that there is nothing to be gained from paying a salary. The couple files joint returns so half of the family income is taxed to each of them, regardless of who earns it. However, these owners do not realize that putting a spouse on the payroll *can* add tax-sheltered dollars to the family treasury. As an employee, your spouse is entitled to a variety of tax-sheltered benefits. Here are some of the more important ones:

Group life insurance: The corporation can purchase life insurance for your spouse—along with other employees—and it can deduct the premiums. And the premiums covering the first $50,000 of insurance are not income to you or your spouse (see Chapter Seven for details).

Pension and profit-sharing benefits: This is probably the biggest benefit of all. The corporation gets a full deduction for what it contributes for your spouse each year. And your spouse realizes no income until he or she actually cashes in on the fund. So his or her retirement nest egg grows tax-free. And when your spouse does retire, the retirement funds receive favorable tax treatment.

Business-paid travel expenses: It's tough to deduct a spouse's expenses on a convention trip. But if he or she is an employee, it is easier to show a business purpose for attending the convention. Then, your spouse's convention expenses would be deductible—the same as are your expenses (see Chapter Six for details).

Here are two deductions that are available on your personal tax return when both you and your spouse have earnings:

IRA deductions: You can contribute only an additional $250 (on top of your own $2,000 IRA contribution) for a non-working spouse's IRA. But if your spouse is on the payroll, (and earns a minimum of $2,000) you can contribute and deduct $2,000 for his or her IRA—$1,750 more of deductions on your joint return.

Marriage penalty deduction: A working couple is entitled to a special deduction to offset something called the "marriage penalty." The joint income of a working couple is taxed more heavily if they are married than if they are not. However, married couples are allowed a deduction of 10% of the lower earning spouse's income, up to a maximum deduction of $3,000.

Important point: If your business is run as a sole proprietorship, you can't get a marriage penalty deduction; the tax law denies the deduction for amounts paid by a self-employed taxpayer to his or her working spouse. On the other hand, if you operate your business as a sole proprietorship, you do not have to pay Social Security tax on your spouse's earnings (you must pay this tax if you're incorporated). Your spouse is entitled to a $2,000 IRA contribution whether salary is paid by a corporation, partnership, or sole proprietorship.

How Tax Savings Can Help Self-Employeds Get Corporate Health Insurance Benefits

Small business owners often incorporate to get tax-free benefits. One of the most popular is health insurance coverage. Premiums are fully deductible by the corporation and completely tax-free to employees. Self-employeds generally cannot take advantage of this benefit. They have to pay for medical coverage with after tax dollars. Reason: The tax break for health insurance premiums is reserved for employees, and an unincorporated business owner is not considered an employee.

To make matters worse, taxpayers can't take a deduction for their health insurance premiums on their individual tax returns unless they itemize and their total medical expenses exceed 5% of their adjusted gross income. Is there anything self-employeds can do to get company-paid medical coverage?

▶ **EASY SOLUTION:** There is a Government-approved way for many self-employeds to save on medical coverage. It's an indirect approach that yields a direct benefit [Rev. Rul. 71-588, 1971-2 CB 91].

How it works: The self-employed puts his spouse on the payroll. Since she probably already works in the business, it's just a matter of making her an official employee. Then he sets up a medical plan in writing for employees of the business. Since the plan also covers employees' spouses, the business owner now has the benefit of an employee fringe benefit. As long as the spouse is a bona-fide employee, the owner can deduct the health premiums as a business expense.

Important: This tax idea will work only if the spouse/employee—not the business owner—is covered by the health insurance policy. The spouse is the employee.

▶ **ADDED BENEFIT:** The business does not have to pay the health insurance premiums of all employees. Medical insurance coverage is not subject to the non-discrimination rules that generally apply to medical reimbursement plans. So the medical insurance plan can pay just the premiums on the policy taken out on the employee spouse.

HOW THE TAX LAW PROVIDES FAST AUDIT-PROOF DEDUCTIONS FOR EQUIPMENT PURCHASES

Today's depreciation setup—known as the Accelerated Cost Recovery System, or ACRS—is designed to stimulate capital investment. It allows taxpayers to recover the cost of equipment, vehicles, machinery and buildings faster than with the old system of depreciating the item over its useful life. The ACRS system applies to property placed in service after 1980.

How the system works: The cost of most equipment and machinery can be recovered over a five year period. The cost of cars, light-duty trucks and research and experimentation equipment can be recovered over three years. Buildings placed in service after May 8, 1985 have a 19-year writeoff period (15 years, if placed in service after 1980 and before March 16, 1984; 18 years if placed in service between March 16, 1984 and May 8, 1985).

The law provides tables to indicate the percentage of cost that can be deducted each year for each class of property. A taxpayer simply takes the total cost of the property placed in each class and multiplies it by the percentage stated in the tables.

> **Example:** XYZ Corp. purchases and places into service $20,000 of three year property and $40,000 of five year property in 1986. The recovery percentage for the first year for three year property is 25%; for five year property, it is 15%. Result: XYZ's cost recovery deduction in 1986 is $11,000 (25% of $20,000 plus 15% of $40,000).

Other simplified rules: The ACRS system makes no distinction between new and used property. The cost for both are recovered at the same rate. In addition, a taxpayer can recover the entire cost of an item over the recovery period. Reason: Salvage value is ignored for cost recovery purposes.

Furthermore, ACRS adopts the half-year convention—in other words, for a calendar year taxpayer, all property placed in service during the year is considered placed in service July 1. For example, five year property purchased for $10,000 and placed in service on December 31 of this year qualifies for the same first year writeoff as five year property purchased for $10,000 on January 1.

Special rules: Although ACRS generally creates a more simplified system of cost recovery, it does add a number of complications. The first—and most important—complication is that the—

> ▶ **OLD RULES ARE STILL ALIVE:** ACRS replaced the old depreciation system only for property placed in service in 1981 and later. Property placed in service before 1981 will continue to be depreciated in the same way as in the past. Thus, for most businesses, both ACRS and the old depreciation system exist side-by-side.

Because of the significantly higher deductions available under ACRS, many taxpayers may be tempted to try to convert property purchased before 1981 into ACRS purchases. However, it is difficult to do so. Generally, ACRS will not be available for property in use during 1980 unless (1) the property is transferred after 1980 and (2) both the owner and the user (if different from the owner) change. So a sale-leaseback will not convert property purchased before 1981 into property eligible for ACRS.

Other cost recovery periods are available: A taxpayer does not have to use the standard ACRS system of three, five, ten, 15, 18 and 19 year recovery periods with accelerated recovery percentages in the early years. The straight-line method of cost recovery can also be used either over the regular recovery period or longer recovery periods. For example, a taxpayer may use a five or 12 year recovery period for three-year property, and a 12 or 25 year period for five-year property.

If a recovery method other than the standard ACRS method is elected for one piece of property in a recovery class, it must be elected for all property in that class placed into service during that year. So if straight-line is elected for a machine in the five year class placed into service in 1986, all five year property placed into service in 1986 must be recovered using the straight-line method.

Special expensing deduction: Instead of depreciating property under ACRS, a business can elect to treat all or part of the cost of qualifying property as a currently deductible expense. The current dollar limitation on the amount of capital cost that can be expensed is $5,000 a year. All or part of the cost of a number of assets may be expensed, but only up to the dollar limitation. *Important:* If expensing is elected, the investment credit can't be taken for the expensed portion of the property's basis.

Don't Forget Sales Tax When Figuring Your Equipment Writeoff

What is the best way to treat the sales tax you pay on equipment purchases? In most states you have a choice: You can currently deduct (''expense'') sales tax or capitalize it. The sales tax is deductible currently—even if paid on the purchase of capital equipment that must be depreciated. (But if your state imposes sales tax on the seller, the tax must be added to the equipment's cost and recovered through depreciation deductions—even if the tax is separately stated and paid by you.)

The way you choose to recover your equipment costs also should be the best way to handle the sales tax. If you come out ahead expensing your equipment, a current sales tax deduction should give you the greatest tax savings. If you do better capitalizing your equipment, capitalize your sales tax also.

▶ **TAX BONUS:** If you expense your equipment's cost, you may be able to get a current deduction greater than the full $5,000 expensing limit. You can separately deduct *all* the sales tax paid on the purchase in addition to $5,000 of the equipment's cost.

Another reminder: Don't forget your freight and installation costs when figuring your cost for depreciation or expensing. If you do, you're a double tax loser Reason: You're cheating yourself out of tax dollars now, and when you later sell the equipment, you'll owe more tax—your basis is reduced by the amount of depreciation you could have taken, even if you did not take it.

HOW TO MAKE THE MOST OUT OF THE 10% INVESTMENT CREDIT

One of the biggest tax breaks for all businesses—large or small, incorporated or not—is the 10% investment credit. A $10,000 purchase of business equipment or machinery can mean an out-of-pocket outlay of only $9,000; Uncle Sam pays the other $1,000. That, in essence, is the tax magic of the 10% investment credit.

How it works: Broadly speaking, the credit allows a company to subtract from its tax bill a portion of its investment in new—and (to a limited extent) in used—depreciable property (except buildings). Thus, if the tax before credit is $10,500 and the credit is $2,500, the tax payable is cut to $8,000—that is, it's a direct *dollar-for-dollar reduction in the tax.*

The amount of the investment tax credit depends on the cost recovery period for the property placed in service: 10% of the cost of eligible five-year, ten-year or 15-year public utility property; 6% for in the case of three-year property. However, if you claim the full investment credit, you must reduce the property's depreciable basis by one-half the credit claimed. Alternatively, you may elect to reduce the investment credit by 2%—for example, from 10% to 8% for five-year property, from 6% to 4% for three-year property—and take depreciation deductions based on the property's full cost.

> **Example:** Baker Co., a manufacturer of small tools, placed the following assets in service at various times during this year—and figured its investment credit on them as follows:

Asset	Recovery Period	Cost (basis)	Applicable Percentage	Tax Credit
Light duty truck	3 yrs.	$15,000	6%	$ 900
Office furniture	5 yrs.	10,000	10%	1,000
Business machinery	5 yrs.	20,000	10%	2,000
				$3,900

What property qualifies for the credit? Eligible property is called "Sec. 38 property" and, as defined, is the keystone of this tax break. Let's see exactly what types of assets qualify.

(1) *Tangible personal business property.* This includes such items as factory machinery, office equipment, trucks and the like. But it generally doesn't cover land or improvements such as buildings and other permanent structures.

▶ **IMPORTANT:** Local law definitions are not controlling. Many assets qualify for the credit even though classified as fixtures.

Examples: *(1) Grocery counters, display racks and shelves, electric signs, refrigerators, and so on.* Furthermore, things such as gasoline pumps and hydraulic car lifts are eligible for the credit, even though they are attached to the ground.

(2) *Elevators and escalators.*

(3) Certain tangible *real-property-like assets* (except buildings) tied closely to (that is, an "integral part" of) manufacturing, production, or extraction, or used in furnishing transportation, communications and certain utilities.

(4) Certain *research and storage facilities* used in connection with manufacturing, production and so forth—even though not an integral part of the activity. Thus, there's a credit for a farmer's silo, oil and gas storage tanks, and wind tunnels. There have been difficulties in the past in deciding exactly what constitutes a qualifying "storage facility." The tax law now specifically provides that it includes a facility for the bulk storage of *fungible* commodities (including those in a liquid or gaseous state).

"Special purpose buildings": Buildings generally do not qualify as Sec. 38 property. This includes such assets as apartments, factory and office buildings, warehouses, and the like. But certain "special purpose buildings" do qualify— that is, a structure so closely related to the equipment it houses that its life ends with that of the equipment.

"Structural components"—in general. Structural components generally do not qualify for the credit. Examples include "integral parts" of a building such as a central air conditioning or heating system, and plumbing, wiring and lighting. Also, walls, floors, doors, windows, and other "structural components."

Recapture: For investment credit property placed in service after 1980, a "two-percent" recapture rule applies. As pointed out, there is a 6% investment credit for 3-year recovery property and a 10% credit for 5-year recovery property. That comes out to 2% a year—and that's how recapture works. Each full year the property is held before disposition reduces recapture by 2%. If the property is disposed of after a full year, for example, only 4% of the credit for 3-year property is subject to recapture—only 8% in the case of a credit for 5-year property—and so on.

HOW YOUR BUSINESS CAN DEDUCT MORE THAN IT SPENDS ON EQUIPMENT PURCHASES

The big benefit in tax shelters is that investors can often write off more than they invest. Business owners can get the same benefit without investing in a tax shelter. Whether or not your business is incorporated, you can make an everyday outlay to maintain or expand operations and—

▶ **DEDUCT MORE THAN YOU SPEND:** The deduction and credits for the purchase of equipment and furnishings can far exceed the cash outlay in the year of purchase.

Result: An excess writeoff that can shelter other income from tax.

▶ **THREE PART SHELTER:** The tax shelter is built on three breaks written right into the tax law: (1) You can elect to expense—to deduct currently—up to $5,000 of equipment and furnishings purchased each year. The portion of your cost that isn't expensed is eligible for (2) the 10% investment tax credit and (3) fast depreciation writeoffs.

Key points: You get the same three breaks—in the same amounts—whether the equipment is put into service in January or in December. And the tax savings are the same if you pay all cash or finance most of the purchase price.

To see how you can come out net dollars ahead, let's look at an—

Example: Reliable Sales Corp. is in the 18% tax bracket (i.e., it has taxable income between $25,000 and $50,000). In June, 1986, it purchases $10,000 of office equipment. Reliable makes a $2,000 downpayment and pays another $1,000 during the year.

Reliable takes a 1986 expensing deduction of $5,000. In addition, it can claim a 10% investment credit on the $5,000 of equipment cost that isn't expensed. In the 18% bracket, the $500 credit is the equivalent of $2,778 in deductions.

The office equipment has a five-year depreciation under the tax law. So, in 1986, the Reliable is entitled to a depreciation deduction equal to 15% of $4,750 ($10,000 cost less $5,000 amount expensed less one-half the $500 investment credit). This works out to a depreciation deduction of $712.

▶ **MULTIPLE WRITEOFF:** Combining expensing, the investment credit deduction equivalent and the depreciation deduction, Reliable gets a total writeoff of $8,490 on its 1986 return. In other words, the corporation not only can write off the $3,000 it lays out in 1986—but another $5,490 as well.

Interest-free loan from Uncle Sam: Just as with a tax shelter investment, this excess writeoff goes to offset some of Reliable's other taxable income. Again as with tax shelter investments, the quicker the corporation claims its depreciation deductions on the equipment, the less it will have in later years—and the bigger its tax bill will be then. But in the meantime, Reliable can use the tax savings from its multiple writeoff for expanding its business. It is as if it had received an interest-free loan from Uncle Sam.

HOW THE RIGHT KIND OF LEASING ARRANGEMENT CAN HELP YOU TAKE TAX-SHELTERED PROFITS OUT OF YOUR COMPANY

A Tax Court decision points up how an owner of a closely-held company can set up a special tax shelter opportunity. The owner can lease property to the company. If the rent is tied into the gross sales of the company, the owner can effectively get—

▶ **DEDUCTIBLE DIVIDENDS:** An owner wants to take advantage of every opportunity to pay out corporate earnings that are deductible—for example, a bonus earned as a company executive that's keyed into company profits. On the other hand, if the earnings are paid out as dividends, the earnings are taxed twice—once to the corporation and again to the owner. And they're not deductible by the corporation.

In this case, the owner used rents instead of bonuses to receive deductible earnings. He had his corporation pay him rent based on a fixed payment *plus* a percentage of company sales—something very close to a distribution of earnings.

Facts of the case: The Davis Company, a food distribution corporation, needed a new warehouse, but couldn't obtain financing to build one. So the company's shareholders, Mr. and Mrs. Davis, bought land, built a warehouse and leased it to the company. The lease was a 20-year net lease (the company paid all property taxes and maintenance costs).

Under the lease terms, the company was to pay the Davises an annual rent of $60,000 plus 1% of the company's annual gross sales in excess of $4 million. The year the lease was signed, the company's gross sales were only $2.3 million, and the Davises received only the $60,000 of fixed rent. But eight years later, sales had climbed to almost $10 million and the Davises received a total of $118,000.

The Government disallowed the company's rent deduction in excess of the $60,000 fixed payment. It contended that the percentage was excessive and was nothing more than a disguised dividend.

▶ **TAXPAYER VICTORY:** The Tax Court disagreed with the Government. It held that the company's entire $118,000 rent payout was deductible [Davis & Sons, Inc., TC Memo 1981-178].

Reason: There was a legitimate business purpose behind the leasing arrangement. When the company couldn't get financing for the needed facility, the Davises had to get it themselves and put up the building. Percentage leases are common in commercial real estate. Mr. and Mrs. Davis, as investors, were entitled to use the same technique with their company that they would use with any other business tenant.

True, the lease deal turned out to be a big success—receipts from the percentage arrangement were almost as high as the original base rent. But, said the Tax Court, the Government couldn't use hindsight to knock down the original lease agreement. When the lease was drawn up, its provisions were fair.

▶ **KEYS TO DEAL:** A Davis-type leasing arrangement will work—it will draw off company earnings to the shareholder on a tax-deductible basis—only if (1) there's a business reason for the deal and (2) the lease terms are reasonable. Best advice: If you want to lease property to your company, have an appraiser tell you what a fair rental value would be in an arm's length transaction. And by all means see your professional advisers before making a move.

HOW YOUR BUSINESS CAN TAKE TAX ADVANTAGE OF A SPECIAL KIND OF MUTUAL FUND

Corporations—the giants as well as the small incorporated business—get a big tax break that's not available to individuals. If your business invests its "loose change" in stocks, the dividend income is almost all tax-free.

▶ **BASIC BREAK:** Your corporation pays no tax on 85% of the dividends it receives on stock it owns in other companies. Put another way, only 15% of its dividend income is subject to tax. As a result, the effective corporate tax rate on dividend income can be no higher than 6.9%. It's even lower for small corporations— as low as 2.3%.

Comparison: Your corporation's interest income and short-term capital gains are fully taxable. The tax rate is the same here as it is on business profits—ranging from 15% on the first $25,000 of taxable income to 46% on taxable income above $100,000.

So when it comes to investing corporate cash, dividend-paying stock has a built-in tax advantage. From a tax point of view, the more dividends, the better. In fact, there are mutual funds designed to help you take advantage of this special tax saver.

How a typical fund works: The fund invests primarily in dividend-paying stocks, with the remainder invested in interest-bearing obligations. Most of the stocks are preferred issues and pay so-called variable dividends. These are dividends tied to the yield of Treasury securities and adjusted periodically to reflect current rates. Unlike preferred stock that pays a fixed dividend, these shares are less likely to fluctuate in value with changes in interest rates because they always pay the going rate. Investors may choose to have the dividends automatically reinvested or paid out in cash.

The mutual fund itself pays no tax. It distributes the dividends it receives to the corporate investors. And dividends distributed by the fund are treated as dividends by the recipients. So they are 85% tax-free to your corporation. (Distributions attributable to capital gains or interest income do not qualify for this tax break.)

Q: Can't your corporation do the same thing as the mutual fund?

A: Of course. A corporation can invest directly in common or preferred stocks whose dividends qualify to the 85% corporate dividend deduction. However, many businesses prefer investing through these special mutual funds for the same reason many individual investors prefer mutual funds—namely, professional management and diversification of investment dollars.

▶ **FINAL POINT:** Whether you invest directly or through a fund, in the final analysis, your net return depends on the success of the underlying investments. If they go sour, no special tax break will help. You'll want to consult with your investment adviser before making a move.

HOW TO GET THOUSANDS OF TAX-FREE DOLLARS FROM YOUR COMPANY BY USING AN INTEREST-FREE LOAN

An interest-free loan has to be one of the best bargains around. Instead of borrowing from a financial institution and paying sky-high interest, you borrow from a friendlier lender—your corporation—and pay zero interest. The dollars you save amount to a significant dollars and cents benefit:

> **Example:** You want to buy a new home and will need to borrow an additional $50,000 to help finance the purchase. If you get a mortgage from the bank for, say, 15 years at 12½% interest, you will end up paying about $59,783 in interest. If you get the same loan from your company—and pay zero interest—you wind up with an average "cash bonus" of about $3,985 a year for 15 years.

From the tax view point: You are considered to have received taxable compensation equal to the foregone interest—the interest your company could have charged, but didn't. However, you are also entitled to an offsetting interest deduction for the interest you would have ordinarily paid on the loan—but didn't. Bottom line: a tax-free fringe benefit.

Caution: The interest-free loan should either be a demand loan (that is, repayable in full on demand by the company) or a term loan conditioned on continued employment.

However, if a regular term loan (not conditioned on employment) is used, then the deal isn't as attractive.

Here's why: You get your compensation income and interest deduction with a term loan—but they don't come at the same time. Under the tax rules, the entire compensation element on an interest-free term loan is taxed to you the year the loan is made. But your deduction for the interest element is spread out over the term of the loan. So in the year the loan is made, you will have all of your taxable compensation, but only a small interest deduction to offset it. On the other hand, a term loan is better for your company: It gets a big upfront compensation deduction, while the interest income is spread out over the term.

Another break: Unlike many other tax-sheltered fringe benefits, your company does not have to make interest-free loans available to all employees. It can limit coverage to a select few. However, if you and the other employees receiving loans are also shareholders, watch out: If the deemed payment from your company is made to you in your shareholder capacity, the payment is *not* compensation; it's a dividend. And a dividend is *not* deductible by your company.

In addition, the tax rules say that, if you are a more-than-5% shareholder, the deemed payment will be treated as a shareholder loan unless you can present "clear and convincing evidence" that the transaction is solely compensatory in nature.

Of course, having the payment treated as a dividend is not the end of the world. True, your company loses its deduction. But you still have your interest deduction to offset your dividend income—in effect, a tax-free dividend. However, to avoid any dividend complication in the first place, here's—

▶ **WHAT TO DO:** Consider the following moves: (1) Have the company spell out in the corporate minutes that the loan is being provided for compensatory reasons and give a rundown on the valuable services you have provided the company; (2) Be sure to maintain your traditional dividend policy while the loan is outstanding; (3) Show that the company has a policy of providing employee loans by offering interest-free loans to key employees who are *not* shareholders.

Note: A no-interest company loan, whether made to an employee or to a shareholder, may qualify for this—

▶ **EXCEPTION:** There are no tax consequences to a no-interest loan if (1) total loans between the company and the taxpayer are less than $10,000, and (2) tax avoidance is not a principal purpose of the loan.

HOW YOU CAN DEDUCT SOME HOME EXPENSES AS BUSINESS EXPENSES

A number of important tax law changes enable many more taxpayers to claim office-at-home deductions on their tax returns. In effect, this type of deduction enables you to transform part of your nondeductible household expenses into dollar-saving deductions.

Background: The tax law allows someone who conducts business out of a home to deduct home expenses (such as utilities and maintenance) related to that business. In general, you can deduct these expenses only if (1) a part of your home is used regularly and exclusively as (2) your "principal place of business" or as a place to meet with customers in the normal course of your business. And if you use the home-office as an employee, it must be for the convenience of your employer.

Originally, Government regualtions said that the business had to be your primary business. But now the Government says you can have a separate principal place of business for each of your businesses—so a side-line business run out of your home can qualify for the deduction.

A portion of your home must be used exclusively for business. However, the portion need not be a separate room. It can be just the part of a room where your desk and business supplies are kept.

Caution: You get no deductions if your activities are not substantial enough to constitute a business. For example, managing your stock portfolio isn't enough. On the other hand, running a part-time consulting business out of your home clearly qualifies.

Let's say you or your spouse conducts a profit-making enterprise out of your home. Which expenses can you deduct, and how do you figure your deduction?

Answer: First off, any expenses directly connected with your business—i.e., supplies, telephone, postage—are 100% deductible. In addition, you can also deduct part of home-maintenance and repair expenses that are related to your office-at-home. Examples: Utilities, insurance, trash removal, even some home repairs (e.g., repairs to the home heating or air conditioning system). Finally, you can also claim depreciation deductions for the portion of your home that is used for business (if you rent your home, you deduct part of the rent).

How do you allocate these home expenses to your business? *Answer:* You allocate either on a percentage of area used or on a percentage of rooms used. Thus, if a home is 1,500 square feet, and the office at home is 150 square feet, then you can deduct 10% of home expenses that relate to the business conducted at the home. If your home has eight rooms about the same size, and one room is used as an office at home, then one-eighth of the home expenses are deductible.

Casualty losses: If you suffer a casualty loss to the business part of your home, you can write off the loss as a business expense. Of course, a casualty loss to the personal part of your home can be written off as an itemized deduction. But personal casualty losses are deductible only to the extent that your total losses (counting only losses in excess of $100 per casualty) exceed 10% of your adjusted gross income. On the other hand, casualty losses that are deductible as business expenses can be completely written off—the $100 per casualty reduction and 10% floor simply don't apply.

Furnishings: Let's say you need a desk in your office-at-home and you move a desk out of the family den. Then the desk becomes depreciable business property—just like the equipment your company buys. Your basis for figuring your depreciation deductions is the lower of (1) the original cost for the desk or (2) its fair market value at the time you convert it to business property.

Repairs: You can fully deduct the cost of repairs to your office-at-home. And repairs that benefit the entire home (e.g., roof repairs) are deductible to the extent your home is used for business.

▶ **ANOTHER DEDUCTION:** If you're like many business people, you do a great deal of business over your home phone. The good news is that the cost of these calls is deductible, whether or not you qualify for other "office-at-home" deductions. How much? Well, only the cost that's attributable to the percentage of business use of the phone. If you have only one phone at home this allocation can be a tedious chore.

▶ **WHAT TO DO:** To simplify figuring your deduction, install a separate phone at home for your business use. This will pinpoint your deduction and eliminate difficult allocation problems.

KEY STRATEGIES TO SLASH YOUR PAYROLL TAXES

Social Security and unemployment taxes have become a big part of the cost of running any business—large or small. But by making some small changes in your payroll setup, you may be able to put a dent in your tax bill.

#1—How Two Corporations Can Sometimes Operate as Cheaply as One

An owner of more than one business often operates each as a separate corporation. This is usually done for a non-tax reason. One cannot be held liable for the debts of another if they are separate corporations. But dividing up your businesses among different croporations can also have important tax consequences.

▶ **PAYROLL TAX TRAP:** Unless you handle things right, you could wind up paying more Social Security taxes than if your businesses were combined in one corporation.

Here's why: There's a limit on how much Social Security tax an employer must pay on each employee's wages. For 1986, the limit is 7.15% on the first $42,000 of wages—or a maximum tax of $3,003. But if an employee works for two different employers, each must compute the Social Security tax—and each one could wind up paying up to $3,003.

Result: If an employee of yours works at two or more of your businesses—and they are operated as separate corporations—each corporation is generally treated as a different employer. So your total Social Security tax payment on the shared employee could exceed the normal $3,003 maximum.

▶ **WHAT TO DO:** Instead of each corporation paying wages separately to the shared employee, make one corporation the "common paymaster" and have it make the payments for the other corporations.

New result: Under the Social Security tax rules, if one corporation acts as a common paymaster for "related" corporations, only the common paymaster corporation will be treated as the employer for shared employees. So even though an employee may work for two or three of your corporations, you will owe no more than the one-employer maximum on Social Security taxes.

Example: The Green family owns two stores that are operated as two separate corporations. Mrs. Green is the treasurer for both corporations. Her total compensation for the year is $60,000—one-half from each corporation. Without a common paymaster, each corporation would have to pay $2,145 in Social Security tax on her salary (7.15% of $30,000). That would mean a total of $4,290 for the two corporations. But with a common paymaster the family businesses come out—

Payroll tax dollars ahead: For Social Security purposes, the corporation that is the common paymaster is treated as Mrs. Green's sole employer. So the corporation is only liable for $3,003 in Social Security tax. That's a Social Security tax savings of $1,287 on Mrs. Green's wages.

More tax savings: Green's stores may share other employees in addition to Mrs. Green. As long as an employee's total salary for the year exceeds $42,000, your corporations come out ahead with a common paymaster.

When are corporations "related"? Your corporations come within the tax law definitions of "related." The tax law says corporations are related if any one of the following tests is satisfied at any time during the calendar quarter: (1) The corporations are members of a group where more than 50% of the stock of one corporation is owned by one or more of the other corporations, (2) 50% or more of one corporation's officers are concurrently officers of the other corporations, or (3) 30% or more of one corporation's employees are concurrently employed by another corporation.

Important: As we said, the common paymaster must be one of the related corporations. The Government says it is not sufficient if an individual (say, the treasurer of the related corporations) simply serves as payroll agent for the corporations [Rev. Rul. 81-21, 1981-1 CB 482].

> ▶ **WHAT TO DO:** The corporation designated as common paymaster should pay each shared employee his or her full salary, drawing it from a single bank account. The designated corporation should also be responsible for keeping the books and payroll records on the shared employees.

If your corporations use a common paymaster, but have overlooked the payroll tax break, you can get a do-it-yourself tax refund.

> ▶ **HOW TO HANDLE IT:** Overpayment on the employer's share of Social Security tax deposited earlier in the year can be used to offset Social Security taxes due on a later quarter's return. In addition, to get the refund the employer must reimburse the employee for his share of the overwithholding and then claim a credit for both portions on the quarterly return. Be sure the paymaster gets a receipt from the employee.

#2—How To Get Big Unemployment Tax Savings Next Year By Making A Small Voluntary Contribution This Year

You can reduce your unemployment tax liability for next year—and thus increase your working capital—by making a voluntary contribution to your state unemployment tax fund this year. Nearly half the states allow such payments.

> ▶ **BUILD UP YOUR RESERVES:** The key to this strategy lies in increasing your unemployment tax account's reserve just enough to push it into a lower rate bracket.

In some cases this can be accomplished for $100 or less—and the savings can be much larger.

To see how a voluntary contribution works in practice, let's look at this—

Hypothetical example: Baker Company, in State X, has a taxable annual payroll of $250,000 and a net credit of $24,750 in its unemployment tax account. At this payroll-to-credit ratio, the company pays a tax of $1,500 a year. But if the company had a credit of $25,000 (just $250 higher than the current figure), its tax bill would be cut in half—dropping to $750.

▶ **TAX-SAVING MOVES:** When permitted by state law, the company may make the extra payment of $250 so it can earn a lower tax rate and cut its tax bill in half. *Net savings:* $500.

Q. How can I tell how large a voluntary contribution is needed to reduce my tax rate?

A. Your state will notify you of the reserve balance in your unemployment insurance account. This, when compared with your average payroll (in some states, average taxable payroll) will tell you your reserve ratio. At least annually, states publish a table showing how the tax rates line up for employers with different reserve ratios.

Key point: The balance in your account must be near the lower limit of a tax bracket for a voluntary contribution to be economical. For instance, say Baker needed to make a voluntary contribution of $1,000, or even $800 to put itself into the next tax bracket. That would be larger than the potential tax saving.

▶ **WHAT TO DO:** Condition acceptance of your voluntary contribution on an actual decrease in your unemployment insurance tax rate. To be deductible for Federal income tax purposes, the contribution must reduce your tax rate.

Q. When I reduce my tax rate, I also reduce the flow of funds into my unemployment insurance account. Couldn't this lead to higher taxes in later years?

A. Yes. The voluntary contribution strategy may give you a tax deferral instead of an outright tax saving. Some of the tax reductions may be "recaptured" in later years through higher tax rates. But "volunteering" now could be an excellent way to conserve cash that may be vitally needed next year.

Chapter 6

How To Tap An Overlooked Source Of Big Tax Deductions

Many self-employed business people and employees must do a lot of business traveling and entertaining, but many are missing out on the full deductions they're entitled to. For example, how many people in business know how to deduct part of the cost of a vacation, write off the cost of home entertainment, or how to take their spouse along on a business trip and deduct part of the cost? Do you know there are two ways to deduct your business auto expenses, and how to cope with the latest, tough recordkeeping rules?

This Chapter shows the practical day-to-day applications and dollar-saving possibilities hidden away in the T&E rules—and how to comply with the rules with a minimum of time and trouble.

HOW TO GET BIG TAX WRITEOFFS FOR YOUR BUSINESS CAR

A taxpayer who uses his car for business can figure his deductions using one of two methods. The first is easy to use but restricts your deductions. The second yields a maximum writeoff but requires more recordkeeping.

Method #1—Automatic mileage deduction: Also known as the standard mileage allowance, this is a simplified, Government-approved method for figuring your car expenses. Instead of deducting some or all of your actual business expenses, you deduct a flat amount for each business mile you drive during the year.

The amounts are changed from time to time by the Government. But here are the current figures: 21¢ a mile for the first 15,000 business miles driven during the year and 11¢ for each annual business mile above 15,000. In addition, after the car has been fully depreciated, you can deduct 11¢ for each business mile. You can also claim an investment credit for the business portion of the car's cost, as long as business use exceeds 50% of total use.

> **Example:** Mr. Johnson buys a new business car. He drives 30,000 miles each year, 20,000 of which are on business travel.

Result: If Johnson uses the automatic mileage method, he can deduct $3,700 in each of the first three years—15,000 miles at the 21¢ rate and 5,000 miles at the 11¢ rate. The amount of Johnson's deduction is audit-proof. The government says he can deduct it regardless of what his actual expenses are.

Under the automatic mileage rules, a car is considered fully depreciated after a cumulative 60,000 miles have been deducted at the 21¢ rate. So, beginning in the fourth year, Johnson will be limited to a deduction of $2,200 each year—20,000 miles at the 11¢ rate.

Q: Which expenses can't you deduct if you use the automatic deduction?

A: You cannot deduct any of your fixed and operating car costs allocable to business use. In other words, you don't get any separate deductions for gasoline, oil, repairs, licenses, insurance and depreciation; these are all built into the mileage deduction. But you can deduct parking fees and tolls in addition to the mileage deduction, as long as they are paid in connection with business travel.

Q: What sort of records do I have to keep if I use the automatic mileage method?

A: You have to keep records showing when and where you have traveled, how many miles you traveled, and the business purpose of the travel. However, you do not have to keep track of out-of-pocket car expenses such as gas, oil, maintenance, and so forth.

Method #2—Actual expense deduction: With this method, you can deduct the entire cost of operating a car you use exclusively for business. This includes more than the cost of gas, oil, repairs, insurance, etc. You are also entitled to depreciation deductions. If your car was placed in service after 1980, you can write off 25% of its cost in the first year, 38% the second year, and 37% the third year, if the car is used solely for business. You are also entitled to an investment tax credit for the year you place a business car in service.

New dollar limits: Dollar limits are imposed on the tax breaks for business cars placed in service after June 18, 1984:

● If the car was placed in service after June 18, 1984, and before April 3, 1985, the investment tax credit cannot exceed $1,000. And depreciation deductions cannot exceed $4,000 in the first year and $6,000 in subsequent years.

● If the car was placed in service after April 2, 1985, the investment credit cannot exceed $675, first-year depreciation is limited to $3,200, and annual depreciation in subsequent years is limited to $4,800.

The dollar limits are reduced proportionately to the extent a car is used for personal travel during the year. If you use your car for both business and personal purposes, you keep a record of all your expenses and deduct the portion allocable to business use. This is done on the basis of mileage. If business use of a car placed in service after June 18, 1984, does not exceed 50% of total use, you get no investment tax credit. And the business portion of the car cost must be recovered using a special depreciation schedule (10% the first year, 20% in years two through five, 10% in the sixth year). The dollar limits for depreciation (see above) work in conjunction with the new 50% requirement.

> **Example:** A taxpayer who buys a $20,000 car on January 1, 1986, and uses it 40% for business can't claim an investment credit. He can only write off $8,000 of the cost over the extended depreciation period (40% of $20,000). And he can only depreciate $800 of the cost in the first year (lesser of 10% of $8,000 or 40% of the first-year limit of $4,000).

An employee who uses his own car on employer business must prove the business use of the car is for the employer's convenience and is a condition of employment. If he doesn't, the employee is denied the credit and cannot claim ACRS depreciation deductions for the car. However, the employee may use the automatic mileage deduction and write off 21¢ for each of the first 15,000 business miles he travels during the year, plus 11¢ for each additional business mile.

Special Rules for Leased Business Cars

While there are dollar caps on the investment credit and depreciation deductions for business car owners, there are no dollar caps as such for taxpayers who lease business cars. The taxpayer writes off that portion of the lease payments allocable to business use (i.e., if 80% of total mileage is for business use, the taxpayer deducts 80% of his lease payments).

However, the tax law does reduce the tax benefit from lease deductions if the taxpayer rents a "luxury car" or does not use the leased car predominantly for business. The reduction applies to autos leased after June 18, 1984. For autos leased after that date and before April 3, 1985, a "luxury car" is one worth more than $16,500 when the lease is signed. For autos leased after April 2, 1985, a "luxury car" is one worth more than $11,250 when the lease is signed.

How the new rules work in a nutshell: The leased car user is required to include a specified amount in gross income—a "deduction offset." This deduction offset reduces the effective tax savings a taxpayer gets for leasing a car for business use. The exact amount of the deduction offset is figured using a series of tables set forth in IRS Reg. 1.280F-4T(d) and IRS Reg. 1.280F-1T. See your tax adviser for details.

Your Recordkeeping Chores

The recordkeeping required for out-of-pocket expenses depends on how you use the car:

● When you use the car around town for business trips—visiting local suppliers and customers, for example—you should keep receipts (when available) for items such as gas, oil, tune-ups, and so forth. You do not have to keep a log of such expenses.

● When you are out of town on business and travel by car, you have to keep records that list time, place, business purpose and amount of your car expenses. And you have to keep receipts of all $25-and-over expenditures.

Q: Do I have to keep a record of my business mileage?

A: Yes. You must keep a record of business mileage whether you use your car around town or drive it on an overnight trip away from home.

Your record (kept in a diary, log, or other recordkeeping system) must include the following entries:

(1) The date of the use.

(2) The name of the car user (required only if the user is someone other than the regular driver).

(3) The business trip's mileage. You can record the beginning and ending odometer reading or simply enter the number of miles traveled.

(4) The business purpose of the travel.

One entry is enough for a round trip or for a period of uninterrupted business use. Incidental personal use (e.g., going for lunch) is not considered an interruption of business use. The entry should be made "at or near" the time of the business travel. The IRS says that once-a-week entries meet this requirement.

One more recordkeeping step: You must also record your car's odometer readings at the beginning and end of each year. Reason: Deductions for a car used for both business and personal purposes are based on the ratio of business mileage to total mileage. In addition, if you do not use a car put in service after June 18, 1984, more than 50% of the time for business, you lose the investment credit and must use a five-year rather than a three-year writeoff period. And if you lease a car, your rental deduction is reduced if you do not use the car more than 50% for business. The easiest way to compare business mileage to total mileage is by having those beginning and ending odometer readings. At year end, you simply add up total business miles traveled from your diary pages and divide the result by your total miles for the year (ending mileage less beginning mileage). That gives you the ratio of business use to total use.

If Your Company Supplies You With A Business Car

If you use the company car for business driving only, there aren't any tax consequences for you. However, if you use the company car for personal driving (commuting, weekend trips, etc.) then you will be taxed on the value of your personal use. The value is measured using one of four methods:

Method #1—Actual cost: Here, the yardstick is what it would have cost you to lease a comparable car from a third party (e.g., a commercial car leasing company). The annual lease cost is then multiplied by the employee's personal use percentage (based on mileage).

> **Example (1):** XYZ Corp. leases a fleet of business cars for three years. Smith uses one of the cars, valued at $15,000, 60% for business and 40% for personal driving. Because of its fleet discount, XYZ Corp.'s annual lease cost for the car is only

$4,200. But if Smith rented the car on his own for three years, it would cost him $4,600 a year.

Result: Under Method #1, Smith's annual compensation income for personal use of the car is $1,840 (40% of $4,600).

Method #2—Table Amount: This method is a Government-approved short-cut. The employer and employee can value personal use with reference to a special Government table. The amounts approximate annual lease cost for four-year leases and include maintenance and insurance. The fair market value of the car is determined as of the date the car is made available to the employee. If the car was made available to him prior to 1985, the car's fair market value on January 1, 1985 is used.

> *Example (2):* Same facts as in Example (1) except that Method #2 is used. Smith's compensation income would be $1,740 (40% of $4,350, the annual lease value of a $15,000 car).

Method #3—Commuting Value: This is a special method that may be used only if the employer (1) requires the employee to commute in the car for business reasons and (2) has a policy limiting personal use of the car to commuting. This method cannot be used by employees who own a 5%-or-greater interest in their companies. If these requirements are met, the employee can value each one-way commute at $1.50.

Method #4—Cents-per-mile: Under this special method, the number of miles driven by an employee is multiplied by a standard mileage rate: 21¢ per mile for the first 15,000 miles and 11¢ for each additional mile above 15,000. These figures include the cost of gas, so if the employee pays for gas himself, the figures are reduced by 5½¢ per mile.

Some Of Your "Commuting" Expenses May Really Be Deductible "Transportation" Expenses

There's a distinct difference between transportation expenses and travel expenses. Basically, transportation is local in nature. What's more, it has a narrower, more on-the-job flavor than does travel. For example, a transportation expense is limited to the actual cost of the ticket you buy or the fare you pay, e.g., taxi fare and tips, train, plane, bus and subway rides. It does not include "travel items" such as meals and lodging.

If you use your own car, then the cost of gas, oil, maintenance, tolls, garaging and the like (as far as they are tied in with business) can be deducted. So can depreciation, to the same extent.

What about commutation? The cost of getting to and from your job and home is a personal expense and not deductible. This is true whether your job is 7 blocks or 7 miles distant from your home. Nor does it matter that public transportation is not available, or that you may be physically disabled and can't use normal transportation methods. Sounds rough, doesn't it? It is—but it's not hopeless.

What looks like "commuting" may be deductible. Never give up a tax deduction simply because the facts seem to fit into a general rule denying it. It sometimes pays to take a second look. For instance, what at first glance looks like commuting may still be deductible in certain settings.

> **Example 1:** Let's assume your residence and job are in Baltimore, Md. You go on temporary assignment to supervise a job about 25 miles from Springfield, Mo. There's no place to live near the job, so you have to stay in a Springfield hotel. You can deduct the costs of going to and from work while in Springfield. These are necessary business expenses in getting to and from a temporary assignment—they're not commuting. And, of course, you can deduct the costs of the round trip to Springfield (from Baltimore), and meals and lodging while in Springfield—these are travel expenses.

> **Example 2:** You live and work in Chicago and your company has two offices. You often travel from home to Office 1, then to Office 2, then back home in the evening.

Result: The trip between Office 1 and Office 2 is business travel. Only the travel from your home to Office 1 and from Office 2 to home are considered commuting. Reason: A trip between two business locations is treated as a business trip.

> **Example 3:** Many times, while you are on your way to the office each morning, you stop and visit a customer's office.

Result: Your customer's office is considered a business location, so that the portion of the trip between your customer's office and your office becomes a business trip. In other words, by stopping at your customer's office, you have effectively converted part of your personal commuting into a business trip. That portion of your trip from home to the customer is, of course, not deductible.

> **Example 4:** You are taking a refresher course to bring yourself up to date on the latest developments in your field. You drive from your office to your classes at a local college near your home.

Result: Your trip between your office and class is business travel. Reason: Again, you are traveling between business locations. The place where you take work-related courses is considered a business location.

WHY BUSINESS TRAVEL YIELDS YOU MORE DEDUCTIONS THAN BUSINESS TRANSPORTATION

The cost of business travel is deductible. So is the cost of business transportation. But there is a big tax difference between the two.

▶ **KEY POINT:** Deductible transportation is limited to the cost of getting from one business location to another (e.g., taxi fare). It is only one of many costs that make up the cost of travel. Deductible travel is the cost of transportation—plus meals, lodging and the other expenses incidental to the trip.

For example, Mr. Green travels from Michigan to Texas to meet with his company's suppliers. He is fully reimbursed by his employer. All of the following are deductible by his company as travel expenses:

● The cost of getting from his home to the airport, and on the return trip, getting from the airport to his home.

● His air, rail or bus fares.

● Baggage charges and the cost of shipping special material such as samples and displays.

● Taxi fares or other transportation costs between the airport or station and his hotel and between his hotel and his Dallas work location (and back).

● Meals and lodging while in Dallas.

● Cleaning and laundry expenses in Dallas.

● Any tips he pays along the way to porters, hotel people and waiters.

● Telephone and telex charges.

Travel costs are deductible whether you are a self-employed professional or businessperson, a partner, or an employee of a corporation. If you are self-employed or are not reimbursed for the expenses, you get the deduction. If your company reimburses you for travel expenses, it gets the deduction and the reimbursement is tax-free to you.

Q: Can I deduct the cost of travel on every business trip?

A: Definitely not. It's fully deductible travel only if you are away from your tax home—your main place of business—on an overnight trip.

How to account for your business travel expenses: The government allows business travel deductions only if you keep a record of ALL your expenses while on travel status. The records, made in your diary at or near the time the expense was incurred, must show the following:

(1) The time (dates you left and returned for each trip and number of days on business);

(2) The place (the name of your city or other destination);

(3) The business purpose of the travel; and

(4) The amount of each separate expense.

How To Get A Trouble-free Deduction for Meals While Away on Business

You can claim a deduction for meals while away from home on a business trip without having to record the amount of the expense or keep receipts for the meals.

The automatic deduction is $14 per day for a stay away from home in one general area lasting fewer than 30 days, and $9 for each day if the travel requires a stay of 30 days or more. You need only prove time, place and business purpose of the travel.

There are a number of special rules that must be followed in connection with the new automatic deduction.

The 30-day period: A taxpayer is considered to be away from home on business, when figuring the 30-day period, even though he leaves the business location for a brief time—for example, a weekend trip home or a recreational side trip. So you may exceed the 30-day limit, and thus be subject to the lower $9 limit even though part of the time is spent at home.

▶ **SILVER LINING:** You are entitled to the automatic meal deduction for those days spent at home or on recreation. So, in effect, you can deduct the meals you eat at home.

Reimbursed expenses: An employee who is reimbursed for his meals can use the automatic deduction only if (1) the employee is reimbursed a separate amount for meals (not given a per diem allowance, which covers both meals and lodging), (2) he includes the reimbursement in income, (3) he does not have to account to the employer for the actual cost, and (4) he is not a more-than-10% shareholder in the company.

First and last day of the trip: Taxpayers are not necessarily entitled to a full $14/$9 deduction for meals on the first and last day of a business trip away from home. You must make an allocation based on the amount of time actually spent away from home.

Actual expenses: A taxpayer of course, has the option of choosing between the automatic method and the actual expense method of figuring his meal expense deduction. But if he elects to use the new automatic deduction, he must use it to compute his meal deductions for the entire year.

▶ **FINAL POINT:** The convenience of the automatic meal deduction may be more than offset by the modest amounts allowed. What's more, a taxpayer is allowed only the $14/$9 amount regardless of where his business takes him—it is the same for every city in the country. So look things over carefully before you go the automatic deduction route.

HOW TO MIX BUSINESS AND PLEASURE AND COME OUT A BIG TAX WINNER

You are about to leave on an important business trip. You have been working hard and deserve a special reward. So your employer tells you to add a company-paid vacation to your upcoming business trip. For example, if the trip is going to take you to Denver for a week to call on customers, spend the weekend at nearby Aspen at the company's expense.

Payoff: Your company's payments for the business portion of the trip—the air fare to Denver and back and the meals and lodging in Denver—is a "tax-free working condition fringe benefit." What that means: You don't pay tax on the business portion. Only the remainder of the payments (the personal portion of the trip) is taxable income to you. However, if the trip were solely a company-paid vacation—you went just to Aspen—the entire cost would be taxable to you. In other words, by combining the vacation with a business trip, you have converted the value of the air fare there and back from taxable compensation to a tax-free reimbursement.

▶ **KEY TEST:** Your company must show that the primary purpose of the combined business-pleasure trip is business. One of the key factors used in determining a primary business purpose is time—the more time you spend on business, the better chance you have of proving a primary business purpose. The ultimate question is: Would you have made the trip to Denver even if you didn't get the vacation?

Q: Suppose my wife and two children come along on the combined business/pleasure trip and the company picks up their tab. Any breaks there?

A: The company's outlay for your family's expenses is fully taxable to you. However, you may not have to declare as much income as you think.

▶ **BASIC RULE:** You can exclude from tax the amount it would have cost you to go alone. And that can be substantially more than your share of the total family travel cost.

Example: Mr. Brown must go on a four day business trip for his company to New Orleans. If he goes alone, the trip would cost $1,200 (including air fare, meals and lodging). However, if he takes his spouse and two children and adds on three days to see the sights, the total cost comes to $2,200. (He gets family rates for the air fare and hotel room.)

▶ **LOW-COST VACATION:** His exclusion is not $550—one-fourth of the $2,200 the company spends. The full $1,200 is tax-free to Brown. The $1,000 extra the company spends on his vacation is taxable compensation to Brown. Brown's employer, of course, gets a deduction for the entire $2,200.

Protecting yourself—and the company: The company's reimbursement for the business portion of the trip—travel, meals and lodging while on business—is tax-free to you and deductible by the company only if the primary purpose of your trip is business.

The taxable personal portion of the trip is deductible by the company only if the company treats it as compensation. Your company can elect to treat the taxable portion of the trip (and other taxable fringe benefits) as paid on a pay period, quarterly, semi-annual or annual basis.

Caution: The employer cannot retroactively treat a business trip as compensation. For example, if the government audits a company's return and determines that a combined personal/business trip does not meet the primary purpose test, the company loses its deductions for everything but the business portion of the meals and lodging. Suppose an employee takes a company-paid trip but spends only two out of seven days on business. The company deduction is limited to the two day's worth of meals and lodging. Everything else is not deductible. The company cannot save its deductions by going back and claiming the balance of the trip was really "compensation." The employee, on the other hand, will be hit with full compensation income on the value of the trip.

▶ **WHAT TO DO:** Your company should set up strict recordkeeping guidelines for combined business-vacation trips. Separate records of business and vacation expenses must be kept. And the company should receive business expense records plus receipts that prove the primary business purpose of the trip and the amounts spent on the business portion.

Q: Does the combined business/personal trip work for partners and self-employeds as well as for corporate employees?

A: Yes it does. The same basic principles apply no matter how the business is organized. For example, the self-employed taxpayer simply takes a tax deduction on his or her return for the business portion of a combined business/pleasure trip. The partnership claims the tax deduction when compiling partnership taxable income. The personal portion is treated as if it were a salary payment to the partner.

How To Take A Government-Paid Personal Weekend Trip

You are out of town on business for a few weeks. A weekend arrives and you'd rather be home with your family. What's more, there's even a dollar saving in taking a quick round trip home. The air fare is less than your weekend hotel bill and meals. So you take the trip home and your company reimburses you for your cost.

Tax result: Your company takes a deduction for the reimbursement. And as long as you make an adequate accounting to your company, you don't have to report the expenses or reimbursement on your tax return. In other words, you get a tax-free, company-paid personal weekend trip. And the government approves of the idea.

To quote the Revenue Service: Travel expenses (including meals and lodging en route) from the area of your temporary place of work to your hometown and return are deductible "if they are no more than it would have cost you for meals and lodging had you stayed at your temporary place or work. If they are more, your deduction is limited to the amount you would have spent at your temporary place of work" [IRS Pub. 17, "Your Federal Income Tax"].

Example: You live and work in Miami. Your company sends you to New York on business for two weeks. You fly home to spend the intervening weekend with your family and your company picks up the tab. You leave New York on Friday evening and return on Monday morning to complete your assignment.

Your fare from New York to Miami and back is $200. To stay in New York over the weekend would have cost $225.

Result: Your weekend trip to Miami—your purely personal trip home—is fully deductible by your company and tax-free to you. Reason: The cost of the trip was below what it would have cost you to stay in New York.

Q: Suppose my round trip flight to Miami costs $250—I go first class. What is the story on my flight home?

A: The company can still deduct $225 of your fare—the amount a weekend stay in New York would have cost. And this portion of the air fare is tax-free to you. The $25 balance of the company-paid air fare is, however, taxed to you as compensation.

Caution: Be sure to check out of your hotel before you leave on the weekend trip and re-register when you return. Reason: You can't deduct the cost of the room and the trip. The Government says that if you pay for your hotel room over the weekend, the deduction for the trip home is limited to the amount you would have spent for only meals had you remained out-of-town instead of flying home.

Important: You must keep records of your meals and lodging costs while you're away from home on a business trip. These are necessary to get your T&E writeoffs. But the records are even more important if you take trips home during your stay. Reason: The records are the proof you must have to show what it would have cost you not to go home—and, thus, how much of your trip home is deductible.

HOW TO GET TRAVEL DEDUCTIONS FOR THE COST OF LOOKING AFTER INVESTMENT PROPERTY

Business travel expenses aren't the only deductible travel expenses. You can also deduct the cost of traveling necessary to "manage, conserve or maintain" investment property.

Actual case in point: An investor who lived in St. Louis owned three unimproved lots in Charlotte, North Carolina. Local ordinances required him to keep the lots clear of trash and underbrush, but he was unable to hire anyone in Charlotte to do the work for him. So he went to the area twice a year, did the work himself, and deducted what he spent for travel, meals and lodging. The Government said he wasn't entitled to deductions. But the Tax Court disagreed.

▶ **TAXPAYER VICTORY:** The work was necessary for the maintenance and management of the investment properties. Therefore, the investor was entitled to deduct the cost of doing the work, including his travel expenses [Harris, TC Memo 1978-332].

The tax principle involved in this case has wide application. For example, say you own a vacation home or condominium for rental and eventual sale. It's essential that you visit the property periodically to discuss problems with the property manager. You also replace damaged furniture and arrange for necessary repairs. Your traveling costs are deductible.

▶ **TAX RULE:** The cost of an investor's travel is deductible whenever the primary purpose of the trip is to do work necessary to maintain investment property.

Q: I'm an active real estate investor who owns several properties. I'm always on the look-out for new ones. Often, I try to mix my real estate business with pleasure. While I'm scouting for a possible new acquisition, I take some time out to relax and enjoy the area. What's the story on my travel expenses?

A: As long as the primary reason for your trips is to further your real estate business, you can enjoy the following—

▶ **TAX BREAKS:** (1) If the income property is acquired, the travel costs are added to your tax basis for the property. (2) If the property is not acquired, the travel costs are currently deductible.

How do you show the primary purpose of the trip is business? The time spent on business versus time spent on pleasure is critical.

Case in point: Mr. F owned five rental properties in his home town. He intended rental income to be his primary source of income at retirement. He took several trips during which he combined business with pleasure—he vacationed while he looked for new properties.

First, F traveled to Palm Springs and spent one day there investigating a townhouse. Later, he spent a week in Reno vacationing, two days of which were spent investigating real estate. The next year, F spent three days in Palm Springs investigating real estate, which he bought.

Result: F can deduct the first trip to Palm Springs since it was solely to investigate real estate and the property was not bought. The cost of the second trip to Palm Springs is added to the cost of the Palm Springs property he bought.

However, the cost of travel to and from Reno is not deductible. Reason: Only two days out of seven were spent on real estate business. But any direct expenses attributable to investigating real estate while in Reno (meals, lodging, gas etc. during the two days he spends on real estate business) are deductible [Fairey, TC Memo 1982-219].

HOW TO GET TROUBLE-FREE DEDUCTIONS FOR YOUR BUSINESS ENTERTAINMENT EXPENSES

The tax law recognizes that entertainment of prospective and existing clients and associates is a necessary cost of doing business. That's why business entertainment is deductible. But the rules in this area are surprisingly complex. Entertainment is deductible only if (1) it meets one of two tax law tests, and (2) the proper records are kept.

Tax Law Tests For Entertainment

As a general rule, entertainment is deductible only if it is (1) directly related to, or (2) associated with, the active conduct of your trade or business.

An entertainment expense is "directly related" if business is actually discussed and you have more than a general expectation of deriving a business benefit from the meeting. An expense is "associated with" your business if it precedes or follows a substantial business discussion. If you meet either test, you're in the clear:

● If your company reimburses you for the expense, it gets a deduction. And if you make a satisfactory accounting of the expense to your company, you don't have to include the reimbursement in your income.

● If you lay out the expense yourself and aren't reimbursed, you get the deduction.

If the expense meets neither test, there's generally no deduction.

What is an Entertainment Expense?

"Entertainment" covers a lot more than buying a meal or drinks for a business client or customer. It also includes amusement or recreational activities, whether or not the activities can be called "advertising" or "public relations." Generally, the term includes entertaining business guests at such places as restaurants, night-clubs, country clubs, theaters, sporting events, and so forth.

Let's run down some of the more common entertainment expenses and see how the rules work.

"On the Town"

What's the story on theater tickets, nightclubs, ball games and the like? The tax law is extremely rough on expenses such as these, if you have the "direct relationship" rule to contend with. After all, it's not easy to show that you conducted business discussions on these occasions. However, there is—

▶ **A WAY OUT:** If the theater party, nightclub treat, ball game or what have you directly precedes or follows a substantial and bona fide business discussion, and if the expense is "associated with the active conduct of [your] business," the cost is deductible. What's more, the business treat itself can be for goodwill. How soon must it precede or follow the business discussion? Answer: Unless the customer comes from out of town or other unusual circumstances exist, the entertainment will normally have to take place on the day of the business discussion.

Let's take a look at a few examples—and see, specifically, what is and isn't deductible.

Example (1): Some business prospects arrive in town Monday evening. You take them to the ball game and a night club. All day Tuesday you and they enter into substantial bona fide business discussions. Tuesday night, you're back at the night club. Result: Your entertainment expenses are deductible.

Example (2): Prospective local customers come to your office for lengthy discussions. That evening you treat them to dinner and the theater. Result: Your entertainment expenses are deductible.

Example (3): Jones, a valued customer, comes to the big city for a vacation. And it's all on you, including a few trips to the local night spots. And, why not? Over the course of any given year, Jones spends thousands and thousands of dollars with your firm. You're simply trying to retain his goodwill. Sad result: You can't deduct a penny—the entertainment didn't precede or follow any substantial business discussions.

Example (4): You go to a business convention. In between and after the business meetings you entertain your business associates and prospective customers. Happy result: The cost is deductible.

▶ **WATCH OUT:** If the entertainment is extravagant or lavish under the circumstances in which it is provided, you lose the deduction for the extravagant portion even if it's directly related to or associated with your trade or business. What's "lavish and extravagant?" The law doesn't spell it out—it's handled by the Revenue Service on a case-by-case approach. The same goes for "lavish and extravagant" travel expenses.

Pretty drastic, isn't it? And, remember, the "associated with" rule is the easy one, too. If the entertainment doesn't directly precede or follow substantial business discussions, as it doesn't in Example (3) above, you are left with just—

▶ **ONE LAST HOPE:** You'll have to prove that the entertainment was *directly related* to your trade or business. Moreover, *you must attend the function or send a representative.*

▶ **WATCH THIS:** Strictly goodwill entertainment is *out* under the "directly related" test. You must actually discuss business. What's more, you have to show more than a general expectation of realizing income or other business benefit at some indefinite future date. However, you *don't* have to close the business deal at the time of the entertainment.

Your **drinks and dinner:** There is a general rule holding that, even where all the tests are met and the deduction is allowed, it's limited to the difference between what you spend on yourself and your guests and what you'd normally spend on yourself.

Example: You take a customer out to dinner and spend $20 per person. If your own meal would normally come to $6, this rule limits your deduction to $34. Now, though, you get—

▶ **A BREAK:** The Revenue Service says it will *not* enforce this rule except in cases of abuse. Result: The entire $40 is deductible.

The "quiet business meal" rule is the big exception to the strict entertainment rules. Here's how it works: Say you take a customer or a client to dinner. Or, perhaps you prefer to take your customer to a hotel bar or cocktail lounge for a few drinks. As long as your guest is a business associate, you can deduct the tab *whether or not you discuss business,* make a sales pitch, or even if it's only for goodwill. The only limitation is that the atmosphere must be conducive to a business discussion. For example, a distracting influence such as a floor show would knock out the deduction. In addition, if you took the customer to a cocktail lounge where you arranged to meet with a lot of people, you'd probably also miss out on the deduction. And, of course, reciprocity deals—you buy mine today, I'll buy yours tomorrow—are out.

How to Back Up Your Deductions For
Business Entertainment

Every time you entertain a business client or associate you must list the following items in your T&E expense diary:

● The date of the entertainment, a description (e.g., "dinner") and where it took place.

● The amount of the expense. Some expenses can be aggregated—for example, you can have one entry for drinks, dinner and tips at a restaurant.

● The business reason for the entertainment, or the nature of the benefit to be gained.

● The business relationship to you of the person you entertain. If you entertain a number of people, you need not list all their names if their business relationship to you is evident. For example, if you take the principal officers of ABC Corp. to a ball game, you can simply describe your guests as "principal officers of ABC Corp." On the other hand, if you entertain both business and non-business guests at the same time, you must differentiate between the two categories of guests in your diary.

▶ **YOU MUST HAVE PROOF:** You must be able to prove the amount of any $25-or-over business-entertainment expense. The best form of proof is a receipt—for example, one from a restaurant or nightclub. A credit card slip will also suffice.

How to Entertain At Home And Enjoy Some Tax Breaks, Too!

The tax rules specifically permit deductions for the cost of home entertainment. If you pay for it, you get a deduction on your tax return. If your company pays, your company gets a deduction, and there's no tax cost to you.

▶ **KEY TAX BREAK:** You can write off the cost of entertaining business associates at your home if the entertainment directly precedes or follows a substantial business discussion.

What's more, this break is not limited to just a relaxing evening with a customer (although, of course, that's deductible, too). You can host a party for a customer, invite a few friends and still deduct a big share of your expenses. As long as the entertaining is not "extravagant"—and the Government says going first-class is not necessarily extravagant—it's deductible.

Example: Mr. Brown, a big customer of yours, and two of his junior execs are in town. After an afternoon of negotiations at your office, you invite the three of them and their wives to a party at your home. You also invite three other couples—just good friends. So there will be a total of 14 people at the party.

Result: Since the party directly follows a substantial business discussion, it qualifies as deductible business entertainment. And how much can you deduct? All the expenses except those attributable to your six non-business guests.

Let's say you hire a caterer for the party—cost $170. Liquor comes to around $50. And you ask the maid to work overtime to help out—another $20. Total cost of the party: $240. So you can write off $137 ($240 less 6/14 of $240).

Q: Is there any way to deduct home entertainment expenses that don't precede or follow a business discussion?

A: Sure. Say you have a customer and his wife over for dinner—and there's no business discussed before, after or during the meal. You can deduct the cost of the meal, even though it's only for goodwill. Reason: It's a "quiet business meal." When you entertain at home in an atmosphere conducive to a business discussion, the cost is deductible—even though no business is actually discussed.

HOW TO HANDLE RECORDKEEPING IF YOU ARE REIMBURSED FOR T&E EXPENSES

If you are an employee, you are probably reimbursed for what you spend on company travel and entertainment. The company, in turn, probably requires you to keep records and account for your expenses before it actually reimburses you. On the other hand, you may be an executive of your company who is reimbursed or given an expense account and is not required to make an accounting.

An employee's recordkeeping responsibilities depend on whether or not he is required to account for T&E expenses to his employer and how the reimbursement arrangement is set up. What's at stake: Reimbursements that are not accounted for properly are taxable to the employee. Here are the details:

How Accounting to Your Employer Brightens Your Tax Picture

The employee who adequately accounts to his employer for travel and entertainment in order to receive reimbursements benefits in two ways. As a general rule:

(1) The employee does not have to report either the expenses or the reimbursement on his tax return.

(2) An adequate accounting to his employer relieves him of the need to retain records and receipts. The burden of proof for T&E expenses shifts to the employer. The employer, in turn, relies on employee records and receipts to substantiate its deductions.

In essence, the employee is accounting to the company, instead of to the Government. He must either turn over his records to the company or prepare an expense account sheet from his records. He may have to submit receipts as well. It's a good idea for a company to assign T&E reimbursement and audit responsiblities to a company executive who does not normally incur these expenses. This way, the company isn't likely to run into the problems of an executive auditing his or her own reimbursement claims.

The type of recordkeeping required of the employee depends on how the reimbursement arrangement is set up.

Reimbursement At Government-Approved Rates

Recordkeeping is simplified if the employer uses Government-approved per diem allowances. The employee keeps a diary of time, place, mileage (in case of auto travel) and business purpose of his expenses. He does not have to account for the amount of his expenses. Nor is he required to keep receipts. Preparing an account sheet from his diary constitutes an "adequate accounting." The various Government-approved rates are as follows:

● The per diem rate is $44 for away-from-home travel within the U.S. In a high-cost location, the per diem rate equals the rate paid by the Federal Government to its employees on travel status at the location.

● The meals-only rate is $14 a day while on travel status within the U.S. The rate falls to $9 a day if the travel requires a stay of 30 days or more. The meals rate applies only if (1) lodging is provided in kind by the employer, or (2) the employer makes a direct payment to the provider of the lodging, or (3) there are no lodging expenses.

• The per diem rate for travel outside the U.S. can be the same as the per diem paid by the Federal Government to its employees traveling to the foreign location.

• The automatic mileage allowance is 21¢ per mile for an employee's use of his own car for company business.

As we said, the employee who uses a Government-approved rate does not have to keep track of the amount of his travel or transportation expenses. Nor does he have to keep receipts. And he does not have to retain a copy of his records after he has made an accounting to his employer. However, as with most rules, there are exceptions.

The first exception applies when the employee expects his expenses to exceed the reimbursements and wants to deduct the excess on his tax return. This excess can be deducted only if the employee keeps complete records (including the amount of each expense) and the necessary receipts and keeps copies of everything after he has made an accounting to the employer.

The second exception comes into play when the employee is related to the employer. Examples: A member of the family (e.g., son who is employed by his sole proprietor father), or an employee who owns more than 10% of the employer company's stock. A related employee must keep complete records and receipts, and retain copies of everything. Reason: He remains open to audit even though he has made an adequate accounting to his employer.

▶ **EXCEPTION TO EXCEPTION:** A related employee who receives a mileage reimbursement of 21¢ a mile or less does not have to make diary entries of the amount of each expense. Nor does he have to obtain receipts—even though he is related. He is treated the same as an employee. He keeps a diary that lists time, place, mileage, and business purpose. In addition, after he has accounted to the employer, the related employee need not retain a copy of his auto-use log.

Reimbursement of Actual Expenses

An employee must keep complete records and make a full accounting to his employer whenever he is reimbursed for his actual travel or transportation expenses. He must also make a full accounting if his reimbursement exceeds the Government-approved figures. In addition, full recordkeeping and accounting is always required for business entertainment. Reason: There is no approved Government reimbursement figure for business entertainment.

▶ **RECORDKEEPING REQUIREMENTS:** Again, the employee keeps complete records: time, place, mileage (in case of auto use), business purpose and amount of each expense for away from home travel and business entertainment. The expense account sheet he prepares for his employer must list all of these elements. He must also obtain receipts for all lodging expenses and all other $25-or-over T&E expenses and turn the receipts over to the employer.

Q: Should an employee retain copies of his T&E diary and receipts after he accounts to the company?

A: In general, there's no need to retain receipts. Reason: By making the proper accounting to the company, the employee is relieved of making an accounting to the Government. There are two exceptions:

(1) If the employee's expenses exceed his reimbursement, the employee must retain copies of his diary and receipts in order to claim a deduction for the difference.

(2) If the employee is related (e.g., he is a more than 10% company owner), he must keep copies of both his diary and receipts. Reason: He may be called upon to provide the government with the same records and receipts he gave the company.

Note: If the employee's reimbursement exceeds his T&E expenses, he must report the difference as income on his return.

If Employee is Reimbursed But is Not Required To Account to His Employer

A company may reimburse some of its employees for T&E expenses without requiring an accounting. For example, if the president of a closely held company does a lot of business travel and entertainment, he may simply be given an expense allowance. He's not required to explain how he spent the money since he would, in effect, be accounting to himself.

Tax consequences: The employee must declare the allowance as income on his personal tax return and then claim his actual travel and entertainment expenses on Form 2106.

▶ **RECORDKEEPING REQUIRED:** An employee who is not required to account to his employer for his T&E expenses must keep complete records of his expenses in order to deduct them on his tax return. He must also keep receipts for all lodging expenses, for other $25-or-over travel and entertainment expenses and for local transportation expenses, where available.

Chapter 7

How To Boost Your Income And Expand Your Wealth—Without Getting A Raise

Even a good-paying job and successful investments don't guarantee a comfortable living these days. Reason: A good-sized chunk of your income is drained off by taxes—as much as 50¢ on your top dollar. Fortunately, there's a ready-made solution in the form of tax-free or tax-favored employer-paid benefits and perks. These benefits, which are specifically approved by the tax law, allow you to boost your effective income without getting a raise.

The most powerful employer-paid fringe is the company retirement plan. Employer contributions are fully deductible by the employer and are not currently taxed to the employee. Since there's no tax dilution, more money accumulates—and boosts family wealth. This Chapter shows you how to squeeze the biggest possible tax shelter from your company's retirement plan (or your own plan, if you're self-employed).

While a retirement plan may be the number one fringe, it is far from the only tax-favored company benefit you can enjoy. As you'll see, there are a number of employer-paid benefit plans that can pay your personal bills—says your medical bills, your child's education, and so forth—all on a tax-sheltered basis.

THE TAX-SHELTERED WAY TO PROVIDE FOR YOUR RETIREMENT

For the majority of Americans who get paychecks, a good pension or profit-sharing plan is the best fringe benefit of all. In effect, the company sets aside part of your compensation and invests it—with the aid of competent financial specialists—for your retirement. This part of your compensation is tax-sheltered: The money set aside for you by the company does not appear on your W-2, and is not reported on your tax return. And your retirement account grows free of federal and state tax erosion until you make withdrawals.

Neither a profit-sharing nor a pension plan will do everything that you would like it to do. With a pension setup, you know how much retirement income you'll have from the plan. But you can't withdraw any funds before retirement, and you don't have a direct share in the company's success. With a profit sharing plan, you can pick up more money when the company is doing well, and you can withdraw funds prior to retirement. But you are not protected if there's a slump in your company's business, and you won't know precisely how much money you will accumulate by the time you retire.

How a Pension Plan Allows You to Foretell Your Retirement Future

A pension plan bases annual contributions on not only compensation but also age and years of past service. That's why older employees with many years of service are better off with a pension plan.

How a pension plan works: A pension plan is designed to provide a participant defined benefits (a pension) upon his retirement. So the employer's contribution is not related to company profits. Instead, the contribution is the amount actuarially necessary to provide the determined benefit. The maximum annual pension benefit can't exceed the lesser of $90,000, or the average of the employee's three consecutive highest years of compensation.

There are three basic types of pension plans.

1. *Fixed benefit plan:* After retirement you receive a definite percentage of your salary each year. For this purpose, your salary is (1) your average annual compensation during your entire employment or (2) an average of your compensation during a stated number of years before retirement. Obviously, for employees the second option is better. *Reason:* Your pay during your final work years should be higher than your average pay. So your pension will be based on a higher salary. Your compensation is the primary factor in a fixed benefit plan. The number of years of service doesn't enter into the computation of benefits. However, the plan may require employees to work for a minimum number of years of service before being eligible to participate.

2. *Unit benefit plan:* Under this plan, your years of service do enter into the computation of your pension benefit. You receive a unit of pension benefit for each year of credited service. The annual unit benefit can be expressed as a percentage of compensation or as a stated dollar amount.

Percentage of compensation: Each year you earn a pension benefit that is a percentage of your compensation. For example, in a one percent unit benefit plan, an employee with 25 years of credited service would be entitled to 25% of his compensation as an annual pension. In many plans, the percentage-of-compensation figure increases after an employee's salary exceeds a certain level.

> *Example:* A plan provides a pension of 1% of the first $10,000 of annual compensation plus 1¼% of any excess. An employee with 40 years of credited service and an annual compensation of $25,000 would be entitled to an annual pension of $11,500 computed as follows:
>
> 40% (40 × 1%) × 10,000. . . . . = $ 4,000
> 50% (40 × 1¼%) × 15,000. . . . . = $ 7,500
> Annual pension. $11,500

Stated dollar amount: The stated dollar amount is multiplied by your credited years of service under the plan. For example, if the annual unit of credit is $200 and you have been an employee for 30 years, you would be entitled to a pension of $6,000 per year.

3. *Money-purchase benefit plan:* A money-purchase plan calls for a stipulated annual contribution by the employer. The money is held either in trust or by an insurer. No specific dollar benefit is formulated in advance as under the fixed or the unit benefit plans. Instead, you receive whatever retirement benefit the total contributions (plus earnings) will purchase at retirement. A simple money purchase plan, therefore, recognizes no element of past service. For this reason, a money-purchase plan generally favors younger workers, while a fixed-benefit plan favors older ones. The maximum annual deductible contribution for each plan participant is the lesser of 25% of compensation or $30,000.

> **Example:** In a 15% money purchase plan, the employer contributes 15% of your compensation each year. Assuming your annual compensation is $40,000 and there are 20 years until you retire, the employer would contribute $120,000 for your pension. This amount plus your share of fund earnings would then be available at retirement to provide your pension.

Your pension rights: All formal retirement plans must give employees specified vested rights in their benefits. The vested portion of an employee's benefit represents the part he can walk away with even if he quits or is fired before retirment. The nonvested portion is forfeited by the departed employee and remains in the plan.

A company can choose a vesting schedule from among three that meet Government approval. One example is 5 to 15 year vesting: After five years, an employee is 25% vested; after 6 years, he is 30% vested. The vested portion goes up 5% for each subsequent year until the employee is 100% vested after 15 years.

To sum things up, from the employee's standpoint, a pension plan has three positive features:

1. You know what your pension income will be;

2. Your right to a pension benefit is safe (most pension plans are insured by the Pension Benefit Guarantee Board, a Federal agency).

3. Your employer must put money away for your retirement regardless of the level of its prosperity.

There are also a few minuses. Generally speaking, you cannot tap your pension money before retirement and cannot control how the pension fund invests its money.

Tax Treatment of Pension Income

If your employer funds the entire cost of the retirement plan, your pension checks are fully taxable. However, if the plan requires you to make contributions from your own pocket to supplement the company's plan contributions, you can recover your invested dollars without any tax cost. If your pension income for the first three years comes to less than the total amount you contributed, then your pension checks are tax free until you fully recover your contributions. From that point on, all of your pension is taxable. If you don't meet this three-year rule, the part of each pension check representing your employer's contribution will be taxable and part representing your own contribution will be tax free (your employer will let you know how much of each pension check is taxable).

Extra tax complication: Your employer is required to withhold Federal income tax on your pension checks (other types of retirement plans are affected as well) UNLESS you—

▶ **CHOOSE NO WITHHOLDING:** You can elect not to have the withholding provision apply to your pension. The company issuing the pension checks must notify you of your right to "elect out" of withholding and give you the necessary forms.

If you do not "elect out" then tax is withheld just as if your pension check were salary. In other words, the amount withheld will depend on the number of exemptions you claim on your withholding certificate.

Should you have your employer withhold on your pension checks? There's no set answer. The one thing withholding has going for it is convenience: You may not have to worry about filing estimated tax payments, or coming up with a big sum of cash at tax return time.

How a Profit-Sharing Plan Lets You Share in Your Employer's Success

In a profit-sharing plan, your employer contributes part of its annual profits for investment, accumulation, and eventual distribution to you and your fellow employees. Since contributions are tied to your employer's profits, you have a direct share in its financial success (on the other hand, you may suffer in the years the company doesn't do well).

Tax benefits for employees: You don't pay a cent of current tax on the employer's contribution. In addition, your contributions grow tax-free in your account. These two tax benefits make it possible for rank-and-file employees—as well as executives—to accumulate a tax-sheltered fortune for their retirement.

Example: ABC, Inc. has a profit sharing plan that calls for annual contributions from profits, but not in excess of 10% of each employee's salary. Assuming sufficient profits, Worker A with a salary of $20,000 gets $2,000 a year, Worker B earning $40,000 gets $4,000, and Worker C earning $60,000, gets $6,000.

Let's assume each worker joins ABC's plan at age 40, and that ABC has enough profits each year to make the full 10% profit-sharing contribution. If the plan's money is invested at an 8% rate, then Worker A will have $157,909 in his account at age-65 retirement, Worker B will have $315,818, and Worker C will have $473,726.

How profits are shared: A company has much leeway in controlling the profits to be shared. For example, it can provide for a flat percentage of pre- or post-tax profits to be contributed to the plan. It may have a sliding scale formula that increases contributions as profits rise, or it may provide that profits are to be shared only if and to the extent that company profits exceeds a predetermined level. Generally, a company may deduct contributions equal to 15% of payroll.

Vesting: An employer setting up a profit-sharing plan must, as a general rule, provide for complete vesting of each year's contribution to an employee's account by the end of the fifth plan year after the year the contribution is made. The simplest vesting method: After six years of employment, the employer's contribution for the first year of employment is 100% vested: after seven years, the second year's contribution is also 100% vested: after eight years, the third year's contribution is 100% vested: and so forth.

Allocation among employees: Usually each contribution is allocated among the accounts of the employees in proportion to their compensation. Thus the basic share of a $30,000 employee would be twice that of a $15,000 employee. The maximum deductible contribution per plan participant is the lesser of $30,000 or 15% of compensation.

Summing up: From the employee's standpoint, a profit-sharing plan has these advantages:

1. If things go well for your employer, you share in its success.

2. Your retirement fund is safe. *Reason:* The profit-sharing funds must be held by an independent trustee for your benefit.

3. You may have some control in how your retirement funds are invested. For example, you may have the choice of receiving annual interest on your account accumulation, or investing your funds in a diversified stock-market portfolio (or dividing your money between the two options).

4. Many profit-sharing plans allow employees to withdraw all or a portion of their vested units before retirement. So your profit-sharing account may be a ready source of funds for family emergencies or major purchases.

Disadvantages: There is the risk that a company won't be able to make profit-sharing contributions in a severe business downturn. And you don't know how much your retirement benefit will be.

WHEN AND HOW CAN YOU TAKE CASH OUT OF YOUR RETIREMENT PLAN?

Now that you've seen the advantages of a company retirement plan, you'd like to know how you can get your money out. As a general rule, you can take cash out of a retirement plan at any time (assuming that you have a vested interest). But you can't defer withdrawals as long as you wish. Once you reach age 70½, you must begin making withdrawals according to a tax law-approved schedule. Here's a summary of the rules on distributions:

Withdrawals prior to age 59½: You can make cash withdrawals from a company retirement plan or a Keogh plan prior to age 59½ without paying a penalty tax. However, retirement plan participants who own 5%-or-more of the company must pay a 10% penalty tax on any pre-age-59½ withdrawals. And 5%-or-more owners who belong to a Keogh plan are prohibited from making pre-age-59½ withdrawals.

Withdrawls after age 59½: You can withdraw part or all of your vested interest in the plan without paying a penalty, even if you are a 5%-or-more-company owner.

▶ **IMPORTANT:** A retirement plan is not required to permit withdrawals during employment—and most types of pension plans won't distribute any money before the employee reaches a certain age. Even those plans that do permit withdrawals may impose a penalty to discourage employees from tapping funds prior to retirement.

Withdrawals at age 70½: As a general rule, your entire interest in the plan must be distributed by April 1 of the year following the year in which you reach age 70½ or retire, whichever is later. Two other alternatives: (1) A plan can distribute benefits in the form of an annuity over your life (or the joint lives of you and your designated beneficiary, including non-spouses). Or (2) the plan can make installment payments over a period of time no longer than your life expectancy (or joint life expectancies).

Special rules for owner-employees: The distribution of benefits of any employee who owns more than 5% of the company must begin by April 1 following the year in which he reaches age 70½, even though the employee has not yet retired.

Your life expectancy (or joint life expectancy of the employee and spouse) can be redetermined once a year. (There can be no redetermination in the case of a life annuity.) Annual redeterminations assure a lifetime stream of retirement benefits. However, the present value of payments projected to be paid to you during your life must be more than 50% of the present value of all payments.

Distribution upon employee's death: The speed at which the plan must distribute benefits after your death depends on whether or not distributions began prior to death.

Distributions did not begin before death: As a general rule, the distribution of benefits must be completed within five years after death.

▶ **IMPORTANT EXCEPTION:** Any portion of your interest that is payable to a designated beneficiary can be distributed over the life expectancy of the beneficiary. The distribution must, however, generally begin within one year after your death.

If the designated beneficiary is your spouse, the distribution of benefits does not have to begin until the April 1 following the year you would have reached age 70½. The distribution can then be over the life expectancy of the spouse. If the spouse dies before payments commence, the benefits must be paid out within the one-year and five-year rules mentioned above.

Distribution did begin before death: The payout of remaining benefits can be longer than five years in this situation. The payouts need only continue as per the payout schedule in effect prior to death.

HOW TO BOOST YOUR AFTER-TAX INCOME FROM PROFIT-SHARING PAYOUTS

There are three basic ways to tap your profit-sharing account at retirement:
(1) Withdraw the entire account balance in one lump sum.
(2) Take the cash over a period of years (through an annuity, for example).
(3) Take some of the account in a lump-sum at retirement and take out the rest in the form of an annuity, or in installments.

While your personal needs may dictate how you handle your payout (e.g., you need a large sum of cash to buy a retirement condo), taxes will play a large part in the decision. Here's how the tax law affects your profit-sharing payout options, beginning with—

How Lump-Sum Distributions Get Special Tax-Sheltered Treatment

If you take out your profit-sharing cash in one lump sum at retirement, you qualify for special and favorable tax treatment. To qualify, however, your entire account balance must be distributed to you within one year.

If you became a member of a profit-sharing plan before 1974, you can figure your tax using one of the two options shown below. If you become a member of the plan after 1973, only the first option is available:

Option #1—Ten-Year Averaging: The entire lump-sum payment is taxed as ordinary income separate and apart from your other income. However, the tax is computed as if the income had been received over ten years instead of all at once. And if the payout is less than $70,000, part of the payout may be tax-free due to something called the minimum distribution allowance.

Note: You must have been a plan member for at least five years to qualify for ten-year averaging.

▶ **HOW AVERAGING WORKS:** You take the entire lump-sum distribution (less any minimum distribution allowance) and divide it by ten. To the result, you add $2,480 and compute tax on the total using the tax rates for single individuals (regardless of what filing status you claimed on your return for that year). You multiply the result by ten to arrive at the tax on your profit-sharing payout. This tax is then added to the tax on your other income for the year.

Option #2—Part Capital Gain, Part Ten-Year Averaging: Your payout is divided into two portions. The first portion is composed of profit-sharing accumulations attributable to your years in the plan before 1974. The other portion is made up of accumulations attributable to your plan years after 1973. Each portion is taxed differently.

Pre '74 portion—is taxed as long-term capital gain. That is, only 40% of this amount is taxable. Since it's capital gain, the amount can be offset by capital losses.

Post '73 portion—is taxed under the ten year averaging rules shown under Option #1.

Either option will produce a smaller tax than you'd pay if the distribution were treated as salary income. But the tax bite can still be very substantial.

▶ **Example:** Let's suppose Mr. Smith entered a profit-sharing plan after 1973 and has a $200,000 profit-sharing account balance at retirement. At current tax rates, ten-year averaging results in a tax of $36,922. So almost 18.5% of the payout is washed away.

If Mr. Smith had joined the plan, in, say, 1965, he can use the part capital gain, part ten year averaging option. But if the capital gain portion of the payout is very large, Smith might be subject to another tax—the special alternative minimum tax. (This is a complicated tax that hits taxpayers with substantial amounts of "tax preferences," such as long-term capital gains. If you are in this situation, you should consult a tax professional to assess the situation properly.)

Why Spreading Out Your Plan Payout Can Leave You Big Dollars Ahead

If you don't need a large sum of cash at retirement, and plan to live off your retirement account earnings, then you will probably be better off not using a simple lump-sum distribution. Instead, you should take the profit-sharing cash over a period of years. One way to do this is to use an—

▶ **IRA ROLLOVER ACCOUNT:** An IRA rollover account is basically an Individual Retirement Account set up to receive the payout from your retirement plan. (Regular IRA plans are covered in Chapter Eight.)

There is no limit on the amount of cash you can put into an IRA roll-over account. Big tax advantage: If you take a lump-sum payout from your profit-sharing plan and roll over the entire sum within 60 days of receipt, you owe no current tax on the payout. The tax is payable only as you withdraw cash from the IRA. (Withdrawals must commence by April 1 of the year following the year in which you reach age 70½.)

Dollars and cents: Let's go back to our example of Mr. Smith. Without an IRA rollover, his $200,000 profit-sharing withdrawal (using ten year averaging) will dwindle down to $163,078 after taxes (gross distribution less $36,922 tax). Invested at 9%, that sum will earn Smith $14,677 a year.

If he rolls over his account balance into an IRA, the entire $200,000 will be available for investment. If the IRA earns the same 9%, Smith's annual income will be $18,000.

Tax angles: All amounts withdrawn from an IRA are taxed as ordinary income, and aren't eligible for special tax breaks (other than regular income averaging). However, by spreading out his IRA withdrawals over, say, ten years, Smith will in effect be averaging out the tax over ten years. Since the typical retiree's tax rate is low, Smith may not only spread out the tax, but cut it as well.

IRA Rollover Or Ten-Year Averaging—Which Is Right for You?

Assuming you are at or near retirement when the payout is made, the general rule is this: If you plan to take the money eventually in a lump-sum, do it at the time of the payout and avail yourself of ten-year averaging. If you want to use the money as a source of annual income, roll the payout over into an IRA and take the tax deferral. But this is not a decision to be made lightly. If you roll over into an IRA and have a substantial cash need in a few years, you can end up paying a lot more tax. Reason: Once you roll the payout over into an IRA you lose the ten-year averaging break forever.

> *Example:* Let's use Mr. Smith's situation again. If Smith elects ten-year averaging on the entire $200,000 payout, his tax is about $37,000. Smith invests the remaining $163,000 in tax exempt bonds paying 8%. Alternatively, Smith could have rolled over the entire $200,000 into an IRA, invested in, say, CD's yielding 10%.

Now let's say that in two years Smith needs the money—all of it. The lump-sum payout has grown to $190,000. The IRA contains $242,000. But how much Smith nets after tax is a different story. Smith can cash in his $190,000 of municipal bonds without paying a tax (assuming he has no gains when he disposes of the bonds). But his IRA withdrawal is fully taxable. The $242,000 could be diminished by as much as 50%, leaving Smith with only $121,000.

Of course, Smith may be able to use regular income averaging to ease the tax bite, but he still won't come out as well as with ten-year averaging.

Moral of the story: Don't automatically assume that because you are not going to draw on a retirement plan payout at once that the right move is to roll it over into an IRA. Lump-sum tax treatment is a powerful dollar-saver. You shouldn't discard it until you are certain what your eventual plans for the payout are.

Still another option: You can ask your profit-sharing plan trustee to buy an annuity for you. The full balance in your profit-sharing account is available for investment in the annuity. None of the payout is subject to tax at this point. You pay tax, of course, on the full annuity payment each year as you receive it.

Result: You accomplish essentially the same thing as you do with the IRA rollover. However, there are a few differences: With an annuity, your annual income is fixed and when the annuity stops (when you die, or, in the case of joint and survivor annuity when you and your spouse are both gone), there's nothing left over for your heirs. On the other hand, with an IRA rollover account, you retain control. You can take advantage of rising interest rates by switching your money around (or lock in high interest with a CD when rates start falling). Finally, if you don't exhaust the rollover account's principal, your heirs will be left the balance when you pass on.

▶ **WATCH THIS PITFALL:** If you want an annuity, be sure the trustee of the profit-sharing plan buys it for you. Don't take a lump sum and then buy the annuity yourself. If you do, you may be taxed on the entire lump-sum distribution, and will have far less to invest in your annuity.

How To Receive Cash Plus An Annuity And Still Get A Big Tax Break

Many employees nearing retirement want their profit-sharing account to do two things: Supply a lump sum of cash (to buy a retirement condo, take a world tour, etc.) *and* provide them with a source of income during retirement.

▶ **GOOD NEWS:** You can accomplish both goals—and retain tax breaks—by getting part of your profit-sharing payout in cash, and part in an annuity.

Tax break #1: You can use special ten-year averaging on the ordinary income portion of the payout (generally, the payout attributable to post-1973 plan participation). *Reason*: You are considered to have received a lump-sum payment (your entire balance) even though the annuity portion of the payout won't be paid until future years.

Tax break #2: Even though the annuity is considered to be part of a lump-sum distribution, the employee doesn't pay tax on the annuity until he receives the payments.

The tax on the ordinary income portion of the distribution is computed on the cash plus the current actuarial value of the annuity. The amount of tax is then reduced by the portion of the tax attributable to the value of the annuity.

Result: Although the annuity contract is taken into account as part of the lump-sum distribution, it is not currently taxed. You pay tax on the annuity when you receive payouts.

Key point: The annuity contract is disregarded for purposes of computing the tax on any capital gain portion of the payout (i.e., the portion attributable to the pre-1974 plan participation).

Q. What if I take half my $200,000 payout in cash and roll over the $100,000 balance into an IRA?

A. This won't work as well. The $100,000 rolled over to the IRA is tax-free. However, the $100,000 balance is fully taxable and is not eligible for ten-year averaging.

How To Get the Best Possible Retirement Annuity

The United States Supreme Court has ruled that a retirement plan that gives employees the option of taking payouts in the form of an annuity must make the same annuity payments for men and women. Prior to the decision, the annuities could, on the same size payout, give higher yearly benefits to a man than to a woman. That's because, on average, men have shorter life expectancies than women, and, therefore, have less time to collect benefits.

Retirement plan annuities now must be figured from unisex annuity tables. The result is that female employees choosing a lifetime annuity option will receive higher benefits than before; male employees will receive less.

Thanks to the ruling, female employees who want an annuity payout are probably ahead of the game if they stick with their plan's annuity. But male employees who want an annuity can make out better if they take a lump-sum payout, roll it over into an IRA, and buy an annuity on their own through the IRA. (IRA annuities can be purchased directly from insurance companies.)

The IRA annuity can continue to pay higher benefits to men than women— assuming the same age and investment. Reason: IRA annuities are not subject to the Supreme Court decision. The decision only affects annuities paid through an employer-sponsored retirement plan.

Special Rules Protect Your Spouse's Right To Your Retirement Plan Benefits

Married couples are usually partners when it comes to family property. So a surviving spouse's rights in the property are protected on her mate's death. A spouse can't be completely disinherited. But that wasn't always the situation when it came to retirement plan benefits. All too often, a surviving spouse was unpleasantly surprised to discover that she was left without a penny of her partner's benefits. In effect, the benefits died with him.

But this won't happen any more since the law now practically guarantees that a surviving spouse will receive benefits from her working mate's retirement account.

To accomplish this goal, a spouse's consent is now needed for a wide variety of pension decisions during the plan member's lifetime. In addition, a spouse is entitled to certain benefit payments after her husband's death.

Important: The rules are very complex and can cause many complications. For example, you may be hamstrung in employment and retirement plan moves you want to make during your lifetime. In effect, your spouse may have a veto power over your plans. What's more, if you're not careful, you and your spouse may not receive the benefits in the form you thought you would get them.

Spouse's consent for lifetime decisions: As we said, the law now protects a surviving spouse's rights to the partner's retirement benefits. To fulfill that objective, a plan member's spouse has been given an important say in a variety of fundamental retirement plan decisions. Let's take a look at some of the spouse's more important veto powers.

• Early retirement: If a marrried plan member's accrued benefit exceeds $3,500, he cannot receive early retirement benefits (before the normal retirement age or age 62) without the consent of his spouse. Reason: Early retirement results in lower pension—and survivor—benefits. So the spouse's consent is necessary to protect his or her interests.

▶ **PAYOUT EXCEPTION:** A married plan member may elect a joint and survivor annuity prior to normal retirement age without the spouse's consent.

This early retirement rule can have a wider impact than expected. Spousal consent may also be necessary if the plan member wants to change jobs or simply make a withdrawal while employed.

• Plan loans: A spouse must now consent to loans from the pension or profit-sharing plan by the plan member. Reason: An unpaid loan that's secured by a participant's retirement account reduces benefits payable to the couple. So, once again, the spouse's consent is necessary to protect his or her share of plan benefits.

Spouse's protection if employee dies before retirement: Retirement plans must now automatically pay a surviving spouse a "pre-retirement survivor annuity." The surviving spouse has the right to begin receiving this annuity at the plan member's earliest retirement age under the plan. If benefits exceed $3,500, the surviving spouse can delay receiving benefits if he or she so desires.

Potential pitfall: Some profit-sharing plans pay death benefits in a lump-sum to a surviving spouse. And that may appeal to you and your spouse. But under the rules, the profit-sharing plan must pay out the benefits as a pre-retirement survivor annuity. That means the annuity must be at least one-half the plan member's account balance. So your spouse will get only half the money up front; the rest is an annuity that may not start for years.

It's possible for the spouse to request a lump-sum after the plan member's death, but he or she may not think of it at that time.

▶ **WHAT TO DO:** You and your spouse can waive the annuity and elect the lump-sum payout. Both you and your spouse must consent to the waiver and the new payout form.

If a spouse consents to the waiver of the annuity and allows a change in beneficiary under the plan, the plan member cannot later change the beneficiary without the spouse's consent.

Spouse's protection during retirement: A joint and survivor annuity is now the required payout for all pension plans and most profit-sharing plans. Only exception: A profit-sharing plan that offers only a lump-sum payout.

Again, if the retiring plan member wants any other form of payout—maybe a lump-sum—his spouse must formally waive her right to the survivor benefit.

> ▶ **SEE YOUR ADVISER:** It is an absolute must that you sit down with the person who administers your plan and discuss the spouse payout rules. He or she can help you decide what payout forms are best for you and your spouse after considering your circumstances.

He or she can also be sure that any consents and waivers that your spouse agrees to are properly executed. For example, a waiver of the pre-retirement survivor annuity must be written and witnessed by a plan representative or a notary public.

HOW KEOGH PLANS CAN HELP SELF-EMPLOYEDS BUILD TAX-SHELTERED WEALTH

A Keogh plan is simply a retirement plan for self-employed business people or professionals. If you run your business or practice as a sole proprietorship or a partnership, you can set up your own—

> ▶ **TAX-SHELTERED RETIREMENT PLAN:** (1) You get a deduction for what you put into your Keogh retirement fund; (2) the earnings from the fund build up tax-free; and (3) you pay no tax until you retire and withdraw your money.

It's possible to be a company employee and a self-employed business person at the same time. For example, you may draw down a regular salary and also do some freelance consulting work on the side. You're covered by a retirement plan at your regular job. But what about your outside earnings? Can you set part of them aside in a retirement tax shelter? Sure. The most obvious way is to set up an IRA and contribute up to $2,000 of your consulting earnings to it. The salary-only employee can, of course, set up an IRA. But can you do better than that.

> ▶ **MORE TAX SHELTER:** You can set up a Keogh plan, too. To the extent your outside earnings are from self-employment, they qualify for the same Keogh breaks that full-time self-employed get.

How To Cash In On The Most Common Type Of Keogh Plan

So-called "defined contribution" Keogh plans have always been more popular than pension-type Keogh plans. *Reason*: They are simpler to administer. The contribution is figured as a percentage of each participant's earned income. Your retirement benefit depends on how well your contributions are invested.

A defined contribution Keogh can be either a profit-sharing type plan or a money-purchase type plan. In a profit-sharing Keogh, you are obligated to contribute a set percentage of profits to participants' accounts (yours and your full-time employees, if any). In a money-purchase pension Keogh, you must make a specific contribution to each participant's account each year, regardless of the level of profits.

The maximum deduction for a money purchase Keogh contribution is $30,000 or 20% of self-employment income, whichever is less. For profit-sharing Keoghs, the deduction is the lesser of $30,000 or 13.043% of self-employment income.

Here's an example of how a defined contribution Keogh plan allows you to sock away big dollars for a comfortable retirement—and get big current deductions to boot.

Mr. Smith is a 40-year-old self-employed businessman with earned income of $65,000, and taxable income of $50,000 after all deductions and exemptions. This year, he sets up a Keogh plan and contributes $6,000 (less than the maximum with either a profit-sharing or a money-purchase Keogh). Let's assume he makes the same contribution each year—and has the same annual income and deductions—until he retires at 65.

Tax shelter result: Smith saves over $2,000 every year in Federal income taxes due to the Keogh contribution. At 1986 tax rates for married filing jointly, here's how this works out:

Tax on $50,000 taxable income (without Keogh)	$10,764
Less tax on $44,000 taxable income	
($50,000 less $6,000 Keogh contribution)	8,755
Net annual tax saving	$ 2,009

Wealth-building result: Smith's Keogh contributions grow free of tax erosion until retirement. If the money earns 8% a year, Smith's annual $6,000 contribution will swell to about $473,700 by the time he retires at age 65.

Keogh contributions can be invested in many ways. Some examples: You can set up your Keogh plan at a local bank, which acts as trustee and invests the funds for you. You can purchase nontransferrable annuity contracts from an insurance company. Or you can invest your Keogh money in mutual funds or in a wide variety of investment programs offered by brokerage houses.

Question: When can I make my contribution to a Keogh plan?

Answer: If your Keogh plan was opened before the end of your taxable year, you may make your contribution any time before your income tax return for that year is due (including extensions).

Question: When and how will my Keogh retirement account be taxed?

Answer: Income taxes on both your Keogh contributions and the plan's earnings are payable only when funds are withdrawn from your retirement fund. If the funds are taken out in one lump sum at retirement or disability, you are eligible for the same tax breaks available to lump-sum withdrawals from corporate plans. If the withdrawal is spread over your retirement years, the tax will also be reduced sharply. That's because your income will probably be lower then—and, in addition, when you reach age 65, your personal income tax exemption doubles.

Question: Do I have to include my employees in my Keogh plan?

Answer: In general, the answer is yes. And you must contribute in the same proportion for participating employees as you do for yourself. Contributions you make for your employees are fully deductible by you.

Here are two ways to reduce Keogh plan funding costs without cutting into your personal benefits.

Method #1: You can gear contributions to the maximum percentage of your earnings that you plan to contribute. For example, suppose you plan to put away a sum of $15,000 each year in your own Keogh plan account. Let's say that $15,000 represents 7½% of your earned income. Result: You can limit contributions you must make for employees to 7½% of their salaries.

Method #2: You can "integrate" your Keogh plan with Social Security. In simple terms, part of the employer's share of the Social Security payroll tax is a kind of credit towards retirement plan contributions on behalf of rank-and-file workers. The Social Security tax you pay reduces the amount you must place in lower-earning workers' Keogh plan accounts. You are allowed to make bigger Keogh plan contributions for higher-earning employees.

Caution: If your money-purchase or profit-sharing Keogh plan is "top heavy" (more than 60% of the contributions or benefits go to key employees), you must make a minimum cash contribution of 3%-of-salary to the Keogh accounts of rank-and-file workers. A similar minimum-benefit rule applies to pension-type Keoghs.

Question: Can I make contributions to a Keogh plan if I am already covered by my company's retirement plan?

Answer: The answer is "Yes" if you have outside income—for example, earnings from freelance consulting work. In this situation, you can set up a Keogh plan for yourself, even if you are the only "employee" and even if you are covered by another retirement plan. However, if you have no outside earnings, you may not make contributions to a Keogh plan.

Question: Can I include my spouse in my Keogh plan?

Answer: If your spouse is your paid employee, he or she must be covered by the plan, and you must make contributions for the both of you.

Why a Pension-Type Keogh May Be a Better
Tax Shelter for Older Self-Employeds

There are two basic types of Keogh plans—the more common profit-sharing plan and the defined-benefit plan. With the standard Keogh, you can contribute and deduct annually up to 13.043% of your self-employment income or $30,000, whichever is less.

▶ **BIGGER TAX SHELTER:** A defined-benefit Keogh allows an older self-employed taxpayer to make bigger deductible contributions and receive a bigger retirement fund than he would with a basic profit-sharing plan.

Reason: Defined-benefit Keoghs pay a set amount at retirement (thus, defined benefit), like a corporate pension plan. The benefit can be as much as the average of his three highest consecutive years of self-employment income, with a $90,000 cap. Sufficient amounts must be contributed to the plan every year in order to accumulate enough to pay the fixed benefit. Since an older self-employed is nearing retirement, there is a relatively short time to accumulate the necessary funds. Thus, the annual deductible contributions to the defined benefit Keogh can be quite large.

Example: Mr. Smith is 55 and will retire at age 65. He starts a sideline consulting business this year. His consultant fees are $10,000 a year.

• Basic Keogh: Smith can contribute and deduct $1,304 a year to the plan. Assuming 10% growth each year, his plan will be $20,787 at age 65. That would allow him to buy an annual life annuity of $2,198 at 65.

• Defined-benefit Keogh: According to the rules, Smith can be paid a $10,000 pension (his yearly self-employment income). To fund that pension, Smith contributes and deducts $5,547 each year (assuming 10% growth and level funding).

▶ **SEE YOUR ADVISER:** Consult with your retirement adviser before setting up your Keogh plan. Reason: While a defined-benefit Keogh can offer you a generous tax shelter, it also has some drawbacks.

To begin with, you pay much higher administrative costs for a defined-benefit Keogh than for a basic Keogh plan. And you are obligated to make contributions to a defined-benefit Keogh each year—even if you have no self-employment income. You are under no such obligation with a profit-sharing Keogh plan.

HERE'S A TAX-SHELTERED RETIREMENT PLAN THAT WON'T SADDLE YOU WITH RED TAPE AND PAPERWORK

Pension and profit-sharing plans have one drawback for the smaller company, partnership or for the sole proprietor: There are administrative expenses and special minimum-funding rules that can make the plan too expensive to maintain. That's why one type of plan is attracting attention.

▶ **SIMPLIFIED PLAN:** A Simplified Employee Pension Plan combines the simplicity of an IRA with the generous contribution limits of a formal pension plan.

SEPs allows employers to use IRAs to build tax-sheltered retirement funds for themselves and their employees with minimum headaches and costs.

How it works: Each covered employee sets up his own IRA at, for example, a bank, insurance company or brokerage house. Then the company makes contributions to each employee's IRA account. The maximum deductible contribution to each employee's account is 15% of compensation or $30,000, whichever is less. However, in the case of an unincorporated business, the maximum deductible contribution to each partner's or owner's account is equal to 13.043% of his or her net business income or $30,000, whichever is less. The company's contributions are deductible, and they are effectively tax-free to the employee (the employee declares the contribution as income and takes an offsetting deduction). The contributions grow and compound tax-free until withdrawn. The rules that apply to IRA withdrawals also apply to SEPs (see Chapter Eight for details.)

There are, of course, some rules the company must follow. Probably the most important is that a SEP must not discriminate in favor of company owners or highly paid employees. A SEP cannot be set up just for the owner and his key employees. Generally, *all* employees have to be covered (with exceptions for certain workers, such as those who are employed part time).

The company does not have to make the maximum contribution, and it does not have to make contributions every year. But it cannot contribute a higher percentage for some employees than for others. The contributions must bear a uniform relationship to total compensation (up to $200,000) of each employee.

▶ **ANOTHER PLUS:** SEP plans can be set up so that employees can make their own deductible contributions to the plan. As with an IRA, each employee can contribute up to $2,000 of his or her earnings to the account. These contributions are completely tax deductible on the employee's tax return. Alternatively, the employee can set up a separate IRA, and contribute to that account. Either way, the employer's contributions to the SEP do not reduce the size of the deductible contribution that the employee can make on his own.

HOW TAX-FREE FRINGE BENEFITS HELP
YOU GET AND KEEP MORE FOR YOUR FAMILY

Fringe benefit plans provide an unusually tax-favored method of supplementing your cash compensation. Properly set up, benefits received under these plans are not taxable to you (at least not currently). And the cost of providing the benefits is a currently deductible business expense to the company. Thus, they enable you to realize what amounts to a tax-free or tax-deferred increase in salary.

To illustrate the power of tax-free fringe benefits, let's assume a worker earning $40,000 is offered a $2,000 raise, or, in the alternative, $2,000 of tax-free fringe benefits. The $2,000 raise is fully subject to Federal income taxes and Social Security taxes. Assuming the worker's taxable income is, say, $35,000, the raise shrinks to $1,297 after taxes. In contrast, the $2,000 in fringe benefits buys $2,000 of family benefits. As we'll see, company-paid fringes can provide you and your family with life insurance, health insurance, money for college—even help buying a home—all on a tax-free basis.

How an Employer-Paid Medical Plan Can Keep
You Feeling Tip-Top—At No Tax Cost

Medical costs keep going up. But as your income goes up, it gets harder and harder to get a tax break from your medical bills. Reason: You can deduct medical expenses only to the extent they exceed 5% of your adjusted gross income (generally, gross income less IRA contributions, marriage penalty deduction and employee business expenses).

▶ **HOW TO GET RELIEF:** A company-paid medical reimbursement plan can take this major financial burden off your shoulders. Such a plan can put thousands of dollars in your pocket *absolutely tax-free*. And the company, for its part, can deduct every cent it pays to cover the cost.

Example: Let's assume Arlene Smith has a $50,000 adjusted gross income and $1,850 in medical bills. If she paid the medical bills out of her own pocket, she couldn't deduct a penny—her $1,850 of medical expenses do not exceed 5% of her $50,000 adjusted gross income.

Better way: Smith's company sets up a medical reimbursement plan that reimburses her for these expenses. She gets, in effect, $1,850 in tax-free dollars at an after-tax cost to the company of $999 (if the company is in the 46% tax bracket). If Smith is in the 33% tax bracket, she'd have to get a salary increase of about $2,760 to net $1,850. And the salary increase would cost the company about $1,490 (if it is in the 46% tax bracket).

Question: Can an employer be selective about the employees it covers with a medical reimbursement plan?

Answer: As a general rule, the answer is "No." The plan must meet broad coverage requirements similar to those for qualified pension plans. In general, 70% of the employees must be plan members. And the plan may not provide greater benefits for key execs than for the rank and file. For example, a plan can't provide benefits in proportion to compensation.

However, note that the anti-discrimination rules apply only to self-insured plans (the company itself pays the medical bills as they come in). A company can escape the tough rules by buying a health-insurance policy that covers only the top-echelon employees. The premiums are deductible by the company and both the premiums and reimbursements are tax-free to the employees.

How a Company-Paid Medical Checkup Can
Give You a Tax-Free Bill of Health

All businesses want to keep their employees in "good working order" just as long as possible. For this very sound reason, more and more companies provide their personnel with an annual complete medical checkup. The company foots the bill by either paying the physician or reimbursing the employee.

▶ **IT'S TAX-FREE:** The reimbursement the employee receives from the company for the physical—medical diagnostic procedures—is tax-free income. That's true even if the physical isn't available to all employees, but is limited to a chosen few.

What are "medical diagnostic procedures?" They include routine medical examinations, blood tests, and X-rays. But the testing for or treatment of a specific complaint or symptom doesn't qualify as a diagnostic procedure. (A routine dental exam with X-rays is a diagnostic procedure, but X-rays and treatment for impacted wisdom teeth aren't.) In addition, an activity undertaken for exercise, fitness, nutrition, recreation, or the general improvement of health doesn't qualify.

▶ **MORE THAN MEDICAL EXPENSES:** Travel reimbursements primarily for a diagnostic procedure are also exempt from tax. Incidental expenses for food and lodging, however, are not exempt.

Important: Only physicals for *employees* are tax-free. Company-paid examinations for members of an employee's family are taxable to the employee (unless otherwise covered under a medical reimbursement plan).

How Your Company Can Provide You With Life Insurance At Rock-Bottom Cost

Everyone comes out ahead with company-paid group-term life insurance. That's why it's such a popular fringe benefit. Your company saves taxes—the premiums are deductible—while it picks up the tab for one of your most important personal expenses. You on the other hand, pick up what is, in essence, tax-free income. The first $50,000 worth of group-term coverage is tax free to the employee. It's like getting a tax-free raise to pay the premium.

You are taxed only on the value of employer-paid coverage in excess of $50,000.

And there are these other advantages:

● Generally, you do not have to pass a medical examination to qualify for coverage.

● You can usually purchase additional coverage at favorable group rates.

● Your employer can deduct the premiums it pays as a business expense.

You must report as income only the cost of the coverage in excess of $50,000, less any contributions you have made. This cost is computed by using the following Government table:

Age Bracket of Insured	Monthly Cost per $1,000 of Protection
Under 30	$ .08
30-34	.09
35-39	.11
40-44	.17
45-49	.29
50-54	.48
55-59	.75
60-64	1.17

Example: Mr. Smith is 48 years old, married and has taxable income which places him in the 38% tax bracket. His life is insured under an employer-paid policy for $100,000. Half of that is tax-free because of the exclusion for the premiums paid for the first $50,000 of coverage. The cost of the other $50,000 is computed as follows $.29 × 50 × 12 = $174 (i.e., montly cost for age 48 times thousands of dollars in coverage, times months in the year).

Result: Mr. Smith pays only $66.12 ($174 × 38%) in taxes for $100,000 in employer-paid insurance.

If Smith and his employer share in paying the premiums, the taxable cost of his insurance coverage does not include the payments Smith makes. For example, if Smith pays $150 in premiums, his taxable income for the insurance coverage is reduced by $150. The same rule applies even if Smith assigns the insurance policy to his spouse and she pays the premiums for the extra coverage.

Added break: An employee's spouse and children may be included in an employer-paid group-term plan. The cost of the insurance coverage is tax-free to the employee as long as the cost is "incidental" (even if the employee is covered for $50,000 or more). The cost of coverage is incidental if the amount of insurance for the spouse and children does not exceed $2,000 each.

Important: If you are a company owner, you can't set up a group-term plan that covers only you and your key people. Generally, the plan must benefit all employees. But the amount of insurance coverage per employee can vary with the employee's salary. So as an owner-employee, it is possible for you to get more insurance coverage than your employees.

How To Get A Tax-Free Reimbursement For Your Child's School Expenses

Educating a child these days usually costs a great deal more than keeping the child healthy. Your company can reimburse you tax-free for his or her medical expenses. But what's the story on reimbursements for your child's education?

Answer: Unlike medical reimbursements for your child, there's no special tax law break for your child's education. So the payments you receive are treated like compensation—deductible by your company, taxable to you.

But this doesn't mean there aren't any favorable tax angles to education reimbursements. In fact, the Government has specifically approved a special kind of—

▶ **TAX-SHELTERED EDUCATION REIMBURSEMENT PLAN:** Your company makes contributions over a period of years to a trust set up for your child. When your child enters college, the trust pays some or all of the child's school expenses. If your child doesn't go to college, trust benefits are forfeited.

Result: You pay no tax when the contributions are put in the trust—the tax is postponed until your child actually incurs college expenses and the trust makes payments. So a college fund grows for your child and you have no current tax worries. And the company gets a deduction when the trust makes the payments [Rev. Rul. 75-448, 1975-2 CB 55].

How Your Company Can Provide You With No-Cost Child Care

The child-care credit is an extremely valuable tax break for working people (see Chapter Ten). However, the child care break still leaves you out of pocket for part of the cost. But, with the help of your company, you can get—

▶ **NO-COST DEPENDENT CARE:** Your company can set up a dependent care assistance plan and pick up the tab for the exact same expenses that are eligible for the child care credit. If the plan follows the blueprint spelled out in the tax law, (1) the company deducts the full cost, and (2) it's completely tax-free to you. Payoff: Instead of being out of pocket for a large part of every child-care dollar, you are not out of pocket one red cent.

Example: Mrs. Brown recently got a job. As a result, she and Mr. Brown will incur $4,000 in child care expenses in 1986 for their two young children.

▶ **IDEA IN ACTION:** Mrs. Brown's company sets up a dependent care assistance plan and reimburses her for the child care expenses. Result: Since the reimbursements are tax-free, all of the $4,000 she gets can go to pay the expenses. Mrs. Brown has effectively shifted her entire child care cost to the company.

If instead Mrs. Brown's company had given her a $4,000 salary increase to pay for the child care expenses, $2,000 would come right off the top in taxes (we're assuming the Browns are in the 50% tax bracket). So the Browns would have to find an extra $2,000 to make up the difference. The child care credit would help: The Browns would be entitled to a tax credit of $800 (20% of $4,000). But they would still have to dig into their pockets for another $1,200. With the dependent care assistance plan, the $1,200 can stay in their pockets.

Icing on the cake: There is a dollar limit on the amount of job-related dependent care expenses that can qualify for the child-care credit: $2,400 for one qualifying individual, $4,800 for two or more. There is no dollar limit on payments under a dependent care assistance plan. (The payments, however, cannot exceed the earned income of the lower-earning spouse.)

Important: A dependent care assistance program cannot qualify for favorable tax treatment if the plan discriminates among employees. No more than 25% of the dependent care assistance paid during the year can go to employee shareholders who own more than 5% of the company's stock.

Employer-Paid Financial Counseling Fees— An Increasingly Popular Fringe Benefit

More and more people are making use of financial planners to map out family investments and taxes. A number of employers have instituted a unique sweetener to the fringe benefit picture. It's the employer-paid financial counseling fee.

Here's how it works: Key executives are provided with the services of a firm of financial advisors. This firm gives the employee investment and tax advice aimed at making his money work for him most profitably. The bill is picked up by the employer.

The tax picture: The Revenue Service says that his fringe benefit is really extra salary. So, the employee has to include it in income and his company has to withhold income taxes. However, there's usually—

▶ **NO ADDED TAX:** If the employee pays for investment advice or tax advice out of his own pocket, it's deductible. So when the employer pays for it and the employee includes it in his income, he gets a deduction here too [Rev. Rul. 73-13, 1973-1 CB 42]. And, since the company has already paid the withholding on this fringe benefit, the extra withholding serves as a dollar-for-dollar credit against the employee's tax.

▶ **WHAT TO DO:** Make sure the financial consultants provide you with a written statement indicating that their services were rendered for investment and tax advice. And retain it in your files should the Revenue Service require you to justify the deduction.

How To Sharpen Your Business Skills With Tax-Free, No-Cost Education

Like many other hard-working executives and employees, you may be going back to the classroom. Your goal: To sharpen your business skills and improve your job performance. To encourage this back-to-school trend, your company can reimburse you and your fellow employees for out-of-pocket tuition and textbook expenses in job-related courses.

Your company gets a better-trained employee, plus a deduction for the reimbursement to boot. And you get a tax-free education.

▶ **BIG TAX BREAK:** The Government says that educational reimbursements for job-related courses are not "wages." So the payments are free from income tax withholding and payroll taxes [Rev. Rul. 76-71, 1976-1 CB 308].

If the employee is paid directly and accounts to his company, he doesn't report the payments on his tax return. He simply states that the payments didn't exceed his expenses. And if the company makes the payments directly to the school, the employee doesn't even have to do that.

For the reimbursement to be tax-free, however, the employee must pass the—

> ▶ **TAX LAW TEST:** If the studies maintain or improve an employee's skills in his current business, or he must take the courses to keep his present job, the company reimbursement is tax-free. On the other hand, if the courses help the employee qualify for a new business, or satisfy the minimum requirements for his present job, any reimbursement the company gives him is taxable as compensation. Reason: It's purely a personal expense unrelated to his job.

As you can imagine, it's not always clear whether an education expense falls into the job-related or personal category. For example, a course that helps you qualify for a new business may also improve your skills in your present job. Is the course job-related or not?

Let's look at the tax law test as it has been applied in a couple of specific situations.

● Education improving your present job skills: Generally, you cannot receive a tax-free reimbursement from your employer for education expenses that qualify you for a new trade, business or profession—even if the courses help you perform your present job. However, you are not prevented from receiving a tax-free reimbursement merely because the courses lead to a specialized or advanced degree in your profession. As long as the courses improve or maintain your present job skills, or are required by your company to keep your present job, your educational expense reimbursement may still be tax-free.

> **Example 1:** Mr. Smith, personnel manager at XYZ Corp., goes to night school to improve himself in personnel practices. The courses he takes also lead him to a degree of "Master of Arts in Personnel Administration." Since the education sharpens his skills as a personnel manager, the courses are job-related [Rev. Rul. 69-199, 1969-1 CB 51].

● Education on an informal basis: An educational expense reimbursement can cover more than just the cost of formal classroom education. It can also cover education received in an informal setting.

> **Example 2:** When the president of XYZ Construction Co. died, Mr. Lage took over the top spot. Lacking experience in certain aspects of management, Lage hired a management consultant as his tutor.

It's job-related. The tutoring improved Mr. Lage's managerial skills required in his job. The fact that the education took place outside the classroom didn't make it a personal expense. Mr. Lage's tutor was a recognized expert in his field, and that's all that mattered [Lage, 52 TC 130].

Question: Can an employer offer job-related educational reimbursements to just its key employees?

Answer: Yes, it can. The company need not offer reimbursements to all of its employees.

How Your Company Can Help You Buy A Home At A Discount—Tax-Free

Home prices continue to climb in many areas. Fortunately the company must be able to help you out with a program that allows key employees to purchase homes in the same general location as the company, at a substantial discount.

Is the employee price break subject to tax? No, says the IRS in a private letter ruling. The discount is, in effect, tax-free income.

Result: An impressive fringe benefit for the key people in your company—including, of course, yourself—with an attractive tax benefit added on.

Facts of the ruling: XYZ Co. rented out some homes it owned near its facilities to employees of the company. The company decided to offer the homes for sale to some key employees with certain restrictions: The home had to be used as a single-family residence; and, the employee also had to give the company an option to repurchase the home within 60 days of one of the following triggering events: the employee died, terminated his or her employment, ceased to use the home as a principal residence, or notified the company of his or her intention to sell. So, in effect, the company was granted a right of first refusal on the home.

The company had an expert outside appraiser determine the fair market value of the houses in a normal market. Then that amount was reduced by 15% by a formula under the plan. The formula took into account factors that would not be present in an ordinary deal: the option, the absence of a broker's commission, and the restriction on the single-family residence. The company was required to repurchase the home under the same formula.

Tax breaks: The employee-homeowner can deduct the real estate taxes and the mortgage interest. And if the company exercises the option to repurchase, the employee's gain from the sale of the home qualifies for the sale-and-replacement tax deferral for principal residences and for the once-in-a-lifetime $125,000 exclusion. And most important, there's this—

▶ **TAX-FREE BENEFIT:** The 15% difference in the purchase price and the normal fair market value does not represent taxable income to the employee.

Reason: Where property is subject to a restriction which never ends—here, the repurchase option—and can be sold only at a price determined under a formula, a special rule comes into play. The price determined by the formula is deemed to be the fair market value of the property (unless the Revenue Service can establish to the contrary) [Ltr. Rul. 7943070].

Question: What happens if the company fails to exercise its option during the 60-day period?

Answer: The Revenue Service would treat that as a cancellation of the restriction. Result: The employee would then have taxable income equal to the difference between the current fair market value of the home and the formula price at the time of cancellation. However, the tax law gives the employee a chance to prove that he or she hasn't received any income. How do you prove it? Here's—

▶ **HOW TO DO IT:** The employee must submit a written statement from the company indicating that the company did not intend to treat the cancellation of the restriction a compensation and that no deduction will be taken for the cancellation. The statement must be filed by the employee with the employee's income tax return for the year in which the cancellation occurred [Reg. §1.83-5(b)].

Chapter 8

How To Use IRAs To Multiply Your Family's Wealth

The Individual Retirement Account (IRA) is one of the most popular tax shelters around. According to the Revenue Service, taxpayers claimed some $32.3 billion in IRA deductions in a recent year. The reasons for the IRA's success are simple—it is easy to set up and it works!

You can set up an IRA and make deductible contributions to it in any year that you (1) have earnings from employment or self-employment, and (2) have not reached age 70½. If you meet these two easy conditions, you qualify for a—

▶ **TWO-WAY TAX SHELTER:** (1) You can contribute as much as $2,000 a year to a regular IRA and deduct every dollar. (2) The interest or other income credited to your account is not taxed currently—your entire account compounds tax-free until you withdraw it.

In effect, the tax dollars you save as a result of the IRA deduction finance part of your investment. The higher your tax bracket, the more of the money going into your IRA is coming from the Federal government. And you don't have to pay back the ''loan'' until you withdraw the money from your IRA.

Example: Mr. Brown is a single taxpayer with no dependents. His taxable income for 1986, after taking into account his exemption and deductions, is $30,000. Without an IRA, Brown's Federal income tax will be $5,833. But if he contributes $2,000 to an IRA by April 15, 1987, his taxable income will be reduced to $28,000. Result: His taxes are cut to $5,233—$600 less than without the IRA. So, in effect, Brown has put only $1,400 of his own money into the IRA. Uncle Sam has loaned Brown the $600 balance. The "loan" isn't repayable until Brown starts taking cash out of the IRA.

You can invest your IRA money in many different ways, ranging from bank accounts or CDs to money market funds or even a self-directed stock portfolio. You can be as aggressive or conservative in investing your IRA funds as you are with your other investments. And you can move your IRA funds from one investment to another as economic conditions or your own circumstances or preferences change.

HOW TO SET UP YOUR IRA TAX SHELTER

There are three basic ways to establish an IRA account:

1. Custodial or trust account: These IRAs are usually set up at a bank, savings and loan, credit union, mutual fund or brokerage firm. The contributions can be invested in savings accounts, mutual fund shares or any other asset that's an acceptable investment for a qualified retirement plan.

2. Annuity or endowment contract: You can use your contributions to purchase an annuity directly from an insurance company. You can also purchase an endowment contract with incidental life insurance features. Only the premium attributable to the retirement savings portion of the contract is deductible.

3. A self-directed account: With this plan you make your own IRA investment decisions. A self-directed account is usually set up as a trust account with a broker.

Q. How much can I contribute to an IRA each year?

A. Your annual deductible contribution to a regular IRA is limited to the lesser of (1) 100% of your earned income or (2) $2,000 in the case of single taxpayers, $2,250 for marrieds where only one spouse works, $4,000 for marrieds where both spouses work.

Special break: A divorced spouse can now treat taxable alimony payments as "earned income" for purposes of the IRA deduction. Thus, a divorced person who receives, say, $8,000 in alimony, can make an annual deductible IRA contribution up to $2,000 even if he or she has no earnings from employment or self-employment.

Q. What happens if I contribute more than the allowable limit?

A. To the extent the contribution is not permitted, it's an "excess contribution." That means it's not deductible and is subject to an annual excise tax. But there are two ways to correct an excess contribution.

▶ **WHAT TO DO:** (1) If you make an excess contribution in any year, you can withdraw the excess by April 15 of the next year and not pay a penalty. (2) You can limit the excise tax to just one year by contributing *less* than the maximum the following year (assuming you're eligible to contribute in that year).

Q. How late in the year can I make my annual IRA contribution?

A. You can make your contribution in the *next* year. Of course, the earlier in the year you make your contribution the faster your tax-sheltered nest egg grows. But you can wait as late as your tax return date (April 15 of the following year) to make a contribution for the year. In fact, you can wait as late as the tax return due date to both set up your IRA *and* make a contribution.

Q. Suppose I mail my IRA to a bank before the April 15 deadline and it arrives at the bank after the deadline. Which date controls—the date I mailed the contribution or the date the bank received it?

A. The postal service is treated as an agent of the bank under the general law of contracts. So IRA contributions made by mail are deemed to be timely if the envelope is *postmarked* by the April 15 due date, regardless of when they are actually received.

Q. What happens to the contribution after I put it in the IRA?

A. The full amount put into an IRA accumulates tax-free until it's withdrawn. So each year you have more dollars earning more dollars. To see what this can mean in dollars-and-cents, let's look at a—

> **Simplified example:** Mr. Brown is 40 years old and in the 50% tax bracket. He wants to put $2,000 of his *pre-tax* earnings aside each year to supplement other retirement income. Let's see what Brown will have by the time he's 65 if he puts money in a—

Bank account at 10% interest: Each year he will be able to deposit an after-tax net of only $1,000. And his 10% annual return is actually only 5% after he pays the tax collector. Result: At age 65, Brown will have about $50,000 in his account.

Individual Retirement Account at 10% interest: Because he can deduct his contribution, Brown puts the full $2,000 in his IRA each year. And his 10% annual return is completely sheltered from tax. *Result:* At age 65, Brown will have about $216,000 in his IRA. Of course, there is a tax bill to pay on that accumulated amount. But even if half goes to the tax collector, Brown will still be left with over $100,000. And Brown may be able to boost his after-tax take by spreading out his IRA withdrawals over his retirement years.

Q. Must I make IRA contributions each year?

A. *No*. If you don't want to contribute in a given year, you can skip it. It's all up to you—you can skip, increase or decrease contributions at your option. But if you don't make a contribution—or contribute less than you could have—you can't make it up in a later year.

Q. Must I make contributions each year to the same IRA?

A. No. You can set up as many IRAs as you want. For example, you can put your IRA contributions in a mutual fund IRA one year and in a savings account IRA the next. Or you can split a year's contribution between two or more IRAs. As long as your total contribution doesn't exceed the annual maximum, you're okay.

Q. Are trustee's fees deductible?

A. Trustee's administrative fees can be deducted only if they are billed separately and paid in connection with your IRA. They are claimed as a miscellaneous itemized deduction.

Q. Can I claim an IRA deduction before the IRA contribution is made?

A. Yes. You can claim an IRA deduction on a return filed before April 15 provided you make your contribution before the April 15 tax return due date.

HOW YOUR IRA MONEY WILL GROW

The chart below shows the nest egg you will accumulate by investing $2,000 each year at various interest rates. To figure the accumulation on an annual contribution of $2,250 (spousal IRA), multiply the accumulation figure by 1.125; for annual contributions of $4,000 ($2,000 for each working spouse), multiply the appropriate accumulation figure by 2.

Total Amount Accumulated In Your IRA

AT THE END OF	7½%	8%	8½%	9%	9½%	10%	11%	12%
10 Yrs.	$ 28,294	$ 28,973	$ 29,670	$ 30,386	$ 31,121	$ 31,875	$ 33,444	$ 35,097
15 Yrs.	$ 52,237	$ 54,304	$ 56,464	$ 58,722	$ 61,080	$ 63,545	$ 68,811	$ 74,550
20 Yrs.	$ 86,609	$ 91,524	$ 96,754	$102,320	$108,244	$114,550	$128,406	$144,105
25 Yrs.	$135,956	$146,212	$157,336	$169,402	$182,492	$196,694	$228,827	$266,668
30 Yrs.	$206,798	$226,566	$248,429	$272,615	$299,375	$328,988	$398,042	$482,665

Note: The chart assumes you deposit your annual IRA contribution at the end of each year. If you deposit your IRA contribution at the beginning of each year, your accumulation will be larger because your money is compounding for a longer period of time. To figure the accumulation if you deposit IRA funds at the beginning of each year, simply multiply the appropriate figure by one plus the interest rate. Example: If you deposit $2,000 at the end of each year, your IRA will grow to $96,754 at the end of 20 years if the account earns 8½% each year. If you make your $2,000 deposit at the beginning of each year and the account grows at 8½% per year, you will have $104,978 at the end of 20 years ($96,754 times 1.085).

Q. Can I move funds from one IRA to another?

A. Yes. You can transfer funds from one IRA account trustee directly to another trustee without limit (but check with both trustees before doing so). Alternatively, you can withdraw your IRA funds and transfer them yourself to another investment. The difference is that the IRA funds come into your hand. This is called an—

▶ **IRA-TO-IRA ROLLOVER:** There are no tax consequences to such a rollover provided the money is redeposited in another IRA within 60 days. And for each IRA you own, you are permitted to make a tax-free rollover only *once a year*.

If you fail to stay within these limitations, the transfer will be taxed to you as a regular IRA withdrawal and what you put in the second IRA may be subject to tax penalties as an excess contribution. On the other hand, you need not make a complete rollover of the distribution to secure tax-free treatment. You can make a partial IRA-to-IRA rollover. The part rolled over is tax-free. The part you put in your pocket is taxable.

▶ **IMPORTANT:** You can avoid the once-a-year rule if the trustee of the old IRA (e.g., the bank holding your CD) agrees to transfer the funds directly to the trustee of the new IRA (e.g., the mutual fund in which you intend to reinvest the funds). It's a good idea to find out about the availability of trustee-to-trustee transfers before you open your IRA.

Q. How are regular IRA withdrawals taxed?

A. IRA withdrawals are taxed as ordinary income in the year you make them. If you use an annuity contract as an IRA, each annuity payment is taxable as you receive it. IRA distributions, whether received in a lump sum or not, are not eligible for the 10-year-averaging treatment that's available for payouts from corporate or Keogh plans. However, you can use regular income averaging.

Q. Can I make withdrawals whenever I want?

A. Yes. But if you make a withdrawal too soon—or too late— you may owe a penalty tax in addition to the regular income tax. If you make a withdrawal before age 59½, it's subject to a 10% excise tax. However, this doesn't apply in cases of death or disability. You must begin making certain minimum withdrawals by April 1 of the year following the year you reach 70½. To the extent your withdrawals fall short of these minimum amounts, there's a 50% excise tax.

How To Squeeze Top Family Tax Savings Out Of Your IRA Contributions

If your spouse does not work outside the home for pay, you can set up a "spousal" IRA on his or her behalf and contribute an additional $250 a year. The annual contribution limit for your IRA and your spousal IRA is the lesser of $2,250 or 100% of your earnings. You have flexibility in allocating deposits. As long as no more than $2,000 is contributed to either IRA account, you can divide the contributions as you wish. A joint account is not allowed. However, you and your spouse can have rights of survivorship in the other's account.

There's no restriction on the amount of investment income a spouse can have and still participate in a spousal IRA. But if he or she has one penny of income from employment or self-employment, you cannot contribute to a spousal IRA. (Incidentally, the date the earnings are received—not the date the work was done—is the controlling factor in determining if a spouse had earned income during a year.)

▶ **ON THE BRIGHT SIDE:** A *working* spouse can set up his or her own regular IRA—or simply begin using a spousal IRA as a regular one. He or she can contribute 100% of earnings, up to $2,000. In other words, if you and your spouse both contribute the maximum, you can put away and deduct $4,000 each year.

Many two-earner families may not be able to put away a full $4,000 each year. Where the total contribution from both spouses is less—$1,500, $2,000, or $3,000—a little astute planning can lead the way to big tax savings:

> **Example 1:** Mr. Reese is 54½ years old and Mrs. Reese is 48 years old. Their wage earnings are about equal. They plan to make a $3,000 IRA contribution this year. How should they split up the contribution?

Tax-saving answer: Mr. Reese should make a $2,000 contribution to his IRA, and Mrs. Reese should put $1,000 in hers. Reason: Mr. Reese can make penalty-free withdrawals from his IRA in just 5 years—when he reaches age 59½. On the other hand, Mrs. Reese will have to wait 11 years to get her IRA money out penalty-free.

> **Example 2:** Mr. Smith earns $50,000 a year; Mrs. Smith, $30,000. They file a joint return. The Smiths want to contribute a total of $2,000 to an IRA this year.

Tax-wise move: Mr. Smith—the higher-earning spouse—should make the $2,000 IRA contribution. At stake is the so-called "marriage penalty deduction." This deduction allows a working couple to deduct 10% of the lesser of $30,000 or the "qualified earned income" of the spouse with lower earnings. IRA contributions are one of several deductions subtracted from earned income to arrive at qualified earned income.

If Mrs. Smith makes the contribution, the Smiths get a working couple deduction of only $2,800 (10% of $28,000 qualified earned income). If Mr. Smith makes the contribution, the Smiths get the maximum $3,000 deduction (10% of $30,000 qualified earned income)—or $200 more.

HOW YOU CAN TRANSFER FUNDS FROM A COMPANY RETIREMENT PLAN TO AN IRA—BEFORE RETIREMENT

Employees now have more control than ever before over their company-paid retirement plan account.

▶ **BIG TAX BREAK:** You can now roll over funds from your company retirement plan to an IRA while still working. The rollover is completely tax-free. Under prior law, a retirement plan to IRA rollover worked only with "lump-sum distributions" made on account of your leaving the job, reaching age 59½, or disability.

The funds you roll over from your company retirement plan can be invested in any of the options available to other IRAs. The rollover is completely separate from your regular IRA contributions. So you can still make a $2,000 deductible contribution regardless of how much money you roll over.

Special rules: In order to qualify for the tax-free rollover break, the distribution must represent at least 50% of your retirement plan account balance. But if your company has several retirement plans, the amounts in the various plans don't have to be aggregated for purposes of the 50% rule. This is a one-shot deal for each plan. You can't repeat it later with the same plan and still get tax-free treatment. You must complete the rollover from the company plan to one or more IRAs within 60 days. And your retirement plan is not required to allow distributions during employment.

Important: Once you have made a rollover of this type from a company retirement plan, future withdrawals from that plan are no longer eligible for ten-year forward averaging or capital gain treatment (See Chapter Seven). But of course ordinary income averaging will still be available.

AN IRA CAN BE A TAX-SAVING FORTUNE-BUILDER— AT ANY AGE

Don't let anyone tell you that "it's too late to start building wealth through an Individual Retirement Account." This is almost never true. In fact, in some respects an IRA is even better for older taxpayers than for younger ones.

▶ **BONANZA FOR ALL AGES:** As long as you have earnings from work— whether you're self-employed or an employee, full-time or part-time—you can set aside in an IRA and deduct from your income up to $2,000 a year ($2,250 if you have a non-working spouse; $4,000 if both spouses work). Chances are good that these amounts will even be increased in years to come. But whatever the amount of your annual set-asides, they grow and compound tax-free until withdrawn.

To see how an IRA can work for you—regardless of your age—let's look at four typical situations.

1. At age 55: Mr. Brown is a business executive, and his wife is not employed. The Brown's top-dollar of income is taxed in the 50% Federal tax bracket. Brown is 55 and expects to retire in ten years.

Brown puts $1,125 into a bank CD every year. These are after-tax dollars, so Brown must earn $2,250 in order to have the $1,125 to invest. The certificate pays 10% interest annually, but Brown nets only 5%—the rest is siphoned off in taxes. Net result: After ten years, the Browns won't have much to show for their investment—a total of just $14,858.

▶ **TOP WEALTH-BUILDING MOVE:** Brown sets up an IRA at his bank and contributes $2,250 to it each year for ten years. The contributions are also invested in bank CDs paying 10%.

The entire $2,250 contribution goes to work for him each year. Since his contribution is deductible, there is no tax depletion. And with tax-free compounding, there is a quick buildup of funds.

Payoff: By the time he reaches 65, Brown will have $39,445 in his IRA. (The difference is almost as dramatic in lower tax brackets.) Of course, Brown has to pay tax on the IRA accumulation when he withdraws it. By that time he will be retired and presumably be in a lower tax bracket. But let's assume the worst. He's still in the 50% bracket and half his IRA accumulation goes to taxes. He still does almost 30% better with the IRA than without it.

2. At age 59½: Mrs. Potter is a self-employed businesswoman and figures she will work another five years—until she is 65. Potter wants to keep her funds liquid in case a business or personal emergency arises.

An IRA is tailor-made for taxpayers like Mrs. Potter. Like the 55-year old Mr. Brown, she can get a fast cash buildup, thanks to the IRA tax shelter. But Potter gets something more.

▶ **SPECIAL IRA EDGE OVER 59½:** Taxpayers must pay a penalty if they want to get their IRA money back before they reach age 59½ (absent death or disability). It's 10% of the IRA withdrawals and is in addition to the regular income tax. Since Mrs. Potter is already age 59½, she is not subject to the penalty tax.

3. On Social Security: Mr. Lee is a 65 year old widower. He receives a pension of $22,000 a year and draws $6,000 in annual Social Security benefits. He also receives a $2,000 director's fee for serving on the board of directors at the company where he formerly worked.

Everything we said about Mrs. Potter holds true for Mr. Lee if he contributes his director's fee to an IRA. But Lee gets an extra benefit. Not only does he shelter his fee from tax, he also—

▶ **SHELTERS SOCIAL SECURITY:** A portion of Social Security benefits are subject to tax when taxable income plus one half of the benefits exceed certain thresholds—$25,000 for singles, $32,000 for marrieds. By contributing his board of director fee to an IRA, Lee avoids having the fee included in the threshold amount. So his other income and one-half of his benefits don't exceed $25,000—and he owes no tax on his benefits.

4. Over age 70½: Mr. Wilson, age 72, earns $3,000 a year from part-time work. Mrs. Wilson is age 65 and isn't employed.

An IRA would offer the same advantages to Mr. Wilson as it does to Mr. Lee. But Mr. Wilson is 72 and the tax law prohibits a taxpayer from making IRA contributions for himself starting in the year he reaches 70½. Is Wilson out of luck? No, he's not.

▶ **GOOD NEWS:** Wilson can still make deductible contributions to an IRA set up for Mrs. Wilson. Reason: When a taxpayer's spouse isn't employed, he can set up an IRA for himself and one for his spouse. He can contribute and deduct a total of $2,250 to the IRA's on a joint return—but no more than $2,000 to any one IRA.

The key here is that the tax law does permit a taxpayer to make a contribution to his nonworking spouse's IRA—even when he can't make one for himself because he's over 70½. So, until Mrs. Wilson reaches age 70½, Mr. Wilson can contribute and deduct as much as $2,000 each year on her behalf.

THREE WAYS TO MAKE A FULL IRA CONTRIBUTION
WHEN YOU HAVEN'T $2,000 TO SPARE

You do not have to contribute to an IRA every year. And when you do, you do not have to contribute the maximum allowed by law. But it is worth going out of your way to do so. A $2,000 contribution generates a $2,000 deduction. If your family's taxable income is $37,000 before the IRA contribution, you'll save $560 in federal income tax at 1986 rates; if it's about $48,000, the deduction saves $660.

Several "creative financing" techniques can squeeze out IRA investment money even if your finances currently appear as bloodless as a stone.

1. *Tap your company plan:* If your company has a profit-sharing plan to which you've made *nondeductible* voluntary contributions, the stage is set to fund an IRA without spending a dime. Withdraw $2,000 of your voluntary contribution to the company plan and put it into the IRA.

This is a can't-lose proposition as far as taxes go. You owe no tax on the withdrawal because it is treated as a nontaxable return of capital up to the amount of prior contributions. And the IRA contribution is, of course, deductible. In essence you've shifted retirement funds from your profit-sharing plan to an IRA, and picked up a bonus $2,000 deduction along the way.

2. *Float a tax loan:* Using a tax refund to fund your tax deductible IRA is like using Goliath's own weight to throw him. Oddly enough, Goliath's rules permit this [Revenue Ruling 84-18, IRB 1984-6]. A taxpayer should be able to claim a deduction for an IRA contribution made after the tax return is filed if the contribution is made no later than the tax return due date.

> *Example:* The Fullers are in the 38% bracket. They want to make a $2,000 IRA contribution for 1986, but have only $1,240. A $2,000 IRA deduction would create a $760 refund and provide the cash needed to make a full IRA contribution. The Fullers file their 1986 Form 1040 in January, 1987, and claim their $2,000 IRA deduction. They get their refund check and actually make the IRA contribution by April 15.

Important: Once the deduction is claimed it is crucial that you carry through and make the contribution by April 15. And note that any extensions you get for your tax return filing date do *not* extend the deadline for making an IRA contribution. Failure to contribute in time (or to file an amended return) can lead to severe penalties.

3. *Borrow the contribution:* A fast way to raise your IRA investment is to borrow the money from a bank, or other source of credit. For instance, let's say Mr. Green recently took out a loan from a bank. He used the loan to make a contribution to an Individual Retirement Account. Result: The Government says the interest Green pays is deductible [Ltr. Rul. 8527082].

> ▶ **Reason:** Expenses allocable to tax-exempt income are generally not deductible. But the Revenue Service says that this rule does not affect the current deduction

of interest where the loan proceeds are contributed to an IRA. Reason: The interest is an expense allocable to the loan, not to IRA income.

Q. Suppose this isn't a one-shot affair. Suppose Green repeats the process each year. Could Green still deduct the interest?

A. He should be able to. The Government certainly did not say that Green's borrowing had to be limited to one year.

▶ **IDEA IN ACTION:** In the first year, let's say Green borrows $2,000 to make his IRA contribution. But in subsequent years, the tax savings from the prior year's IRA contribution are used to reduce the extra amount that must be borrowed that year. Green makes deductible interest payments on the outstanding loan balance each year.

The loan balance and interest payments will increase each year. But the IRA contributions also grow and compound. The IRA earnings are tax deferred: there is no tax due until they are withdrawn at retirement.

Of course, the interest charges come out of the taxpayer's pocket each year, while the IRA earnings stay out of reach until the taxpayer reaches age 59½ (or death or disability). But the taxpayer more than makes up for this when the IRA funds are finally withdrawn. The IRA accumulation will be large enough for the taxpayer to repay the loan, recoup the interest expense and still have thousands left over. Another plus: The funds that would have gone into the IRA, if there had been no borrowings, remain in the taxpayer's pocket.

Example: Mr. Green, age 40, is in the 50% tax bracket. This year, he borrows $2,000 from a bank to make an IRA contribution putting up, say, stock as collateral. (He can't use the IRA itself as collateral.) Next year he borrows another $1,000 from the bank and combines it with the $1,000 in tax savings from the prior year's IRA contribution to make a $2,000 IRA contribution. In following years, Green follows the same strategy. The interest on the loans is 12% per annum. But, since interest is deductible, the after-tax interest charge is only 6%. Green earns 10% on his IRA contributions compounded annually. The chart on the next page shows how he comes out over 20 years.

Let's say that Green retires at age 60 and withdraws his entire IRA account. Assuming he is still in the 50% tax bracket that year, he will pay $63,001 in taxes on the distribution (50% of $126,002). After repaying the $21,000 outstanding balance on his loan and recouping his after-tax interest payments (total of $13,800), Green ends up with $28,201 free and clear.

▶ **BETTER WAY:** Instead of withdrawing his entire IRA balance in the year he retires, Green withdraws just enough to pay off the loan. He rolls the rest over into an IRA annuity.

If Green withdraws $42,000, he'll be left with $21,000 after tax—just enough to pay off the loan.

Year	Accumulated Borrowings	Annual After-Tax Interest	IRA Accumulation
1	$ 2,000	$ 120	$ 2,200
2	3,000	180	4,620
3	4,000	240	7,282
4	5,000	300	10,210
5	6,000	360	13,431
6	7,000	420	16,974
7	8,000	480	20,871
8	9,000	540	25,158
9	10,000	600	29,874
10	11,000	660	35,061
11	12,000	720	40,767
12	13,000	780	47,044
13	14,000	840	53,949
14	15,000	900	61,543
15	16,000	960	69,898
16	17,000	1,020	79,088
17	18,000	1,080	89,196
18	19,000	1,140	100,316
19	20,000	1,200	112,547
20	21,000	1,260	126,002

Result: Green rolls over the $84,002 balance ($126,002 minus $42,000) into an IRA annuity. Assuming that, he selects a 10-year fixed period annuity, he will receive about $9,759 a year to supplement his retirement income. Assuming that, with annuity payments rather than a lump sum payout, Green's marginal tax rate drops to 33% after retirement—he's getting an annual after-tax yield of $6,507. In a little more than two years he will recoup his interest payments and after ten years, Brown will have $51,270 free and clear.

Important: If Green is counting on his IRA as a primary source of retirement income, he would be better off contributing $2,000 out of his own pocket and skipping the loans. But if he can put the $2,000 that would have gone to the IRA into another good investment, he can end up with the best of both worlds at retirement—the income from his other investment plus the money from his IRA.

AN IRA ALTERNATIVE THAT RUNS ITSELF

At the same time that IRAs became available to taxpayers who were members of a company pension or profit-sharing plan, another avenue for accumulating retirement savings opened up for them. As an alternative to making contributions to an IRA, you can make deductible voluntary contributions to your company plan, provided the plan permits this.

▶ **WHICH IS RIGHT FOR YOU?** A company plan may offer the convenience of contributing by payroll deduction. Also, because of the large amounts involved, a company plan may be able to get a better return on its investment than you can safely achieve investing on your own. Finally, the plan investments are professionally managed. On the other hand, with an IRA you call the shots. You can move your funds from one IRA investment to another as the changing economic times dictate.

There are a lot of similarities between voluntary contributions and IRAs. In general, the maximum deductible contribution an employee can make to either an IRA or as a voluntary contribution to a company plan is $2,000. Contributions to either setup grow tax-free, and you can't make withdrawals before age 59½ without penalty (except for disability). When you do withdraw your money at retirement, the payouts qualify for regular income averaging only.

There are, however, three areas where the IRA and the voluntary deductible contribution differ:

1. *Contributions for non-working spouse:* If your spouse doesn't work, you can contribute and deduct $2,250 to a spousal IRA. You can divide the contribution as you wish as long as no more than $2,000 is contributed to the account of either spouse. On the other hand, your maximum contribution to a company plan would still be limited to $2,000. The other $250 would have to be contributed to a separate spousal IRA.

2. *Tax-free rollover:* Amounts in an IRA generally cannot be rolled over into a company retirement plan. But deductible voluntary contributions to a company plan can be rolled over into another employer's retirement plan. The rollover is permitted, however, only if the second employer's plan (1) permits such rollovers on a nondiscriminatory basis, and (2) continues to treat your rollover as a deductible voluntary contribution.

3. *Time for withdrawals:* You must begin withdrawing money from an IRA in the year you reach age 70½ or face a big penalty. But funds from your deductible voluntary contribution account don't have to be withdrawn at any certain time.

Final point: Check with the administrator of your company plan to see when contributions must be made. While you can contribute to an IRA up to the tax return due date of the year at issue, the company plan may not offer this flexibility. Contributions made in 1986—even before April 15—may have to be treated as 1986 contributions.

HOW TO GET A TAX-FREE, INTEREST-FREE LOAN
FROM YOUR IRA SOURCE

You *can* borrow money from your Individual Retirement Account—and do it tax-free and interest-free. That may come as a surprise: As a general rule, the tax law prohibits borrowing from an IRA. Loans are treated as "premature distributions," subject to a 10% penalty tax, as well as the regular income tax on distributions. However, in two situations, the tax law does permit you to have access to your IRA funds on a tax-free, short-term basis. Technically speaking, these are not considered loans, so they don't violate the prohibition against borrowing. But the bottom line is that you do get temporary use of your money. In our book, that amounts to a loan.

▶ **LOAN STRATEGY #1:** You can roll over part or all funds from one IRA into another IRA. The key here is that you have 60 days to complete the rollover. Meanwhile, you can put the funds to any use you want.

Example: Mr. Smith, age 40, has two IRAs, one at his bank and one at a stock brokerage firm. Smith gets a stock tip that he is certain will give him a chance to make a quick profit. But he lacks the funds to invest.

▶ **IDEA IN ACTION:** Smith makes a withdrawal from the IRA at the brokerage firm and invests in the stock. Within 60 days, he sells the stock, pockets his profit and rolls the remainder (an amount equal to his original IRA withdrawal) over into his bank IRA.

Result: The only tax Smith owes is the tax on his stock profit. Because Smith rolled his IRA withdrawal over into another IRA within 60 days, it's tax-free. There is no penalty tax and no regular income tax. (Note: Rollovers from one IRA to another are permitted only once in a one-year period and, of course, there is no deduction for the rollover.)

▶ **LOAN STRATEGY #2:** An IRA withdrawal is "premature" only if you are under 59½. If you are 59½ or older, there is no penalty tax. The withdrawal is, of course, subject to the regular income tax. However, if the withdrawal doesn't exceed $2,000, you can redeposit the money by the tax return due date for the year of the withdrawal and get a standard IRA deduction that offsets your taxable distribution (assuming you are still working and eligible to make IRA contributions). Net result: The tax-free use of your money for much longer than 60 days.

Example: Mr. Jones, age 60, has an IRA at his bank. Jones promised his grandson a home computer as a graduation present in 1986, but is short of cash.

▶ **IDEA IN ACTION:** Jones withdraws $2,000 (or any lesser amount) from his IRA and uses it to pay for the home computer. Then on or before April 15, 1987, he puts the money back in his IRA.

Result: Since Jones is over age 59½, there is no penalty tax on the IRA withdrawal. But he does have to report the $2,000 withdrawal on his 1986 tax return as a regular IRA distribution.

However, Jones has also made an IRA contribution—even though the "contribution" was merely a redeposit of the funds withdrawn earlier. And, because he made this contribution before the due date of his 1986 return, he can claim a $2,000 deduction for the contribution on his 1986 return (assuming he hasn't made any other IRA contributions for 1986). So the deduction will wash out the taxable income he has on the withdrawal—making it effectively tax-free. (Jones can, of course, withdraw more than $2,000, but he won't be able to shelter the excess with an IRA deduction.)

HOW TO USE YOUR IRA TO BUILD A FORTUNE FOR YOUR FAMILY

How you invest your IRA contributions is one of the most significant financial decisions you will ever make. That's a tall statement about something whose main attraction right now is a tax deduction. But the numbers speak for themselves: An annual IRA contribution of $2,000 invested at 10% will grow to $362,000 after 30 years. If the same annual contribution is invested at 9%, you'll have $297,000 at the end of 30 years.

A mere one percent difference in investment yield is magnified to a 22% difference in eventual income. It's easy to see that a tax-deferred IRA not only compounds your interest, it compounds your strokes of genius—and carelessness—as well.

Where to start your fortune: 60% of IRA deposits are currently in savings accounts and certificates of deposit at banks and savings and loan associations. It's possible that your IRA should be numbered among them. But it is unlikely that plopping down your IRA at the closest bank—even to get a toaster—is the right move. Banks differ, too. That $362,000, which was compounded *annually*, would be $422,000 if the bank compounded interest *daily*. With $60,000 you can buy a lot of toasters, even in the year 2015.

What You Can—And Cannot—Invest In

Some IRA investments are ruled out by law, others by plain common sense.

By law, you can't invest in life insurance. The ostensible purpose of an IRA is to provide retirement income for you, not a death benefit for your family.

By law, you cannot invest on margin: This is the equivalent of pledging IRA assets as security for a loan, which is a prohibited transaction. You must pay full value for stocks, bonds and other securities. If you hold stocks in an IRA, you cannot sell the stocks short, since it involves "borrowing" stock. Commodity contracts, which are highly margined, are ruled out entirely.

By law, you cannot invest in collectibles: The Government wants IRA savings invested in the economic mainstream, not in stamps, coins, vintage wines, etc. The restriction on "collectibles" also eliminates purchases of gold and silver bullion, or certificates representing bullion. (You can, however, invest in gold or silver through mining company stocks.)

Common sense rules out investments that are not enhanced by being placed in a tax-sheltered IRA. Tax-free municipal bonds, for instance, usually pay a percentage point or two less than taxable bonds. In a tax-deferred IRA there is no tax difference between municipals and taxable bonds, so municipals are inappropriate. Tax-sheltered investments such as real estate and oil and gas also lose some lustre in an IRA since writeoffs for depreciation, mortgage interest, intangible drilling expenses, etc. are useless.

A Buyer's Guide To IRA Investments

Before you select an investment, ask yourself one crucial question. What kind of money manager am I? In other words, how much time and inclination do you have to handle your money. Where you should invest depends to a great extent on your answer. For instance:

"No interest at all." Then you're probably best off with a get-it-and-forget-it investment such as long-term bank CDs, high grade corporate zero coupon bonds, or treasury receipts. You may also consider an annuity.

"Some interest." Moving your IRA funds between a bank's fixed rate six-month CDs and its money market deposit account (or variable rate CD) may be your best strategy. When you feel interest rates are on the way up, you can ride them in the variable rate investment. When they've peaked or are on the way down, you lock in the current high rate by putting your funds in a CD.

"Much interest." A family of mutual funds may be your best bet. You can switch at little cost from a money market fund paying daily interest to stock and bond funds that offer different profit strategies. You decide your overall investment aims; the funds' managers select the specific securities.

"Great interest." If you are enthusiastic about following your IRA investment on a daily basis, then a self-directed account with a broker may be for you.

Keep in mind that as you grow older and your IRA grows bigger your interest in managing the funds in it may increase. At the same time, more options open up. Reason: Some investments carry significant fixed fees and commissions. While they are prohibitively expensive for a $2,000 IRA, they are not very onerous for a $10,000 or $15,000 account. On the other hand, as you near retirement some investments develop drawbacks that you may want to avoid.

Bank certificates of deposit: Most bank IRAs are invested in certificates of deposit. These are issued for a fixed term—usually from three months to five years—and pay a fixed—or less commonly, a variable—rate of interest. Bank CDs are insured up to $100,000 by an agency of the Federal Government and are extremely safe. Compare CDs on the basis of "effective annual yield." This reflects the bank's compounding policy (e.g., quarterly, monthly, daily).

As a general rule, the longer a CD's maturity the higher the interest rate it pays. But while there are low or nonexistent administration fees, there are also stiff penalties for cashing in a CD prematurely.

Banks are permitted to impose stiffer penalties than those required by government regulations. So it pays to take a close look at the fine print. The current *minimum penalties* for early withdrawal are as follows:

- *Three months' interest (often six months')* on a CD with a term of one year or more.

  - *One month's interest* on CDs with a term of one month to a year.

  - *All interest* on CDs with a term shorter than a month.

Banks can waive early withdrawal penalties for depositors who are age 59½ or over. Profit angle: If this is your bank's policy and you meet the age requirement, select a CD with the longest maturity and highest yield.

Penalties are not stone walls: If interest rates rise sharply after you buy a long-term CD, it may pay to absorb the penalty for early withdrawal and transfer the money to a CD paying higher interest. You can ask the bank to calculate the differential for you.

> **Example:** You invest $2,000 in a four-year CD paying 10%, compounded annually. A year later, you can invest in a three-year CD paying 13%. If you hold the old CD to maturity, you have $2,928. If you switch to the 13% CD, you have $3,102— *even after paying the $50 penalty.*

Money-market accounts: A *money market mutual fund* pools the investments of its shareholders and invests in bank CDs, Treasury bills, banker's acceptances and the commercial paper of large corporations—all short-term money-market investments. A money market fund's interest rate changes from day to day. (For more on money market funds, see Chapter Two.)

A *money market deposit account* is offered by banks. It sounds the same, and in many ways acts the same, as a money market fund. But the deposit account is fundamentally different. Unlike the money market fund, the bank deposit account is federally insured up to $100,000. Also, many banks do not charge a fee to open and maintain an IRA money market deposit account. Most of the funds do. The interest rate paid by a money market deposit account changes weekly or monthly. It may or may not be pegged to an index of what money market funds are paying. The rates, however, tend to be slightly lower than you would get for a two-to-five year CD. But banks attempt—and by and large they've succeeded—to keep their money market rate competitive with rates offered by the mutual funds.

So why set up an IRA with a money market fund? One reason is that some banks don't permit IRA investments in their money market accounts. Another reason, and a good one, is that many money market funds are a part of a larger family of mutual funds. For a small fee or no fee at all, you can switch your IRA to a stock mutual fund or a bond fund in the same family, depending on where you feel the profit opportunities are greatest. If you feel that both stocks and bonds are headed down, you can switch back to the money market fund and earn the going rate of interest on your money.

Caution: Some money funds charge a fee of $5 or $10 to open an IRA. Most charge a fee of $20 or less per year to maintain the account. These fees substantially cut your yield if you are investing a small amount.

Example: You put $800 into a money market fund IRA. It earns an annual return of 9%. If an administration fee of $10 is charged against your account, your net yield is cut dramatically to 7.75%. Make sure that a management fee is charged to you whenever possible, not to your IRA. Request that the account trustee bill the fee separately and pay it by separate check. *Result:* The fee is tax deductible as an expense for the production of income. And you have that much more money working tax-free in your IRA.

Stock mutual funds: The nearer you are to drawing on your IRA for retirement income, the *less* advisable it is to invest in a stock mutual fund (see Chapter Two for details on how these funds work). In other words, leave yourself time to ride out a bear market and capitalize on the expected long-term growth in stock values.

On the other hand, if you are within five—or even ten—years of retirement, you have to consider that a short-term drop in stock values could mean that you will have to sell mutual fund shares at a loss. In an IRA, you get no tax benefit from this loss.

Corporate bonds: The denominations of corporate bonds are usually too large to make them practical for an IRA. But the minimum investment for bond mutual funds and unit trusts (as low as $1,000) puts them in range. Such funds also reduce your risk by diversifying your investment over a number of bonds. See Chapter Two for details on their operation. Bond values fluctuate with interest rates. So the same considerations that apply to stock funds apply—though to a lesser degree—to bond funds.

One type of corporate bond, however, is tailor-made for IRAs and other tax sheltered investors.

▶ **THE ZERO COUPON BOND:** These bonds are sold at a deep discount from face value and pay no periodic interest. Their yield is the difference between the price paid and the face value which you receive at redemption. For instance, a $5,000 bond that matures in 16 years may cost $1,250. When you buy it, you lock in a known annual return of 9.05%.

Zero coupon corporate bonds are available in maturities ranging up to 33 years. But since you receive no income until maturity, it's essential that you invest only in bonds of reliable corporations.

Treasury receipts: These are, in effect, zero-coupon Treasury bonds (see Chapter Two for details). Since the underlying investment is guaranteed by the U.S. Government, treasury receipts are safer than zero-coupon corporate bonds.

The disadvantage of Treasury receipts is that they are truly a long-term commitment—on your part as well as the U.S. Government's. The brokers who create stripped Treasury bonds do not promise to maintain a secondary market for them. Reselling them may be difficult. A fair price is not assured. And that may mean you are locked into a relatively low return if interest rates rise above the rate at which you bought.

On the other hand, if interest rates go down, you continue to receive an above-market return on every cent you have invested. You don't have to reinvest proceeds at a lower rate.

Ginnie Mae Certificates: A Ginnie Mae Certificate represents ownership in a pool of mortgages. Payment of interest and principal are guaranteed by the Federal government. An individual certificate costs $25,000 (with $5,000 increments above that). That puts it out of the IRA league. However, for as little as $1,000 you can buy a unit in a Ginnie Mae trust or invest in a mutual fund which buys Ginnie Mae certificates exclusively. See Chapter Two for more details on Ginnie Maes and a description of how funds and trusts work. The return on Ginnie Mae certificates is attractive. The Government guarantee is also appealing. But for the IRA investor there are some—

▶ **SPECIAL CONSIDERATIONS:** The commission cost for investing in a unit trust is pretty high. A 4% charge is not unusual. Moreover, since the Ginnie Maes pay out a constant stream of principal and interest, you should make sure the payout is reinvested in a safe, high-yielding alternative investment. (Mutual funds reinvest earnings in other Ginnie Maes; unit trusts often "rollover" payments into a money market account.)

The value of your mutual fund shares or trust fund unit will fluctuate with interest rates. You may receive less than your principal investment if you are forced to sell when rates are high.

Annuities: Annuities are issued by life insurance companies and sold by their sales staff or other agents. They offer a unique advantage:

A life annuity assures you that you will never outlive your capital. You—or you and your spouse if you wish—are guaranteed a fixed monthly income for life.

An IRA annuity must provide for flexible premium payments. In other words, you can contribute $2,000 a year, $700 the next. You can also change the timing of your payments, from quarterly to semi-quarterly or annually—or vice-versa. How large your monthly annuity payments will be depends on how much you contributed, how good a return the insurance company earned on its investments, and your life expectancy at the time the payments begin. (Payments are lower if the annuity is for you and your surviving spouse.)

Fixed rate and variable rate annuities: All annuities guarantee a minimum annual return. A *fixed rate annuity* also guarantees a maximum return for the first year or two. This may be as high as 12%. After this initial period the return on your annuity contributions depends on the insurance company's return on its investments. In the past, annuities have realized a poor return compared with other investments. So be especially careful of multi-year projections based on the rate offered in the first year. With a *variable rate annuity* your return varies with the investment you choose. You can have the insurance company invest your contributions in a money market fund, a stock fund, or a fixed income growth fund. You can usually switch between these investments.

Fees are a major consideration when you invest in an annuity. A so-called "front load" may reduce your contribution by 8% or 9%. There may also be a small annual maintenance fee. "Back load" annuities usually charge a larger annual fee—$25 to $30. And they impose a hefty surrender charge—7% to 8%— if you withdraw early from the annuity. This charge decreases each year so that after about the tenth there is no penalty for withdrawal. (As we noted earlier, the annual fees are deductible if they are separately billed and separately paid.)

▶ **WORD TO THE WISE** There doesn't seem to be any compelling reason to invest your IRA in an annuity if you aren't near retirement age. It is always possible, if you decide that an annuity is right for you (and remember, it involves giving up a possible legacy to your heirs), to rollover your IRA funds into a single-premium annuity just before you retire. It is entirely likely that until that time, careful investing on your part will produce a larger IRA nest egg—and hence, large annuity payments— than the expensive ministrations of an insurance company.

A self-directed IRA: You can open an ordinary fixed custodian IRA account with a broker and invest in long-term securities such as Ginnie Maes, Treasury bonds and receipts, "load" mutual funds, what have you. Alternatively, you can open a self-directed IRA in order to buy and sell individual securities at a faster pace.

A self-directed account will involve high fees: Usually $25 to $30 to set up the account and an annual maintenance fee of $35 to $50. (You will want these tax deductible fees separately billed to you, not to your IRA.) In addition, you pay the regular broker's commission on trades.

A self-directed IRA is for the younger investor or the investor whose retirement income is secured apart from his IRA. There's another—

▶ **SPECIAL CONSIDERATION:** An initial IRA contribution of $2,000 or even $4,000 is too little with which to open a self-directed account, especially since you cannot buy securities on margin. You will be forced to buy lower priced stock or to buy odd lots that will eat up your investment in commissions. So you should not open a self-directed IRA until it has accumulated at least $10,000 in another investment.

THE TAX WISE WAY TO TAKE CASH OUT OF YOUR IRA

Tax savings is often a matter of timing—and that's certainly the case when it comes to your IRA withdrawals. To a large extent, you can control the amount of tax you will pay on your IRA cash.

Withdrawals before age 59½: This is the worst possible time to take money out of an IRA. Reason: The withdrawal is hit with both regular income taxes and a 10% penalty tax. For example, if you are in the 33% federal tax bracket (for taxpayers filing a joint return in 1986, taxable income between $37,980 and $49,420), you will pay 43¢ in tax on every dollar you withdraw. And that's just federal tax—state and local income tax will cut your take even more.

Withdrawals after age 59½ and before retirement: Once you reach age 59½, your IRA is like a tax-sheltered savings account. Your annual contributions to the IRA are tax deductible and your account earns tax-sheltered income. And you can withdraw money without paying a 10% penalty tax.

▶ **TAX SAVING STRATEGY:** If at all possible, avoid withdrawing IRA cash before you retire. Reason: You are likely to be in a much higher tax bracket during your working years than during your retirement years. So a pre-retirement withdrawal will be taxed at a higher rate.

Withdrawals after you retire: This is the best time to take money out of an IRA. And, at this point, you can pretty much write your own ticket when it comes to withdrawals.

• You can take out all your money in one lump sum. From the tax point of view, however, this is not a very good idea. Reasons: You don't get any special tax breaks on a lump-sum withdrawal—it's taxed as ordinary income, just like interest or dividends. And a large withdrawal may propel you into a higher tax bracket or even result in a federal income tax on part of your Social Security retirement benefits (see Chapter Nine).

• You can make periodic withdrawals from your IRA to supplement your other retirement income, withdraw each year's interest (leaving the principal intact), or set up a systematic withdrawal program. For example, you can use the money in your IRA to purchase an annuity that will make fixed monthly payments for your lifetime (single-life annuity), or for your lifetime and the lifetime of a beneficiary, such as a spouse (joint life annuity). Or you can arrange for fixed installment payments over a period of years.

• Of course, if you are living comfortably on your Social Security checks, company retirement plan and earnings on your other assets, you don't have to tap your IRA funds at all. You can simply let the IRA accumulate tax sheltered dividends or interest until you are age 70½.

• **At age 70½:** The tax law requires you to begin taking money out of all your IRA accounts at this point, whether or not you are retired. You have three payout choices:

(1) A lump-sum payout of everything in your IRAs.

(2) You can purchase an annuity that will make fixed payments for your life or the lives of you and your designated beneficiary. For example, let's assume a taxpayer has accumulated $30,000 in his IRA accounts. If the taxpayer is a male, the money will buy a single-life annuity paying about $342 a month. If the taxpayer is a female, the cash will buy a single life annuity paying about $300 a month (because of a female's longer life expectancy at age 70). Advantage of the annuity method: You will never outlive your IRA income. Disadvantage: After you die (or after you and your designated beneficiary die), the payments stop. There's nothing left for your heirs.

(3) You can arrange for your IRA balance to be paid out in installments. The installments can last for a period of time that does not extend beyond your life expectancy, or the life expectancy of you and your designated beneficiary.

How to figure your payouts under the installment method: There are three ways to take payouts if you use this method.

● *Method #1:* If the installment payments are for your life only, your life expectancy at age 70 is the key factor. If you are a female, your first annual payment must be at least 1/15th of your account balance (a female's life expectancy at age 70 is 15 years). In the second year, your payment must be at least 1/14th, the third, 1/13th, and so forth, until everything is paid out of the IRA. If you are a male, your first annual payment must be at least 1/12.1 of your entire account balance (12.1 years is a male's life expectancy at age 70). In the second year, your payment is 1/11.1 of the account balance, and so forth.

▶ **HUSBAND AND WIFE:** You can arrange for installment payments to last as long as the combined life expectancy of you and your spouse. Joint life expectancies are shown in the table below:

Owner of Individual Retirement Arrangement	Age of Spouse (In year you became age 70½)												
	61	62	63	64	65	66	67	68	69	70	71	72	73
Female-Multiple	21.6	21.1	20.7	20.3	19.9	19.6	19.2	18.9	18.6	18.3	18.0	17.8	17.5
Male-Multiple	23.0	22.4	21.8	21.2	20.7	20.2	19.7	19.2	18.7	18.3	17.9	17.5	17.1

Owner of Individual Retirement Arrangement	Age of Spouse (In year you became age 70½)												
	74	75	76	77	78	79	80	81	82	83	84	85
Female-Multiple	17.3	17.1	16.9	16.7	16.6	16.4	16.3	16.2	16.0	15.9	15.8	15.8
Male-Multiple	16.7	16.4	16.1	15.8	15.5	15.2	14.9	14.7	14.5	14.3	14.1	13.9

Example (1): If Anne Smith is age 70, and her husband is age 71, their combined joint life expectancy is 18 years. Their first annual payment must be at least 1/18th the balance in Anne's IRA, the second, 1/17th, etc.

Method #2: If you want to stretch out your IRA payments for a longer period of time, you can have your IRA trustee base annual installments on your *recalculated* life expectancy each year. Generally, the longer you live, the longer you're expected to live. So you can spread your required distributions over a longer period of time.

Result: Smaller distributions to you, and more money stays in the tax-sheltered IRA for your children or grandchildren.

Example (2): Same facts as in Example (1), except that Anne Smith asks for installment payouts based on recalculated life expectancies. In the first year, her payout will be 1/18th the account balance (same as in Method #1). However, in the second year, her payout will be 1/17.6 of her account balance (the combined life expectancy of a female age 71 and a male age 72 is 17.6 years).

Method #3: You can base the minimum required distribution on the longer life expectancy of you and your child or grandchild, instead of your spouse. Result: Still smaller required distributions to you, and more for your heirs.

There are, however, limits to this method. Withdrawals must be set up so that you are expected to receive at least 50% of your IRA over your lifetime (the general rule for annuities as well as installment payments). In addition, you cannot base installment payments on a recalculated life expectancy. That's strictly an option for a husband and wife (or for a taxpayer who bases payouts on his own life expectancy).

If You Die Before Receiving Everything In Your IRA

The rate at which the IRA must distribute benefits to your designated beneficiary depends on whether or not distributions began prior to death.

• Distributions did not begin before death: As a general rule, your IRA account can be paid out to your designated beneficiary over his or her life or life expectancy. The distribution must, however, generally begin within one year after you die. Of course, your beneficiary can ask for an accelerated payment schedule.

If you name your spouse as your designated beneficiary, the distribution of benefits does not have to begin until April 1 of the year following the year you would have reached age 70½. The distribution can then be over the life or the life expectancy of the spouse.

• Distribution did begin before death: The payout of remaining benefits need only continue as per the payout schedule in effect prior to death.

Estate taxes: All IRA benefits are subject to estate taxes. But if the IRA owner's spouse is the beneficiary, the unlimited marital deduction will shelter the entire payout from estate taxes regardless of the size of the IRA account (see Chapter 13). If the beneficiary is not the IRA owner's spouse, the entire account balance will be included in the decedent's estate. Keep in mind that by 1987, the unified estate and gift tax credit will shelter up to $600,000 from estate taxes.

Chapter 9

How Social Security Helps You And Your Family—Both Now And In The Future

The Social Security system has provided retirement benefits to millions of qualified workers for some 50 years. But monthly checks for retirees represent only part of the benefits available to workers and their families under Social Security. The system also provides payments to disabled workers and to survivors of deceased workers. And while it is possible to plan for retirement, there's no telling when an accident or illness may strike, leaving a worker and his or her family in need of financial help.

That's why now is a good time to take a close look at what Social Security can do for you. This chapter shows you how to get and keep the most Social Security benefit dollars. You'll find details on the benefits you and your dependents are eligible for, how to qualify, and how to reduce—or even eliminate—the Federal income tax on Social Security benefits. Also highlighted are the key facts you need to know about the Federal health-insurance system known as Medicare.

HOW TO QUALIFY FOR RETIREMENT BENEFITS

You are eligible for most Social Security benefits only if you are "fully insured." You become "fully insured" when you meet the quarters-of-coverage requirement. Quarters of coverage refers to the number of calendar quarters (three month periods) in which you earned a minimum amount as an employee or a self-employed worker. (In 1986, the minimum amount is $440 a quarter.) The exact number of quarters of coverage needed to be fully insured depends on your age. Your age in years translates into the required quarters.

▶ **BASIC FORMULA:** In general, forty quarters is the most you need. Specifically, count the number of years after 1950 (or after the year in which you turn 21, if later) up through the year you become 61. The number of years equals the number of quarters of coverage needed to be fully insured.

For example, if you reach age 61 in 1986, you have 36 years after 1955. That means you need 36 quarters of coverage, or nine years of work. If you reach age 61 in 1990 or later, you need the maximum forty quarters of coverage.

Being "fully insured" entitles you and your family to benefits when you retire. You are in "currently insured" status when you have at least six quarters of coverage. That means your survivors are entitled to benefits if you die before becoming "fully insured."

When you qualify for retirement benefits: You can retire any time on or after your 65th birthday with full Social Security benefits, if you were born before 1938. If you were born in 1938 or later, you must wait beyond your 65th birthday to draw full retirement benefits. The normal retirement age is gradually raised to 67 over a 27-year period, depending on your birthdate. The first two columns in the chart that follows show what your normal retirement age will be.

At-A-Glance Guide to Your Retirement Benefits Under the Social Security Law

Born	Retirement with full benefits at age:	Early retirement (age 62) % of full benefit available to retirees	Benefit increase for each year worked after normal retirement age
1924-and before	65 years	80.0%	3.0%
1925-1926	65 years	80.0%	3.5%
1927-1928	65 years	80.0%	4.0%
1929-1930	65 years	80.0%	4.5%
1931-1932	65 years	80.0%	5.0%
1933-1934	65 years	80.0%	5.5%
1935-1936	65 years	80.0%	6.0%
1937	65 years	80.0%	6.5%
1938	65 & 2 months	79.2%	6.5%
1939	65 & 4 months	78.3%	7.0%
1940	65 & 6 months	77.5%	7.0%
1941	65 & 8 months	76.7%	7.5%
1942	65 & 10 months	75.8%	7.5%
1943-1954	66 years	75.0%	8.0%
1955	66 & 2 months	74.2%	8.0%
1956	66 & 4 months	73.3%	8.0%
1957	66 & 6 months	72.5%	8.0%
1958	66 & 8 months	71.7%	8.0%
1959	66 & 10 months	70.8%	8.0%
1960-and after	67 years	70.0%	8.0%

If you retire early: Your minimum—or early—retirement age is 62, regardless of your normal retirement age. The third column in the above chart shows how much of your full benefit you will receive at age 62, depending on when you were born. For example, if your normal retirement age is 66 (you were born between 1943 and 1954), you will receive 75% of your full benefit if you retire at age 62.

If you retire before your normal retirement age, your monthly benefit will be less than your Primary Insurance Amount, or PIA. The PIA is the benefit you would have received had you retired at normal retirement age. What's more, as a general rule, your benefit is reduced permanently. In other words, if you retire at age 62 (and don't go back to work afterwards), you won't get higher benefit checks once you reach your normal retirement age.

If you retire early, your full benefit is reduced by 5/9 of 1% for each month you receive benefits before your normal retirement age. For example, if your normal retirement age is 65, and you retire at age 62, you receive 80% of your PIA; at age 63, you get 86.6%; at age 64, you get 93.3%.

How much money you are entitled to receive: At your normal retirement age, you receive your full benefit (PIA). How large your PIA will be depends upon your average earnings during the years you were covered under Social Security. When you are ready to retire, the Social Security Administration will calculate your monthly payment. Under current law, after you retire, your benefit goes up each year to compensate for any increases in the cost of living.

1986 benefits: The maximum monthly benefit payable to a worker retiring at age 65 is $760. It's $630 if he or she retires this year at age 62 (roughly 80% of the benefit he would have received if he retired in 1989 at age 65). These top benefits are payable to workers whose annual wages or self-employment earnings equaled or exceeded the Social Security wage base each year. The wage base is the maximum amount of earnings that are subject to Social Security taxes. The wage base, which was just $3,600 in 1951, goes up each year. The wage base for 1986 is $42,000.

A worker who has earned average wages each year (the national average for 1985 is estimated to be $16,595) receives $576 each month if he retires this year at age 65 and $482 if he retires at age 62.

Forward projections: The Social Security Administration has supplied us with estimates of monthly retirement benefits payable in future years. The figures are expressed in current dollars (i.e., there's no allowance for inflation).

Retirement at Age 65 in Year	Maximum Monthly Benefit	Benefit Payable to Workers With Average Earnings
1990	$784	$581
1995	$856	$618
2000	$958	$666
2005	$1,066	$714

Delayed retirement: If you continue to work past normal retirement age, you will receive an increase in your monthly payment. The increase is 1/4 of 1% for each month that you work past normal retirement age, or 3% a year. The increase is not available for work past age 70. (If you reached age 65 before 1983 and continue to work, the increase in your benefit is 1/12 of 1% per month, or 1% per year.)

Over time, the present 3% per year increment—for each additional year worked past the normal retirement age—increases to 8%. Column four in the chart at the top of the previous page shows you the details.

Keep in mind that any post-retirement-age work improves your earnings record. Your years of high earnings after normal retirement age displace earlier years when you earned less. This boosts the basic benefit when you eventually file for Social Security. The 3% per year increment is applied to this already expanded benefit.

Post-retirement employment: Many retirees who are receiving Social Security payments want to supplement their benefits with part-time income. But there is a limit on how much you can earn from a job or self-employment and still collect your full Social Security retirement benefit. The annual earnings limit changes from year to year. For 1986, for example, the limit is $5,760 for retirees under age 65, and $7,800 for those age 65 through 69. You lose $1 of benefits for each $2 you make over the earnings limit. Important: There is no earnings limit for retirees age 70 and over. In other words, once you reach that age, you can earn any amount and still collect full Social Security benefits.

> **Example:** Jane Able, age 66, retires in 1985. In 1986, she gets a part-time job that pays $9,000 a year. Result: She loses $600 in Social Security benefits, figured as follows:
>
> Earnings from employment $9,000
> Less earnings limit   7,800
> $1,200
>
> Lost Social Security benefits ($1,200
> divided by two) $600

▶ **NEW BREAK ON THE WAY:** Beginning in 1990, those over normal retirement age lose $1 in Social Security benefits for every $3 of earnings above the annual limit. Since the annual earnings limit increases each year as average wages go up, retirees will be able to earn higher amounts without forfeiting benefits.

Strategy Pointers For Retirees

There are a number of twists and turns in the Social Security rules that can mean more benefits when you retire. Here are three important pointers:

#1—Special break for the year of retirement: For the year of retirement, your earnings during that year prior to retirement do not affect the benefits you are eligible to receive for the balance of the year. You get full benefits for any month your wages don't exceed the monthly exempt amount and you don't perform substantial services in self-employment. The monthly exempt amounts for 1986 are $650 if you're 65 through 69 and $480 if you're under 65. Important: After your first year of retirement, your annual earnings become the test.

> **Example:** Anne Jones, age 65, earns a total of $8,000 from January through May, and retires at the end of the first week of June 1986. She receives a final paycheck of $400. Result: She gets full monthly Social Security benefits beginnning with June, since her earnings for that month do not exceed $650.

#2—Retiring early can make good dollar sense: For example, let's say Bob Smith will be entitled to a monthly benefit of $700 if he retires at age 65. If he

retires at age 62, he will receive 80% of that amount, or $560 each month. On the surface, it doesn't make sense for Smith to retire early. In reality, however, if Smith can *afford to* retire early at age 62, he may well come out ahead.

Reason: In the three-year period between age 62 and 65, he will receive a total of $20,160 in Social Security benefits ($560 a month times 12, times 3 years). If he waits until age 65 to retire, he will have to wait until age 77 to recoup these dollars. Here's why: If Smith begins collecting benefits at 65, he'll get $8,400 per year—$1,680 more than he gets if he retires at age 62. Disregarding any cost-of-living increases, it will take 12 years of benefits at the full rate to get back the $20,160 he'd receive between age 62 and 65. In other words, Smith will have to live past age 77 to come out ahead.

#3—Going back to work after you retire can boost your benefits: As we said, if you retire early, you will receive a reduced retirement benefit. And, as a general rule, the basic benefit rate is fixed—it doesn't go up once you reach normal retirement age (currently age 65).

▶ **IMPORTANT EXCEPTION:** The reduction is based on the number of months you actually receive full benefit checks before age 65. So any month you receive a benefit check that is reduced because of excess earnings does not count against you. When you reach age 65, the Government recomputes your benefits to arrive at your final benefit amount.

Early retirement strategy: If you're undecided about early retirement, here's what you may want to do: Apply for early Social Security benefits. Granted, your benefits will be lower than your PIA. For example, you get 80% of your PIA if you retire at age 62. But when and if you go back to work before 65, you may be able to boost your permanent benefit at age 65. Reason: The months for which you receive a smaller benefit check because of the earnings limit don't count against you when figuring benefit reduction at age 65.

For example, if Mr. Able retired in 1985 at age 62, worked in 1986, and earned enough to have 12 months of earnings-reduced benefits, he will be entitled to 86⅔% of his PIA (100% less 24 months times 5/9 of 1%) in 1988 when he is 65.

RETIREMENT BENEFITS FOR SPOUSE AND CHILDREN

When you retire, you may not be the only member of your family who receives a monthly check from Social Security. If you are "fully insured," the following dependents are also entitled to payments:

1. Your spouse. Your husband or wife gets 50% of your Primary Insurance Amount if he or she applies at age 65. The amount is reduced by 25/36ths of 1% for each month a spouse applies before 65. For example, if a spouse applies at age 62 the benefit is 37½% of the PIA. Note: Age 62 is the earliest age a spouse can collect benefits based on your record.

2. A spouse of any age who is caring for an eligible child under 16. Here, the husband or wife receives 50% of a spouse's PIA, even if he or she is younger than age 62. A spouse of any age also qualifies for a 50% benefit if he or she is caring for a child disabled before age 22.

3. An eligible child. A child under age 18 (or under 19 if in high school), or a child of any age if disabled mentally or physically before age 22, is entitled to 50% of your PIA.

▶ **FAMILY BENEFIT LIMIT:** Any amounts that your dependents receive will not reduce your monthly payment. However, the total of your family's payments cannot exceed what is called the Family Maximum Benefit. This is the limit on the amount of benefits any one family can receive, based on the earnings record of one worker. The limit varies with each family, depending on your Primary Insurance Amount.

Coordinating Benefits When Both Spouses Worked

If you're married and both you and your spouse work, you can receive retirement benefits based on either your own work record or your spouse's. When you're eligible for retirement benefits on more than one record, you receive the benefit that is the larger of the two.

For example, in a family where both the husband and wife have worked all their adult lives and have had high earnings, the wife's own benefit is likely to be higher than the benefit she would receive as a spouse (50% of her husband's normal retirement age payment).

Or suppose the husband is younger than the wife, and both have earnings records. The wife can go ahead and retire on her own record. When her husband retires, she can switch to spouse's payments, if they are higher than her own.

▶ **WHAT TO DO:** When you apply for retirement benefits, ask your Social Security Office to figure out whether you get a higher payment on your own record or on your spouse's.

How to apply: You can apply for Social Security benefits either in person or over the phone. Once you've been interviewed by phone, the rest of the process can be completed by mail.

When applying in person, you need to bring with you the following records: Your Social Security card or a record of the number; proof of age (birth or baptismal certificate, military record, if any, or passport); your W-2 Forms for the last two years (or copies of your last two federal income tax returns if you were self-employed); children's birth certificates, if you're applying for them; and marriage certificate, if you're applying for benefits under your spouse's earnings record.

How to safeguard your benefits: It's important to make sure your Social Security tax dollars are doing what they're supposed to do—building future Social Security benefits.

▶ **WHAT TO DO:** Check to see if your earnings have been properly credited to your Social Security account. If some haven't—or if they've been recorded incorrectly—you will pay for it in reduced benefits when you retire.

Your move: Ask your local Social Security Office for a copy of Form OAG7004. Fill out the Form and mail it to the Social Security Administration at the address supplied on the form. You will receive a statement of earnings and the number of quarters of coverage with which you have been credited.

▶ **IMPORTANT:** There is a time limit involved when it comes to correcting any mistakes you may discover. Generally, an earnings record can't be corrected if the request is made more than 39 1/2 months after the year in which the wages were paid. So a checkup at least once every three years is a good move.

DISABILITY BENEFITS

Workers who suffer a severe injury or physical or mental illness are entitled to help from Social Security in the form of monthly disability checks. But the requirements are tough.

Requirement #1. A person must have a minimum period of work to qualify. The number of calendar quarters required depends on age. If a worker is disabled after age 30, the number of quarters required ranges from 20 to 40. And at least 20 quarters of work (or five years) must have been performed in the ten years prior to disability. A worker disabled before age 31 needs fewer quarters to qualify, but the minimum number is six.

Requirement #2. The illness or injury must be expected to last at least twelve months or result in death. Medical certification is required.

Requirement #3. The worker must be unable to perform "any substantial gainful work." This is defined by the Social Security Administration as work (even on a part-time basis) that "involves the performance of significant physical or mental duties which are productive in nature." If the worker is able to perform such work, he or she is denied benefits, even if not employed. Work that pays more than $300 a month is considered "substantial and gainful." If it pays less than $190 a month, the work is not substantial and gainful. If the pay is between $190 and $300, the determination of whether the work is substantial and gainful is made on a case-by-case basis. There are, however, a number of exceptions:

● More lenient tests apply to a blind person whose vision is worse than 20/200 with glasses or who has a field of vision of 20 degrees or less. First, work is *presumed* to be substantial and gainful only if it pays an amount in excess of the monthly earnings limit for a 65-or-over retired person ($650 for 1986). Second, blind people between age 55 and 65 are entitled to disability benefits as long as they are unable to perform the same work they did before their blindness. A finding that they are *able* to perform substantial gainful work will not result in a loss of benefits. However, benefits stop for any period that the blind person actually engages in substantial work (as defined above).

● A special rule applies to a "trial work period"—up to nine months of work following a disability. Benefits are paid during this period regardless of the level of earnings. If the worker recovers fully within the trial work period, benefits are continued for the month of the recovery, plus two more months. After the nine-month period is up (and the worker does not recover fully), the Social Security Administration determines if the worker is able to do substantial and gainful work. If the answer is "yes," benefits continue for three more months, then stop. If the answer is "no," the benefits continue.

Requirement #4: A worker on disability must accept vocational rehabilitation. If he or she refuses such rehabilitation, then disability payments are cut off.

Figuring the disability benefit. In general, the amount of a worker's disability payment is determined as if he or she had retired in the year the disability began. As with retirement, the exact disability payment depends upon the earnings record. Payments will not begin until the sixth full month of disability. If a worker is still disabled at age 65, his or her disability payments will be changed to retirement payments. After 24 months of disability, the worker is entitled to medicare.

Family benefits: A disabled worker's family members are also entitled to disability benefits. Eligible family members are the same as those qualifying for benefits on account of a worker's retirement (see p. 227). In general, family benefits cannot exceed 150% of the worker's benefits.

Still another restriction: Disability benefits are subject to the same annual earnings limits that apply to retired workers (for 1986, it's $7,800 for those age 65 or over, $5,760 for those under 65). The earnings test is applied separately to each family member receiving disability benefits. For example, suppose a worker with a wife and two children is disabled in 1986. The wife is the only family member employed during the year. Result: She loses $1 in her disability benefits for every $2 she earns over $5,760. However, disability benefits for the other family members are not affected by her work.

▶ **INESCAPABLE CONCLUSION:** Social Security disability benefits are of limited help to a worker who suffers a debilitating illness or injury. Anyone interested in protecting the family should carry private, long-term disability insurance. It's as important as life insurance. There's no reduction in disability payments for private insurance payments; there *is* a reduction for workmens compensation payments.

HOW A FAMILY QUALIFIES FOR SOCIAL SECURITY SURVIVOR BENEFITS

If a worker dies during employment, his or her spouse and children are entitled to what is in effect Government-paid life insurance benefits. These benefits, which can last for many years, will help cushion the financial shock of losing the family breadwinner.

How the family qualifies: The worker must be either fully or currently insured at the time of death.

How to figure "fully insured status." Count the number of years after 1950 (or after the year the worker turned 21, if later) up through the year before death occurs or the year the worker turned 61, if earlier. That number of years is the number of work quarters needed.

A worker is currently insured if he or she has a minimum of six quarters of covered employment earned during the last 13 calendar quarters before death.

Family benefits: If a worker satisfies the less-demanding currently insured requirements at death, the following dependents are eligible to receive survivor benefits:

● A spouse (or divorced spouse) of any age caring for an eligible child under age 16 or disabled before age 22. The spouse receives 75% of the worker's PIA.

● A child under age 18 (or under 19 if in high school) or disabled before age 22. The child receives 75% of the worker's PIA. If both parents are dead, the child's benefit is based on whichever earnings record is greater.

If the worker was fully insured at death, the following dependents also qualify for payments:

● Surviving spouse, age 60 or over. At age 60, the spouse receives 71.5% of the worker's PIA. This amount gradually increases to 100% for spouses who apply at age 65 or older. To qualify, the spouse must have been married to the decedent for nine months (except for death due to accident or military duty), or be the parent of the worker's natural or adopted child.

● Disabled surviving spouse, age 50-59. Here, the survivor receives 71.5% of the worker's PIA.

● Dependent parents, age 62 or older. A dependent parent receives 82.5% of the deceased worker's PIA. In order to qualify, the parent must be receiving at least one-half of his or her support from the worker at the time of his or her death, and cannot remarry (unless the new spouse is entitled to benefits). If both parents qualify for survivor benefits, each receives 75%.

Important: Survivor benefits are subject to the same annual earnings limitations that apply to retirement and disability benefits (see p. 227).

HOW TO COPE WITH THE INCOME TAX ON SOCIAL SECURITY BENEFITS

A portion of Social Security benefits (retirement, disability or survivor payments) is now subject to Federal income tax. Affluent retirees will pay income tax on one-half of their Social Security benefits. Other retirees will pay tax on a smaller portion of their benefits. Most retirees escape the extra income tax altogether.

How it works: The benefits are subject to tax only if a special gross income base exceeds $25,000 (for single filers) or $32,000 (for joint filers) or zero for marrieds filing separately. The special gross income base consists of: (1) a retiree's adjusted gross income (generally, gross income subject to tax less deductions the typical retiree doesn't take anyway); (2) interest not subject to tax; and (3) one-half of Social Security benefits.

If the total of these items exceeds the $25,000/$32,000 figures, then there is an income tax on the lesser of: (1) one half of Social Security benefits; or (2) one half of the excess of the special gross income base over the threshold amount.

> **Example:** Mr. and Mrs. Smith are over 65 and have pension income from their employers. In 1986, they have $26,000 in fully taxable pension income, $5,000 in taxable dividends and interest, and $2,000 in tax-free municipal bond interest. They also receive $10,000 in Social Security benefits.

Here is how the Smiths would calculate the portion of Social Security benefits subject to income tax.

Adjusted gross income	$31,000
Municipal bond interest	2,000
One-half of Social Security benefits	5,000
Special gross income base	38,000
Less threshold amount for joint filers	32,000
Excess	6,000
One-half of excess	3,000

The Smiths' Social Security benefit subject to tax is $3,000 since that figure is less than $5,000 (one half their benefits).

The bottom line: Assuming the Smiths do not itemize deductions, their tax for 1986, with the inclusion of $3,000 in Social Security benefits, is about $4,562. Without the benefits tax, they would owe $3,812.

Result: The Smiths' income tax bill for 1986 is $750 more ($4,562 less $3,812). Put another way, the Smiths lose 7½% of their $10,000 Social Security benefit.

The chart on the next page shows how much income besides Social Security you can have before your benefits become subject to tax. As year-end approaches, you may want to defer income to the following year (hold up on an IRA withdrawal, for example) to minimize the tax bite on Social Security payments.

How You Can Slash—Or Maybe Eliminate—
The Tax on Social Security Benefits

There are a number of investments that either don't trigger the tax on Social Security benefits or may result in a smaller tax. The first group yields current cash income that is partially tax-free (actually it's your cash investment being returned to you over a period of time).

SINGLE			MARRIED FILING JOINTLY		
Annual Social Security benefit	Social Security benefits not taxed unless other income exceeds—	One-half of benefits taxed if other income is at least—	Annual Social Security benefit	Social Security benefits not taxed unless other income exceeds—	One-half of benefits taxed if other income is at least—
$ 4,200	$22,900	$27,100	$ 9,000	$27,500	$36,500
4,800	22,600	27,400	9,600	27,200	36,800
5,400	22,300	27,700	10,200	26,900	37,100
6,000	22,000	28,000	10,800	26,600	37,400
7,200	21,400	28,600	12,000	26,000	38,000
7,800	21,100	28,900	12,600	25,700	38,300
8,400	20,800	29,200	13,200	25,400	38,600
9,000	20,500	29,500	13,800	25,100	38,900
9,600	20,200	29,800	14,400	24,800	39,200
10,200	19,900	30,100	15,000	24,500	39,500
10,800	19,600	30,400	15,600	24,200	39,800
11,400	19,300	30,700	16,200	23,900	40,100
12,000	19,000	31,000	16,800	23,600	40,400

Current Income Investments

● Annuities: These investments are long-time favorites of retirees because they provide a steady stream of income. They also offer a tax-saving feature: Part of each payment is a tax-free return of your investment in the annuity contract. This part of the payment is not included in your modified adjusted gross income and therefore does not subject you to the tax on benefits.

● Ginnie Maes: These are mortgage-backed securities that allow you to get a return that reflects the relatively high interest rates home buyers are paying. Plus, they are backed by the full faith and credit of the U.S. Government. Each month you receive payments that are akin to annuity payments in the sense that part of the payment is a tax-free return of capital and part is taxable income. Result: Your return of capital doesn't trigger the benefit tax.

● Rental properties: If you own rental property (e.g., a two-family house), you also receive current cash (rent) that is partially (or maybe entirely) tax-free. Reason: You are entitled to depreciation deductions, which, in effect, allow you to recover the cost of the property. They shelter some or all of the rent from tax. While depreciation reduces rental income from tax—and therefore shelters Social Security benefits from income tax—it does not reduce your cash income. Reason: It is not a cash expense, like property taxes, repairs, utilities, or mortgage interest.

Deferred Income Investments

The second group of investments avoids the benefit tax by postponing taxable income to a future date:

• U.S. Savings Bonds: Series EE bonds don't trigger the tax. Reason: The tax on Series EE Bonds is postponed until you cash them in or they mature. The interest they earn each year goes untaxed until then.

• Growth stock: The appreciation in value of your stock holdings is not taxed until you sell the stock. So your net worth may be increasing dramatically without resulting in your Social Security benefits being taxed.

▶ **GOOD NEWS WHEN YOU SELL:** Only 40% of the profit from stock you've held for more than six months is subject to tax. Since the profit is long-term capital gain, the other 60% of your profit is tax-free and doesn't expose your benefits to tax.

• Market discount bonds: A bond you buy for less than its par value is said to be selling at a market discount. The amount of the discount is not subject to tax until the bond is redeemed or sold.

If the bond was issued on or before July 18, 1984, your discount is low-taxed capital gain and is 60% tax-free. But if the bond was issued after that date, the gain from a sale or redemption is fully taxable to the extent it's attributable to the market discount.

▶ **IMPORTANT TAX DIFFERENCE:** Investments that are originally issued at a price below the stated redemption value are called original issue discount investments (OIDs). Prime example: Zero coupon bonds. You owe tax each year on the accrued growth of an OID, even though you may receive no interest from the bond during the year.

So an original issue discount bond can increase the tax on your benefits each year while putting no dollars in your pocket until a later date.

With the deferred income investments, you may have to declare a substantial amount of taxable income the year the tax is due. But even so, you could probably pocket more Social Security benefits than if your investments were currently taxable. Reason: No more than half of your Social Security benefits can be subject to tax, regardless of how high your income is for the year. You can come out ahead by paying tax on 50% of your benefits in one year, instead of paying tax on a smaller portion of your benefits year in and year out.

Example: Mr. and Mrs. Smith have $28,000 of pension income and receive $10,000 a year in Social Security benefits. They can either invest in certificates of deposit that will pay $3,000 a year in interest, or they can buy a market discount bond that is redeemable in five years at a $15,000 profit. If the Smiths invest in the CDs, they will pay tax on 20% of their Social Security benefits ($2,000) each year. If they invest in the market discount bond, they pay no tax on their benefits until the year the bond is redeemed. At that time, they pay tax on the full 50% of their benefits ($5,000).

Result: Over the same five-year period, the Smiths would pay tax on $10,000 of benefits if they invest in CDs, but on only $5,000 of benefits if they invest in the market discount bond.

Other strategies: There are tax moves that allow you to time your income and deductions. They can sometimes be used to lower your modified adjusted gross income and thus decrease—or eliminate—the tax on your benefits:

● IRA/Keogh contributions: If you have earnings and are not yet age 70, you may be able to make IRA and/or Keogh contributions. These contributions are tax deductible and lower your modified adjusted gross income. Of course, if you exceed the earnings limit—currently $7,800 for those at least 65 but not yet 70, $5,760 for those under 65—you also reduce your benefits.

● Timing your retirement: Let's say you will retire in the near future. It's just a matter of when—either late this year or early next year. For purposes of figuring your monthly benefit check, it doesn't make any difference when you retire during the year. Reason: The excess earnings test is figured on a monthly basis for the year you retire. You can't lose your benefits for the year because of high earnings in a few months. But for purposes of the benefit tax, the general rule is—

▶ **RETIRE EARLY NEXT YEAR:** All your earnings in the year of retirement count towards the $32,000/$25,000 base. There is no monthly earnings break here. So if you retire late this year, half of your benefits may be subject to income tax. But by delaying retirement until early next year, you may not owe a penny of tax on that year's benefits.

HOW TO MAKE THE MOST OF YOUR MEDICARE COVERAGE

With the cost of health care rising 15 percent a year, Medicare remains one of your most significant retirement benefits. Its health-care coverage *is* extensive, but as you'll see, a lot of medical expenses just aren't covered. Inescapable conclusion: You will need supplemental health insurance coverage during your retirement years.

Medicare consists of two parts: (1) Hospital Insurance (Medicare Part A) which is financed through the Social Security taxes you pay as an employee or a self-employed; and (2) Supplementary Medical Insurance (Medicare Part B) which is financed jointly by monthly premiums paid by subscribers and by payments from the Federal Government.

Medicare Part A: Hospital Insurance

Hospital Insurance benefits are available without cost to anyone 65 or older who is entitled to Social Security retirement or survivor benefits, or to Railroad Retirement benefits. This includes the age-65 spouse, widow, or widower of the person who is (or would have been) entitled to Social Security benefits.

Individuals under 65 are also eligible for Medicare after receiving Social Security or Railroad Retirement disability benefits for at least two years, or if they have chronic kidney disease and require dialysis or a kidney transplant.

Key point: You are entitled to Hospital Insurance benefits at your normal retirement age (currently 65) whether you retire or decide to continue working. There are no income limitations.

Automatic entitlement: At normal retirement age, you are automatically enrolled in the Hospital Insurance Plan *if* you apply for and are entitled to receive your Social Security benefits. You do not have to file an additional application for your Medicare coverage. Here's—

> ▶ **WHAT TO DO:** Contact your local Social Security office at least three months before your 65th birthday to apply for your retirement insurance benefits. That way you'll be sure to receive your Medicare card in time for your first month of eligibility.

If you decide to continue working past 65, you must apply for your Medicare coverage. You won't be covered automatically. And if you retire early—at, say, age 62—you won't receive your Medicare coverage until you reach 65.

Covered services and benefits: Your Medicare hospital insurance covers four basic types of care: In-patient hospital care, in-patient care in a skilled nursing facility, hospice care and home health care. Each provides a different service and, not surprisingly, the benefits you receive for each also differ.

1. In-patient Hospital Care: In-patient hospital care covers the cost of a semi-private room, meals, regular nursing services, drugs, anesthesia, lab tests, x-rays, rehabilitation services and any other services the hospital ordinarily provides including blood—except for the first three pints.

The length of your covered stay is called a *benefit period.* It begins with your first day of hospital treatment and ends on the 60th day after your release. You will be charged a deductible each time you begin a new benefit period. Your hospital benefits are as follows:

● First 60 days: You pay $492 deductible; Medicare pays remaining covered costs.

● Next 30 days: You pay $123 a day; Medicare pays remaining covered costs.

● 60 reserve days: You pay $246 a day; Medicare pays remaining covered costs.

The deductible is adjusted periodically to keep it in line with rising costs. You have a lifetime reserve of 60 days to use as you see fit, but they do not become available until you have exhausted the first 90 days of any "spell of illness." Reserve days may be used only once; they are not renewable.

Although the coverage seems extensive, a severe illness requiring a long-term hospital stay can be catastrophic.

Example: A patient who has been in the hospital for three months finds out he needs additional care for another 45 days. What would his minimum costs be for 135 days of hospitalization? (1) $492 deductible for the first 60 days; (2) $123 a day for the next 30 days, or $3,690; and (3) $246 a day for the next 45 "reserve days," or $11,070. Total cost: $14,760. And that doesn't include the cost of the first three pints of blood, if needed, private nursing care, or those physicians' fees or other services you may be required to cover under Medicare Part B.

Here's something else to keep in mind. Once a patient has used up his reserve days, he becomes liable for *all* hospital costs for that benefit period. Unlikely? Maybe. The patient's expenses could fall within a new benefit period, if he has been out of the hospital for more than 60 days. If not, one lengthy illness or injury could have major financial repercussions.

2. In-patient Skilled Nursing Facility Care: Benefits are also available if you have been hospitalized at least three days and are transferred to a skilled nursing facility for in-patient care within 30 days of your hospital stay. Most nursing homes are *not* considered skilled nursing facilities. Skilled nursing facility benefits are as follows: For the first 20 days, Medicare pays all covered costs; for the next 80 days, you pay $61.50 a day (Medicare pays remaining covered costs).

3. Hospice Care: Hospice care for terminally ill patients can now take place in the home, or in an in-patient hospice setting (a special care facility for the terminally ill).

To qualify patients must be certified as terminally ill. There are two 90-day periods and a subsequent 30-day period of eligibility. An individual must also waive all rights to Medicare payments for the following services: care provided by a hospice other than the one designated by the patient; and any Medicare services related to treatment of the terminal condition for which hospice care was elected.

4. Home Health Care: Either Medical Insurance or Hospital Insurance will cover an *unlimited* number of home health visits by a home health agency if: (1) the care includes part-time skilled nursing care or physical or speech therapy; (2) the patient is confined to home; (3) a doctor determines that the patient needs home health care and sets up a care plan; and (4) the agency providing the services is participating in Medicare. Medicare will also cover medical supplies (except drugs) and equipment, social services or the part-time services of a home health aide (but not homemaker services).

Medicare Part B: Supplementary Medical Insurance

If you're entitled to Hospital Insurance (Medicare Part A) you are automatically enrolled in the Supplementary Medical Insurance Plan (unless you decline the coverage). If you choose to participate, there's a monthly premium charge. The amount, which changes each January, is $15.50 through December 31, 1986. If you're receiving monthly Social Security benefits, the premium will be deducted from your monthly benefit check; otherwise, you'll be billed quarterly.

Medicare Part B coverage is a bargain you shouldn't pass up. The benefits are extensive and the cost is relatively low, since the Federal Government pays almost three-quarters of the actual cost.

Covered services: Medicare Medical Insurance can help pay for: (1) doctors' and surgeons' fees and services; (2) out-patient hospital services (such as visits to an emergency room); (3) out-patient surgical services; (4) out-patient physical therapy, speech pathology and rehabilitation services; (5) home health care and; (6) certain other health services and supplies not covered by Medicare Part A, including such things as splints, casts, home dialysis equipment, dental surgery, radioactive isotope therapy, and drugs that you cannot administer yourself.

Basic payment rule: You pay the first $75 of covered medical expenses each year. Medicare pays 80 percent of the "approved charges," after payment of the deductible. You pay the remaining 20 percent. The "approved charges" for covered services in your area may be lower than what most doctors or suppliers charge. This means that you (or your private insurance carrier) may be liable for any costs that exceed the approved charge.

▶ **WHAT TO DO:** Ask your doctor or supplier if he or she will accept *assignment* of your bill, i.e., agree to accept Medicare's approved charge as payment in full for services rendered. Medicare will then pay 80 percent of the approved charge and your doctor will only bill you for the remaining 20 percent (and for any part of the deductible you may not have met).

Here's what can happen if your doctor doesn't accept assignment: Let's say he charges you $900 for surgery, but Medicare only approves a $600 fee. If you have not already met the $75 deductible, you must first apply it to the $600, reducing it to $525. Medicare will then pay 80 percent of the $525, or $420. Itemizing the charges, you will have to pay: (1) the $75 deductible; (2) the $105 balance of the approved charge (20% of $525); and (3) the $300 unassigned charge. Your total cost for the surgery is $480. Remember this doesn't include any costs you may incur for hospitalization.

How to file your claim: Medicare payments are handled by private insurance organizations (such as Blue Cross and Blue Shield) under contract to the Federal Government. For doctor bills, you must submit a Patient's Request for Medicare Payment Form, also called Form 1490S, to your carrier. But if your doctor will accept assignment, he or she submits the bill directly to your Medicare carrier. If you receive care from a participating hospital, skilled nursing facility, home health agency or hospice, this facility will send a claim for payment directly to your Medicare intermediary. You'll receive a notice (Explanation of Medicare Benefits) showing the services Medicare paid for and the costs that were not covered—costs you may be responsible for.

Services Medicare Doesn't Cover: Here's a partial list of items Medicare usually will not pay for: (1) routine physical check-ups and tests; (2) private duty nursing; (3) custodial nursing home care; (4) private room in a hospital unless medically necessary; (5) eyeglasses and eye examinations and hearing aids and hearing exams; (6) routine dental care; (7) drugs and medicines you purchase yourself with or without a prescription (except when receiving benefits for hospice care); (8) routine immunizations; and (9) care received outside the U.S.A. except, under certain conditions, in Canada and Mexico.

How To Buy Supplementary Private Health Insurance

At this point you may be wondering how you're going to protect yourself from the gaps that exist in Medicare's coverage. For many people, the answer is to buy protection from a supplementary private health plan.

First step: If you are covered currently by a health insurance policy, (employer paid, individual, or group) find out if it is convertible into a supplemental Medicare policy when you reach 65. This may well be the most convenient solution to the problem. If you can't convert your current policy (or its age 65 terms are unsatisfactory) you must arrange for supplemental insurance for your retirement years. Here's what's available:

1. Supplemental Hospital Insurance: Look for a policy that pays some or all of the deductibles and payments you are responsible for under Medicare Part A. There may or may not be a limit on the number of days covered for a hospital stay. Stay away from an indemnity policy or a hospital income policy that pays you a specified amount for each day you're in the hospital. Reason: The policy may not cover you for the deductible and co-payments you must make under Medicare Part A.

2. Supplemental Medical Insurance (for Medicare Part B): You should purchase one of two types of supplemental insurance. The first, a UCR (usual, customary and reasonable) policy, may pay all or part of the doctor's bill not covered by Medicare. The UCR rate is usually higher than Medicare's approved charge. The second type pays the 20 percent co-insurance that Medicare doesn't cover. It may also pay the Part B deductible. You should stay away from an indemnity policy that pays you a fixed amount for a given medical service. Like the hospital indemnity policy, it is not geared to Medicare at all.

3. Catastrophic or Major Medical Insurance: This type of policy helps cover the cost of a severe, long-term illness or injury. Most have a large deductible and may not cover the deductibles and payments a patient must pay under the Medicare System. Nonetheless, experts consider this type of policy to be a very worthwhile investment.

4. Health Maintenance Organizations (HMOs): Health Maintenance Organizations provide both insurance and health care service. You pay a membership fee and then receive your medical care from doctors and suppliers affiliated with the HMO. For Medicare-covered services there are usually no separate charges for deductibles or payments.

You may also obtain nursing home coverage or specified disease insurance, but neither is a substitute for Supplemental Medical, Catastrophic, Major Medical or HMO insurance. Whichever policy you decide to purchase, here are some items you ought to watch out for:

1. Check for preexisting condition exclusions (and don't be misled by assurances that a medical exam is not required—you still may not be able to get insurance if you have a health problem).

2. Don't rush to replace existing coverage—new policies often impose waiting periods before coverage begins.

3. Find out the limits the policy puts on benefits whether expressed in dollar amounts or number of days of coverage. And above all—

4. Don't buy too much coverage. You generally will *not* be paid twice for the same medical bills. It is also financially unwise to try to cover every conceivable pain or illness you might suffer.

If you would like help in deciding whether to buy supplementary health insurance or need additional advice on your Medicare benefits or eligibility, here's—

▶ **WHAT TO DO:** Contact your local Social Security office or the Health Care Financing Administration to obtain free copies of the *Guide to Health Insurance for People With Medicare* and *Your Medicare Handbook*.

Chapter 10

Family Tax Tactics That Yield Big Dollar Savings Year After Year

Members of your family can be an important part of your tax-saving, wealth-building strategy. Prime example: Income splitting. By taking some income out of your high tax bracket and shifting it to lower-bracket family members, you accomplish two important goals: (1) you cut the overall family tax bill; and (2) you accumulate more cash for important family goals, such as the education of your children.

This Chapter explains this effective and simple tax-cutting device and also covers the many other ways your family can save you taxes. You will see how to get and keep the biggest number of dependency exemptions for your family members, and how to qualify for the filing status that means the lowest rate of tax for you and your family. And if you have child-care expenses, this Chapter will show you how you're in line for even greater tax savings through the child-care tax credit.

HOW GIFTS TO YOUR CHILDREN CUT YOUR FAMILY'S INCOME TAXES

The easiest way to cut the family income tax bill is to make outright gifts of property to your children. The gift can be cash, stocks, bonds, even assets such as real estate. However, even in this simplest of all tax-cutting methods, there are a few complications to avoid. Let's start with—

The Tax-Wise Way to Give Income Property To A Child

A gift of income-producing property to a child is a two-way winner. Since you no longer own the property, you pay no tax on the income it produces. Your child is taxed on the income generated by the property, but at his low-bracket rates. Result: Your family keeps more of the income, and Uncle Sam gets less.

The popularity of this income-splitting technique has led all the states to adopt the Uniform Gifts to Minors Act. The Act cuts to a minimum the red tape of giving securities. You make the gift and name yourself as custodian. The mechanics are simple. For example, suppose you want to give some of your stock or other securities to a child. You merely re-register the securities in the child's name, with the parent as custodian. Generally, the following language may be used:
"_____ (name of donor/parent) as custodian for

_____ (name of minor child) under the _____ (State) Uniform Gifts to Minors Act.'' No other trustees, guardians or court procedures are necessary.

While your child is a minor, you manage the property. You can sell, reinvest and collect income and accumulate it or apply it for the child's benefit. When your child reaches majority (age 21 for Uniform Act purposes in some states, age 18 in others), he or she gets the property outright. No trustees, guardians or courts are involved. And all the while, you're piling up tax savings.

> **Example:** Father owns 150 shares of XYZ, Inc. The stock pays annual dividends totalling $1,600. In Father's 50% bracket, $800 of that is taken by taxes. Father decides to give the stock to 12-year-old Son. He simply re-register's the stock in the name of "Father, as custodian for Son."

Result: Of the $1,600 in dividends, Son can shelter $1,080 with his personal exemption and another $100 with the dividend exclusion. (The zero bracket amount—the standard deduction—can't be used to shelter your dependent's investment income.) Assuming he has no other income, Son's tax bill on the remaining $420 is $46.20 (at 1986 tax rates). That's a family tax saving of about $754.

▶ **DIVIDEND TAX SHELTER:** Don't pass up the $100 dividend exclusion when you make your gift. Even when you give rental or other income-producing property not covered by the Uniform Act, you get the benefit of the exclusion if you also give securities that yield at least $100 in dividends.

There are things you have to watch, but with a little ingenuity—and with help from a professional tax adviser—you can handle them.

Income tax: Income from the gift spent by the custodian on items you're legally obligated to provide for your minor child are considered taxable income to you.

Let's say Father is the custodian and uses $1,000 of the XYZ dividends to pay part of Son's tuition. In effect, Father is getting an extra $1,000 that he can use to discharge his support obligations to Son. Therefore, the $1,000 is taxable to him and not to Son.

▶ **WHAT TO DO:** Whenever possible, pay your child's bills out of your own pocket. By banking or reinvesting the income from the gift, you can avoid income tax while your child's nest egg builds up even more.

Gift tax: Gifts made to a minor under the Uniform Act are subject to gift tax. However, your potential gift tax liability can be eliminated by the $10,000 gift tax exclusion and your unified gift and estate tax credit [see Chapter Thirteen for details].

▶ **DOUBLE THE GIFT TAX BREAK:** Your spouse also has a unified gift and estate tax credit and an annual gift tax exclusion. By joining together in a gift to your child (a so-called split gift), you and your spouse double the unified credit and the gift tax exclusion. Result: You lower or eliminate the tax bill on your gift.

Estate tax: There is a problem when a parent-custodian makes a gift of securities, names himself custodian and dies before his child reaches majority. In that situation, the courts have said that the gift is included in the parent's taxable estate. *Reason:* A custodian has the power to terminate the custodianship and give the property to the child outright. That means it is still the parent-custodian's property for estate tax purposes (Stuit, 28 AFTR2d 71-6289).

▶ **WHAT TO DO:** Name someone else as custodian. If the gift isn't made jointly, your spouse will do fine. If the gift has been made jointly, another family member or friend, or even a bank can be named. The problem arises only when the giver of the gift is also the custodian. If you're making a gift to your grandchildren, you can name one of their parents as custodian, and get the same tax-saving result.

If you've already made a gift and named yourself custodian, consider resigning and designating a successor. In some states that could involve a court proceeding, but it should be a routine one. In any case, you'll want to discuss the problem with your attorney before you commit yourself.

How to Build A College Fund For Your Child With the Tax Law's Help

Let's say you want to set aside money for your child in order to provide him or her with a fund for college. Obviously, you don't want the child to have immediate access to the funds—that money's earmarked for education. The simplest way to accomplish your goals, and use tax dollars to finance part of the college fund, is to use a custodial account. This type of account complies with the provisions of the Uniform Gifts to Minors Act. The money you place into the account belongs to the child, but withdrawals can be made by the custodian for the benefit of the child. The money in the account will go directly to the child when he or she reaches majority (usually age 18).

Tax-saving result: You cut the family tax bill by shifting the interest income out of your bracket into the child's lower bracket. The tax dollars saved will compound and grow along with your cash gift and build up a much larger education fund.

Tax-saving idea in action: Your daughter will be ready for college in around ten years. You can afford to set aside $6,000 right now to help pay for her college costs. We'll assume you're in the 33% tax bracket (for 1986, taxable income between $32,270 and $49,420).

● If you purchase long-term CDs in your own name earning, say, 8% interest, your effective, after-tax yield is only 5.36%. In ten years' time, you will have accumulated $10,114—that's after taxes.

• If you put the money aside in a custodial account for your daughter, and the account earns 8% per year, your child will have about $12,950 at the end of ten years. Reason: Assuming your daughter has no other unearned income (e.g., dividends and interest), she will pay no tax on each year's interest buildup. She can use her personal exemption ($1,080 for 1986) to shelter the annual interest from tax.

Dollars and cents result: Your daughter has $2,836 more for college—courtesy of Uncle Sam.

▶ **TAX-SAVING TIP:** Be sure to get a Social Security number for your child and give that number to the bank officer when you open the custodial account. Otherwise, the bank will list your Social Security number on the account and will report your child's earnings as your own on a Form 1099 sent to the Government.

Finally, when you open the account for your child, be sure it's a *custodial account*, not a trust account. Reason: A trust account is opened in your name, as "trustee" for the child. You make withdrawals as you see fit and the account balance automatically goes to the child at your death. Tax result: The interest earned on the account will be taxable to you, not the child, because you retain clear control of the funds.

THE TAX-WISE WAY TO BUY U.S. SAVINGS BONDS FOR YOUR CHILDREN

U.S. Savings Bonds are a good way to put your money away for your children's future. But your family's tax bill on these bonds can vary greatly, depending on how you register them. Let's take a look at some common situations.

(1) You register the bonds jointly with your child. (Example: "John Jones or Mary Jones.") There's no gift when the bonds are registered. But if your child redeems the bonds for herself and doesn't have to account to you, you have made a gift at that time. (The gift is the cash your child gets.) If the bonds are not redeemed by your child, they will be included in your estate.

(2) You register the bonds in your name, payable to your child on your death. There's no gift since you, as the registered owner, can redeem the bonds at any time. So the bonds will be included in your estate.

▶ **INCOME TAX BILL:** If you register your bonds either jointly or in your name (payable to the child on your death), you are still considered to be the owner of the bonds. So when you redeem the bonds, the interest is taxable to you—and you alone.

(3) You buy the bonds and register them in your child's name. You've made a gift at that time, but the annual $10,000 exclusion can shelter the gift from tax. And the bonds will not be in your estate, so there are no estate tax problems.

▶ **NO INCOME TAX BILL:** Since your child owns the bonds, the interest is taxed to him rather than to you. And with the right tax moves, your child also may avoid paying any tax.

Tax-saving strategy: Have your child report the interest from the bonds on his tax return each year. (You can elect to report EE Bond interest each year or let it pile up.) The child's personal examption can shelter $1,080 of interest from Federal tax in 1986, and there are no state or local taxes due. So in effect, you've converted the bonds into tax-exempts. And when your child is ready for college, he or she can cash in the bonds without paying any tax.

Question: I bought Savings Bonds years ago in my name. Can I just hand them over to my child?

Answer: No. You must have the bonds reissued in your child's name. All the interest from that point on will be treated as income to your child. But if you haven't been reporting the interest yearly, you must pay tax on all interest accrued up to that point. Caution: If your child reports the interest on bonds each year, he or she must continue the procedure for all future EE bonds he or she purchases (unless the Government okays a switch).

HOW TO PROTECT YOURSELF WHEN YOU HELP YOUR CHILDREN GET STARTED IN BUSINESS

You've always said you would help your child out if and when he went into business for himself—and now it's time to make good on your promise. You're about to make a good sized financial commitment to get the new business off the ground. You expect the venture to do well—otherwise you wouldn't back it. But suppose it doesn't and you don't get your money back? You may get top tax relief—but only if you handle things right at the outset.

Example: Mr. White's son, Ed, wants to start out on his own and open a new business. Although Ed will be sinking his own savings into the new enterprise, he still needs $15,000 cash from his father to make a grand opening.

Gift: Mr. White gives Ed the $15,000 cash. Now the money is Ed's. If he loses it, the tax loss is his—not Mr. White's.

▶ **DOLLAR DISASTER:** Mr. White has lost the entire $15,000 with nothing to show for it taxwise.

Loan: Mr. White loans Ed $15,000. If he defaults on the loans, Mr. White has what is called a "non-business bad debt." As such, the loan is treated as a short-term capital loss under the tax law.

▶ **TAX RULES:** Capital loss deductions are first used to offset capital gains. Only the excess loss (if any) shelters ordinary business income. And then only $3,000 of ordinary income can be sheltered per year (excess losses may be carried forward and deducted in future years).

Note: Business losses are fully deductible in the year they are incurred. However, Mr. White is not in the business of making loans, so the loan could not be treated as a business bad debt.

Important: The courts and the Revenue Service give intra-family "loans" a very close look to make sure that the loans are not really gifts. So extra care should be taken when making a family loan.

▶ **WHAT TO DO:** Formalize any loan transaction. Set up a family loan just as you would with an unrelated party. Provide for a maturity date, interest and the like. Taking promissory notes, for instance, may not guarantee that the loan will be treated as a bona fide debt for income tax purposes—but it sure can help. In any case, be prepared to show that it was the intention of the parties to create a debtor-creditor relationship.

Other steps: (1)You must be able to prove worthlessness; so make real efforts to collect the loan. And keep your proof (e.g., copies of correspondence, the note itself and records of any payments). It's not necessary to go to court to show that a debt is uncollectible. For example, bankruptcy is generally satisfactory evidence of the worthlessness of an unsecured debt. (2) You can deduct the loss only in the year the debt goes bad; therefore, claim the deduction as soon as you can. This sidesteps the possibility that the Revenue Service may claim that the deduction belongs in an earlier (and maybe closed) tax year.

Loan guarantee: Mr. White guarantees Ed's $15,000 bank loan.

▶ **TAX RESULT:** Unless Ed gives his father a reasonable payment in return for the guarantee, Mr. White is out of luck. When he has to repay the loan to the bank and Ed can't reimburse him, Mr. White gets no deduction for his loss. Reason: The loan repayment and guarantee are gifts.

What if Ed pays his father a reasonable amount in return for the guarantee? Mr. White's loss is a short-term capital loss—just as if Mr. White had made the loan to Ed—not much consolation.

Stock: From a tax angle this is the—

▶ **BEST APPROACH:** Mr. White and Ed incorporate the new business. The corporation elects to be treated as an S corporation—in other words any profits or losses are passed through to the shareholders (including, of course, Mr. White). Finally, the new corporation issues "Sec. 1244" stock to its shareholders.

Mr. White gets 100 shares of stock for his $15,000 cash. Use of this type of stock ensures that White will get an ordinary loss for his capital contribution—if Ed's business goes under.

S Corporation treatment: A corporation that elects to be treated as an S corporation pays no federal income taxes. Its taxable income (whether distributed or not) is taxed directly to the shareholders. Just as important, its operating losses are also passed through directly to shareholders. So Mr. White will be able to deduct his share of any loss on his personal return. Generally, a domestic corporation can elect this special treatment if it has 35 or fewer shareholders and no corporations as stockholders.

"Sec. 1244" stock: Sec. 1244 stock is stock issued for money or property by a "small business corporation" (in simple terms, one which has less than $1 million in contributions to capital). This type of stock gives White maximum shareholder protection: If he sells the stock at a loss or it becomes worthless, he gets an ordinary loss deduction. He can use it to offset taxable income on a dollar-for-dollar basis. The maximum allowable loss in any one year is $50,000 (it's $100,000 if stock is owned by husband and wife and they file a joint return).

On the other hand, if White sells the stock at a gain, it's treated as capital gain, just like any other profitable stock sale.

If the business goes under: Let's say that Ed's Corp. goes under in the first year of operation. White can claim a $15,000 ordinary loss on his income tax return and thus reduce his total income subject to tax.

If the business thrives and prospers: Let's say that things go well for Ed, as he and White hope and expect they will. White has several options: He can remain a shareholder and earn income from the corporation; he can make a gift of the stock to Ed (over a period of years, so that the annual $10,000 gift tax exclusion covers each gift); or he can sell the stock to Ed (resulting in low-taxed long-term capital gain, if the stock is held more than six months).

HOW THE RIGHT STOCK GIFT CAN MEAN TAX SAVINGS FOR YOU AND YOUR CHILD

There's a happy event in your family that calls for a large gift—a marriage, birth, graduation, or the start of a new career for a child. With the right kind of giving, it can be a happy time tax-wise, too.

> **Example:** Your daughter Ellen is getting married this month. As a wedding present, you want to give Ellen 100 shares of XYZ, Inc. stock. You've been buying XYZ stock at various times over the years, and have 300 shares. You bought 100 shares at $20 a share, another 100 at $48 a share, and another 100 at $70. XYZ stock is now listed at $50 a share.

You want to do the right thing for Ellen, and for yourself. What are the tax consequences of the stock gift, and which block of stock should you give her?

First of all, there won't be any gift tax on your present, because the tax law allows you to give up to $10,000 to each of as many people as you wish, without a gift tax. (If your spouse joins in the gift, the limit is $20,000 per recipient per year.)

Income tax consequences to Ellen: From your daughter's point of view, getting a gift of stock is not a taxable event. However, when she sells the stock, Ellen has to figure out her taxable gain or deductible loss. To do that, she needs to know her basis in the stock (her "cost" for tax purposes), and her holding period.

Her basis is what *you* paid for shares you give her. Exception: If you paid more for the stock than its market price on the date of the gift, her basis is the market price at the date of the gift. (However, if she sells for more than the market price on the date of the gift, but less than your cost, she has neither gain nor loss.) For example, say you give her the XYZ stock shares you bought for $70 a share. Ellen sells the shares for $20 at a later time. Her basis for figuring her loss is $50 (market value at time of gift), not $70. If she sells for, say, $60, she has neither gain nor loss.

Her holding period, used to figure whether the gain or loss on a later sale is short- or long-term, includes *your* holding period. So if you give Ellen stock you bought six months ago, and she sells the stock one month after the gift, all her profit is low-taxed long-term capital gain. *Reason*: Ellen's holding period is deemed to be seven months (your holding period plus hers), and that's longer than the six-month-and-a-day holding period required for long-term capital gains.

One exception: If Ellen sells at a *loss* and used fair market value as of the date of the gifts as her tax basis, her holding period runs from the date of the gift (and doesn't include your holding period).

Which block of stock should you give to Ellen? Let's divide your XYZ stock holdings into three classes and look at each:

(1) Your low-cost stock: This stock is not a very good choice from the tax viewpoint. If you give Ellen 100 shares of XYZ stock you bought at $20, and she turns around and immediately sells the shares, then she will owe a capital gains tax.

Of course, if you plan on selling the shares soon, anyway, then it's better to have the gain taxed in Ellen's low tax bracket, rather than in yours. But, if that's not the case, you should hang on to these shares.

(2) Your high-cost stock: It doesn't seem wise to give these. Suppose you give Ellen the 100 shares you bought for $70 a share. They are now worth $50 a share, and may stay at that level for a while. If Ellen sells the shares at $50 a share, there's an economic loss of $2,000—the difference between the $7,000 cost, and the $5,000 sales proceeds. But Ellen has to figure her capital loss using $50 per share as her basis (value at time of gift). Result: The $2,000 loss cannot be deducted either by you or Ellen (her basis is the same as the selling price). Nobody benefits from the loss.

▶ **WHAT TO DO:** Sell the shares you bought at $70, yourself. Then give the $5,000 sales proceeds to Ellen. If the prospects for XYZ stock are good, have her purchase 100 shares at $50 per share. Result: You nail down a $2,000 loss, and Ellen winds up with a cost basis of $5,000 for her shares of XYZ stock.

(3) Your medium-cost stock: As another alternative, you can give Ellen your third block of XYZ shares, the 100 shares you bought at $48. If Ellen sells the shares for more than $48, she has a small gain to pay tax on. If she sells for $48, she has neither gain nor loss. If she sells for less than $48, she has a deductible loss.

▶ **HOW TO MAKE A STOCK GIFT:** Give Ellen the stock certificate, and endorse it over to her. Give her the following information: Your date of purchase; price paid; and broker's commission on the purchase (Ellen can add this to her basis).

To establish that your gift does not exceed the annual per-donee gift tax exclusion, be sure to record the market value of the stock at the time of the gift (average of the high and low at which the stock was sold on that date).

HOW TO IMPROVE YOUR FINANCIAL POSITION WHEN YOU HELP YOUR SON OR DAUGHTER BUY A HOME

Many young couples ask their parents for financial assistance when they buy a home. Parents with the wherewithal to do so make a cash gift to the children to help them with the downpayment. But other parents simply can't afford to part with a big sum of cash and have nothing to show for it. Fortunately, there are a number of ways to help your child and improve your own financial position at the same time. Here are three alternatives:

(1) You make the downpayment, obtain the mortgage and buy the home in your own name. Then you rent the home to your child and also give him an option to buy the home within, say, five years. Your rental income offsets the expense of owning the home. And you get—

▶ **TAX SHELTER:** The rental income is taxable. But, like any landlord, you can deduct your out-of-pocket expenses for upkeep and maintenance—insurance, repair costs and the like. In addition, you are entitled to depreciation deductions based on the full purchase price. Result: You may wind up with a tax loss. In other words, your writeoffs may not only shelter your rental income, but some of your other income as well.

More tax shelter: Assuming you eventually sell the home to your child for more than you paid for it, most or all of your profit will be tax-sheltered capital gain— taxed at only 40% of the rate of your regular income.

(2) Your child makes the downpayment and takes out the mortgage. But your child borrows part of the downpayment from you and gives you a personal note in return. The note matures in, say, five years and no payment of principal is required before then.

If the loan to your child (plus any other outstanding loans between you and your child) does not exceed $10,000, you can charge your child low interest—or no interest—without any adverse tax consequences. That's also true for a loan of up to $100,000 if your child does not have more than $1,000 of net investment income in a year. This may very well be the case for the first few years after your child buys a home.

If your child has net investment income above $1,000 in any year the low interest loan is outstanding, you may be hit with taxable interest income under the special family loan rules (see below). But the maximum interest that can be imputed to you under these rules cannot exceed the amount of your child's investment income.

▶ **WATCH OUT:** You may want to charge a market rate of interest on the loan, but let your child defer interest payments until the note comes due. If so, you will be taxed under another tax law provision on the interest that accrues each year—even though no interest is actually paid.

(3) You and your child enter into an ''equity sharing'' arrangement.

How it works: You put up part of the cash needed for the downpayment and buy an interest in the home. You take title along with your child as a co-owner; each of you pays a proportionate share of the mortgage payments and maintenance and upkeep expenses. Your child pays you rent for his use of your portion of the home.

▶ **THREE-WAY WINNER:** (1) By shifting mortgage payments and expenses to you, your child is able to afford a home he otherwise couldn't. The savings more than compensate for the rent he has to pay. (2) You get the tax-sheltered benefits of owning income real estate. (3) And if the home goes up in value, you get a share of the profits—at low capital gain rates—when it's sold.

HOW TO MAKE THE BEST USE OF THE TAX RULES FOR FAMILY LOANS

One of the simplest ways to help out a family member is to make a low-interest or a no-interest loan. And, until recently, the arrangement didn't cause any special tax problems for you. If you loaned money to your child or another relative and charged interest, you simply reported your interest income on your tax return. If you didn't charge interest, you didn't report any income from the loan.

▶ **FAMILY LOAN RULES:** The Tax Law imposes a special set of tax rules on interest-free loans between family members. In general, the rules apply only to family loans made after June 6, 1984. Under the new rules, interest is taxed to the lender—"imputed" is the tax term—even though interest is not actually paid to the lender.

Net effect: You may have to report interest income from a family loan that is interest-free. Or if you did charge interest, you may have to report more than you received during the year.

How the rules work: When you make an interest-free loan, you are treated as having made a cash gift to your child. Your child, in turn, is treated as having used this cash gift to make an interest payment to you. The amount of this as-if gift/interest payment is keyed into Government interest rates.

Result: You are considered to have made a taxable gift to your child (eligible for the gift tax exclusion). And the interest payment your child is deemed to have made is taxable income to you and deductible by your child. Your child has a new deduction, and you have phantom taxable income.

Fortunately, however, the typical family loan is exempted from the harsh effect of these new rules. These are the major escape hatches.

▶ **ESCAPE HATCH #1:** If the loan, plus any other outstanding loans to your child, doesn't exceed $10,000 and your child doesn't use the loan proceeds to buy an income-producing investment, then the new rules don't apply—either for income or gift tax purposes. (Apparently, however, you would still be subject to the gift tax rules.)

▶ **ESCAPE HATCH #2:** If the loan, plus any other outstanding loans to your child, doesn't exceed $100,000, the amount of income imputed to you, for income tax purposes only, is limited. Regardless of the Government interest rate, the imputed income cannot exceed your child's net investment income (rents, dividends, interest, etc. less related expenses).

If your child's net investment income is less than $1,000, no income is imputed to you. However—and this is important—Escape Hatch #2 does not apply at all if tax savings is one of the principal motives behind the loan. The full Government rates will be imputed for both gift and income tax purposes.

Example (1): Mr. Hartley lends his son $10,000 interest-free to pay his college tuition. Hartley has made no other loans to his son.

Result: There are no income or gift tax consequences to the loan. Reason: Since Hartley's son doesn't use the proceeds to acquire an income-producing investment, the loan qualifies under Escape Hatch #1.

Example (2): Same facts as in (1), except that the loan is for $11,000.

Result: Even though Hartley can no longer use Escape Hatch #1, he may still owe no gift or income tax. Reason: Since the loan is not motivated by tax savings, it can qualify under Escape Hatch #2: Assuming the son has less than $1,000 net investment income, no taxable income is imputed to Mr. Hartley. Income is imputed for gift tax purposes, but it can be easily sheltered by the annual exclusion.

Example (3): Mr. Ross makes a $50,000 interest-free loan to his daughter to start a business. She nets around $1,500 a year in bank interest.

Result: Escape Hatch #1 is, of course, not available. Since the loan has no tax avoidance purpose, Ross can take advantage of Escape Hatch #2. No matter what the Government interest rate is, the amount of income imputed to Ross cannot exceed $1,500. As for gift tax purposes, interest at the full Government rate is imputed, but Ross's annual exclusion should cover it.

HOW TO SLASH YOUR TAX BILL BY CLAIMING EVERY POSSIBLE EXEMPTION DEDUCTION

Many taxpayers cheat themselves out of perfectly legitimate deductions that can yield automatic tax savings of hundreds of dollars. We're talking about your personal and dependency exemptions. Good as they are, they are more valuable each year under the "indexing" system. It automatically hikes exemption deductions (as well as other key tax breaks, such as the standard deductions) if the Consumer Price Index goes up. For 1986, each personal and dependency exemption gives you a $1,080 deduction (the deduction was $1,040 in 1985).

Exemptions For You And Your Spouse

You, along with every taxpayer, get an exemption for yourself. In addition, you get another one for your spouse. However, if your spouse has even a penny of gross income, you must file a joint return with him or her in order to claim the exemption.

Furthermore, you get another exemption when you reach 65, and still another when your spouse arrives at that age. For purposes of the extra exemption for age, you are 65 this year if your 65th birthday occurs on or before January 1 of next year.

Finally, there's still another exemption available if a taxpayer is blind; still another if his or her spouse is blind.

Exemptions For You And Your Dependents

You also get an exemption for every person who meets the following five tests:

1. Support test: The rule itself is easy—you must furnish more than one half the support of your dependent. But the application can be tough. For instance—

What is support? It includes any money you give, directly or indirectly, for the person's food, shelter, clothing, education, medical care, allowance, and the like. It also includes goods furnished, at their fair market value. Lodging is measured by the fair rental value of the room, apartment, or house supplied, including furnishings, heat, and utilities. Fair rental value is what you'd reasonably expect to get from a stranger for the same facilities. If you're a tenant yourself, lodging is a proportionate part of your rent. Support doesn't include income taxes (Federal or local), or life insurance premiums. But support does include capital purchases, such as the cost of buying a car.

There's more: Allowances, toys, haircuts, recreation, music, dancing and dramatic lessons, and so on, are also support.

▶ **REMEMBER:** A small amount can tip the scale either way. Make sure of your deduction by keeping accurate, complete records.

2. Gross income test: For 1986, your dependent must have less than $1,080 in gross income. Gross income means all income subject to tax, without taking into account any deductions.

Example: Your mother owns a small building. Rents total $2,400, and she has rental expenses of $1,500. Though net rental income is only $900, her gross is still $2,400 and she fails the gross income test.

Tax-exempt income is not part of gross income. But, if it's used by the dependent for his or her own support, tax-exempt income may kill your deduction under the more-than-half support test.

▶ **TWO EXCEPTIONS:** There is no gross income test for your child or stepchild if he or she is (1) under 19, OR (2) a full-time student of any age for some part of any calendar months during the tax year at some educational institution maintaining a regular faculty and curriculum.

3. Relationship test: Your dependent must be either (a) a member of your household (but not in an unlawful relationship) who had your home as his or her principal place of abode for the entire taxable year, or (b) related to you as your child, or adopted child (or a child placed in your home by a legally authorized placement agency for adoption), or such child's descendant; stepchild; son- or daughter-in-law; parent or other ancestor, stepfather or mother; father- or mother-in-law; brother; sister; stepbrother or sister; half-brother or sister; brother- or sister-in-law. Also, if related by blood: uncle, aunt, nephew, niece.

Reminder: Even if the marriage that gave rise to the relationship in the first place ends, an in-law is still a relative. Furthermore, if you file a joint return, your spouse's relatives (e.g., his or her uncles) become yours, too. Not so on a separate return.

4 Citizen or resident test: Your dependent must be a U.S. citizen or he must be a resident of the U.S., Canada or Mexico.

5. Joint return test: Your dependent, if married, must not file a joint return with his or her spouse. Otherwise, you'll lose him or her as a dependent. You still get a full exemption for a dependent who is born or dies during the year, provided all the tests for claiming the exemption are met for the part of the year the dependent is alive.

Tax-saving tip #1: If your child and his or her spouse aren't required to file any tax return because they have a low gross income for 1986, but file a joint return solely to claim refunds for tax withheld, you keep the dependency exemption for your child (if the other four dependency tests have been met).

Tax-saving tip #2: If your dependent child marries during 1986, ask the newlyweds to file separate returns. That way, you'll salvage a personal exemption deduction for your child.

Special Rules For Divorced Parents

The parent with custody for the greater part of the year gets a dependency deduction for a child, unless there is an agreement to the contrary. The custodial parent can agree, using Form 8331 to release the child's dependency exemption to the noncustodial parent. The amount of support contributed by either parent is irrelevant.

Important: Both a custodial and a noncustodial parent can treat medical expenses each pays for a child as their own expenses for purposes of the medical deduction—even though they may not be able to claim a dependency deduction for the child.

HOW TO NAIL DOWN A DEPENDENCY DEDUCTION WITHOUT PAYING ONE PENNY MORE

Say you provide support to a relative—it could be a niece, grandchild, your married child or a parent. General rule: You can claim a dependency deduction for a relative only if you provide more than half of his or her support.

If you are near this halfway mark, you may figure it is worth your while to add a few more dollars more to what you have already provided this year. That's sound thinking but it may not be necessary.

▶ NO-COST TAX MOVE: Take a few minutes to jot down all the support you contribute—including items of support that are payments to someone other than your relatives. There's a good chance that these overlooked items will push you over the halfway mark. In fact, you may get a dependency deduction without laying out one extra penny. Reason: These are often expenses you were going to incur anyway.

▶ To help out, here's a checklist of 29 items you may be surprised to learn count as support:

1. Home insurance
2. Personal property insurance
3. The cost of a maid or housekeepe
4. Telephone bills
5. Utility bills
6. Child's allowance
7. Automobiles
8. Babysitter payments
9. Charitable contributions
10. Child care payments
11. Television sets
12. The cost of boarding school
13. Music and dance lessons
14. School supplies
15. Medical insurance
16. Student loan payments

17. Lump-sum payments to a rest home
18. Mortgage and property taxes
19. Toys and bicycle repairs
20. The cost of entertainment
21. Vacations
22. Summer camp
23. Swimming pool fees

24. Book clubs
25. Wedding apparel and accessories
26. Haircuts and permanents
27. Vitamins
28. Laundry and dry cleaning fees
29. Long-distance trips to care for a
relative

▶ **OTHER SIDE OF THE COIN:** Say you help your mother pay some of her monthly bills. You thought you would come nowhere near the half-support mark for the year—but after reading our checklist and taking the time to figure things out, you find you'll be just a couple of hundred dollars short at the end of the year. By adding a few extra dollars between now and then—to get you over the halfway point—you can get an extra dependency deduction.

Two Ways to Rescue a Dependency Deduction For Your Working Child

Working during the summer vacation is a good way for children to get their feet wet in the business world. However, you may be risking a—

▶ **$1,080 DEPENDENCY DEDUCTION:** You can't claim a dependency deduction for a child unless you provide more than half of the child's support. If you're not careful, your child's earnings may push him or her over the half-support mark.

Here are some ways you can avoid losing your dependency deduction when your child goes to work this summer.

● *Financed purchases:* Your daughter Jackie earns $8,000 a year from her summer job and the job she has on weekends during the school year. She spends all of her earnings on support. You provide her with only $4,000 of support. Jackie needs a car to get back and forth from work and school. If you buy a $5,000 car for her, the entire $5,000 counts as support you provide to Jackie this year, even though you may only actually pay a part of it now and finance the balance [Rev. Rul. 77-282, 1977-2 CB 52].

Result: You can claim a dependency deduction for Jackie. Reason: You now provide more than half of her support ($9,000 to $8,000).

● *Student loan:* Your son Glen earns $6,000 a year, all of which he spends on support. You provide Glen with $7,000 of support, so you are entitled to a dependency deduction for him. Glen is starting junior college in the fall and needs to take out a student loan of $2,000 to get by.

▶ **WHAT TO DO:** Take out the loan in your own name and give Glen the money. Reason: Amounts financed under a student loan count as support [McCauley, 56 TC 48].

Result: You hold onto your dependency deduction because you provide more support than Glen does ($9,000 to $6,000). On the other hand, if Glen takes out the loan, it will count against you and you will lose the dependency deduction (Glen provides $8,000 of support, you provide $7,000).

There's more: These are just two items that count towards support that you provide your child. There are others—the cost of summer camp and school supplies, to name two more. The important thing to keep in mind is to make sure that you don't dip below the half-support mark.

HOW TO CHOOSE THE RIGHT FILING STATUS

Although it may seem relatively simple, your filing status is one of the most important items on your return. Reason: Your filing status fixes the rate of tax on your income. Married persons who file a joint return and qualifying widows and widowers are taxed at the lowest rates. Taxpayers who are not married generally file as single taxpayers, with one important exception: Taxpayers who qualify as heads of households can use tax rates that are higher than the rates for marrieds filing jointly but lower than the rates for single people. Marrieds filing separate returns are subject to the highest tax rates.

How To Qualify For The Lowest Possible Tax Rates

Your income is taxed at the lowest rates possible if you are (1) a married person filing jointly with your spouse, or (2) an eligible widow or widower.

Married filing jointly with spouse: You can file jointly with your spouse if you were married as of the end of 1986. You may also file a joint return if your spouse died during 1986. You can also claim an exemption for the spouse. If you remarried, file jointly with your new spouse, not with the decedent.

You may not file a joint return if you were legally separated under a decree of divorce or separate maintenance in 1986.

If both you and your spouse worked for pay or were self-employed, filing jointly yields a—

▶ **BONUS TAX BREAK:** You get a special deduction equal to 10% of the lower-earning spouse's earnings. Deduction limit: $3,000.

Joint-return benefits for eligible widows or widowers: If your spouse died during 1984 or 1985, you can get the same benefits as on a joint return, IF:

● You were eligible to file a joint return the year your spouse died; and

● You claim a dependency exemption for a child, stepchild, or foster child who lived with you for all of 1986; and

• You paid more than half the household costs of the home where you live with this dependent.

▶ **TAX-SAVING TIP:** If your spouse died before 1984, you may be able to file as a head of household and pay tax at a lower rate than single taxpayers.

How One-Parent Households Can Cash In On A Big Tax Bargain

Single taxpayers can qualify for a big tax break by claiming head-of-household filing status. A head-of-household's rates are about halfway between the rates for single taxpayers and those for married couples filing joint returns. It will, therefor, become most important for those taxpayers who can qualify for the head-of-household break to make sure they set things up properly so they can nail it down on their 1986 returns. Let's look at the details.

You qualify as a head-of-household if your spouse did not live with you during the last six months of 1986, and you file a separate return. You must also pass the following tests:

• Generally, you must be unmarried and not a "surviving spouse";

• You must maintain, as your home, a household which is the principal place of abode for more than half the year of (1) your unmarried child; (2) a child's descendant; or (3) any relative (including a married child) for whom you can claim a dependency deduction:

• You must contribute over half the cost of maintaining such home; and

• You must not be a nonresident alien at any time during the taxable year.

▶ **IMPORTANT:** An abandoned spouse who maintains a household for a dependent child can claim head-of-household status, even though married and filing separately.

Q: My young grandson lives with me. I provide more than half the cost of running the home, but his mother actually supports him and claims him as a dependent. Can I qualify as a head-of-household?

A: Yes. As long as the relative living with you is a child or a child's descendant and isn't married, you don't have to be able to claim a dependency deduction for him in order to qualify as a head-of-household. The same rule applies to adopted children or stepchildren. It does not apply, however, to descendants of stepchildren.

Q: I support my mother, but she doesn't live with me. Do I qualify as a head-of-household?

A: Yes—as long as you claim her as a dependent and you provide more than half the cost of maintaining her separate household, including a room in a rest home or home for the aged. Reason: Parents are exceptions to the rule that the home must be yours and the child or dependent must live in it.

▶ **EXTRA TAX BREAK:** A taxpayer who can file as a head-of-household gets a larger flat standard deduction (also known as a "zero bracket amount") than a married taxpayer filing separately—$2,480 rather than $1,835.

Single Taxpayers And Marrieds Filing Separate Returns

If you are unmarried, you usually must file a separate return as a single taxpayer. However, if you are a widow or widower, or you have a child or relative living with you, you may be eligible for lower joint-return or head-of-household tax rates.

If you and your spouse file separate returns, you usually pay higher combined taxes than you would pay by filing jointly. Reason: Married filing separately are hit by the highest tax rates.

If you file a separate return, you pay tax on your income only; so does your spouse. You and your spouse must figure tax the same way. So if your spouse itemizes deductions, you must itemize also.

Marrieds Living In a Community Property State

Special rules apply to marrieds living in a community property state (Arizona, California, Idaho, Louisiana, Nevada, New Mexico, Texas, Washington or Wisconsin). You may file separately or jointly. But if you file separately, each spouse must report one half the community income (no matter who earned what). And each may deduct one half the total deductions paid with community income.

Community property laws may be disregarded if you file separate returns, lived apart the entire year, and kept your funds separate.

HOW TO SLASH HUNDREDS OFF YOUR TAX BILL WITH THE CHILD CARE CREDIT

It's common for both parents to hold down jobs in order to make ends meet these days. If there are small children in the household, they have to be cared for during working hours—an expensive proposition. The tax law provides significant relief in the form of an up-to-$960 child care tax credit. Since tax credits reduce your tax bill on a dollar-for-dollar basis, this break is worth far more than a tax deduction, which merely reduces your income subject to tax.

The basics: You can take a tax credit for the first $2,400 of eligible child care expenses if one child or dependent is involved: or for the first $4,800 of expenses if two or more children or dependents are cared for. The credit depends on the income level. It's a 30% credit for taxpayers with an adjusted gross income of $10,000 or less. For those earning more than $10,000, the credit drops 1% for each additional $2,000 of income. However, the tax credit can't drop below 20%.

In practical terms, this means the tax credit is 20% for taxpayers with an adjusted gross income of $28,000 and up. Maximum credit for these taxpayers is $480 if one dependent is involved (20% of $2,400), and $960 if two or more dependents are involved (20% of $4,800).

The amount of child care expenses the credit is based on cannot exceed the lesser of your earned income, or your spouse's. If your spouse is a full-time student, he or she is considered to have earned income of $200 a month if one child or dependent is cared for, or $400 a month if there are two or more children or dependents.

Q: Who can take the child care credit?

A: The tax law grants the credit to a number of categories of taxpayers who spend money on the care of a child under 15, or a spouse or dependent incapable of self-care.

• Families where both spouses work full-time.

• A working widow, widower, or a divorced or separated parent who has custody of a child (or children) under 15. Divorced or separated parents can get the credit even though they don't claim the child as a dependent, as long as their custody period runs longer than the other parent's.

• Families where one spouse works full-time and the other is either working part-time or is a full-time student.

Key point: In order to be a "full-time student," your spouse has to be enrolled in school at least five months out of the year. And that may be a problem if your spouse starts school in the fall.

> *Example:* Mr. Allen has a full-time job and Mrs. Allen is very active in community affairs. The Allens have a housekeeper, Emma. Mrs. Allen is starting graduate school in September and Emma will spend about half of her working time taking care of the Allen's two children while Mrs. Allen is in school. Emma is paid $700 a month.

Q: Will the Allens be in line for a child care credit on Emma's salary in 1986?

A: Not as things stand now. Reason: Mrs. Allen's four months of schooling during 1986 aren't enough to qualify her as a full-time student this year.

> ▶ **TAX-SAVING MOVE:** If Mrs. Allen attends summer school for at least one month, she will meet the full-time student test and the Allens can claim a child care credit for five months of the housekeeper's salary.

And here's a bonus break: The housekeeper's entire salary for five months (subject to the earned income limit of $400 a month) qualifies as a child care

REV:03-20 EXP:03-17 XX

expense as long as part of her job is looking after the children. Result: Mrs. Allen's one extra month of schooling puts the Allens in line for a child care credit of $400 for 1986 (20% x $400 x 5 months).

Q: Which expenses are eligible for the child-care credit?

A: The cost of looking after a dependent under 15 at home and out-of-household expenses such as boarding and nursery school expenses qualify. As a general rule, the direct expense of educating a child doesn't qualify for the child-care credit. But if you send your child away to boarding school, the non-education portion of the school's cost (room, board and supervision before and after the normal school day) does qualify for the credit.

Summer camp: The cost of having a babysitter look after your children during the summer certainly qualifies for the credit. So the cost of a day camp should also qualify. And in a recent case, the Tax Court ruled, and the IRS later agreed, that the cost of a non-specialized summer camp did qualify (Zoltan, 79 TC 490, Acq. 1984-52).

Q: Must the expense be for a small child?

A: No. You can claim the credit for personal care expenses of your spouse, or a dependent of any age, as long as they are physically or mentally unable to take care of themselves.

For example, your spouse may be temporarily laid up with a broken leg. If you hire a housekeeper to look after the house and help your spouse recuperate, her wages, the cost of her meals, and any extra lodging costs you incur qualify for the credit.

Q: Exactly what do in-household expenses encompass? Are they restricted to amounts relating only to actual child (or dependent) care?

A: Not at all. They include all household help expenses—maid, cook, housekeeper, or caretaker. The key condition: The household help's presence allows both parents (or a single person) to go to work.

Q: Do payments made to relatives qualify for the credit?

A: Payments made to any kind of relative qualify for the credit as long as (1) the person claiming the credit doesn't also claim the relative receiving child-care payments as a dependent and (2) the relative is not less than 19 years old and a child of the taxpayer.

Q: Say a family has their first child in mid-year and spends $2,400 on eligible child-care payments that year. Can they get the full credit?

A: Yes, they can. There's no month-by-month allocation required. The full credit would thus be available also in instances where, for example, the parents were employed for only part of the year.

Q: Do taxpayers have to wait until tax return time to benefit from this child-care credit?

A: Not necessarily. The wage-holding tables must take the child-care credit into account. Thus, the taxpayer can file a new W-4 withholding form and get a break on the credit before tax-return time.

▶ **KEEP RECORDS:** It's up to you to prove you're entitled to the credit. So keep adequate records. It's the only way to make sure you'll be able to take full advantage of this valuable tax saver.

Chapter 11

How to Get Bargain-Rate Insurance That Gives You Top-Dollar Protection

Insurance is one of your family's basic needs. You need to carry insurance on your car, your home and your life. Insurance is also a complicated area with its own rules, requirements and vocabulary. As a result, the unwary consumer may overpay for coverage or, worse, be underinsured.

This Chapter shows you how to make intelligent choices about insurance. We explain the types of coverage that are available to you, the pros and cons of each and how to get the most protection for the least amount of money.

HOW TO PROTECT YOUR MOST IMPORTANT FAMILY ASSET

You must carry insurance on your own life if you have dependents who would be left financially insecure if you were to die before accumulating a substantial estate. Ask yourself if your family could get along without your salary or self-employment earnings, and be able to maintain your current standard of living. If not, you need life insurance. If you are among the very few who have enough secure assets (savings accounts, stocks, bonds, real estate) to protect your dependents, or if you have no dependents, you do not need life insurance for family protection. You may want it for other reasons.

Other uses for life insurance: A policy's proceeds can help offset the decrease in a large estate from the estate tax bite. And the proceeds are usually available to the beneficiary immediately, while it might take a year or more to settle and distribute a large estate.

Life insurance can also be a source of additional retirement income. Certain types of policies build up cash values payable at retirement. There are cheaper, and arguably better, ways to save for retirement and other major needs. But for those who find it all but impossible to discipline themselves to save, life insurance can provide a compulsory savings plan.

How Much Insurance Do You Need?

Once you have decided that you need life insurance protection, you are faced with the next logical question. How much? There is no pat answer. How many

REV:04-01 EXP:03-22 XX

children do you have? How old are they? Does your spouse work? Does your retirement plan have a death benefit? Do you have employer-paid group term insurance? How much debt do you have? What is your standard of living? How much have you saved or invested? These and many other highly personal and individual factors must be taken into account to answer the seemingly simple question "How much?"

With a few fundamental facts and some simple arithmetic, you can arrive at the amount of coverage that will provide adequate protection without unduly draining your resources.

First, figure out how much annual income your family would need to maintain an adequate standard of living. Here's a useful—

> ▶ **RULE OF THUMB:** Your family would need about 75% of your after-tax income. Let's assume your after-tax income is $40,000 per year; as a rough estimate your family would need about $30,000 per year. But this rule of thumb will vary with your individual situation. For example, you may want to budget $2,000 per year to pay for your children's education.

Now come the adjustments: (1) Subtract from your $32,000 estimate (living expenses, plus fund for education) the amount of your spouse's after-tax earnings and Social Security Survivors' Benefits your family would be entitled to receive. The amount of these benefits will vary with the size of your family and your earnings subject to Social Security tax (see Chapter Nine for details). Your local Social Security office can give you the information needed to estimate how much your family would receive. For our purposes, let's assume your spouse does not work and that Social Security benefits would total $10,000 per year.

That means that your insurance would have to cover the gap of $22,000 per year.

(2) Divide this $22,000 figure by the rate of interest which you conservatively estimate your family would earn on the insurance proceeds. Keep in mind (1) your family will probably use some of the principal to meet major expenses (2) inflation will take its inevitable toll, and (3) income tax will be owed on the interest earned.

A net interest figure of around 6% seems reasonable, but if inflation picks up or interest rates continue to fall, an adjustment may be necessary.

Dividing $22,000 by .06 gives your approximately $370,000. That's how much your family will need to cover the shortfall, assuming the principal remains intact. Subtract from that all assets you now possess which could produce income for your family—savings accounts, stocks and bonds, real estate, trust funds, etc. (Do not figure in equity in your home unless you want your survivors to sell the home. *Reason:* The equity will not generate any income for them.) If these assets total $70,000, you need $300,000 of life insurance.

(3) Subtract the face value of your employer-paid group-term insurance (say $100,000), and any pension or profit-sharing funds that would go to your survivors in the event of your death (say, $70,000). What's left—$130,000—is the amount of additional insurance coverage your family will need.

Why You Should Periodically Review Your Insurance Coverage

Most people forget about their insurance needs once they've bought a policy. And that can be a big mistake. You may wind up underinsured—or overinsured— if you don't review your insurance coverage every couple of years. Here are just a few of the factors you should consider when you do your review:

Effect of inflation: An annual inflation rate of 4% or 5% a year will wipe out half of a dollar's puchasing power in 12 to 14 years' time. Result: You may wind up under-insured if you do not increase your coverage.

Change in family's financial needs: A family's financial needs will increase as the children approach college age. And, of course, once they're out of the house, your spouse would need less cash to live comfortably.

Rising standard of living: Your fortunes may take a turn for the better over the years. As a result, the level of coverage appropriate when you first obtained insurance may become inadequate later on to maintain your family's higher standard of living.

HOW TO GET THE BIGGEST VALUE FOR YOUR INSURANCE DOLLAR

Mention life insurance to the average person, and his eyes will almost immediately glaze over. Images are conjured up of a mystifying array of policies, options and riders which can be combined in almost endless ways ("tailored to suit your individual needs"). As a result, if you don't know what you need, you may be sold the wrong type of policy.

Life insurance policies can offer protection, savings features, retirement income and many variations and combinations of each feature. Stripped of all the fancy terminology, all life insurance either is pure term insurance or a contract that combines term insurance with other features.

What You Get When You Buy Term Insurance

In simple terms, this type of insurance is just like the policy you carry on your home or car. Its sole purpose is to supply a dollar benefit in the event of a casualty (your death). Your family is protected for the term of the policy as long as you continue paying premiums. Term insurance is the cheapest form of coverage around, and that may be a major consideration for young families on a tight budget.

Coverage can range from one year to 30 or more years. The premiums are determined by your age and sex. Term insurance costs less when you are younger and gets more expensive as you get older. But since most families need less insurance coverage as the years go on, coverage can be reduced as premiums increase.

If you buy term insurance, your best bet is to get *renewable term*. When the policy expires, it can be renewed (usually until age 65) at a rate determined by your age at the time of renewal. It is renewable even if your health condition has deteriorated in the meantime.

Term insurance is also available with a *conversion* option. This enables you to transfer to a whole life plan at a later date without a medical examination.

The least expensive way to acquire term insurance is usually through a group plan. Many employer-paid plans allow you to purchase additional coverage at favorable rates. Group rates are available through professional associations, and are also offered by mail to credit-card users. Unlike many more complex types of life insurance policies, term insurance prices are easy to compare. Shop around at a few reputable companies (or savings banks if they sell insurance in your state) for the best rate.

Types of Term Insurance: Although there are some variations, term insurance policies usually fit into one of three types:

1. Annual term: This type of term insurance lasts for only one year. It is usually renewable (if not, steer clear). Each year when you renew the policy, your premium will increase to reflect your increased age. But the money you save on premiums in earlier years can be used to pay the increased costs as you get older.

Or if your insurance needs have lessened—say, your children are grown, you have more saved or your spouse becomes employed—you can decrease your coverage to save premium costs.

2. Level term: This type is similar to annual term except the policy remains in force for a longer period of time, say, five or ten years. The coverage and the premium payments remain level throughout the term the policy is in force. So the initial annual premiums will be higher than a comparable annual term policy. And the later premiums will be lower. Again, buy only if the policy can be automatically renewed.

3. Decreasing term: With a decreasing term policy, premiums remain level while the face value of the policy declines. The rate of decline may follow the amortization schedule of a mortgage, or may be at a fixed percentage or dollar value per year. Premiums are lower for this type of term policy because its face value declines as the risk to the insurance company increases. Decreasing term is most often used to enable survivors to pay off a home mortgage or other major debt obligations.

▶ **DO-IT-YOURSELF DECREASING TERM:** You can design your own decreasing-term policy by purchasing annual renewable term policies of diminishing amounts during the life of your mortgage. This approach could give you more flexibility if you were to sell the house, or refinance your mortgage.

A newer type of level term is known as "deposit" level term. It is so called because a deposit, usually $10 per thousand of face value, is required with the first year's premium. The deposit is returned to the policyholder, with interest, when the policy expires. But if the policy is cancelled, some or all of the deposit is forfeited.

Deposit term was developed because insurance companies found they were losing money on the high number of policies cancelled in early years—after the company had paid for physical exams, commissions, and administrative costs. By protecting themselves against the risk of early cancellation, the companies hope to keep rates lower.

Should you buy deposit term? If the difference in premiums between a deposit and a level term policy is small, and you think you can get a higher rate of return on your "deposit" elsewhere, probably not. And if there is a chance that you would cancel the policy in its early years—definitely not!

If You Want More Than Pure Protection

Whole life insurance, also known as ordinary life, permanent life or straight life, is what most people think of when life insurance is mentioned. But whole life is more than pure life insurance—it is life insurance protection that builds up a cash value.

▶ **HOW WHOLE LIFE WORKS:** You pay a level annual premium each year for life. The face amount of coverage also remains level and is payable to your beneficiary when you die. That's how the insurance part of whole life works. But part of each whole life premium accumulates tax-free to build up a cash value. That's the reason whole life premiums are considerably higher than the cost for an equal face amount of term coverage.

This cash value can be used in a number of ways:

• The policyholder can borrow against the cash value at less than generally prevailing interest rates. But there are drawbacks: (1) You are paying for the use of your own money, and (2) your insurance protection is effectively decreased by the amount of any outstanding policy loan.

• The cash value can be used to pay premiums if you are unable to meet a payment deadline.

Popular whole life options: Whole life can be purchased with a variety of riders and options at additional cost.

• Waiver of premium: This option keeps your policy in force if you are unable to pay premiums due to disability.

• Guaranteed insurability option: This allows you to increase your insurance coverage by certain amounts at certain ages no matter what your health condition.

• Accidental death: With this rider, the policy typically pays your beneficiaries two times the face amount of the policy if you die as a result of an accident.

Other variations: Standard whole life coverage requires premiums to be paid for your entire life to keep your insurance coverage in force. Other variations compress the time over which premiums must be paid to get lifetime coverage.

● Limited payment life: On this whole life variation, premiums are paid for 20 or 30 years, or until age 65. Since your coverage under these policies lasts for a lifetime, and premiums are paid for only a specified number of years, annual premium payments are higher than those on a regular whole life policy. Cash values also accumulate at a faster rate.

● Single payment life: This variation is an extreme form of limited payment life. One large premium payment is made at the policy's inception which applies to an entire life's coverage. Single payment life is not recommended for individuals. The premium is usually prohibitive, and the money could usually be put to more productive use in another investment. Single premium life is usually purchased by corporations.

Is Whole Life A Good Deal For You?

An insurance salesperson will have two strong selling points about whole life. In contrast to term insurance, the whole life variety offers level annual premiums and a cash value buildup. Upon closer examination, however, these two major benefits may be illusory:

Here's what the salesperson will stress: With a term policy, payments start off low, but go up as you grow older. Thus, if you buy term, you will be saddled with high premiums in the years you can least afford to pay them (your retirement years). In contrast, with whole life, your premiums are the same each year. And payments in your later years will be far less than you'd lay out with term insurance.

Finally, you'll be told that a whole life policy gives you an investment element in the form of cash value buildup.

Here's what you won't be told: When you buy whole life, your payments in the early years will be higher than with term insurance. So, in effect, you are *prefunding* part of the higher cost you would otherwise pay when you are older. You are paying up-front with dollars that are inherently more valuable now than dollars will be twenty, thirty, or forty years in the future.

And, contrary to what you might think, the older you become, *the more expensive the whole life policy becomes*. Reason: The policy's cash value will grow larger as you grow older. But that cash value does **not** increase the amount payable to your beneficiaries if you die while the policy is in force. Instead, it is subtracted from the death benefit payable under the contract. For example, suppose a person has a $200,000 whole-life policy. If the cash value is, say $80,000 when the person dies at age 60, the family will receive $200,000. But the insurance company will only lay out $120,000. The balance of the death benefit is paid with the policy's cash value.

Result: As you grow older, your annual premium payments pay for less and less coverage. So a whole life policy is more expensive as you grow older—just like a term policy.

You can get at the cash value by cancelling the policy when you are older and no longer need the coverage. This may not sound bad—you had the insurance protection when you needed it, and when you no longer need it you get part of your premiums refunded. And you would be right except for whole life's—

> ▶ **MAJOR DRAWBACK:** The investment return on a whole life policy's cash value is usually considerably lower than that of many other sound investments. Critics of whole life have long maintained that most people would do better in the long run by buying term coverage and investing the money saved on the lower premiums.

Point to consider: Saving takes self-discipline that many of us don't have. Well-intentioned people buy term insurance meaning to invest the saved premiums—but never do. For those people, whole life coverage may be exactly what is needed. By paying higher premiums on a regular basis, they are forced to save for the future. On the other hand, people in this category might find the incentive they need to save for the future in this—

> ▶ **TAX-LAW BREAK:** Individual Retirement Accounts give more incentive to save for the future than anyone should need. First, by saving in an IRA you reduce your income tax liability. Second, your investment grows tax-free until withdrawn. Third, you can choose almost any kind of investment vehicle. (For more information on IRA accounts see Chapter Seven.)

Best advice: If you don't trust yourself to save regularly, even with the advantages of an IRA, buy whole life for its "forced savings" feature.

Universal Life—The Latest Wrinkle in Whole Life Insurance

In an effort to overcome the criticisms leveled against whole life, insurance companies recently have developed policies designed to be more flexible and yield a better investment return. The most popular type of new policy is called universal life. It is unique in that it makes a separate accounting of the three elements that make up the usual permanent-type policy, but are usually hidden from the consumer:

(1) The charges for the insurance element.

(2) The charges for the company's expenses (salesperson's commissions, administrative overhead, policy fees, etc.).

(3) The rate of return on the investment element (the cash value).

The rate of return is flexible. It is guaranteed not to be less than a specified amount (usually 4%) but may be more, depending on the company's decision (a "non-indexed policy") or according to an external index, like the yield on 30-day Treasury bills (an "indexed" policy).

The purchaser has a great deal of flexibility, too. He can change the face value of the term coverage component and can increase his premium payments, within certain limits, to build up the investment component of the policy. The cash value can also be used to pay premiums if the policyholder fails to make them.

Best features: A universal life policyholder has access to the cash value without having to borrow against it and pay interest. The cash value can simply be withdrawn, but there is usually a service fee charged on each withdrawal. As long as the policy meets some technical tax-law requirements, universal life also qualifies for the same favorable tax breaks as whole life insurance: The return on the investment component is not subject to tax when earned—it compounds tax-free until withdrawn. And withdrawals are treated like insurance dividends: They are subject to tax only to the extent they exceed the premiums paid.

How to shop for universal life: According to Dr. Robert A. Gilman, Director of Research and Education of the American Institute for Economic Research (Great Barrington, Mass.), universal life, stripped to its essence, represents the "buy term and invest the rest" philosophy. As a result, the consumer should assess its desirability by looking at (1) the cost of pure insurance, and (b) the net return—after charges and taxes—on the investment element (the cash value).

The results can be surprising: A high cost for the pure insurance element can erode the high rate of return on the investment element. And the charges and fees can take a huge chunk out of the return on the cash value.

Here's an example from Gilman: $1,000 is contributed annually to the cash value; there's a one-time policy fee of $500; and an 8% fee on each contribution. The company advertises a gross yield of 10%, but it will pay only 4% on the first $1,000 of cash value.

Bottom line: The effective annual return to the policy holder is .6%—not 6%, and not the advertised 10% rate. The return will go up in the later years of the policy, but the purchaser may never quite achieve the advertised investment yield.

▶ **WHAT TO DO:** Insist that the salesperson give you a clear explanation of all the charges and fees in a universal life policy. And ask him or her for a year-by-year illustration that shows the actual rate of return on the policy's cash value. Finally, the illustration you're shown may be based on the company's current investment experience. Ask for other illustrations that show what happens if the investment yield falls.

How to Shop For Insurance

Insurance agents are powerful salespeople. They have to be since their livelihood depends on commissions. And the commissions are paid out of an insurance buyer's premium payments. Here's how to be an intelligent insurance shopper:

(1) Before you see your agent, do your insurance-needs analysis, and determine how much you can afford to pay each month for coverage.

(2) You should ask about the rating of the company that will write your insurance. If you want to check the rating yourself, look up the company in *Best's*

Insurance Reports, Life-Health, available at your local library. The ratings range from A + or A (excellent) to C (fair).

(3) The agent will undoubtedly give you a computer-generated illustration showing how you'd make out with the policy. Be sure you understand the illustration—and that's no mean feat.

(4) There are two basic types of permanent policies: participating and nonparticipating. If you buy a participating policy, you will receive dividends paid out of the insurance company's profits and savings. The dividends reduce your net premium costs. On the other hand, if you buy a nonparticipating policy, you won't be paid dividends, but your annual premiums may be lower. In inflationary times, a participating policy may well have the edge, since you will be sharing in the insurance company's higher investment earnings.

(5) If you want a participating policy, ask the agent to supply you with data on (1) the dividend projections made by the company 5 or 10 years ago, and (2) the actual dividends paid on past policies. If actual dividends were close to (or in excess of) the projections, there's a greater likelihood that you'll do well on your policy.

> ▶ **FINAL SUGGESTION:** Unless you join a group-term plan, you'll generally have to undergo a medical examination before you get the policy. Visit your own doctor first and see if you have health problems. If you aren't in the best of health, your doctor may suggest ways for you to get back in shape. If nothing can be done about your condition, your agent should be told in advance. He or she may well be able to find a carrier for your special insurance needs.

HOW TO PROFIT FROM THE BIG INCOME TAX BREAKS OF LIFE INSURANCE

As a general rule, there are no special tax complications to carrying life insurance. In fact, there's a tax break if the policy pays dividends. The dividends are considered a reduction of cost and are not taxable. This holds true whether the dividend is paid in cash or is used to reduce premiums. (Of course, dividends become taxable if they cumulatively exceed premium costs.)

Life insurance turns out to be a real tax winner when the policy proceeds are paid out to the insured's beneficiaries: If the payment is made in form of a lump sum, the entire amount is free of income taxes. However, there are a few exceptions you should be aware of:

● Proceeds are taxable if the policy was transferred for something of value (not, however, if the policy was given as a gift).

● Proceeds payable as alimony are taxable.

● If the proceeds are from a qualified pension or profit-sharing plan, the amount equal to the cash surrender value is taxable as a distribution from the plan.

Q. What if the proceeds of a regular life insurance policy are paid out in installments, or in the form of an annuity?

A. Part of each payment—representing interest earned on the proceeds—is taxable. The balance is tax free.

▶ **TAX-FREE BREAK:** If the beneficiary of a life insurance policy is a surviving spouse who elects to receive installment payments under either a life income or a term-of-years plan, up to $1,000 of interest income each year is not subject to income tax.

Important: If a surviving spouse leaves the proceeds with the insurer, and elects to receive payments of interest only, there is no interest exclusion. All payments are fully subject to tax.

Life income option: Under this payment option, the face amount of the policy is divided by the beneficiary's life expectancy. The resulting amount is the part of each annual payment that is a tax-free return of the proceeds of the policy. The remainder of each annual payment is taxable interest.

▶ **TAX BONUS:** The tax-free portion of each payment is fixed when the payments begin. So this tax break stays in place even after a beneficiary outlives his or her life expectancy and collects more than the face amount of the policy.

Term-of-years option: If the beneficiary chooses to receive installment payments for a fixed number of years, the amount of each annual payment that is tax-free is found by dividing the face amount of the policy by the number of years that the payments are to last. The balance of each annual payment is taxable interest.

Here's how the tax-free portion of the installment payment is computed in the case of a surviving spouse who is the beneficiary of a $60,000 policy and receives 10 annual installments of $7,000 each:

Amount held by the insurer (face value)	$60,000
Period over which the proceeds are to be paid	10 years
Tax-free proration of face value ($60,000 divided by 10)	$ 6,000
Widow's interest exclusion	$ 1,000
Total exclusion	$ 7,000
Annual taxable income from $7,000 payment ($7,000 minus $7,000)	0

What if the surviving spouse has a 20-year life expectancy and elects to take the $60,000 in installment payments of $4,500 a year for life? Here's how to compute the portion of the annual payment on which he or she must pay tax:

Amount held by the insurer (face value)	$60,000
Life expectancy	20 years
Tax-free proration of face value ($60,000	
divided by 20)	$ 3,000
Widow's annual interest exclusion	$ 1,000
Total exclusion for widow	$ 4,000
Taxable portion of each installment	
payment ($4,500 minus $4,000)	$ 500

▶ **TAX-SAVING IDEA:** If the beneficiary isn't a spouse, income tax can be avoided by investing the tax-free insurance proceeds in municipal bonds. Since the interest paid by these bonds is tax-free, the beneficiary escapes tax on the payout and on all of the interest it generates.

This idea would also benefit a higher-tax-bracket surviving spouse whose $1,000 annual interest exclusion isn't enough to shelter the full interest payment.

HOW TO CASH-IN ON THE ESTATE-AND-GIFT TAX BREAKS FOR LIFE INSURANCE

Thanks to some important changes in the tax rules, buying life insurance is a better than ever way to protect your family's future. Reason: If you handle things right, your insurance can also be gift-tax free and estate-tax free.

Here are some of the common ways that you can arrange your insurance strategy and the tax consequences of each method.

1. *You own the policy and name your child as the beneficiary:* With this type of insurance setup, you are assured that the proceeds go directly to your child. Obviously, since you purchased and own the policy, you have not made any gift. Naming your child as the beneficiary is not considered a gift of the policy to him or her. Therefore, there is no gift tax due under this arrangement.

Estate tax consequences: Since you own the policy, the proceeds will be included in your estate. True, most small and medium sized estates won't have to pay any estate taxes. But increasing financial prosperity, and inflation, could bring yours over the tax-free threshold.

Instead of your retaining ownership of the policy, there may be a better course of action—

2. *Transfer the policy to your spouse and name your child as beneficiary:* When you transfer an insurance policy to your wife you are making a gift. But the gift is tax-free because the law allows an unlimited gift-tax marital deduction. This simply means that you can transfer an unlimited amount of property to your spouse without having to pay a gift tax. In fact, after you transfer the policy to your spouse, you can generally continue to pay premiums on the policy without worrying about gift or estate tax consequences.

Since you no longer own the policy, its proceeds will not be part of your estate. However, there's one important exception to this rule. The tax law says that an insurance policy given away within three years of death is included in the donor's estate.

▶ **WHAT TO DO:** If you plan on transferring ownership of your policy to your spouse, the sooner you do it, the better. *Reason:* The sooner you make the transfer, the sooner the three-year period will expire.

3. *You own the policy, and name your spouse the beneficiary:* This may be the most common of all arrangements. And, thanks to some big tax law changes, there are no estate taxes to pay.

▶ **UNLIMITED ESTATE TAX MARITAL DEDUCTION:** The tax law gives estates an unlimited estate tax marital deduction. (The estate tax marital deduction used to be the greater of $250,000 or one-half of your adjusted gross estate.)

Result: Whatever you leave to your spouse, including the proceeds of an insurance policy, is estate tax-free. Although technically, the amount of the proceeds are included in your estate, you are entitled to an offsetting deduction equal to the amount that's left to your spouse.

Best advice: Review your insurance setup—and your entire estate—with your professional adviser. We've covered only the most common types of arrangements. Yours may well differ, or your particular personal situation may require another approach.

HOW TO PROTECT YOUR HEALTH—AND YOUR WEALTH

Health care costs continue to rise at an alarming rate. The cost of even routine surgery and a short hospital stay is staggering. To protect yourself in the event of illness you need health insurance. The foundation of your health insurance coverage should be—

▶ **GROUP HEALTH INSURANCE:** Group health coverage is by far the best buy available. Premiums are up to 40% lower than comparable individual coverage. Most employers offer some type of health insurance plan to their employees. Many pay the entire premium—and it's a tax-free fringe benefit to the employee. Some employers share the cost with employees, or pay for basic coverage only. In the latter case, extended coverage is usually available to the company's employees for an additional premium.

Best bet: Purchase whatever coverage is available through your employer's group plan. It's invariably cheaper than individual coverage.

Group health plans are also available through many professional associations, labor unions, and fraternal groups. Basic coverage usually includes:

● Hospital expenses: Covered items generally include the cost of a semi-private hospital room and board, and nursing services, drugs, operating room fees, bandages and dressings, and lab fees associated with a hospital stay. Benefits vary from policy to policy. The covered length of a hospital stay generally ranges from 21 days to one year. The length of coverage is the major factor determining the cost of this type of insurance.

● Surgery: Surgical coverage pays a doctor's fee for covered procedures up to the amount spelled out in the policy. Anesthesia costs are also partially covered under some policies. Some policies' payments are not spelled out—the policy pays a "reasonable" amount for each procedure. While some policies cover only surgery performed in a hospital, others also pay for office surgery.

● Doctor's visits: Physicians' fees for covered hospital visits are paid up to the limit specified in the policy. There is usually a daily limit to these payments, and coverage may be confined to the first part of a hospital stay.

Basic coverage is often quite limited. For example, policies exclude payment for health conditions in existence before the policy was in force; and oral surgery, surgery performed by a podiatrist, cosmetic surgery, and long-term psychiatric hospitalization are generally not covered.

Perhaps the most important form of health insurance is major medical coverage. As its name suggests, it provides coverage in the event of a major illness. Major medical payments take over when basic coverage ends. There is usually a deductible of between $100 and $1,000 for each individual covered (some plans have a combined family deductible). Once the deductible is satisfied the policy pays a percentage of medical costs (usually 80%) up to one limit and 100% of costs thereafter up to the policy's top limit. The insured is responsible for payment of the deductible amount and 20% of the costs up to the first limit which usually ranges from $2,500 to $5,000. The top limit on major medical policies generally ranges from $50,000 to $250,000.

Another type of health insurance is disability coverage, which partially compensates you for lost income due to extended illness. This is available for both long and short terms. These policies pay a percentage of your monthly earnings (usually 60%) up to a specified monthly maximum. Payments under these policies begin after an "elimination period"—usually six months after the disability begins. Disability benefits are paid in addition to what you may receive from Social Security and usually cover less severe disabilities than does Social Security.

Make Sure Your Health Insurance Premiums Are Buying the Most Protection

You may have employer-paid group health insurance which you supplement with one or more individual policies. If you do, there's a good chance that you are paying more than you should for your coverage. That's because most health insurance policies have a—

▶ **COORDINATION OF BENEFITS:** If your policies have overlapping coverage, you will not be able to collect on each, even though you are paying full premiums on each. The primary insurer will pay up to its policy limit and the secondary insurer will be responsible for additional payments if its limit on the covered item is higher. As a result, the premiums you pay on overlapping coverage are wasted.

What to do: Check over your policies, and eliminate any duplicate coverage on the extra plans. Be sure that the supplementary plan does what it is supposed to—give you *extra* coverage for the extra cost.

Another important thing to consider in this regard is duplicated extended benefits under group health plans. Your spouse and dependent minor children are covered under your employer's plan. If your spouse is employed and also has a group plan, check the details of each group plan. Purchase extended coverage selectively. If both plans have prescription drug riders, pay only for the one that gives you the best coverage. If extended hospitalization coverage is available under both plans, choose the plan with the best coverage, and pay only one additional premium.

HOW TO PROTECT YOUR MOST VALUABLE ASSET

Almost no one fails to insure his home—the single most valuable asset for most people. But it is estimated that half of America's homes are underinsured. Most of these homes were adequately insured at one time, but rising construction costs and home values have eroded the coverage. To be sure your home is adequately protected, you need to know some basics about homeowners insurance and about a couple of dangerous pitfalls.

The three most common types of policies are:

1. *Basic:* This least expensive form covers the holder against personal liability and damage or loss due to fire or lightning, windstorm or hail, explosion, riot or civil commotion, aircraft, smoke, vandalism or malicious mischief, theft and breakage of glass that is part of the building.

2. *Broad:* This covers all of the perils in the basic policy, but adds several more, such as damage from the weight of snow, sleet and ice, building collapse, and accidental discharges of a broken plumbing system. Note that you're covered for damages, but not for replacement of the items that caused the damages. The broad policy is the most common form of homeowner coverage.

3. *Special:* This is the broadest and most expensive form of homeowner insurance. It covers most perils except earthquakes, landslides, flood, surface water, waves, sewer backup, seepage, war and nuclear radiation.

Each of these policy types provides liability coverage to protect you if someone is injured on your property. The standard liability limit is $25,000, an amount insufficient to protect most homeowners. At least $100,000 of liability coverage is generally recommended. The extra protection you get is well worth the small additional premium involved.

Homeowners with substantial assets should also consider an "umbrella" policy to protect against large liability claims. The premium on an umbrella policy is very low. Payments from the policy pick up where homeowner's liability coverage ends; the policy's limits generally run upwards of one million dollars.

Each standard policy contains limits on payments for losses of certain types of personal property, such as cash, precious metals, jewelry, furs, and silverware. And standard policies generally do not cover art objects, antiques, or business equipment in your home. If you need coverage for these items, you can purchase a "floater" or a rider to your policy.

Like auto collision and comprehensive coverage, most homeowner policies contain a deductible. It is usually quite low—you pay, say, the first $100 of each loss before the insurance company becomes liable. A cost cutting technique is to increase the deductible amount to, say, $500, thereby reducing premium cost and increasing the degree to which you are self insured. The important thing is that you are still protected against major disasters.

Homeowner policy premiums do not vary as greatly from one insurer to another as those on auto insurance policies, but it still pays to shop around once you have decided upon the type of coverage you need. Costs will also depend upon such factors as the type of home (wood frame or brick), the area, the distance from a fire hydrant or firehouse, whether the home is equipped with smoke detectors, and, of course, the amount of coverage required.

How to Avoid Costly Home Insurance Pitfalls

When you bought your home you probably insured it for its full value. But even if the home is only a few years old, you are probably under-insured if you have not increased your coverage. If your home were totally destroyed you would collect the face value of the policy—not enough to replace your home. But that's only the beginning. If your home is partially damaged you could fall into the—

▶ **CO-INSURANCE TRAP:** To receive full payment for partial damages, you must carry insurance equal to at least 80% of the *replacement* cost of the home (excluding the land and foundation). If your coverage is less than 80%, you bear part of the risk of each partial loss—you become a co-insurer with the insurance company. The percentage of the loss that you bear depends on how far below the 80% your total coverage is.

Example: You bought your house for $48,000 ten years ago and insured it for its full value. The house, now valued at $80,000, is partially damaged by a kitchen fire. The repairs cost $6,000. Since your home is insured for less than 80% of its replacement value ($64,000), you receive only a percentage of the $6,000. You are only insured for 75% of the required amount.

Result: The insurance company pays only 75% of the repair cost—$4,500. The other $1,500 is your responsibility.

▶ **WHAT TO DO:** Purchase inflation protection to protect yourself from this trap. With this feature, the face value of your policy increases by a certain percentage at regular intervals, or is keyed to a construction cost index for your area. This should give you the protection you need, but it's still a good idea to check your policy every year or so to be sure your coverage keeps pace with inflation and increased home values.

Even if your home is insured to its full value, you may run up against the—

▶ **COVERAGE GAP:** The personal possessions stored inside your home may be drastically under-insured.

Here's why: In general your homeowners policy will provide coverage on your personal property based on a percentage of your coverage. Most policies protect this property in a total amount equal to 50% of the coverage of the house.

In other words, if your home is insured for $60,000, your personal property is insured for half that amount or $30,000. Is that adequate?

Crucial step: One way to come up with the answer is to *make a detailed inventory.* Then if your possessions have greater value than the 50% figure, you can increase the amount of coverage on unscheduled property or buy a floater policy to cover personal articles.

Making an inventory involves more than just listing possessions. You should also take photographs of each room. These pictures coupled with cancelled checks and bills to verify values are helpful in documenting claims. You may also wish to keep photos or descriptions of smaller possessions such as art, jewelry, or antiques. These are useful in case of theft as well as in loss by fire. Update your inventory periodically—say, every two years. Keep a copy of the inventory and other records in a safe place.

Another smart move is to—

▶ **HIRE A PROFESSIONAL APPRAISER:** Find out what your home is really worth today so you can accurately and adequately increase your insurance. (Just adding $10,000 or $15,000 more coverage probably won't be enough.) An appraiser's fee can run up to a few hundred dollars but, when you consider the thousands of dollars involved it can be one of the wisest investments you can make.

You'll find appraisers in the Yellow Pages. Look for those whose names are followed by "MAI" (Member of the Appraisal Institute) or "SRA" (Senior Residential Appraiser).

▶ **CAUTION:** Homeowner policies do not cover you for the full purchase price of damaged, destroyed or stolen personal possessions. They pay only the depreciated value—cost *less* depreciation. Suggestion: Buy personal property replacement-value coverage. This additional coverage will pay you enough to replace the lost personal items.

WHAT TO LOOK FOR WHEN BUYING AUTO INSURANCE

The most important function of auto insurance is not to protect you against financial loss if your car is damaged or stolen. Its primary function is to protect you against potentially gigantic liability claims if you are involved in an accident—claims that could wipe out your entire nest egg. This type of auto insurance is—

▶ **LIABILITY INSURANCE:** This protects you against claims resulting from an accident for which you are found to be at fault. It compensates injured parties for both personal injury and property damage resulting from an accident.

Auto liability coverage is broken down into two major components: bodily injury and property damage. The bodily injury portion provides one coverage limit for injuries to one person, and a higher limit for injuries to two or more people. Many states require 10/20 coverage. This will pay a single accident victim up to $10,000 for damages resulting from bodily injury, and limits payment to $20,000 if more than one person is injured.

With judgments of hundreds of thousands of dollars now being commonplace, (and millions not unheard of), the required minimum liability coverage is insufficient to protect anyone with any assets from financial disaster. Required property damage limits—often as low as $5,000—are also too low to protect you against a major claim.

It will do you little good to have minimum liability coverage when a single misjudgment on your part (or on the part of anyone else who drives your car) can result in a seven-figure judgment against you.

▶ **WHAT TO DO:** Do not stint on liability coverage. Carry a minimum of 100/300/25 ($100,000 single bodily injury; $300,000 group bodily injury; $25,000 property damage) coverage. Higher limits are highly advised if you have a substantial amount of assets to protect against the claims of an injured party. Surprisingly, the cost of the additional coverage is not prohibitive—especially in relation to the devastating losses from which you are shielding yourself.

Many states have adopted forms of no-fault insurance. In these states, each insured's company compensates him or her for economic losses resulting from injuries, up to certain limits. An injured party who receives payment for physical injuries cannot sue the driver at fault for damages unless the injuries exceed the no-fault limits. But since these limits are generally extremely low, it is still essential to carry additional liability insurance.

Other Types of Auto Insurance

Collision coverage: If your car is damaged in an accident, collision coverage pays for its repair. Remember, the "other guy" may not be insured—or there may not be another guy. If you sideswipe your garage, for example, there's no one else to collect from. Premium costs are based on factors such as the age, sex, marital status, and driving record of the car's driver, and the type and cost of a car. Rates also vary tremendously according to the area in which you live or drive—urban rates are much higher than rural. (The same holds true for other types of auto insurance.) Insurers rate cars according to the cost of repairs. Collision coverage will cost more on a car that is more costly to repair.

Collision coverage is always sold with a "deductible". The deductible is the amount of repair cost which the owner pays for before the insurance company becomes liable. In some areas the minimum deductible on these policies is $200—the owner pays the first $200 of any repair bill. A higher deductible substantially reduces the premium for collision coverage.

The insurance company pays for repairs above the deductible amount, but with this—

> ▶ **IMPORTANT LIMIT:** The insurer will not pay for repairs that exceed the car's book value. For example, if repairs to a damaged car will cost $2,000, but the car is worth only $1,500, the insurance company will pay only $1,500 less the applicable deductible.

If you borrow from a bank or finance company to buy a car, the lender requires you to carry collision (and comprehensive) insurance to protect its loan collateral. If the car is totally destroyed, the lender collects the amount outstanding on the loan from the insurer. The balance of the insurance payment goes to you.

Comprehensive coverage: This pays for losses from the theft of a car or from damages as a result of fire, vandalism, falling objects, flood, and the like. Some comprehensive policies also pay for towing charges resulting from an accident or breakdown. There is usually a separate deductible on glass breakage, and premiums can be reduced by a general comprehensive deductible. Premiums can also be saved by limiting comprehensive protection to fire and theft losses.

Like collision coverage, the policy will not pay for repairs in excess of the car's value.

Uninsured motorist coverage: It is estimated that upwards of 20% of today's drivers are uninsured—even where insurance is mandatory. Many of these are the highest-risk and least responsible drivers on the road. Uninsured motorist coverage helps compensate you, your family, and other passengers in your car for damages from injury caused by an uninsured motorist or a hit-and-run driver. You are also covered if you are hit while walking or riding a bicycle. Payments under this type of coverage are usually limited to the minimum mandatory liability coverage required by state law; but in some states higher coverage limits are available.

Medical payment coverage: This provides limited coverage for medical expenses incurred by the car's owner and passengers as a result of an accident, regardless of who is at fault. This also covers family members who are injured while riding in someone else's car, or who are injured by a car while walking.

These policies are typically coordinated with other health insurance you may have: payments will meet your other health insurance's deductible and pick up after your other health coverage is exhausted.

Smart Strategies to Cut the Cost of Auto Insurance

There are a couple of things you can do to ease the jolt every time you see your bill for auto insurance. The first is to make sure you are paying the lowest possible rate for your auto coverage. The second is to see that you are not paying for unnecessary coverage. Here are cost-cutting tactics:

#1: It pays to shop around for the best deal on auto insurance rates. This may sound like shop-worn advice. But it's as true today as it was ten or twenty years ago. Insurance firms are competitive; their rates do differ. It's possible that you could knock 10% or 15% off your costs by changing insurance carriers.

▶ **WHAT TO DO:** Call your local consumer protection agency or the state's insurance department and ask for a list of comparative auto insurance prices. If you can't get a list from the officials, ask your insurance agent to quote you rates from several insurers. Or call several agents and see how their quoted rates compare.

#2: Buy the right kind of car. Though far less publicized than mileage ratings, *insurance ratings* of car models do exist—and can save you money. An insurance rating is an objective evaluation of how much it costs to repair a particular car.

If your insurer uses ratings for accident costs, it can mean a difference of as much as 40% a year in collision premiums for two similarly priced cars.

And don't buy a super-high performance car with many flashy extras. Insurers will suspect that you mean to speed and charge you more.

▶ **BUYING SMART:** Ask your insurer for a list of accident cost ratings for car models you have in mind. The information on insurance ratings will help you factor in the cost of insurance when you make your car buying decision.

#3: Ask if you qualify for a discount. There are a number of situations where an insurer will give you a break. Here are some examples:

● Most insurers give a discount for a two-car policy. So if you have two cars, insure both with one company.

● If you have an accident-free driving record, use it to the hilt. Many companies give discounts for this. Deal with one that does.

● If your under-age-25 child uses the car, you're in high-premium territory. But many insurers give discounts for good student drivers. Your child's completion of an approved driver training course can lop 5% to 15% off your liability and collision premiums. And if your child is away at college much of the year (and carless), ask your insurer what sort of break you get.

● If you buy a car with an air bag (it inflates upon collision to protect passengers), you'll probably pay a lower auto insurance bill.

● If you own an older car that's paid for, cancel the collision coverage and the comprehensive coverage. If you want some protection, keep the fire and theft portion of the comprehensive policy.

#4: Custom-tailor your policy. Tell your insurer what *you* need and *you* want. The typical car policy consists of several types of coverage. You may cut costs by reducing or deleting coverage you don't need.

For example, comprehensive insurance protects against fire, theft, vandalism and ''natural cause'' accidents resulting from, say, bad weather. You can lower the comprehensive premium by raising the deductible, i.e., the amount of damage you would pay for if you file a claim.

Key questions: Is your car frequently parked in high-crime areas? Is the car attractive to potential car thieves? Is a ''natural cause'' accident likely? If your answers are ''no'' here's—

▶ **WHAT TO DO:** Consider reducing the comprehensive premium by increasing the deductible. If your family owns two cars, you may even want to eliminate comprehensive coverage entirely on the older car—in other words, "self-insure" it.

The same moves apply to collision coverage as to comprehensive. But the potential savings are greater beause collision is more expensive.

Should you cut your liability coverage? The answer is probably ''no.'' Liability covers personal injury and property damage to others for which you (or another person driving your car) are held liable. Applying your cost pruning shears here, and cutting liability coverage to the minimum required by your state, could be—

▶ **A SHORTSIGHTED MOVE:** Judgments of several hundred thousand dollars are not uncommon in personal injury cases. So it is a reasonable precaution to have substantial liability coverage. Moreover, the top dollars of liability coverage cost little. If $300,000 of coverage costs you $574 a year, cutting it to $100,000 would save only about $60—a little more than 10%.

Can you save on medical payment insurance? The answer here depends on how good your other medical insurance is. Your auto policy medical insurance covers medical and hospital costs incurred by you or your passengers as the result of an accident. This may needlessly duplicate hospitalization insurance you and your family have from another source. So all you may want to cover with this insurance is passengers.

Chapter 12

How To Care For An Aging Parent Without Draining Your Financial Resources

The good news: Thanks to advances in medical science, people are living longer lives. The bad news: The cost of living to a ripe old age has gone through the roof. And that means there's a good chance that eventually you will be footing at least a portion of your parents' bills.

There are a number of ways you can avoid a heavy financial burden and help your parents remain independent and self-sufficient. And the time to discuss these options is *now*, while your parents are still healthy. Don't wait for a crisis to strike before you create a blueprint to assist Mom and Dad. This chapter will show you how to help your parents: use a durable power of attorney to protect themselves in the event of illness or infirmity; write a living will; unlock the equity in their homes; and choose a nursing home. You'll also see how the tax law can help reduce the cost of supporting a parent.

HOW A DURABLE POWER OF ATTORNEY CAN HELP KEEP YOUR PARENTS' AFFAIRS IN ORDER

Although your parents may not want to think about it, they could possibly lose their ability to handle their affairs due to an accident, age, illness, or infirmity. Even if the impairment is only temporary, it could leave the entire family in a real dilemma. Reason: If, let's say, your father is sick, his property and business are left in a state of limbo—except to the extent it is jointly owned with your mother.

▶ **WHAT TO DO:** Your parents should consider giving someone they trust a durable power of attorney. Such a power, which can either survive or become effective upon impairment, allows the person named in the document to act on their behalf. Many states have adopted specific legislation that provides for a durable power of attorney.

Important: There is another type of power of attorney—a regular power of attorney. But it just won't do in this situation. Reason: The person designated as the agent under a regular power loses his ability to act when the princpal becomes impaired. The agent's powers become null and void. In legal terms, they "lapse."

There are two alternatives to a durable power of attorney. But they both have shortcomings:

• Property can be transferred to a trust now. Since the trust owns the property, the trustee's authority to act survives any impairment. But therein lies the rub: Your parent loses control over your property between now and when the trust is needed.

• Nothing is done now and the state appoints a guardian or conservator if and when there is an impairment. Of course, there would have to be a judicial determination that your mother or father is unable to handle his or her affairs. That can take time, during which there is a gap in the management of the assets. And once a guardian or conservator is appointed, he is given very little discretion regarding investments and the disbursement of assets. He may even be under a duty to wind up a business at the earliest convenient moment. As a result, the business may be sold off, and at less than top dollar (it's a forced sale).

If a durable power of attorney is chosen and it is effective from its inception, there is no gap in the management of the assets. If, on the other hand, the power is to take effect only upon impairment, there can be a gap in management.

▶ **SMOOTH TRANSITION:** The durable power of attorney agreement should define what kind of impairment triggers the power. The standard should be reasonably objective, but nevertheless allow for some discretion. Perhaps a self-perpetuating committee of physicians, including your parents' personal physician, could make the determination.

Payoff: In addition to keeping the family's financial affairs in order, a durable power of attorney can allow the named agent to make some important moves that can slash the estate tax bill. For example, he or she can buy flower bonds to help pay the estate tax. Or the agent can set things up so the business qualifies for several key estate tax breaks. The agent can even continue a long-established pattern of gift-giving that can also slash the size of the taxable estate.

▶ **SEE AN ATTORNEY:** An attorney can draw up the power of attorney to meet your parents' needs—naming the person of their choice, maybe limiting the agent's powers or the length of the power. An attorney will also be sure that all state law requirements regarding the power are satisfied. The attorney will also know if special bank forms are necessary.

WHY IT MAY BE BETTER FOR YOUR PARENTS TO HAVE TWO WILLS

A growing number of people now have two wills—the usual one and a second so called "living" or "mercy" will. A living will instructs a person's family and physician that if he becomes terminally ill and incompetent, he does not wish to be kept alive by extraordinary life support systems. The will can specify the measures that are ruled out.

Twenty-two states and the District of Columbia have passed acts that give living wills legal validity. While there are some differences in each state's law, most statutory language is quite similar.

Taking that into consideration, here are some guidelines that should increase the chances of your mother or father's wishes being respected by a physician and, where necessary, enforced by a court.

1. Competence: The living will must be in writing and executed while your parents are of sound mind. With one exception (Idaho), a person does not need to be terminally ill in order to execute a living will.

2. Witnesses: The will must be witnessed by at least two adults. Among other requirements, the witnesses generally cannot be related to your parents by blood or marriage, be entitled to any part of their estate or have a claim against it, or be their attending physician.

This is done to establish that they did in fact sign the document, and more importantly, did so of their own free will.

3. Authentication: The living will should be notarized as further proof of the seriousness of their intent.

4. Status: The more recently the living will has been executed, the more likely it is that a physician or a court will accept it. A living will should be re-dated and initialled at least once every five years to make it clear that the directions are unchanged.

Is it binding? According to most statutes, a doctor with a moral, legal or other objection is under no obligation to withdraw life-sustaining procedures. However, the patient or his or her family may ask that another doctor, who will honor the document, be brought in. Therefore, the answer to the question is, as a practical matter, "yes."

▶ **WHAT TO DO:** Make sure that your parents discuss the contents of the living will with their doctor before they sign it. If an agreement cannot be reached, another, more sympathetic doctor may be sought out.

As a rule, the provisions of a living will take effect only when: (1) A diagnosis of terminal illness has been made, (2) death is imminent, and (3) life-sustaining procedures are being implemented or are contemplated.

For your information: The jurisdictions that have living will acts are: Alabama, Arkansas, California, Delaware, District of Columbia, Florida, Georgia, Idaho, Illinois, Louisiana, Kansas, Mississippi, Nevada, New Mexico, North Carolina, Oregon, Texas, Vermont, Virginia, Washington, West Virginia, Wisconsin, and Wyoming. Eighteen others, including New Jersey and New York, have legislation pending.

In states where such a statute does not exist, the living will still may be taken as a strong indication of a patient's desires.

Sample Living Will

Here is a sample living will that can be adapted to fit your parents' needs. Keep in mind that some states require that a form specified in their statutes be used. Others request the adoption of particular language.

TO MY FAMILY, PHYSICIAN, LAWYER, AND OTHERS WHOM IT MAY CONCERN:

Death is as much a reality as birth, growth, maturity and old age—it is the one certainty of life. If the time comes when I can no longer take part in decisions for my own future, let this statement stand as an expression of my wishes and directions, while I am still of sound mind.

If the situation should arise in which there is no reasonable expectation of my recovery from extreme physical or mental disability, I direct that I be allowed to die and not be kept alive by medications, artificial means or "heroic measures." I do, however, ask that medication be mercifully administered to me to alleviate suffering even though this may shorten my remaining life.

This statement is made after careful consideration and is in accordance with my strong convictions and beliefs. I want the wishes and directions here expressed carried out to the extent permitted by law. Insofar as they may not be legally enforceable, I hope that those to whom this Will is addressed will regard themselves as morally bound by these provisions. Optional specific provisions:

1. Measures of artificial life-support in the face of impending death that I specifically refuse are:

a) Electrical or mechanical resuscitation of my heart when it has stopped beating.

b) Nasogastric tube feeding when I am paralyzed or unable to take nourishment by mouth.

c) Mechanical respiration when I am no longer able to sustain my own breathing.

2. I would like to live out my last days at home rather than in a hospital if it does not jeopardize the chance of my recovering to a meaningful and sentient life or does not impose an undue burden on my family.

3. If any of my tissues are sound and would be of value as transplants to other people, I freely give my permission for such donation.

DURABLE POWER OF ATTORNEY (optional):
I hereby designate   to serve as my attorney-in-fact for the purpose of making medical treatment decisions. This power of attorney shall remain effective in the event that I become incompetent or otherwise unable to make such decisions for myself.

Reprinted with the permission of: *Concern for Dying, 250 West 57th St., New York, N.Y. 10017, (212) 246-6962.*

HOW YOUR PARENTS CAN UNLOCK THE CASH IN THEIR HOME

Your parents' home is probably the best investment they ever made. It may be worth two, three or four times what they paid for it. The problem: As your parents get older, their "investment" isn't doing them much good. Reason: Unless they sell the house or refinance it (both propositions that may not be acceptable), their equity is locked in. In short, they are "house-rich" but "cash-poor."

And just think what your parents could do with the equity they've built up in the home. They could invest it and use the interest or dividends to supplement other retirement income. Part of the cash could be used to put in ramps, handrails, elevators or bathrooms which will enable your parents to continue to live self-sufficiently.

A California outfit, the Family Backed Mortgage Assoc., Inc. has come up with a setup that allows parents to turn their homes into cash—and gives the children important benefits as well. It's called the—

▶ **"GRANNIE MAE" PROGRAM:** This arrangement permits parents to live in their home for the rest of their lives and get a steady stream of income, based on their age and the value of their home. When they die, the home goes to their children outright.

How it works: The Grannie Mae setup consists of two separate transactions: a sale followed by a long-term lease.

The sale: Parents sell their home to their children. The children finance the purchase with a cash downpayment and a mortgage from a Grannie Mae-approved lender. The sale proceeds go toward the purchase of an annuity from an insurance company.

The annuity pays the parent a monthly income for life (or for the joint lives of both parents). The amount of the annuity payments depends on the average life expectancy of the parent at the time of the sale. There is a guaranteed minimum number of payments. So if the parent dies before the life expectancy tables say he or she was supposed to, the insurance company will make the annuity payments to the estate for the remainder of his or her life expectancy.

The long-term lease: After the house is sold, the parent becomes a tenant and the child becomes the landlord. The lease is automatically renewable each year for as long as the parent (or surviving spouse) wishes to live in the home. And if the child sells the home, the parent doesn't lose the right to stay there. The buyer takes the home subject to the lease.

▶ **KEY TO THE DEAL:** As tenants, your parents pay rent to you. The rent is based on the appraised value of the home and usually ranges annually from four to nine percent of the value. Depending on their life expectancy, the annuity income should exceed the money being paid out for the rent.

Example: Mrs. Worth is a 65-year old widow. She sells her home to her son for $100,000 under the Grannie Mae program. The sale proceeds are used to purchase an annuity that pays her $13,200 each year. After the sale, Mrs. Worth pays her son $6,000 in rent each year. So she's ahead by $7,200. And she also keeps the money she would otherwise pay out for property taxes, major maintenance costs, and home-owners' and hazard insurance—her son, "the landlord," is responsible for those. Let's assume these added expenses come to $2,000 a year.

Result: Mrs. Worth nets an extra $9,200 each year from the sale-leaseback.

▶ **WHAT'S IN IT FOR THE CHILD?** You, of course, eventually get full possession of the home. And since your parents have sold the home, there won't be any
estate tax on it. But there is another important break for you: current income tax
savings.

The tax law gives big breaks to landlords. You can currently deduct out-of-
pocket expenses and get an annual writeoff for depreciation. Payoff: These deductions may not only shelter the rental income from tax—but some of your other
highly taxed income as well.

Important: While the Grannie Mae program offers many benefits, obviously
it's not for everyone. For example, if you are in a relatively low tax bracket, the
tax savings may not be that substantial. There are mortgage fees, administration
costs and the like that must be considered. And the rental payments you receive
should at least equal what you're paying out for the mortgage, taxes, insurance,
utilities, and so forth. Otherwise, you'll be in the red. You and your parents will
want to talk things over carefully with your legal and financial advisers before
taking any action.

HOW TO CHOOSE A NURSING HOME

Choosing a nursing or convalescent home for a parent is an important responsibility. In many cases, it will be up to you to do the necessary research and make
the decision. Understandably, this is not an easy job, especially if you find
yourself asking, ''can we find some other sort of arrangement? Are there alternatives?'' This section will help answer some of these perplexing questions.

Step one: Ask your family doctor about the type of facility your parent will
need. You may also want to ask a social worker and other health care providers
for their opinions as well. Here are just three of the types of facilities that may be
recommended to you:

● Minimum care. These facilities are for people who do not need actual
nursing or medical care, but can, with some assistance, see to their everyday
needs.

● Intermediate care. This type of arrangement is for those who need some
nursing care. Registered nurses are on duty at least part of the day.

● Lifetime care. Patients pay a flat entrance fee plus a monthly fee for use of a
living unit, meals and various health benefits for the rest of their lives. It goes
without saying that this type of home is the most expensive.

Step two: Evaluate your parents' financial situation—and your own, as well.
You may find that your parents are uncomfortable discussing money matters with

you. If that's the case, get your brothers and sisters together and leave your parents out of it for the time being.

Dollars needed: Tally up your parents' Social Security payments, pensions and other retirement income, Medicare coverage, house, car, investments and other assets. Subtract from the amount, your parents' yearly living expenses *plus* what will be required for in-house care or a nursing home, for example.

Then ask yourself, with the money situation as it is currently, can they or we, cover any deficit? You'll also need to find out whether Medicaid or Medicare will pick up any of the cost. We'll discuss this further in step six.

Step three: Pay a visit to each home. Make some of those visits unannounced and at off hours, e.g., early in the morning, late at night, and at meal times. Look for the following:

- Clean and comfortable rooms and meeting areas.

- Facilities and staff for rehabilitation and/or physical therapy. See if those facilities are being used.

- Condition of the patients.

- Well-lit and unobstructed halls, stairs and bathrooms, all equipped with handrails.

- Clearly marked exits that are not locked on the inside, closed fire doors, and automatic sprinkler systems.

- Beds that have curtains for privacy and conveniently located call bells for the nurses.

- Nutritious, well-prepared meals. If possible, order a tray while visiting and try the food yourself. If there's a printed menu, see whether the meal matches it.

- Bulletin boards or display cases showing notices for programs and activities. An activity director on the staff is a plus.

- Warm, friendly and interested staff members.

Step four: Talk to each home's administrator. Here are some of the questions you should ask:

- Does the home and the administrator hold current state licenses? (This is must.)

- Are special diets or therapies provided if the patient needs them? (Also a must.)

- Is a full-time physician on staff? Licensed physical therapist? Registered dietician?

- Are rooms shared on the basis of patients' preferences and compatabilities?

- Are there planned recreational programs and outings?

● Do the aides (those that have the most direct contact with the patients) get training from the professional staff?

● How much does the home charge per day? Are there extra charges for wheelchairs, bedpans, medicines, etc.,?

● What is the staff/patient ratio and how many of the staff are licensed professionals?

Step five. See what the doctors and families of patients have to say about the facility.

Step six: Find out if your parent qualifies for Medicare or Medicaid assistance. But be forewarned—

> ▶ **MEDICARE MAY BE NO CARE:** It's important to note that nursing home care will not be covered by Medicare unless it's associated with recuperation for an acute condition (the patient must have been hospitalized for at least three days). And even if that requirement is met, coverage is limited to 100 days (see Chapter Nine for more details).

Medicaid will help you out, but there's a catch. State welfare agencies generally require that virtually all the patient's resources (and his or her spouse's) be exhausted before financial assistance is tendered. What's more, intra-family transfers of the patient's assets are disregarded if the transfers take place in the two-year period before a Medicaid claim is made. In other words, you cannot pauperize your parent (by transferring assets to other family members) and thereby qualify him or her for Medicaid.

> ▶ **WHAT TO DO:** If you foresee the need for your parent to be placed in a nursing home for long-term care, you should discuss the situation with your family lawyer.

Other Ways To Care For Your Parents

If you decide that it is better for your aged parent to stay in his or her own home—or your home—you should consider hiring a home companion/helper. However, if your parent requires medical attention, you will need a home health aide, licensed practical nurse or a nurse's aide. Medicare will pay the full cost of medically necessary home health care.

For a price, a health care agency will place certified bonded personnel in the home. To earn its fees, the agency does the original screening and takes care of tax withholding. Although agencies can save you time and effort, their expense may be prohibitive, and the results by no means guaranteed. So, you may want to—

> ▶ **DO IT YOURSELF:** Talk to friends, family, neighbors and members of organizations you belong to for referrals. You can also place ads in the local newspapers. A week is generally a long enough period of time to generate responses.

Use the phone interview to screen out the obviously unacceptable candidates and to get background information on those that may be suitable. You'll want to know how much experience they've had, their last employers (two references are standard) and their availability. Leave the rest of your questions to the initial face-to-face interview.

The first interview: Here are some of the points you should raise in the first meeting you have with potential home companions:

• Give applicants a detailed description of the routine that is currently followed at home. (Once you've hired someone, put this routine into writing and discuss it again.) Don't make the job seem easier or harder than it really is. Remember, you're looking for someone willing to make a long-term commitment.

• Describe your parent's physical and mental limitations.

• Ask the applicants how they would respond to different emergencies.

• Discuss the types of activities that they might be interested in sharing with your parent.

• Establish from the start the groundrules for living in the home.

The second interview: A second interview is the time to let your parent evaluate the applicant. For your part, pay close attention to the attitude the potential home companion has toward your parent.

Let's say you've hired someone as a live-in companion for your parent. Now you're an employer. And with that new role comes increased paperwork: You are responsible for:

(1) Withholding Social Security from the employee's pay and for making your own matching contribution to the Federal government on a quarterly basis.

(2) Paying Federal and state unemployment taxes.

(3) Withholding Federal income taxes (only if the employee and you agree).

(4) Obtaining a workers' compensation rider to your homeowner's policy.

(5) Applying for an Employer Identification Number. Call the IRS and ask for the Employer Identification Request form.

▶ **WHAT TO DO:** Call the Social Security and Internal Revenue Offices with your questions. They'll help you get through the maze of government regulations and assist you in filling out the required forms.

For more help: Home health care agencies are listed in the phone book. You can also write to Home Health Service and Staffing Association, 815 Connecticut Ave., N.W., Suite 206, Washington, D.C. 20006. The National HomeCaring Council at 235 Park Ave. So., New York, N.Y. 10003 is another source of home companions and home-health aide services.

Home-Sharing For Older People

Shared-housing arrangements are becoming an increasingly popular alternative for older people who want to stay in a home environment, but cannot live alone. Nearly all these programs are funded and run either by local government or by private foundations. The vast majority match up an older person or couple, usually 60 and older and frequently the owner of the home, with a person the same age or younger. That person must be willing to pay for part of the home's maintenance, work in exchange for rent or provide companionship. The match-up organization generally does quite extensive counseling with prospective sharers and charges a nominal fee. The housing counselor will ask your parents, for instance, why they want to share their home and what they expect to get out of the arrangement—both monetarily and psychologically. (Managing the house and setting the rent are up to the individuals involved.) After the counselor finds a good match, the two people meet. If they decide to live together, the counselor will follow up on them for a number of months after.

Cluster housing: Rather than match up two people in a single home, cluster housing promotes group living for the elderly. Under this setup your parent would live with pehaps eight other people in a house bought by either individuals or community-sponsored coalitions. While some of these houses merely have separate bedrooms for the occupants (kitchens, bathrooms, etc., are shared) others are divided into separate, self-contained apartments.

▶ **FOR MORE INFORMATION:** Contact the National Shared Housing Resource Center, 6344 Greene St., Philadelphia, PA 19144 for the different types of shared housing arrangements available in your community. Local social service agencies may also be able to help. The "College Connection," run by the Consolidated Capital Foundation, in Emeryville, California is another option. It arranges for college students to exchange ten hours of work per week for a room in an older person's home.

HOW TO CLAIM A FULL DEPENDENCY EXEMPTION FOR A RELATIVE YOU SUPPORT ONLY PARTIALLY

You have been successful in your business or profession, and you feel that you have a special obligation to provide for your parents in their old age. Your brothers and sisters feel the same way, so you all chip in to help your parents make ends meet. You're glad to do it. But this sometimes creates a—

Tax problem: Say you and your brothers and sisters together are contributing most of Mother's support. But none of you, individually, contribute more than half. The basic rule is that a taxpayer gets a dependency deduction for a parent only if he or she provides more than half the parent's support. But the tax law provides a way for someone in the family to get the exemption even though none of you meet the more-than-half test.

▶ **TAKE TAX ACTION NOW:** Set things up so that your family can take advantage of a "multiple support agreement." This agreement lets you and your brothers and sisters decide which of you can take the exemption for, say, your mother. And you can trade off the exemptions so that over the years everybody gets a chance to claim the deduction.

Here Are The Key Requirements

1. Mother must have received over half of her support from you and your brothers and sisters;

2. Each of you must be able—except for contributing half of her support—to claim her as a dependent. (This means that Mother can't have more than $1,080 in gross income for 1986.)

3. No one of you can contribute singly more than half your Mother's support;

4. If you're the one who's selected to take the exemption, you must contribute more than 10% of support.

5. Anybody else who gives more than 10% support must agree not to claim an exemption for Mother in the year you claim the exemption. This entails filling out Form 2120 (Multiple Support Declaration), available at any IRS office.

▶ **ADDED TAX BREAK:** The one who claims Mother as an exemption can also treat medical payments made on Mother's behalf as a deductible medical expense on his or her tax return.

Example: Each year, Joseph Smith and his brothers Charles and Andrew contribute $4,000 each for the support of their aged mother, Clara Smith. Of the total $12,000 each year, $1,500 is for doctor bills. By agreement with his brothers, Joseph (being the one with the highest income tax bracket) is going to claim Clara as a dependent. Also by agreement, $1,500 of Joseph's total $4,000 contribution is allocated to the $1,500 in doctor bills.

Smith claims his mother as a dependent on page one of Form 1040 and deducts his payment of her doctor bills as a medical expense on Schedule A, Form 1040. Charles and Andrew each complete a copy of Form 2120. This Form is available at any Internal Revenue Service office. Charles and Andrew each enter their own Social Security number and address in the same manner as they make these entries on their own Form 1040s. If they are married, their spouses also sign the Form. Joseph files both his brothers' Form 2120s with his tax return. A sample Form 2120, made out by Charles, is reproduced below.

Q: Let's say I share the support of my parent, together with my brothers and sisters. But my parent's yearly income from investments is way over the $1,080 limit so she can't be claimed as a dependent. Any tax breaks here?

A: You can still deduct your parent's *medical* expenses on your return. Here's how: Have your brothers and sisters designate you as the one entitled to deduct the

Form **2120**
(Rev August 1984)

Department of the Treasury—Internal Revenue Service

Multiple Support Declaration

OMB No. 1545-0071
Expires 8-31-86

During the calendar year 19_____, I paid more than 10% of the support of

Clara Smith

(Name of person)

I could have claimed this person as a dependent except that I did not pay more than 50% of his or her support.

I understand that this person is being claimed as a dependent on the income tax return of *Joseph and Mary Smith*

(Name)

611 Front Street, Littletown, Mass.

(Address)

I agree not to claim an exemption for this person on my Federal income tax return for any tax year that began in this calendar year.

Charles Smith   *003 03 0066*

(Your signature)   (Your social security number)

March 11, 19   *313 Anderson Avenue, Covington, Mass.*

(Date)   (Address)

Form **2120** (Rev. 8-84)

medical expenses. The family uses the same multiple support agreement it would use if a dependency exemption were being claimed for the parent.

▶ **TAX ACTION NOW:** If your family chips in to support a family member this year—and a dependency exemption won't be claimed—designate one of the supporting members to pay nothing but medical expenses. You can all share the total costs equally. But if one person pays the medical bills and the others pay non-medical items, that one person gets a bigger medical expense deduction.

YOUR FAMILY MAY SAVE TAXES BY *NOT* USING A MULTIPLE SUPPORT AGREEMENT THIS YEAR

As we've seen, a family can come out tax dollars ahead with a multiple support agreement. But this isn't always the case. Some families—maybe yours—may be better off without the multiple support agreement. To see why, let's look at a—

Typical family situation: John Smith and his four brothers and sisters provide all of their mother's support in 1986. They each contribute $1,000—for a total of $5,000. Mrs. Smith's medical expenses run about $2,500 a year.

If the Smiths use a multiple support agreement: Let's say the Smiths agree to let John claim Mrs. Smith as a dependent. The other brothers and sisters fill out Form 2120 at tax return time, stating that they will not claim Mrs. Smith as a dependent for this year. John attaches these Forms to his own return. *Result*: John gets a $1,080 dependency exemption and deducts his share of the medical expenses ($500). So by using the multiple support agreement, the Smith family picks up $1,580 in deductions. But—

The family is still missing out on an extra $2,000 in deductions: Reason: Nobody gets any tax benefit from the remaining $2,000 of Mrs. Smiths's medical expenses. The $500 John pays can be deducted on his return. But the other four brothers and sisters can't deduct what they paid.

Of course, if John thinks ahead, he can make sure his $1,000 support contribution goes entirely toward Mrs. Smith's medical expenses. At least that can increase his medical deduction by another $500. But the family still loses the tax benefit of the other $1,500 in medical expenses.

▶ **TOP TAX STRATEGY:** The Smiths should take turns providing all of Mrs. Smith's yearly support. In other words, each brother and sister pays the full $5,000 in support every fifth year.

New result: Each family member can deduct *all* of Mrs. Smith's medical expenses when his or her turn comes up to provide support. John deducts a total of $3,580, instead of the $1,580 he'd deduct under a multiple support agreement.

How Medicare and Medicaid Can Help You Get a Dependency Deduction

One of your aging relatives may be getting medical benefits through Medicare and Medicaid. Those benefits can help you, too—if you're trying to claim a deduction for the relative. It's all because of—

▶ **WHAT'S CALLED SUPPORT:** The benefits do not work against you when determining if you meet the more-than-half support test for a dependency deduction. So you may be able to provide less than half the actual dollar support of a relative and still get a dependency deduction.

Example: Mr. Brown contributes $4,000 to the support of his 65-year old Aunt Corey in 1986. Her only other income is $3,000 in Social Security benefits, which she spends on her own support. Corey also gets Medicare benefits of $2,500 and Medicaid benefits of $1,500. Total annual support: $11,000.

Result: Aunt Corey is Brown's dependent and he is entitled to a $1,080 deduction for her on his return. Reason: Her total support for tax purposes (Social Security and what Brown gives her) comes to $7,000—the Medicare and Medicaid don't count. So Brown's $4,000 contribution is more than half of Aunt Corey's total support. If Medicare and Medicaid did count, Brown would have to provide more than $5,500 to get a deduction. (Note: If a relative has $1,080 or more of gross income, you can't claim a dependency deduction for her. But nontaxable Social Security, Medicare and Medicaid don't count towards the gross income test.)

▶ **WATCH THIS:** The annual boost in Social Security benefits for a dependent relative may call for a similar increase in your support payments. Reason: you must provide more than half the relative's support in order to claim him or her as a dependent. Social Security benefits spent by the recipient are considered to be provided for his or her own support. So protect your dependency deduction by maintaining your total support payments at the more-than-half level.

For example, an additional few dollars of support paid to an elderly relative may allow you to retain a $1,080 dependency deduction—worth $540 if you are in the 50% income tax bracket.

How to Use The 'Unit Rule' to Buy Two Dependency Deductions For The Price Of One

If you help support your parents, you may be able to get two dependency deductions for the money you contribute towards their support.

Here's why: For dependency purposes, unless you can prove otherwise, both parents are treated "as a unit." Everything Dad and Mom receive—whether from you or elsewhere—is assumed to be received equally by both.

Case in point: Total support of Smith's retired parents came to $4,100. Of this, he paid $2,100, and his parents' Social Security benefits provided the other $2,000. It's assumed that everything Dad and Mom received—both from their son and otherwise—is spent equally on each. Since Smith provided more than half their support together, he gets dependency deductions for both.

But the rule works both ways: Let's say your parents receive $2,520 in Social Security benefits. You give them another $1,300. Under the unit rule, you get no deduction at all because you're not providing more than half of either parent's support. But you can salvage one deduction—for your Mother, for example—by getting around the unit rule.

► **WHAT TO DO:** Allocate your support payments solely to Mother and keep careful records proving your allocation. This salvages Mother's exemption. Reason: Because you've specifically allocated your support payments, the unit rule does not apply.

The best way for you to handle things is to pay Mother's expenses directly for clothing, medical bills and the like. Ask Mother to obtain bills made out to her for the expenses, and you pay them by check. Make sure you keep both the bills and the remitted canceled checks as proof. *Added benefit:* This way you not only nail down Mother's exemption, but you can add the medical expenses you paid for Mother to your own in computing your medical deduction.

► **WATCH THIS:** Meeting the more than half support test may require more cash every year. One reason: Social Security benefits are geared to the cost-of-living index. And they keep going up. That means you might have to chip in extra cash to hold on to your dependency deductions.

HOW YOU CAN WRITE OFF THE ENTIRE COST OF NURSING HOME CARE

There's no question that the cost of staying at a hospital as an in-patient is a deductible medical expense. But suppose that someone—say, your dependent parent—is forced to live in a nursing home that provides medical care. Is that cost deductible?

Tax law test: The law says that if the medical care is "a principal reason" for your parent's presence at the nursing home—it doesn't have to be *the* principal reason—the cost of the nursing home qualifies for the medical deduction.

> *Example:* Mr. Smith, age 77, suffered an incapacitating stroke and was unable to care for himself either mentally or physically. Because of his ongoing need for constant care and attention, he was placed in a nursing home where he is assisted by a full-time nurse.

> ▶ **FULLY DEDUCTIBLE:** The Government says that the entire cost of the nursing home is a deductible medical expense. Reason: The expenses were incurred primarily for Smith's medical care and were essential to his medical care.

And remember, you can deduct the medical expense you pay for your parent if you provide more than half his or her support.

Chapter 13

How To Leave Your Family In The Best Possible Financial Shape

This chapter will NOT give you a "do it yourself" estate plan. *Reason:* The process of providing for your family's future is far too important to be handled by a non-professional. The best advice we can give you is to see a lawyer, one you can trust with your most intimate personal and financial details. The legal fee you will pay will be one of your family's best investments.

What we *will* show you are the preliminary steps to take—and decisions to make—right now, before you see your lawyer:

1. How to prepare an inventory of assets to be left to the family.

2. The basics on how to plan the division of your property.

3. How to prepare your final letter—this tells your family what needs to be done when you die.

4. How to make the most of today's liberal estate and gift tax rules. Federal estate and gift taxes play an important role in many a family's estate plan. We'll show the basics of today's estate tax setup and explain some tax-saving strategies you and your lawyer may wish to consider.

WHY YOUR FAMILY NEEDS A WILL

Regardless of the size of your estate and the kind of property you own, the best way to protect your family's interests is for you and your spouse to have a will. Reason: If you do not prepare a will, four of the most critical decisions affecting your family's future will be made by someone else—by laws in your state or by a court.

Who Will Get Your Property?

If you die without a will, a state law will decide for you. In most states, the distribution of a decedent's assets follows a rigid schedule:

● The spouse gets one third to one half of the property. The balance is left to the children.

● If there are no children, the spouse usually gets the decedent's property and shares the other half with the decedent's parents, brothers and sisters.

● If a person has no family, his or her assets wind up in the state's coffers. The state will not distribute any property to, say, friends of the decedent or to the decedent's favorite charities.

▶ **WHERE THERE'S A WILL:** You can divide your property as you see fit and make specific bequests of property to specific family members. (Of course, even if *you* don't leave something to a surviving spouse, the *law* will give your spouse a share of your estate.) And if your nearest relatives are, say, cousins and there's no love lost between you, you can leave your property to friends or favorite charities.

Who Will Raise Your Children?

If you and your spouse die without a will, then a court will decide who will raise your children. The procedure for selecting a guardian is time-consuming and costly—and a costly waste of cash that could otherwise be used to raise the children. They could wind up in the custody of family members whose lifestyle and beliefs do not coincide with yours. Furthermore, a guardian has to account to the court in writing for every penny spent. He or she is not allowed to lay out cash for anything beyond the bare necessities of life without a court order (which entails further expense).

▶ **WHERE THERE'S A WILL:** You can direct that your children be raised by a person you trust. You need not appoint a family member. For example, you can appoint a lifelong friend as guardian. And your will can also give the guardian the right to spend money on the children without court approval.

Who Will Administer Your Estate?

If you die without a will, a court will decide who will manage your estate. It may be a family member, someone selected by the court, or if no one wants to do the job, a Public Administrator. The Administrator is in charge of many important duties, such as locating all of the decedent's assets, paying off all debts, filing tax returns, and overseeing the distribution of assets. The court may not pick the right person for the job—after all, it doesn't know your family like you do. And the Administrator will have to put up a bond, which is paid by the estate.

▶ **WHERE THERE'S A WILL:** You can pick an administrator—called an Executor—who will do the job the way you'd want it done. And you can relieve your Executor of the need to post a bond.

How Much Tax Will Your Estate Pay?

If you die without a will, your property will be distributed in accordance with state law, with no regard for tax savings. Depending on the size of your assets, your family may wind up with a state inheritance tax as well as a federal estate tax.

▶ **WHERE THERE'S A WILL:** If you have a will, and a professionally prepared estate plan, you can reduce, or even eliminate inheritance and estate taxes and leave more to your family members.

PROBATE—WHAT IT IS AND HOW TO AVOID IT

At one time or another, someone may have told you that leaving a will is a sure way to trap your family in the expenses of a probate proceeding. This process—and how to avoid it—is the subject of many books and articles, and the source of much confusion and misunderstanding for a lot of families.

What it is: Probate means "to prove." It is the court proceeding that proves that a will is genuine. The court determines the will's validity, sees that property is distributed according to the decedent's instructions, interprets ambiguous language in the will and settles disputes between heirs. The court also oversees the payment of debts owed by the decedent to creditors, the collection of debts owed to the decedent, and selects or appoints a guardian for the decedent's children.

A probate court may also step in when a person dies without leaving a will and does not own the bulk of his or her important assets as a joint tenant with someone else (technically, a joint tenancy with rights of survivorship).

The probate process is costly and slow. It involves attorney's fees and court costs. There are still more costs involved if the court finds it necessary to appoint an administrator for the estate or a guardian for the children. It may take as much as one or two years for heirs to receive their property.

How to avoid probate costs: The smaller the value of assets a person owns at death, the better the chance of avoiding probate. There are three basic ways you can reduce the amount of property that will be included in your estate at death, and at the same time ensure that your property will be distributed according to your wishes:

1. Give property away as gifts during your lifetime.
2. During your lifetime, you can set up trusts that will take effect when you die. The trust document will spell out how the trust assets should be distributed.
3. Own property jointly with another family member, such as your spouse or children. The property can include such items as your home, other real estate, stocks, bonds, etc. "Joint tenants with rights of survivorship" is the legal term.

Result: When you die, property held in trust or held jointly passes "outside your will." The jointly held property passes automatically to the surviving joint tenant. The property held in trust goes to the trust beneficiaries according to the trust document. And, of course, the property you gave away during your lifetime is not included in your estate.

A word of caution: The solutions to the probate problem may not always work or may not be advisable in your family's situation. Prime example: Holding property in joint tenancy. There are many instances where it is advisable to prepare a will and *not* to hold property in joint name. For example, where substantial assets are involved, it may be best not to leave everything to your spouse. There may be big estate tax savings in arranging the disposition of some assets in other ways. And there may be unfavorable income tax consequences to the surviving spouse who sells property that was jointly held (see page 315).

And joint tenancy has no solutions for some other possible problems. Example: Husband and wife both die in an auto accident, or the wife dies a few weeks after the husband. Result: If they don't have a will, the couple's property may be distributed by the state according to rigid, unalterable rules.

SHOULD YOU SET UP A TRUST AS PART OF YOUR ESTATE PLAN?

Many people are under the impression that trusts are for millionaires. That's not necessarily true. A trust can be a valuable estate planning aid for people of modest means as well.

What is a trust? A trust is a legal entity created to hold, invest and distribute property according to the wishes of the grantor (the person setting up the trust).

What you put into the trust is called the *trust property* or *principal*. Any type of property may be the subject of a trust—for example, stocks, bonds, mortgages, real estate, life insurance, business interests, cash, patents, copyrights, etc.

The *beneficiary* is the one who gets the benefit from the trust. It might be your wife, your children, other relatives, charitable or educational institutions, business associates, or others. There can be one beneficiary, or as many as you choose—subject to certain legal limitations.

The *trustee* (a family member, your lawyer, or an institution such as a bank) is charged with the care and management of the trust property, and with the distribution of the benefits to the beneficiaries in accordance with your instructions.

A trust that is written into your will and comes into existence when you die is called a "testamentary trust." In contrast, a will that takes effect immediately is called an "inter-vivos" trust.

Why you may need a trust: A trust can ensure that your hard-won assets will be managed, used and distributed wisely. Here are some typical situations where a trust can help out:

• Some of your beneficiaries may be too young, inexperienced or incapable of managing money or assets. A trust will prevent your assets from being frittered away and, at the same time, provide the income your beneficiaries will need to live on.

• You may want to limit your beneficiary's freedom to dispose of some of your property. For example, you may own a valuable piece of property that has been in the family for a long time. You want the income from the property to go to your children, but you do not want the property to be sold until, say, your grandchildren reach a certain age. A trust will carry out your wishes to the letter.

● A trust can also enable you to accomplish several goals with your assets. For example, you want to provide life income to your spouse or child and then have your assets given outright to other beneficiaries such as grandchildren. Your trust can specify how your assets are to be used, and how they will eventually be distributed.

● People who have remarried may need a trust to provide for children from their first marriage. For example, a trust can provide life income to the second spouse and then, when the spouse dies, distribute its assets to the children of the first and second marriages.

Final word: A trust, like a will, is not a do-it-yourself proposition. Talk things over with your lawyer. Explain why you think you need a trust, and the property available to fund it, and the lawyer will take care of the rest. And be sure to get an estimate of what it will cost to set up and administer the trust before you proceed.

SHOULD YOU CHANGE YOUR WILL OR MAKE A NEW ONE?

A will is not an irrevocable document. You can amend it, or even tear it up and start again, if the old will does not reflect your current family and financial situation.

Have you changed your mind about how you want to leave your property? You need a new will if you are not satisfied with the way your old will divides your estate. You can divide assets differently in the new will. And you can change it again later on, if you wish. It's the *last* will you make that counts.

Has your family situation changed? You need a new will if there have been births, deaths, marriages, divorces, or remarriages in your family. In some of these cases, your old will may no longer be legally valid. A new will gives you the opportunity to tie up loose ends and avoid problems.

Has your financial situation changed? You need a new will if you are substantially better off—or worse off—than when you made your old will. You may want to leave more to some family members, or add people or charitable, educational, cultural, etc. institutions to your list. On the other hand, to make sure your principal beneficiary is cared for, you may want to cut down or eliminate other gifts.

Does your will reflect the latest tax laws? You need a new will if your old will and general estate plan does not reflect the latest liberalizations in the tax laws. With proper planning, these new breaks can significantly ease or possibly remove the federal tax burden on your estate. In some cases, tax saving strategies in old wills not only don't work, but can actually expose your estate to a higher tax. In many cases, a new will and estate plan is an absolute must.

How to change your mind: If extensive changes are required, your lawyer will probably draft a new will for you. The old one should be torn up. If your changes are minor, your lawyer can make an amendment to your existing will (in legal terms, a "codicil").

> ▶ **WARNING:** Do not make the changes yourself. If you make alternations in the will (crossing out names, inserting changes) the probate court will ignore them, or worse yet, declare the entire will invalid. Any changes must be made by your lawyer.

HOW TO FIND A LAWYER

The easiest way to find a lawyer is to ask family members, business associates or friends to recommend one. There are several other sources:

● Most state, county or local bar associations have a lawyer referral service. It will provide you with a list of attorneys who specialize in wills and estate planning.

● You can go to your local library or courthouse and consult the *Law Directory*, published by Martindale-Hubbell. The *Directory* lists most U.S. attorneys by state and city, contains biographical data about the practitioners in each firm and also lists specialties.

● Your bank, or bank's trust department, can also provide you with a list of suitable attorneys. The clerk of the probate court in your county can also supply you with a list.

Discuss fees up front: The cost of drafting the will and other estate planning services should be discussed at the *initial meeting* with the lawyer. Find out what the lawyer will charge and what the services include. For a routine will, the lawyer should be able to quote a price. For larger, more complex estates, the lawyer may charge you on an hourly basis (average: $60-$100 per hour).

If the attorney charges by the hour, get an estimate of how long it will take to get the job done. If the cost is substantial, see if the attorney will accept installment payments of the fee, say on a monthly basis. Also, more and more professionals accept payment by credit card; you may want to pay the bill in this manner.

WHAT TO DO BEFORE YOU SIT DOWN
WITH YOUR LAWYER

A lawyer's time is valuable—and yours is too. So before you go to your lawyer to draft a will and estate plan, you should have a clear idea of the assets you own, how you will dispose of them, and who will manage your estate. The material that follows will help you get things in focus.

How To Assemble An Inventory Of Your Property And Assets

Get some sheets of paper and take advantage of this easy guide to locating and itemizing your assets. Then keep it in a safe place until you see your lawyer.

CONFIDENTIAL ASSET INVENTORY CHECKLIST

1. Family And Personal Information

- ☐ Name; address; date and place of birth
- ☐ Occupation; employer's name and address
- ☐ Spouse's name; date and place of birth
- ☐ Child(rens) name(s), date(s) and place(s) of birth
- ☐ Other people you want to leave property to; addresses and relationship to you
- ☐ If you have a will, the date it was last reviewed
- ☐ Location of executed will
- ☐ Executor's name and address

2. Asset Inventory

A. Real Estate—Homes

- ☐ Do you own a home? Location of property; description of property
- ☐ How is it held (joint tenant with right of survivorship, tenant in common, tenant by the entirety, etc.)?
- ☐ Name and relationship of other owners(s)
- ☐ Cost of property (original); present value of property
- ☐ Amount of mortgage(s), other liens; value of your equity interest; total equity in property
- ☐ Property other than principal residence (vacation homes)
- ☐ Insurance on all property above: Kinds of insurance and coverage; policy numbers; amounts; expiration dates; names and addresses of brokers and insurers
- ☐ Name and address of real estate broker

B. Real Estate—Investments

- ☐ Location; description; ownership; cost (including cost and description of improvements); present value (estimated); equity
- ☐ Names and addresses of co-owners; amounts of mortgages and other liens
- ☐ Names and addresses of mortgages; is title clear or not?

☐ Other pertinent information: Original principal balance of mortgage; date when mortgage will be paid off

C. Notes, Mortgages And the Like Owned

☐ Amount and nature of each

☐ Property: Location; description; ownership; valuation

☐ Other liens on this property; names and addresses of associates

☐ Value of your interest; evaluation of collectibility; date and mode of cancellation

D. Business Interests

☐ Name and address; form of conducting business (sole proprietorship, partnership, close corporation)

☐ Shares of stock or percentage of business owned; estimated value

☐ Is there a: Partnership agreement in writing? stockholder's agreement? buy-sell agreement? stock redemption agreement with the corporation?

☐ Net value as a going entity; profitability; liquidity; borrowing capacity; actual and projected cash needs

☐ Continuation prospects (after death); probable cost of liquidation; restrictions affecting your interest; key-man insurance?

E. Employer's Pension, Profit-Sharing, Stock Bonus Plan, Deferred Compensation Agreement and/or Company Benefit Plans, Plus Keoghs and IRAs

☐ Location of: Copies of plans; certificates of participation; account books

F. Bank Accounts, Money Market Accounts, Mutual Funds

☐ Names and addresses of financial institutions

☐ Number of each account; names on each account

☐ Nature of account; how interest accrues on savings account

☐ Amounts at present in each account (or average balance)

☐ Location of bank books, certificates of deposit, check books, statements

☐ For certificates of deposit: Certificate number; how titled; principal amount; interest rate; maturity date

G. Safe Deposit Boxes

☐ Name and addresses of safe deposit company; box number; owner/location of keys; names and addresses of others having access; rented in more than one name?

H. Financial Investments—Stocks and Bonds

☐ Names and addresses of brokerage houses where accounts are maintained; name of person who handles accounts

☐ Stocks owed individually or jointly; stocks owned as custodian for minors; location of stock certificates; estimated value of securities

☐ Other interests: Stock options (same information as above)

☐ U.S. Savings Bonds: Owned individually or with co-owner or beneficiary (names and addresses); face amount of bond; present value

☐ Other corporate, governmental or tax-free bonds: Face amount; coupon or registered; if registered, how titled; interest rate; cost basis; maturity date and other descriptive terms; whether conversion privileges apply; location, if unregistered.

I. Life Insurance And Annuity Policies

☐ Name and address of insurer; number and type of each policy; face amount of each; applicable terms

☐ Names, addresses, relationships of beneficiaries

☐ Rights reserved by owner; loans under policy

☐ Participation in employer's life insurance program (same info as above)

☐ Other types of policies owned: Disability, accident, sickness, hospitalization, etc.; name of insurer; account; number of policies; employer's program

☐ Names, addresses and relationships of beneficiaries; who pay premiums

☐ Policies owned on lives of others; name and address of insurer; number of policy, and amount; cash values; who pays premiums

☐ Locations of all policies above

J. Social Security And Veterans Administration Benefits

☐ Social Security Account number

☐ If veteran: Serial number; branch of service; dates of service

K. Other Property

☐ Money owed you personally (distinct from business credits)

☐ Rights under trusts

☐ Interest in estates of relatives or others

☐ Transfers and/or gifts: Nature and value; date; whether gift tax returns were filed

☐ Facts in connection with: Jewelry; furs; silverware; artworks; books; stamp collections; coin collections; similar property

☐ Value of household furniture; automobiles; boats

☐ All other property or interests not previously covered

☐ Facts relating to insurance on all property above

☐ Cemetery plot: Location; custody of deed; owned in what names; perpetual care or not

How Your Property Will Be Distributed

One way to define your goals is to ask these key questions:

Who will get my property? Your most likely beneficiaries are your spouse, children and grandchildren. You may also want to leave some property to other relatives (such as brothers or sisters), close friends, or charities. Make a list of primary beneficiaries (those first in line to get property) and alternate beneficiaries (they receive property if the primary beneficiaries die before receiving their inheritance). If there's a close family member who will not be receiving anything, *be sure to tell your lawyer.* He can take the steps necessary to prevent a successful contest of your will by that relative.

What practical purpose will my bequests accomplish? Your answers to this question will in turn determine when your beneficiaries will receive your property, and how. Here are some typical responses:

- To provide life income for a family member, such as a spouse.

- To fund a child or grandchild's education or finance a new business venture or practice.

- To pay income for a specific period of years—for example, until a child reaches maturity.

When and how should my property be distributed? Determining when each beneficiary receives his or her property can be complicated. Sometimes the beneficiary will be a minor, who, under the state law *cannot* hold title to an asset until a certain age. You may not want a particular person to receive property until he or she reaches a "mature" age. On the other hand, if you are providing for someone who is handicapped, or otherwise incapacitated, you may want your bequest to be received as soon as possible.

The simplest answer to how each beneficiary shall receive his or her (or its) bequest is: Through a "legacy" or gift of outright ownership. But this will not be the right answer in all cases. For instance, if someone is to receive a bequest in shares at different stated ages, a trust will have to be established.

In other instances, you may wish to make the gift conditional. For example, you may provide that a beneficiary use property for a particular purpose in order to receive the bequest.

When you are deciding what each beneficiary is to receive, especially when you are dealing with your children, keep the following in mind: "Equal treatment" may not be fair treatment. For example, leaving the same amount of property to each child may not be in everybody's best interests.

For example, say two of your children have gone to college, but a third hasn't. You may want to leave the third child an extra amount for education. Or one of your children might be rich and successful while another is struggling to get by. You may want to make appropriate arrangements in your will to help out the less successful child.

▶ **TELL THE CHILDREN:** If your will provides for an unequal distribution of property amoung your children, you should explain your reasons for doing so. Hopefully, you can head off bitterness among your family after your death, and minimize the chances of a will contest by a disgruntled child.

Additionally, in determining what property each of your beneficiaries will receive, it helps to think of your estate first in terms of specific articles of property and specific sums of money, and then in terms of fractional shares or percentages of the estate. Be sure to think carefully about whether there are specific items of personal property, such as family heirlooms, antiques, jewelry, sporting equipment, tools, etc. that ought to be designated for particular persons.

Here's an example that sheds some light on how to sort out the who, why, when, how, and what of splitting your property:

> **Example:** Ted Smith, a successful executive, has a wife in good health who is capable of handling finances. Son is successful in his own business. Daughter, is married to a mailman with a gambling itch. Smith has two grandsons, ages 6 and 7. He also wants to leave something to his deceased sister's son, a godson who has a long term chronic illness, and to his Alma Mater.

His analysis, in abbreviated form, with some tentative conclusions, might look like this:

WHO	WHY	WHEN	HOW	WHAT
Wife	Income	Starting at my death, lasting for her life	Outright	
Son	Simple gift	Immediately after my death	Outright	
Daughter	Supplement to Husband's earnings	Starting at my death, for long term	Some form of trusteeship	
Grandson 1	College fund	Starting at 18	In trust	
Grandson 2		Same as above		
Godson	Help with medical bills	For long term	Purchase of annuity?	
Nephew	Simple gift	Immediately after my death	Outright	
Charity	To fund scholarship in my name	Same as above	Annuity?	

With this basic information, Ted can now go through his Asset Inventory and make some preliminary choices—subject to review by his lawyer—in the WHAT category. For example, if he's got a substantial life insurance policy, maybe the proceeds—together with the family homestead—is enough for the spouse. He can give his son that valuable stamp collection that his dad left him, or, perhaps, leave him the vacation home.

Together with his lawyer, Ted must come up with some way of giving income to his daughter without the possibility of his son-in-law's squandering it. As to his grandchildren, Ted ought to think of giving them money in trust now to provide for their education. After he's through providing for his godson and nephew, maybe there won't be enough left over to fund a scholarship—maybe a simple cash gift will have to do.

Overriding considerations: Ted must make sure there will be enough liquid assets to take care of expenses (funeral, plot, debts) when he dies, and to pay any estate taxes—federal and state—that will come due.

Other Choices To Make Before You See Your Lawyer

You should make a list of potential candidates to fill three important slots: the executor of your estate, the guardian for minor children, and the trustee of any trusts you plan to set up.

Choosing executor and trustee: You need not name an individual to fill these jobs. You can choose a financial institution, such as a bank. Here are the pros and cons of having an individual or institution as executor or trustee.

An institution has these advantages: Professional service and experience; full time attention; permanence; electronic record keeping; expert tax and investment advice. *Disadvantages*: Fees for services; possibility of less attention devoted to smaller estates and trusts, not desirable as business managers of a going business; very conservative money managers; not the same personal contact with your family as an individual would have.

An individual has these advantages: May waive fees; personal knowledge of you and your family; may be better able to run your business; can devote more time to your estate. *Disadvantages*: Not a professional; not able to devote a lot of time to an estate or trust; not adept at record keeping; not an expert in taxes or investing.

If you do choose an individual, you should select someone who will—

- *Be willing to spend the time and effort necessary*. An executor has more work to do than a trustee. The executor must locate beneficiaries, round up assets, pay debts, be responsible for tax returns, and make distributions of your property. These tasks will be done with the assistance of an attorney. But the executor remains legally responsible for their proper execution. So he or she must be closely involved.

- *Have the necessary business know-how*. Will the executor or trustee be able to make sound decisions about your property?

• *Know something of your personal affairs and family relationships.* It could be crucial for the executor to know why you distributed property the way you did. So, while an executor shouldn't have a conflicting interest under your will, he or she should be close enough to you to know what's what.

If you choose a family member or friend for the position of executor, trustee, or guardian, you should also follow these common-sense guidelines:

#1—Choose people who are younger—or at least not older—than you are. This will lessen the likelihood that they will die before you.

#2—Make a list of your prime candidates and a list of backups who will be named as successors. You need successors because your main choices may die, become ill, or back out when they're called on to do the job.

#3—Talk to your primary choices and backups and see if they will accept the job. They should have a clear idea of what will be expected of them.

Choosing a guardian: If you have minor children, you must designate a guardian to take care of them in the event you and your spouse both die. It is especially important to appoint a guardian when there is a relative in either branch of the family who may insist on taking the job, but who you may find unsuitable. You can also appoint a trustee to handle the property you'll leave your children. The guardian and trustee can be the same or different persons—the trustee can even be an institution, such as a bank. Here are some suggestions to keep in mind when choosing a guardian:

• If your children are old enough, ask them who they prefer to live with.

• Your parents may not be good choices. Even if they don't predecease you, they may die before your children are grown up. In that event, your children will be raised by a *third* set of parents (the successor guardians).

• Brothers and sisters can be the right choice, but close friends can do the job as well if they share your outlook on life and child rearing.

Raising your children can place a financial strain upon the guardian. Your will should make funds available to the guardian for the support of the children. Additionally, if you own a larger home than the guardian does, you may provide in your will that the guardian can live in it rent-free. Or you can allow the guardian to sell your home, along with his or her own, and use the proceeds to buy a larger home.

WHERE TO KEEP YOUR WILL

It's customary for the lawyer who drafts your will to keep the original and give you a copy. There usually is no charge for this storage service. Most attorneys will advise against keeping the original copy in your home because there is a statistically greater possibility that it will be lost due to fire or theft.

That may be true. But bear in mind that there may be another reason for the lawyer wanting to retain the original copy. This way the lawyer significantly increases his or her chances of being hired to handle the probate of your estate when your next-of-kin comes to get the original.

▶ **WHAT TO DO:** Hold onto the original and have your lawyer keep the unsigned copy. Make sure the will is stored in a safe, fireproof place where you keep your other important papers. You can buy a safe or a "strong box" for this purpose. Then make sure your lawyer and someone else you trust knows the exact location of the will.

This way, your next-of-kin (or executor-to-be) can bring the will to a lawyer he or she fees comfortable working with, which may or may not be your lawyer. Of course, if your lawyer has a special knowledge of your affairs, say your business, you may *want* his or her firm to handle your estate. If that's the case, indicate your preference in your will or in the letter of instruction (see below) to your family.

▶ **WORD OF WARNING:** Don't store the will in your safe deposit box. That's the worst place to keep a will.

Reason: Strict tax regulations may require temporary sealing of your safe deposit box at the time of your death. Sometimes it can be reopened only in the presence of state officials. State regulations vary, and getting at your will could involve the executor in lots of red tape. Besides being annoying, the loss of time involved may make bequests to an eye bank or other similar gifts useless.

Separate safe deposit boxes, with you keeping your spouse's will and vice versa, is no solution. Beyond the problems raised above, there is the possibility of simultaneous death, and the longshot that the surviving spouse might even destroy the will in the event he or she is unhappy with its contents.

HOW TO PREPARE A LETTER OF INSTRUCTION FOR YOUR FAMILY

One of the best things you can do for your family is to prepare a letter of instruction, explaining what has to be done after you die. It may be the single most important thing you can do to ease the way for your loved ones during a difficult time.

The letter can tell family members or your executor where all your important papers and possessions are located. Also the letter can be an informal way of explaining why certain provisions have been incorporated into your will.

The wishes you express in the letter are not legally binding. But they are morally persuasive on your executor and family members, and generally will be carried out. *Important*: Be sure to show your lawyer a copy of the letter. Reason: If there's any conflict between your instructions and the will, there could be trouble later on.

Besides directions concerning your burial and the ceremony, the letter should contain the following elements:

1. Whom To Contact And What To Do Immediately

Name and telephone of funeral parlor and lawyer, names and phone numbers of family and friends to contact; name and telephone of your company's benefits officer (for final paycheck, pension or profit-sharing benefits, company paid life insurance, etc.); name and telephone of insurance agent (to file insurance claim); contact Social Security (and Veterans Administration, if applicable) for death benefit payable to spouse; obtain multiple copies of death certificate (for filing of claims); begin taking inventory of any expenses associated with death.

2. Other Important Matters To Handle As Soon As Possible

All joint property accounts should be transferred to survivor; cancel credit cards or convert to single name; re-register automobile (and contact auto insurance agent); cancel subscriptions to periodicals and cancel special memberships to organizations.

3. A List Of Where To Find Key Documents And Records

Here's a representative list of items you ought to include here:

Birth certificate	Marriage certificate
Divorce decrees	Separation agreements
List of heirs	List of other relatives
Military service record	Social Security card
Medical record	Tax records
Will, original	Will, copy
Life insurance policies	General insurance policies
Stocks	Bonds
Notes receivable and mortgages	Deeds
Leases	Estate inventory
Bank books	Financial records
Business agreements	Trust instruments
Cemetery deeds	Employee benefit plan statements
Miscellaneous documents and property	Other

▶ **WHAT TO DO:** After you have prepared your final letter, sit down and review it with your spouse or other family members. (Do the same with your will.) The time to clear up any questions is now—when you're around to answer them. Keep the letter where you keep your other important papers. *Good idea*: Attach it to or store it with your will. And take the letter out and review it every couple of years for any possible changes.

HOW YOU AND YOUR FAMILY CAN TAKE ADVANTAGE OF TODAY'S LIBERAL ESTATE AND GIFT TAX RULES

Due to a number of liberalizations, estate and gift taxes will be less of a problem for most people. Estate and gift taxes are totally eliminated for some, substantially reduced for others. However, you must know what to do and how to do it in order to take maximum advantage of the tax law's breaks. Here's an overview of the estate and gift tax rules.

The Federal Estate Tax

This is a tax on the gross estate, less certain deductions. The gross estate includes all property that a decedent owned, or had an interest in at the time of his death, and lifetime gifts over which he "held the strings" (for example, a trust that can be revoked). The estate tax is computed by applying a uniform rate schedule to the sum of (a) transfers at death, plus (b) lifetime taxable gifts made after 1976 (basically, gifts that exceeded the gift-tax exclusion). The estate tax (less any gift tax paid on post-1976 gifts) is then offset dollar-for-dollar by the unified estate-and-gift tax credit (see below).

The Federal Gift Tax

The first $10,000 of gifts made to any person during the course of a year is not subject to any gift tax. This annual exclusion is doubled to $20,000 if the donor's spouse joins in the gift. Gifts in excess of the exclusion are subject to the gift tax, but the gift tax is offset by the unified gift-and-estate tax credit. However, any part of the credit used to shelter a lifetime gift from tax reduces the credit available to offset the estate tax.

▶ **FAMILY TAX SAVINGS:** Lifetime gifts that do not exceed the annual exclusion save estate taxes. Such gifts are removed from the estate, with no dilution of the unified estate-and-gift tax credit. There may even be estate tax savings where the gift exceeds the annual exclusion. This is especially true where the gift is likely to grow in value. Reason: For gift tax purposes, the current value of the gift is used. If left to a beneficiary by will, the property is included in the decedent's estate at its value at that time.

Unified Gift-and-Estate Tax Credit

Simply stated, the unified gift-and-estate tax credit enables a person to transfer a specified dollar amount of property without paying a gift tax or an estate tax. The unified credit increases each year until it reaches a peak of $192,800 in 1987.

Here is a chart showing the gradual increase in the unified credit, and the amount that can be transferred gift- and estate-tax free because of the credit.

Year	Unified Gift and Estate Tax Credit	Amount That Can Can Be Transferred Gift- and Estate-Tax Free
1985	$121,800	$400,000
1986	155,800	500,000
1987	192,800	600,000

▶ **TAX SAVING RESULT:** By 1987, a person will be able to transfer up to $600,000 in property totally free of estate and gift taxes. Another break: When the unified credit is fully phased in, a Federal estate tax return will not have to be filed for any estate of $600,000 or less.

▶ **CAUTION:** Tax planning for estates is still necessary. *Reason*: Although the $600,000 exemption may seem high, remember that it is phased in. In addition, considering rising real estate values and inflation in general, many people whose net worth is currently under $600,000 may have assets worth substantially more than $600,000 by 1987.

Unlimited Marital Deduction

An unlimited amount of property can be transferred to a spouse free of estate and gift taxes. Practical impact: By 1987, the unlimited marital deduction and the unified credit will enable a person to leave up to $1.2 million to his or her spouse and family without paying an estate tax.

Example: Arthur Johnson dies in 1987 and leaves an estate of $1.2 million. He leaves $600,000 to his children, and the balance to his wife. Arthur's estate pays no tax. The unified credit shelters $600,000 of his estate from tax; and the unlimited marital deduction shelters the other $600,000.

Furthermore, his spouse's estate at her death, assuming it consists of $600,000 in assets, will not pay an estate tax, either. *Reason*: The spouse's estate is entitled to a separate unified credit.

▶ **CAUTION:** Under prior law, the marital deduction was limited to the greater of $250,000 or half the decedent's gross estate. Wills that were executed before September 12, 1981, and contain a maximum marital deduction clause geared to the old limited deduction, should be amended immediately, if they haven't been amended already.

Reason: Without an amendment, the property passing to the surviving spouse will be based on the old limited deduction, and a decedent's estate will not be able to benefit fully from the marital deduction.

Joint Property With Right Of Survivorship

Only one half of the value of property held in joint tenancy by a husband and wife is includable in the gross estate of the first spouse to die. However, note that

PROTECTING YOUR FAMILY'S FUTURE

the half included in the estate is not subject to tax because of the unlimited estate tax marital deduction.

Income tax treatment: Generally, the decedent's surviving spouse has an income tax basis that consists of two elements: (1) One half of the original cost of the property (i.e., the surviving spouse's half), plus (2) half the fair market value of the property at the decedent's death (i.e., the half that is included in the estate).

For example, suppose Mr. and Mrs. Smith bought property as joint tenants years ago. The cost was $10,000, and the fair market value at Mr. Smith's death is $100,000. One half of the property value ($50,000) is included in Smith's estate, but is free of tax because of the unlimited estate tax marital deduction. Mrs. Smith's income tax basis for the property is $55,000— $5,000 (half the original cost), plus $50,000 (half the value at death). If Mrs. Smith were to sell the property for $100,000, she would have a taxable long term capital gain of $45,000.

Possible move: If Mr. Smith were to hold the property in his name only (the change in the form of ownership can be accomplished without a gift tax), the property will be included in full in his estate. The property will still be sheltered by the unlimited estate tax marital deduction. However, when Mrs. Smith inherits it, her income tax basis will be a full $100,000 (its value for estate tax purposes). Thus, Mrs. Smith could sell the property for $100,000 and pay no federal income tax.

FIVE STRATEGIES TO GET TOP TAX BENEFIT FROM THE UNLIMITED MARITAL DEDUCTION

Transfers between spouses are exempt from both estate and gift taxes. The marital deduction opens up exciting ways for larger estates to save on taxes— especially when the deduction is combined with the unified credit (which grows each year until it shelters $600,000 in assets in 1987 and later years). However, despite the unlimited marital deduction and the larger unified credit, estate tax planning is still necessary for many families.

Reason: While there is no estate tax when the property passes to the surviving spouse, there may be tax when the property goes from the spouse to the children. The surviving spouse only has the estate tax credit to shelter his or her estate when it passes to the next generation. And, in many cases, that won't be enough.

Example: Mr. Johnson's $1 million in assets are left outright to his spouse. Mrs. Johnson's will provides for everything to be left to the children.

Of the $1 million, $400,000 is subject to estate tax when Mrs. Johnson dies. Estate tax bill: $153,000 (assuming she dies after 1986).

Mr. Johnson's mistake was to waste his own $600,000 exemption. Starting in 1987, combining two credits with the unlimited marital deduction shelters estates as high as $1.2 million. But knowing how to combine the tax breaks is the trick.

Estates of $1.2 Million Or Less

Strategy #1: The obvious strategy for Mr. Johnson is to leave $600,000 to his wife and $400,000 to his children. His estate pays no tax (what passes to his spouse is exempt and the bequest to his children is exempt because of his credit). Nor does his spouse's estate pay tax when her property goes to the children (it is sheltered by her credit).

Strategy #2: The problem with the obvious strategy is that Mrs. Johnson loses the economic benefit of $400,000 after Mr. Johnson dies. Better approach: Mr. Johnson should consider putting the $400,000 in trust for his children with Mrs. Johnson receiving income from the trust during her lifetime. Better result: More dollar support for Mrs. Johnson and still no estate tax when either Johnson dies.

> *Example:* Mr. Johnson leaves $600,000 outright to Mrs. Johnson and gives her the other $400,000 in trust, with the remainder for the children. Mrs. Johnson has the right to the income from the trust, the right to 5% of the principal every year (or $5,000 if that is greater), and the right to receive principal for her health, education, support and maintenance. Her entire estate passes to the children.

The $600,000 passes tax-free from Mr. to Mrs. Johnson (the marital deduction) and then to the children (her $600,000 estate tax credit). And so does the $400,000 in his estate. Reason: His credit exempts the $400,000. And it bypasses her estate, even though she has the limited right to invade trust principal and the right to payments of principal.

This strategy is especially well suited to people who have younger spouses. Where the couple are closer in age there may be a tax problem.

> *Example:* If Mrs. Johnson dies first, Mr. Johnson's estate will pay estate tax (unless he remarries). His estate consists of $1 million, of which $600,000 passes tax-free to his children. The $400,000 balance is subject to tax since his marital deduction is no longer available when his spouse dies. Estate tax bill: $153,000. One way to mitigate this problem is—

Strategy #3: Take advantage of the unlimited gift tax marital deduction. Where feasible, a couple splits ownership of the property down the middle during their lifetimes. Each spouse then leaves his or her estate in trust to the children with an income interest to the other spouse. Result: No estate tax.

> *Example:* Assume the Johnsons are both 50 years old. He owns property worth $1 million, but she owns none. He makes a gift of one half of his assets—$500,000—to his wife. His will provides that the other $500,000 goes to his children in trust. Mrs. Johnson has the right to income, and to receive a limited amount of principal. Upon his spouse's death, the $500,000 in trust goes to the children. Mrs. Johnson's will reads exactly the same way: If she dies first, her $500,000 in assets goes to the children in trust with an interest to Mr. Johnson while he lives.

There is no estate tax no matter which spouse survives. The strategy also assures the surviving spouse the full use of the family wealth as long as he or she lives. If Mrs. Johnson dies first, her $500,000 goes directly to the trust for the children. This amount is sheltered by the unified credit and passes automatically to the children when Mr. Johnson dies. Thus, Mrs. Johnson owns $500,000 outright (what he did not give to Mrs. Johnson) and is entitled to life income from the $500,000 Mrs. Johnson left in trust.

When he dies, the $500,000 left in trust bypasses his estate and goes directly to the children. The remaining $500,000 goes directly to the children under the terms of his will—it is fully sheltered by the unified credit.

What if Mr. Johnson dies first? The results are exactly the same. The children ultimately get everything and no estate tax is paid.

Estates Over $1.2 Million

Strategy #4: An estate tax will be paid when the surviving spouse dies. It's simple arithmetic. The sum of the two $600,000 exemptions is $1.2 million. Anything over that amount is subject to tax—unless you cash in on another expanded and liberalized new tax break.

▶ **LIFETIME GIVING:** You can give each of your children $10,000 every year ($20,000 if your spouse joins in the gift) without paying gift tax or dipping into your unified credit. The $600,000 exemption stays intact to shelter the estate from tax. Result: If enough gifts are made, your taxable estate will be at $1.2 million or below.

Example: Mr. and Mrs. Brown have two children and an estate of $1.5 million. They make gifts of $20,000 to each child for eight years, a total of $320,000. Mr. Brown leaves $600,000 directly to his wife and $580,000 in trust (Strategy #2). $1.18 million goes to the children at her death.

Result: The entire $1.5 million ends up with the children. No tax is paid—either when the lifetime gifts are made or when the $1.18 million passes from the parents to the children.

Strategy #5: Suppose your estate exceeds $1.2 million by so much that lifetime transfers can't bring the taxable estate down to the magic figure of $1.2 million. Or maybe you prefer not to make lifetime gifts to your children. In either case, an estate tax will be paid, but there is a way to minimize the amount of the tax. You can forego the maximum marital deduction and balance the estates. Because of the graduated estate tax rates, by transferring enough assets (either by gift or by will) to make both estates equal, the minimum possible estate tax bill is paid. The sum of the taxes on both estates is less than the tax on the total amount in one estate.

Example: Mr. Allen has an estate of $2.5 million. Mrs. Allen has a negligible estate. If Mr. Allen leaves his entire estate to her, his estate pays no tax. But Mrs. Allen's estate pays tax on the full $2.5 million less the $600,000 exemption. Total tax:

$833,000. If instead he leaves $1.25 million to her and the rest to his children ($255,500 tax) and she then leaves her $1.25 million estate to the children ($225,500 tax), the Allens pick up another $600,000 exemption and stay out of the top estate tax rates. Total tax: $511,000—a tax saving of $322,000.

The strategy of equalizing the estates can be used to good effect even if the surviving spouse has an estate of her own. The trick is to have the surviving spouse receive only enough to balance off the two estates in roughly equal amounts.

HERE'S ANOTHER OPPORTUNITY TO CASH IN ON THE TAX-FREE MARITAL DEDUCTION

All family heads would like to transfer more of their wealth to their families when they write their wills. And they'd like to transfer it at the lowest possible cost.

▶ **GOOD NEWS:** The Government has added another weapon to your wealth-building arsenal. Now you are allowed to give your executor greater flexibility in using an important estate tax break: The marital deduction.

Here's the story: The marital deduction permits you to transfer property to your spouse free of gift or estate tax. In general, the marital deduction is not available for bequests of property where less than a fee simple interest is transferred—what are called terminable interests. For example, if you leave your spouse an income interest in the property during your spouse's lifetime, the bequest does not qualify for the marital deduction.

▶ **KEY EXCEPTION:** An executor can elect to have certain terminable interests qualify for the marital deduction. To qualify, the bequest must give the surviving spouse the right to all income from the property for life, payable at least once a year. In addition, no one can have the power to give any portion of the property to a person other than the surviving spouse during the spouse's lifetime.

Once the election is made, the property becomes subject to estate tax when the surviving spouse eventually dies. Without this election, terminable interests are generally *not* taxed in the surviving spouse's estate.

▶ **PARTIAL ELECTIONS OKAY:** An executor is allowed to elect the marital deduction for only part of an eligible terminable interest in a decedent's estate. In effect, he or she can decide how much of the property is taxed in each estate. The executor decides what part of the terminable interest should get the marital deduction in the decedent's estate (and be taxed later in the surviving spouse's estate) and what part of the terminable interest should be taxed in the decedent's estate (and be exempt from tax in the survivor's estate).

Chapter 14

How to Save Tax Dollars and Time On Your Family Tax Returns

One of the best ways to conserve family cash is to take advantage of all possible deductions on your tax return. This includes most prominently your deductions for medical expenses, interest, taxes, and charitable contributions. The techniques described in this Chapter can add hundreds of dollars to net family income after taxes.

HOW TO MAKE EVERY YEAR A "RECORD YEAR"

Do you keep records of your personal expenses? If your answer is ''no,'' then you're probably missing out on perfectly legitimate deductions that can shave big dollars off your tax bill.

Here's a time- and money-saving suggestion: Keep a current log of your family's personal expenses. That way, you won't miss any deductions and, come tax-return time, you'll avoid that aspirin and black coffee session, shuttling between a hazy memory and a heap of disorganized papers. What's more, you'll probably come up with many items you never previously dreamed of deducting. You'll be surprised at how these little deductions add up.

To help you save these important tax dollars by getting business-like about your personal expenses, we've prepared a special record-keeping form. You can use this format reproduced on p. 322 for noting your daily outlays (we've filled in some sample items to show you how it works).

▶ **TAX TIPS:** (1) When you pay cash, get receipts. These can be preserved in manila folders. (2) When you pay by check, make the check out to the one who is being paid. A check made to "cash" doesn't prove the nature or even the amount of an expense. But a check to a physician, dentist, druggist, and the like, is good evidence. And keep your canceled checks in the manila folders, too.

The wall-calendar way: The calendar on your kitchen wall can also serve as a record-keeping form. You may choose to use this rather than the type of record-keeping form reproduced below. First of all, make sure the calendar is fairly large. All you do is use the date space for the expenses of that day. Naturally, you also put down the why's and wherefore's. Make it a daily habit to transfer all tax information to the calendar. Don't forget—be systematic and do it daily.

Daily Personal Expense Record

Date & Check	To Whom Paid and Why	Amount	Contri- butions	Interest	Taxes	Medi- cal & Drugs	Other Deduc- tions
1/5 #12	Dr. Jones eye exam for wife	$75.00	—	—	—	$75.00	—
1/5 cash	Cab fare; trip to Dr. Jones	8.50	—	—	—	8.50	—
1/7 cash	Alpha Optical; glasses for wife	85.00	—	—	—	85.00	—
1/9 cash	Boy Scouts of America	25.00	25.00	—	—	—	—
1/15 #18	Collector of taxes (real property- home)	1,200.00	—	—	1,200.00	—	—
2/15 #30	Smith's Drug Store (prescrip- tion)	15.00	—	—	—	15.00	—

HOW TO COPE WITH THE TOUGH RULES FOR DEDUCTING MEDICAL EXPENSES

It's difficult getting any tax relief on your family's medical bills. Reason: Medical expenses (prescription drugs, medical care, related travel and insurance premiums) are deductible only to the extent that they exceed 5% of your adjusted gross income.

Net result: You may not get any medical deduction unless you can track down and claim the many overlooked but perfectly legitimate medical expenses that so many of us shell out money for each year. Let's begin with a look at—

Twenty-One Often-Overlooked Deductible Medical Expenses

Deductible medical expenses include more than just hospital and doctor bills. And if that is all you are claiming, you could be passing up valid tax deductions you are eligible for, but just are not aware of. Here's a checklist of 21 Govern-ment-approved medical expense deductions many taxpayers overlook.

1. *Special diets:* The extra cost of a prescribed special diet is deductible if it is (1) solely for the treatment of a medical problem, and (2) in addition to normal nutritional needs. Examples: organic foods [Randolph, 67 TC 35], and high protein meals for hypoglycemia [Von Kalb, TC Memo 1978-366].

2. *Special mattress:* The Government has approved a medical expense deduction for the extra cost of a special mattress designed to alleviate an arthritic condition [Rev. Rul. 58-280, 1958-1 CB 157].

3. *Cosmetic surgery:* The cost of cosmetic surgery is deductible. Unlike most other medical expenses, the surgery need not be recommended by a doctor. A face lift is deductible [Rev. Rul. 76-332, 1976-2 CB 81]. Electrolysis is also deductible [Rev. Rul. 82-111, 1982-1 CB 488].

4. *Acupuncture:* The Government has okayed a deduction for the cost of undergoing acupuncture to alleviate a specific ailment [Rev. Rul. 72-593, 1972-2 CB 180].

5. *Weight reduction:* You can't deduct the cost of a weight reducing program that simply improves your general health and well being [Rev. Rul. 79-151, 1979-1 CB 116]. But you can deduct the cost of a program that prevents or alleviates a specific ailment or illness. Example: A program prescribed for an individual with hypertension, obesity and hearing problems [Ltr. Rul. 8004111].

6. *Hairpiece:* The cost of a hairpiece (or wig) is a deductible medical expense if it is necessary to relieve severe mental distress [Rev. Rul. 62-189, 1962-2 CB 88].

7. *Nursing home:* You often have to pay a lump sum to get your dependent parent into a nursing home. If part of the prepayment is for future medical care, that portion is deductible [Rev. Rul. 75-302, 1975-2 CB 86].

8. *School tuition:* If part of your child's college tuition is for medical care, that amount is deductible [Rev. Rul. 54-457, 1954-2 CB 100]. The charge for medical care, often a sizable sum, is included in a college's "general fee." If you write to the college treasurer, you usually can find out the amount that's allocated to medical care.

9. *Special schools:* You can deduct the cost of sending your child to a special school if the principal reason for his or her attendance is the treatment of a handicap or mental illness; educational services must be incidental. The school must have specially trained personnel and special resources [Sims, TC Memo 1979-499], or there's no deduction [Giovengo, TC Memo 1978-375].

10. *Travelling companion:* You can deduct the cost of bringing someone along on a medically-related trip if your condition makes that person's presence necessary [Ltr. Rul. 8024155.]

11. *Visitation costs:* If your presence is medically necessary, you can deduct the cost of a visit to see your ailing child or spouse [Rev. Rul. 58-533, 1958-2 CB 157]. For example, one parent deducted the cost of going overseas to accompany his child home after an illness [Ltr. Rul. 7813004]. You can also deduct:

12. The cost of a home health spa that alleviates an illness, to the extent it exceeds the increase in the value of your home [Keen, TC Memo 1981-313].

13. Vasectomies and abortions [Rev. Rul. 73-201, 1973-1 CB 140].

14. The cost of computer storage of your medical history [Rev. Rul. 71-282, 1971-2 CB 166].

15. Legal expenses for having a dependent involuntarily committed [Ltr. Rul. 7931059].

16. Additional charges by a restaurant for preparing a salt-free meal [Cohn, 38 TC 387].

17. The installation and monthly cost of a device that adds fluoride into the home water supply on the advice of a dentist [Rev. Rul. 64-267, 1964-2 CB 69].

18. Reclining chair used by a cardiac patient and not otherwise used personally [Rev. Rul. 64-267, 1964-2 CB 69].

19. Auto improvements that are medically necessary—for example, the cost of air conditioning needed to alleviate a child's asthma [Ltr. Rul. 8009080].

20. The excess cost of orthopedic shoes [Ltr. Rul. 8221118].

21. A hair transplant performed by a physician to alleviate baldness [Mattes, 77 TC No. 47].

▶ **REMINDER:** This list is not all-inclusive by any means. But it does show that you can deduct more than just the ordinary expenses. Of course, when you're doing your tax return, don't forget the obvious expenses either, such as the cost of a visit to a doctor, the hospital, and so forth.

How to Get a Medical Deduction for the Cost of Help Around the House

Many taxpayers employ domestic help. The cost, of course, is not deductible. But suppose that same domestic is helping out while you or another family member recuperates from an illness. And the domestic spends part of his or her time performing nurse-like services. Of course, the cost of nursing services is deductible as medical care. But what if the services aren't performed by a registered or practical nurse?

▶ **DEDUCTIBLE MEDICAL CARE:** It's the nature of the service provided, not the status of "registered" or "practical" nurse, that's important. As long as the expenses are medically related, they're deductible.

Example: Mr. Johnson's daughter, Mary, had surgery this year and was confined to bed at home for two months. The Johnsons' regular live-in housekeeper and maid helped bathe, feed, and care for Mary (they had someone else come in and do the housekeeping and washing). They paid a total of $2,000 in wages to the regular housekeeper during the two months. Sixty percent of her normal week was devoted to helping Mary. *Result:* $1,200 (60% of $2,000) is eligible for the medical deduction.

Tax-saving twist: If the Johnsons' medical expenses don't exceed 5% of their adjusted gross income, they may still be able to claim a tax credit for their payment to the housekeeper.

> **Example:** Using the same example as above, let's assume that the Johnsons need somebody to take care of Mary so that they can go to work. So their house-keeper does it. The Johnsons are entitled to a—

> ▶ **TAX CREDIT:** (1) The Johnsons can claim a child care credit of $400 (20% of $2,000). *Reason:* The housekeeper's services enable them to work. And the house-keeper's entire salary counts towards the child care credit as long as part of her job is to care for Mary. No allocation has to be made between her child caring and house-keeping activities.

Note: It is possible for the same expense to qualify for the child care credit and the medical expense deduction. But you cannot claim a tax benefit from the same expense twice.

How You Sometimes Get a Medical Deduction for Long-Distance Travel

Expenses for travel to and from the doctor's office, the hospital, or even the pharmacy, such as cab fares or auto expenses, are deductible. Additionally, if you drive, the Government will allow an automatic 9¢-a-mile deduction, plus tolls and parking. But there's more. You may be able to deduct your expenses for long-distance travel. It all hinges on this—

> ▶ **KEY QUESTION:** Is the trip for your general well being (non-deductible) or the relief of a specific ailment (deductible)?

Case #1: Mr. D suffered a severe heart attack and spent several weeks under the care of a specialist. His doctor advised that it would be beneficial, though not necessary, for him to go to Florida for the winter. Mr. D didn't want to go to Florida but went anyway on the advice of his doctor. Result: No medical expense deduction. Reason: The trip was not primarily for the treatment or cure of an imminent or existing illness. The change of climate would have no curing effect on D's heart condition, but would only aid his general health [Dobkin, 15 TC 886].

Case #2: Mr. C was 72 and suffering from a severe heart condition, stroke and chronic bronchitis. His weakened condition left him susceptible to pneumonia, which he contracted during the winters in South Bend, Indiana. On the advice of his doctor, he spent the winter in Florida. Result: Deductible medical expense. Reason: C went to Florida for the primary purpose of alleviating a specific condition—his bronchitis [Cohn, 38 TC 387].

What kind of travel expenses are deductible? If the trip is essentially for the cure, prevention or alleviation of a specific disease, and therefore deductible, you can deduct more than just gas, oil, tolls, and parking (or the cost of the round-trip train or air fare). You can also deduct the costs of meals and lodging incurred while traveling to and from your destination—both for yourself and for a medically necessary companion.

Case #3: Mr. and Mrs. P's son, Billy, had a spinal ailment. The parents and the boy traveled in their van from their Nevada home to Kentucky so Billy could receive special treatment and operations. The parents claimed a deduction for the family's meals and lodging on the road. The Tax Court said this was a—

▶ **DEDUCTIBLE EXPENSE:** Meals and lodging on trips to sites of necessary medical care come under the heading of "transportation costs," so they are eligible for the medical deduction [Pfersching, TC Memo 1983-341].

Outpatient treatment: Say you'll be staying in a hotel rather than a hospital while receiving out-patient treatment at an out-of-town hospital or clinic. You can deduct the cost of lodging while at your destination, up to a maximum of $50 each night. If a companion accompanies the patient on doctor's orders, the companion's hotel/motel costs also qualify for the $50 per night deduction. (There's no ceiling on hospital costs, of course.) The medical care must be provided by a physician in a licensed hospital or equivalent medical care facility. The lodging can't be lavish nor the trip a disguised vacation.

▶ **WHAT TO DO:** The key to the deduction is the doctor's orders. Get it in writing! Then, keep track of the expenses.

How To Turn One Deduction Into Two

A major illness or injury in the family not only causes pain and mental anguish, it usually puts a substantial strain on the family bank account. When such a calamity does strike, there's not much you can do for the patient except to provide the best medical care possible. There is, however, one tax-saving remedy that can be prescribed for that ailing family budget. It's a—

▶ **DOUBLE DEDUCTION:** With a little know-how you may be able to get extra mileage out of your medical expenditure.

Let's see how it works. Assume that, because of a serious illness in the family, you purchased a hospital bed, a wheel chair, an orthopedic appliance, or the like, at a cost of $300.

Deduction #1: The cost of the medical equipment is a deductible medical expense.

Now, let's look at what happens after the patient fully recovers. The hospital bed and so on are still as good as new.

▶ **WHAT TO DO:** Give them to a charity that can use them. Now you've nailed down—

Deduction #2: The current market value of the gift is fully deductible as a charitable contribution.

▶ **TAX SAVING:** Assuming the present value of the medical equipment is $250, you've cashed in on $550 worth of tax deductions for items which cost you only $300.

HOW TO MAKE THE MOST OF YOUR CHARITABLE DEDUCTIONS

If you itemize your deductions, you list your charitable contributions (e.g., cash donations, out-of-pocket expenditures, traveling expenses, etc.,) on Schedule A of Form 1040 under the "Contributions" section.

But even if you don't itemize for 1986, the tax law allows you to take a deduction for 100% of your charitable contributions.

Here's a table showing how a charitable gift can save tax dollars. The table assumes you file joint return and itemize your deduction.

Taxable Income Before Charitable Deduction	Tax Savings on $1,000 Donation in 1986
$25,000	$220
35,000	280
45,000	330
60,000	380
90,000	420

Whether or not you itemize, you'll want to make sure you are claiming every charitable contribution you're entitled to. Here's a list of often-overlooked charitable deductions:

● Amounts you pay over and above regular membership dues to charitable organizations—e.g., for a sustaining, donor or life membership—generally are deductible contributions.

● If you put up a student in your home, you can deduct up to $50 per month for each month the student attends school.

● Regular dues to charitable organizations may be deductible if your membership privileges are merely nominal and you aren't entitled to any special services. (Note: Occasional social functions you're invited to as an expression of gratitude or for the solicitation of contributions do not count as special services.)

● Dues you pay to a *social* club may be partly deductible as a charitable contribution if some of the dues are earmarked by the club for certain charities. You take the deduction either in the year the club turns over the funds to charity or, if the club treasurer is a collection agent for the charity, in the year you pay your dues.

● The cost of transportation (including commuting) to and from meetings, demonstrations, fund raising or other campaigns for your church, P.T.A., community chest, Red Cross and other charitable organizations is deductible. If you use your own car, the automatic mileage allowance for 1986 is 12¢ per mile plus tolls and parking charges.

● The cost of distinctive uniforms and accessories such as white gloves and shoes for volunteer hospital or Red Cross services or for choir robes and brownie troop uniforms is deductible, provided they aren't suitable for general use.

● The cost of meals and lodging incurred while away from home overnight rendering volunteer services also is deductible.

● The out-of-pocket expenses you incur as an official delegate to a charity-sponsored convention are deductible.

How To Handle Non-Cash Gifts To Charity

Suppose you make a non-cash gift to charity. It could be some closely held stock, antique furniture, a stamp collection, or even used furniture and clothes. How do you prove the amount of your donation, and how do you handle the contribution on your tax return? The answer depends on how much the property is worth:

Gifts of less than $500: You should get and keep a receipt from the charity showing where and when you made the donation, and a description of the property you gave. A receipt isn't required where it's impractical to obtain one (for example, used clothing dropped off at an unattended charity collection center). Whether or not you have a receipt, you should also keep a written record for each item of property showing its fair market value at the time of the gift and how you arrive at the valuation (e.g., estimate or appraisal). Your record should also describe any limits placed on the charity's use of the property.

You claim your deduction for a gift of less than $500 on Schedule A, Form 1040. And you need not describe the gift in an attached statement.

Gifts in excess of $500, but less than $5,000: You're required to obtain a receipt and keep the same sort of records needed for an under-$500 gift. In addition, you must also keep a written record showing: (1) when and how you acquired the property (e.g., purchase or gift), and (2) how much the property cost you (or its basis when you received it).

You claim the deduction on Schedule A, and are required to supply details about your gift on Form 8283 (name of charity, description of property and when given, when and how the property was acquired, your basis in the property, its value at the time of the gift, and how the value was arrived at). Form 8283 must be filed with your return.

Gifts in excess of $5,000 ($10,000 if closely held stock): You need the same elements of proof required for smaller contributions, *plus* a formal appraisal of the property's fair market value at the time of the gift. (Exception: A gift of publicly traded stock, regardless of amount, is treated for recordkeeping purposes as if it were a gift of under $5,000. No appraisal is required.)

You must also file Form 8283 with your tax return for the year in which you claim a deduction for the gift. Special requirements: Page 2 of Form 8283 must be completed. This page consists of a signed acknowledgement from the charity that it received the gift; a detailed description—completed by you—of the property; and a signed certification of the appraiser you used to value the property.

HOW YOUR HOBBY CAN ALLOW YOU TO DEDUCT "NONDEDUCTIBLE" PERSONAL EXPENSES

Years ago, you took up stamp collecting as a hobby (or coins, baseball cards or what have you). You needed something to get your mind off the pressures of your business or practice. Your collection has turned into quite an investment, yet it's still basically a hobby as far as you're concerned. What you may have overlooked during the years is that there are—

Tax savings in hobbies: As a general rule, personal expenses—for example, the expenses connected with a hobby—are not deductible. But if, from time to time, you sell off a piece of your collection—say you get an attractive offer that you don't want to pass up—you are entitled to—

▶ **DEDUCT PERSONAL EXPENSES:** In any year you make money selling your stamps, you can deduct such things as insurance premiums, appraisal fees, publications and other expenses connected with your hobby. In other words, the cost of a personal hobby has now become deductible.

There is a limit, however. Your hobby expenses are deductible only up to the amount of your gross income from the hobby; in other words, the profit from any sales you made during the year. Thus, if you sell a stamp for $1,000 that you bought years ago for $100, your gross income is $900. That means you can deduct up to $900-worth of hobby-connected expenses.

▶ **TAX-SHELTER OPPORTUNITY:** On the one hand, your hobby expenses up to $900 are itemized deductions, and thus fully offset $900 of ordinary income. On the other hand, your $900 profit from the sale of the stamp is long-term capital gain. And since it's long-term capital gain, only 40% of the total profit, or $360, is taxable with your other income.

Result: Your hobby-connected expenses may save you more in taxes than you pay out on the hobby-connected profit.

WHEN ARE YOUR STATE AND LOCAL INCOME TAX PAYMENTS DEDUCTIBLE?

The tax law says that state and local income taxes are deductible on your Federal income tax return. But there is confusion in some taxpayers' minds about—

When these taxes are deductible: You can deduct state and local income taxes on your tax return for the year *they were actually paid.* In other words, on your 1986 return, you can deduct—

● State and local income taxes withheld during the year by (1) your company, or (2) your employer at a second job (even if you are due for a state tax refund for 1986);

● Estimated state and local income tax payments you made in 1986;

● Payments made in 1986 when you filed your 1985 state or local return.

Important: You cannot deduct on your 1986 Federal return those 1986 state and local income taxes unpaid at the end of the year—for example, the tax payment you may make when you file your 1986 state return in 1987. This payment must be deducted on your 1986 Federal return.

Question: I received a refund during 1986 because I overpaid my 1985 state income tax. Does this affect my state income tax deduction on my 1986 return?

Answer: In effect, it does. You still deduct all the income tax you paid during the year on your return. However, you do have to include the refund as income—

▶ **ON FORM 1040:** You enter the amount of the refund on page 1 of Form 1040. The net result is that part of your income tax deduction is offset by the refund. Note: The refund is only reported as income if it's for a year a taxpayer itemized his deductions on his Federal return. So, if, say, your son took the standard deduction in 1985, the 1986 refund is tax-free on his 1986 Federal return.

HOW DISGUISED INTEREST PAYMENTS CAN HELP TO CUT YOUR 1986 TAX BILL

If you are like most taxpayers you have made (or will make) a number of payments during 1986 that are tax deductible interest—but are labeled something else. You can cut your tax bill by locating these hidden interest deductions. Here are some of the most common ones:

Finance charges: Most credit card plans, department store charge accounts, and installment sales contracts impose finance charges on unpaid balances. Any such charges paid during 1986 are deductible as interest.

Prepayment penalties: Most mortgage contracts and installment contracts impose a penalty if you pay them off before the scheduled payment date. These penalties also qualify as deductible interest.

Late payment charges: Utility companies often add a penalty as a late payment charge when a bill goes unpaid a little beyond the due date. That's another payment that's treated as deductible interest.

Loan processing fees (points): Those points paid to the bank to get a mortgage are deductible interest—if they are really points. The payments to the bank must be for the use of the money, not a charge for services rendered. Points paid on a loan for a house that is not your principal residence cannot be deducted in full when paid. They must be deducted proportionately over the life of the loan.

Forfeited interest on time savings account: Say you deposited $5,000 in a four-year, high-interest time savings account a couple of years ago. You paid tax on the interest earned in 1984 and 1985. You need the cash in 1986, so you close out the account. And the bank hits you with a substantial interest penalty for withdrawing early. That forfeited interest is fully deductible. And you can claim this deduction whether you itemize your deductions or take the standard deduction on your return.

Note discount: Say you borrowed money in 1986 and gave a note back to the lender with a face value greater than the amount you received. The discount is deductible, but only in the year—and to the extent that—you made payments. If you made all the payments in 1986, the entire discount is deductible.

Let's say Mr. Smith got a $2,000 loan at 12% from his bank, payable in 12 monthly installments beginning July 1, 1986. The $240 was "discounted," so Smith received only $1,760. If Smith makes six payments in 1986, he can deduct $120 (half the $240 discount) on his 1986 tax return.

YOU AND YOUR LAWYER— SOME OF HIS FEES ARE DEDUCTIBLE

A company or Professional Corporation can deduct its legal fees as a business or professional expense. It's generally thought, however, that you—as an individual—cannot deduct your own legal expenses. But that's not always the case. Even though your legal matter may not be connected with your business, you can deduct your lawyer's fees if the legal services are related to (1) the production or collection of income; or (2) the management, conservation, or maintenance of property you hold for the production of income.

For example, you may deduct fees for any legal services rendered for:

- Recovering damages to income-producing property
- Collecting interest, dividends, rents, or other taxable income
- Advice on your investments
- Managing your real estate
- Obtaining a larger portion of trust income for you (as beneficiary)
- Defending against a reduction of your taxable income

Here too, however, as in the case of business-connected legal matters, to be fully deductible, your lawyer's fee must be ordinary, necessary, and reasonable. And, if it's in the nature of a capital expenditure—for example, it's incurred in obtaining or defending title to property—the fee may not be deducted; it must be added to the cost basis of the property.

> ▶ **IMPORTANT:** It's not necessary that income actually be produced—as long as the matter at hand can reasonably be expected ultimately to either produce taxable income or minimize a deductible loss. But expenses allocable to tax-exempt income (such as a recovery for personal injuries) are not deductible.

Your lawyer and your taxes: The general rule is that legal expenses incurred in connection with tax matters are deductible. What's more, this includes not only Federal taxes, but state and municipal taxes as well. This rule applies not only to formal tax proceedings but, also, to every matter having tax consequences, including tax guidance and advice and the cost of preparing and filing tax returns.

Practical point: Most legal fees cover a variety of services. Some of these may be of a deductible nature; others may not. You have to be able to show which are and which aren't. Here's where your lawyer can really give you a helping hand. Have him itemize the various services he performs and allocate a proper amount to each item. That way you'll be able to prove the amount of business- or tax-related deductible fees.

YOUR CHECKLIST OF DEDUCTIBLE INVESTOR'S EXPENSES

Like many other taxpayers, you are "in the market." But you may not realize that, when it comes to filling out your tax return, there is more to it than just figuring capital gains and losses and determining whether they're long-term or not. There are a number of expenses an investor has in connection with the investment operations, many of which are deductible from ordinary income. Here's a quick checklist:

- Accounting and auditing services
- Fees for preparing any tax return
- Proxy fight costs, provided your investment is substantial
- Custodial services
- Trustee's commissions, e.g., revocable trust created by investor
- Investment counsel and legal fees
- Salaries of clerical help incurred in connection with investments
- Safe deposit box rental
- Subscriptions to advisory publications
- Cost of surety bond on replacement of lost securities
- State stamp taxes (deductible as taxes)
- Service charges connected with a dividend reinvestment plan

▶ **WATCH THIS:** Sometimes the expense is only partly deductible. For instance, if accounting services relate to taxable and tax-exempt income, you must allocate. There's no deduction for the tax-exempt part.

ARE YOU PASSING UP DEDUCTIONS FOR MISCELLANEOUS EXPENSES?

The Instructions to Form 1040 list a number of miscellaneous deductions that can be taken under the "Miscellaneous" section of Schedule A. Included are items ranging from dues to the Chamber of Commerce and gambling losses (up to the amount of winnings) to safe deposit box rentals and job-related education expenses. Expenses that cannot be deducted are also listed (e.g., personal legal fees and the cost of commuting). The Instructions, however, spell out only part of the miscellaneous deduction story. The following are examples of expenses that have been approved by the Government or the courts and are available to tax-payers.

1. Business portion of home phone expenses: Some or all of the cost of a home telephone may be deductible as a miscellaneous expense. It's considered an ordinary and necessary expense of an employee's business. For example, the expense is deductible when you are subject to frequent calls by your employer [Banks, TC Memo 1981-490].

Another example: Mr. Howard, an East Coast executive, often needed to speak with employees on the West Coast. Due to the difference in time zones, Howard made many calls on his home telephone in the evening. Mrs. Howard, a professional writer, also made business-connected calls on the family phone.

The Howards deducted 15% of their telephone expense as a miscellaneous expense. The Revenue Service denied the Howards' claim. But the Tax Court—

▶ **RANG UP THE DEDUCTION:** The Court said that the couple had established that the telphone was needed and used frequently in the course of their respective businesses. The percentage claimed by the Howards was reasonable. Result: Deduction allowed in full [Howard, TC Memo 1981-250].

2. Home security system: A safe deposit box rental is deductible if the box is used to store stocks, bonds or any other valuables held as investments. The rental is not deductible if it is used for storing jewelry or other personal effects. The same rule goes for the cost of a home security system. If the system was installed to protect valuable works of art, jewelry and silverware from being stolen, there is no deduction. However, you are entitled to a miscellaneous itemized deduction if you can prove that the protected property is held for *investment* purposes [Ltr. Rul. 8133033]. Key point: For the system to be deductible, the items being protected—works of art, for example—can be held for both investment and personal reasons, if the *primary* reason is investment related.

3. Cost of looking into real estate investments: The cost of trips made to investigate a prospective real estate investment is added to the cost basis of the property, if purchased. That means the expense can be written off as deductible depreciation on rental property. What happens when you investigate but *don't* buy? Your travel costs are currently deductible.

Actual facts: Mr. Fairey owned several rental properties. He traveled to Palm Springs to look at a townhouse as a potential investment but decided not to buy. Later, Fairey made a second trip to Palm Springs and bought two lots as a result of that trip.

▶ **OWNING PROPERTY IS BUSINESS:** The taxpayer must show that the primary purpose of the trip is business. In his case, Fairey's business was owning properties, so he wrote off the cost of the first trip in the year he made it and capitalized the cost of the second trip [Fairey, TC Memo 1982-219].

Of course, any trips Mr. Fairey took to inspect and manage properties he already owned would be deductible.

4. Appraisal fees: Let's say a taxpayer owns a valuable painting that's destroyed in a fire, and he wants to deduct the loss. Or maybe he decides to donate the painting to charity. Either way, he needs a professional appraisal of the painting's fair market value. The tax law says that appraisal fees for casualty and theft losses and donated property are deductible miscellaneous expenses.

▶ **KEY POINT:** The appraisal fees are deductible as an expense of determining income tax liability. That's why they're miscellaneous deductions—deductible even if the loss of the appraised property is not deductible (because casualty and theft losses don't exceed 10% of adjusted gross income).

5. Deduction for bond premiums: Investors often pay a premium for a bond. In other words, they pay more than the bond's face amount. If a taxpayer buys a $10,000 corporate bond for $11,000, the extra $1,000 is the premium. He can elect to amortize (write off year-by-year) the premium and deduct the amortization as a miscellaneous itemized deduction. If he pays a $1,000 premium on a bond that will mature in ten years, he can deduct $100 a year.

▶ **WATCH THIS:** If he elects to amortize one taxable bond premium, he must make the same election for the premiums on other bonds he owns currently or acquires later. The election does not apply to premiums on tax-exempt municipal bonds. They must be amortized, but they cannot be deducted currently.

6. Home computer: You can claim depreciation deductions for your home computer to the extent it's used for the production of income or for the preparation of taxes. For example, Mr. Smith bought a $2,000 home computer to keep track of his investments, analyze stocks and bonds, and help prepare his tax return. The computer is used 80% of the time for these purposes; the other 20% use is for games, the kids' homework assignments, and so forth.

Result: Smith can depreciate $1,600 of the computer's cost over a thirteen-year period (4% of $1,600 in the first year, 9% in the second through fifth years, 8% in the sixth through twelfth years, and 4% in the thirteenth year). Note: If Smith used the computer more than 50% for business (as opposed to investment use), he could claim a 10% investment credit on the computer *and* write off the business-use portion over just five years.

Caution: Mr. Smith should keep a record of the home computer's usage in order to compute the deduction and defend it in the event of an audit.

And there are more: We have explained some out-of-the way miscellaneous deductions you might forfeit if you deduct only those items listed in the Form 1040 Instructions. There are others, such as: Dues paid to professional societies; subscriptions to professional journals and magazines related to your work; examinations required by an employer; and union dues and expenses. Investment-related fees and unreimbursed business entertainment expenses are two more. What it boils down to is that you can basically deduct any miscellaneous expenses that are connected with job-related education, employment and income-producing property.

HOW TO TAKE THE STING OUT OF THE SPECIAL TAX ON TAX SHELTERS

High income taxpayers have a special tax headache to cope with—the alternative minimum tax. In a nutshell, this tax reduces the tax-cutting effectiveness of tax preference items (so called because they allow "preferential" tax treatment when computing the regular income tax) such as accelerated depreciation on real property.

How the tax works: The alternative minimum tax is targeted at so-called tax preferences (see below). You add up your tax preference items and add that to your adjusted gross income. You then subtract: (1) special minimum tax deductions, and (2) a generous exemption: $40,000 for joint filers and surviving spouses, $20,000 for marrieds filing separately and for estates and trusts, $30,000 for everyone else). What's left over is subject to tax at a 20% rate. The final figure can't be offset by any tax credits (other than the foreign tax credit).

Important: The alternative minimum tax is payable only if it exceeds a taxpayer's regular income tax. It's a tough, complicated measure, but with some astute tax planning, the special tax can be avoided altogether.

Tax preference items subject to the minimum tax: Here are the most important tax preferences:

- Real estate accelerated depreciation in excess of straight line. Each year's excess is a preference.

- The untaxed 60% portion of long-term capital gains.

- Accelerated depreciation on personal property subject to a net lease.

● Percentage depletion in excess of the adjusted basis of the proprty.

● A portion of the intangible drilling cost deduction for oil and gas and geothermal energy.

● The bargain element of incentive stock options.

● Dividends excluded by the $100 ($200 for marrieds filing jointly) dividend exclusion.

● A portion of certain expensed items (including mining exploration and development costs, research and experimental costs, and magazine circulation costs).

Minimum tax deductions. The following items are allowed as deductions to arrive at income subject to the alternative minimum tax:

● Medical expenses to the extent they exceed 10% of adjusted gross income (note that this is double the usual 5% "floor"), and casualty losses (to the extent they exceed 10% of adjusted gross);

● Charitable contributions and wagering losses;

● Interest paid on a loan to buy, build, or substantially rehabilitate either (a) a dwelling used by the taxpayer or a family member during the year, including vacation homes, or (b) the principal residence of the taxpayer.

▶ **SPECIAL RULE FOR CONVERTED PROPERTY:** Suppose you took out a mortgage and bought a principal residence five years ago. Now you use it strictly for income—you rent it out year-round. Can you deduct the interest paid on the converted property for minimum tax purposes? You can, if the debt was incurred before July 1, 1982, and you or a family member used the home when the loan was taken out, or you used the home as a principal residence at that time.

● "Qualified interest." This term includes all amounts otherwise deductible as interest. However, "qualified interest" can only be deducted to the extent of "qualified net investment income" (generally, investment income such as rents, royalties, dividends, interest, net capital gains, less certain investment expenses).

● Deduction for estate taxes (allowable under Sec. 691(c) for taxpayers who have income in respect of a decedent).

Simplified example: Mr. and Mrs. White have a combined income of $150,000. Over the course of the year they made certain tax-sheltered investments (e.g., real estate, oil and gas) that produced a tax loss of $60,000. This brings the Whites' adjusted gross income to $90,000. After other deductions are subtracted, their taxable income is $70,000. 1986 income tax: $18,574

But the Whites' tax-shelter deals yielded tax preferences of $55,000. This is added to their $90,000 adjusted gross income in order to compute the alternative tax. Assuming no alternative tax deductions, only the first $40,000 is exempt from the special tax. The $105,000 balance is taxed at a flat 20% rate. Alternative tax: $21,000.

Result: The Whites must pay the greater of the two taxes—the $21,000 alternative minimum tax. So due to the tax preference items the Whites pay $2,426 more than their regular tax bill.

▶ **WHAT TO DO:** If you are contemplating a tax-shelter investment you should make an alternative minimum tax computation. You may find that the tax preference creates an alternative tax liability and thereby reduces your after-tax return on the investment.

▶ **WHAT TO DO:** If you expect your regular tax to be lower than usual this year, you may want to postpone one or more tax preference items—or accelerate deductions that offset your tax preferences. Let's look at some moves you can make to minimize or eliminate this extra tax.

1. Installment sales of real estate: If you sell real estate on an installment basis, your capital gain on the sale can be spread out over several years as you receive your payments. This avoids the problem of having to take a large amount of gain into income in one year—and thus reduces your chance of getting hit with the minimum tax.

2. Deductions to minimum tax: Some of your itemized deductions cut your income subject to the alternative minimum tax. When you have a lot of preferences—and there's no way to avoid a minimum tax—try to accelerate deductions into the current year to reduce the tax. For example, you might make a charitable contribution this year that you were planning to make in 1987.

3. Paper gain and losses: You can shelter long-term capital gains from the alternative minimum tax by taking down capital losses that offset your gain. For example, if you have a big capital gain from the sale of real estate earlier in the year, you may want to sell, say, stock on which you have long-term losses.

▶ **TIMING IS THE KEY** These are a few of the ways you can cut back or eliminate your alternative minimum tax bill. The key point: Pay special attention to income and deductions relating to tax preference items in a year when your "regular tax" is expected to be small. That's when you are most likely to be affected by the alternative minimum tax.

YOU MAY HAVE TO FILE YOUR CHILD'S RETURN AS WELL AS YOUR OWN

You don't owe tax on your child's income; your child does. And the tax return filing requirements are the same for your child as for adults. Your child must file a return if he or she (1) has $3,560 or more gross income for 1986, or (2) has $1,080 or more in "unearned" income (dividends, interest, etc.) and can be claimed as a tax dependent.

▶ **IT'S UP TO YOU:** The Government says that if a child is too young to file a required return, the parent or guardian must fill out and sign the return for the child. The parent should sign the child's name in the proper place on the return and then write "By (Name), Parent (or Guardian) for minor child" [Rev. Rul. 82-206, 1982-2 CB 356].

Of course, your child may not actually owe any tax when he files. For example, Junior may have a summer job in 1986 and the tax withheld from his paychecks may completely cover his tax liability. Nevertheless, he must still file a return if his earnings exceed $3,560.

▶ **TOUGH RULE:** There is a penalty for failing to file a required return within 60 days of the due date. The penalty is a flat $100—*and it applies even if no tax is actually owed.*

Important: Even if your child's income is below the filing requirements, you may still want you child to file a return. If tax is withheld on your child's 1985 earnings, the only way your child can get a refund is by filing a return.

HOW YOUR DIESEL CAR CAN ENTITLE YOU TO A GENEROUS TAX RETURN BREAK

Taxpayers who buy new diesel powered vehicles are entitled to a—

▶ **SURPRISE TAX BREAK:** Buyers of a diesel-powered vehicle after 1984 and before 1988 may be in line for a little-known tax credit. The credit—a dollar-for-dollar reduction in your tax bill—is available for four-wheel vehicles weighing 10,000 pounds or less regardless of whether the vehicle is put to personal or business use. Amount of the credit: $198 for a truck and $102 for a car.

Background: In 1984, the tax on diesel fuels was raised by 6¢ (from 9¢ to 15¢ per gallon). The increase was intended to offset a reduction in the heavy vehicle use tax. Result: Car and light truck owners would be left paying the higher fuel tax, but not benefiting from the offsetting tax reduction for heavy vehicles. So a credit was created for owners of diesel-powered cars and light trucks. It reimburses them in advance (through a tax credit) for the added diesel fuel tax they will pay over the life of the vehicles.

The credit may be claimed by the first user of the vehicle only. It is not available for used diesel-powered vehicles. The credit is on a per-vehicle basis. So if you buy two diesel-powered vehicles, you are eligible for two tax credits.

▶ **WHERE TO CLAIM THE CREDIT:** You claim the credit on Form 4136, "Computation of Credit for Federal Tax on Gasoline and Special Fuels." The credit is then entered on Form 1040.

HOW TO GET A TAX-SAVING CREDIT FOR SUPPORTING THE CANDIDATE OF YOUR CHOICE

Presidential, local and state elections involve us all as taxpayers. You may be tempted to get involved directly by making contributions to candidates who are sympathetic to your point of view.

▶ **ADDED ENCOURAGEMENT:** You are entitled to a tax credit—a dollar-for-dollar reduction in your tax bill—equal to one-half of your political contributions. There's a credit limit of $100 on a joint return and $50 on an individual return. This is an annual limit; it is not a per-election limit.

Example: Mr. and Mrs. Johnson made a $200 contribution last December to the re-election campaign of their local Congressman. The Johnsons claimed a $100 tax credit on last year's tax return. This July, the Johnsons contribute another $200 contribution to the Congressman's campaign. Result: The Johnsons can claim another $100 tax credit on their current year's tax return.

To qualify for the tax credit, your contribution must be made to a candidate for nomination or election to a Federal, state, or local office. You can contribute directly to the candidate, to a committee set up for the candidate, or to a national, state or local committee of the candidate's national party.

An increasingly popular way for taxpayers to contribute to candidates is through political action committees set up by various organizations—for example, an organization representing manufacturers. These committees collect contributions and distribute money to candidates who support the legislative goals of that particular organization. Contributions made to these political action committees also qualify for the tax credit.

▶ **IMPORTANT:** The Government requires you to back up your credit with written receipts. Receipts should include your name, the date, the amount and purpose of your contribution, and the name of the recipient.

HOW TO HANDLE YOUR ESTIMATED TAXES UNDER THE LATEST TAX RULES

The Tax Law says you must pay estimated taxes if you expect your estimated tax liability for the year (after subtracting credits for tax withheld) plus estimated self-employment tax to be less than $500.

When do you pay? That depends on when during the year you first meet the requirements spelled out above. If they were first met on or before April 1, the first payment is due April 15. The others are due on or before June 15, September 15, and mid-January of the following year. The form to use for estimated tax payments is Form 1040-ES.

What happens if you don't file Form 1040-ES? There is no penalty for not filing Form 1040-ES. However, there's a stiff penalty for underpayments of estimated tax. The penalty is payable for *each* installment to the extent that the installment is less than 20% of the final tax bill.

Surprising fact: Most taxpayers never bother with estimated taxes. Main reason: All tax withheld during the year (on salary, pensions and annuities) is treated as estimated tax payments. Any amounts withheld can be treated as the payment of estimated tax on any one of the four installment dates. So if your withholding for the year comes to at least 80% of your total tax bill, you have paid enough on each installment date to avoid the underpayment penalty.

If you find you are underpaying your estimated tax as the year progresses—you're falling short of the 80% mark—you can still avoid an underpayment penalty without actually making an estimated tax payment.

▶ **WHAT TO DO:** Increase your withholding on salary. Withholding is treated as a downpayment of your estimated tax. Generally you're considered to have paid one-quarter of your total withholding on each estimated tax installment date. So you can wipe out your underpayment even if you increase your withholding near the end of the year.

Are you definitely going to be hit with a penalty if your total prepayments don't equal at least 80%? Answer: No. There are two escape hatches:

Escape hatch #1: You can use the prior year's tax as your estimated tax for the current year. If you make timely estimated tax payments equal to that amount, you aren't liable for the penalty.

Escape hatch #2: You can annualize your income to determine your tax for the year and then pay 80% of that tax in equal installments. To annualize your income, multiply by 12 the taxable income to the end of the period covered by the installment, and then divide by the number of months to the end of the installment period.

Example: Smith has $15,000 of taxable income in the first three months. His annual income at the same rate would be $60,000. If Smith's estimated tax payment on April 15 (plus ¼ of year's withholding) is 20% of the tax on $60,000, he pays no penalty on the first installment of estimated taxes.

▶ **TAX-SAVING CHOICE:** For each installment period, you can use the escape hatch that calls for the lowest possible payment. You need not be consistent from quarter to quarter.

Special relief: The penalty can be waived in cases of casualty, disaster, or "other unusual circumstances". The penalty can also be waived if there is reasonable cause for the underpayment of estimated tax during the first two years after a taxpayer retires after reaching age 62 or becomes disabled at any age.

HOW TO CUT PREVIOUS YEARS' TAX BILLS
BY FILING AMENDED RETURNS

Filling out a tax return means making tax choices—whether to use joint or separate returns, which tax break to use on a home sale and so on and so on. Even astute taxpayers, however, occasionally fail to make the right tax choice on their returns, the one that saves the most taxes. What happens if you now discover you missed the boat somewhere on your previous returns?

Good news: In many cases, you get an—

▶ **AUTOMATIC SECOND CHANCE:** You can change your mind simply by filing an amended return (Form 1040X) reflecting your new choice. No Government approval is needed. Generally speaking, you have until three years after the tax return due date (for example, April 15, 1989 for 1985 returns) to file an amended return.

Here are some examples of why you might want a second chance:

Estimated taxes: Let's say you were due a refund when you filed your 1985 return. But you asked the Revenue Service to credit the refund against the estimated tax payments you owe for 1986. Now, however, you unexpectedly need some ready cash. What do you do? You file an amended return on Form 1040X and request a refund check—instead of an estimated tax credit.

Lump-sum distributions: You received a lump-sum distribution from a profit-sharing plan in 1985. You reported the portion of the payout allocable to pre-1974 plan participation as tax-sheltered capital gain; the rest you treated as ordinary income, eligible for special ten-year income averaging. Now you learn that you could have elected to have the entire payout taxed under ten-year averaging—and that would have produced a lower tax for you. Again, you file an amended return. (Attach a revised Schedule D and Form 4972.)

Income averaging: When you filed your return, you thought your gross income had to go up before you could take advantage of income averaging. Your gross income did not go up—but your deductions did go down. And now you realize that a drop in deductions can also qualify you for income averaging. So you file an amended return and refigure your tax bill using income averaging. (Amend your return on Form 1040X and attach Schedule G.)

Home sale: You sold your home in 1985 and elected to take advantage of the special one-time-only exclusion for over-age-55 homesellers. But you are having second thoughts: You have purchased a new home and think you should save the exclusion for future use. Since your new home cost as much as the sales price of the old one, you can defer the tax on your sale profit under the standard sale-and-replacement break for homesellers. You have three years from the date your return was due or filed (whichever is later) to revoke the election. (Make the change on Form 1040X and attach revised Form 2119.)

Separate returns: When you filled out your 1985 return, you decided to file separately rather than jointly. But you overlooked one thing: the up-to-$3,000 marriage penalty deduction available to working couples if—and only if—they file a joint return. You can claim it by jointly filing one amended return that cancels out your two separate returns. However, the reverse is not true: You cannot switch from a joint return to separate returns.

▶ **IMPORTANT:** When you change your mind on one item, it can sometimes affect something else. For example, some states require that if you file a joint Federal return you must file the same way on your state return. And while you may come out ahead on the amended Federal return, the same may not hold true on your state return. So be sure you look at things from all sides.

INDEX

FAMILY MONEY BOOK